D1453421

UNMODERN PHILOSOPHY AND MODERN PHILOSOPHY

UNMODERN PHILOSOPHY AND MODERN PHILOSOPHY

JOHN DEWEY

Edited and with an Introduction
by Phillip Deen
With a Foreword by Larry A. Hickman

Southern Illinois University Press
Carbondale and Edwardsville

The manuscript by John Dewey presented in this book
was obtained from the Dewey Papers (folders 53/12,
53/13, 53/15–53/18, 54/1–54/3, 54/5, 54/6, 61/12, 61/13,
61/15–61/19, and 61/21), Special Collections Research
Center, Morris Library, Southern Illinois University
Carbondale.

Library of Congress Cataloging-in-Publication Data
Dewey, John, 1859–1952.
Unmodern philosophy and modern philosophy / John
  Dewey ; edited and with an introduction by Phillip
  Deen ; with a foreword by Larry A. Hickman.
    p. cm.
Includes bibliographical references and index.
  ISBN-13: 978-0-8093-3079-9 (cloth : alk. paper)
  ISBN-10: 0-8093-3079-2 (cloth : alk. paper)
  ISBN-13: 978-0-8093-3080-5 (ebook)
  ISBN-10: 0-8093-3080-6 (ebook)
1. Philosophy. I. Deen, Phillip, 1972– II. Title.
B945.D43U56 2012
191—dc23   2011033319

Printed on recycled paper.♻
The paper used in this publication meets the minimum
requirements of American National Standard for Information Sciences—Permanence of Paper for Printed
Library Materials, ANSI Z39.48-1992.∞

Contents

Foreword

n editing and presenting this previously unpublished Dewey manuscript, which was thought to be lost, Phillip Deen has performed an admirable service to readers who are already well acquainted with Dewey's copious publications. His service is perhaps even greater, however, to readers who are not as familiar with Dewey's ideas but have hoped for more a more accessible entry point, available in his own words, into the complexities of the thirty-seven volumes of his *Collected Works*.

Readers of the first sort will be delighted to find in these pages a Dewey who is more supple than the one to whom they are accustomed—more candid, perhaps, but apparently less constrained by the blue pencils of his editors. They will find a Dewey who expands on numerous themes that he introduced and developed in earlier books and essays. In this work, he clarifies old ideas and draws new connections in ways that render them more perspicuous.

The tenth chapter, "Mind and Body," provides several excellent examples. Dewey rehearses and expands themes that he presented in chapter seven of his 1925 *Experience and Nature*, "Nature, Life and Body-Mind." He points out, for example, that ordinary parlance, which treats "mind" as a verb (as in "Mind what I am saying to you" or "I'm minding the children") reveals the poverty of premodern and modern theories that separate mind and matter. Once that separation becomes philosophical dogma, such theories are hard put to explain how the putatively disparate elements can be related. For Dewey, to mind is to care for—to behave in certain observable ways. He also expands his criticism of sense-data theories. He argues that the traditional identification of observation with one of its constituents, sense perception, is one of the great historical philosophical mistakes.

Further, in what Deen appropriately characterizes as a "striking section," Dewey provides an extended discussion of knowing as a form of technology. This section is unique in Dewey's work as I know it. Philosophers interested in technology have long lamented the fact that Dewey's treatment of technology is not presented in any one location but is instead dispersed here and there throughout his writings. Now, in this chapter, we have Dewey's clearest and most succinct remarks about his view of technology and its relation to the role of philosophy in contemporary culture. It is worth noting in this connection that Dewey's view of Francis Bacon is here more nuanced than that of contemporary interpreters who understand him as treating nature as something to be conquered. Dewey reads Bacon as arguing for a kind of transaction with nonhuman nature: nature must first be obeyed if human beings are to achieve those ends that are desirable to common life.

For readers of the second type, those who have hoped for a more easily accessible Dewey, this volume has much to offer. Many of the main themes of Dewey's massive *corpus*, early to late, are presented in a manner that is both clear and well organized. Dewey's criticism of the "reflex arc" concept in psychology; his rejection of the "quest for certainty" that characterized the premodern and modern periods of philosophy; his criticism of premodern and modern treatments of the relations between theory and practice; his attack on scientism; his rejection of the traditional split between human beings and the rest of nature; and his rejection of traditional ethical theories as reductive: they are all here.

This list of criticisms, rejections, and attacks is, of course, negative in tone. In each case mentioned, however, Dewey's revolutionary philosophy takes care to present a constructive alternative. If classical S-R (stimulus-response) theory in psychology is limited or ineffective because based on narrowly selected data and reliance on antiquated mechanical models, then he will replace it with an organic model that emphasizes selective interest and adjustment to dynamic environing conditions. If the modern quest for certainty and the "epistemology industry" that it has spawned are still hung up in the net of the premodern synthesis, then he will supplant those views with a scientific approach that is experimentalist and fallibilist. If premodern and modern philosophies have constructed a metaphysics that projects a problematic relation between theory and practice, then he will reconstruct traditional epistemology as a theory of inquiry that ensures that theory and practice function as partners in the production of new tools and new habits. If positivists have gone too far in claiming that the methods and contents of the sciences are universally applicable, then he will praise the sciences for their many contributions to human life at the same time he emphasizes the importance of wider fields of experience. If traditional philosophy has tended to split human beings off from the rest of nature, then he will reconstruct that account with the help of anthropologists, and perhaps most importantly with the help of his beloved Darwin, in order to demonstrate continuities and evolutionary development. And if traditional ethical theories have tended to be reductive in terms of their exclusive attention to the goods of the utilitarians, the rights and obligations of deontologists, or the virtues praised by Aristotle and others, then he will present an ethics that is experimental and developmental, that treats goods, rights, and virtues as among the many factors that may be called upon as humans take account of problematic situations, imaginatively weighing one claim against another in more comprehensive processes of moral deliberation than the tradition has imagined.

The late Richard Rorty famously remarked that Dewey would be waiting at the end of the road being traveled by Anglo-American analytic philosophy as well as by French philosophers such as Foucault and Deleuze. If Rorty's assessment were in need of additional support, it could surely be found in this volume. Dewey's report to Corinne Chisholm Frost concerning this project, which Deen quotes at length, sums up matters nicely. He will attempt to do something he has not done before, and he has no idea how it will turn out. He will attempt to demonstrate how modern attempts at reconstruction of the metaphysics of Aristotle and the philosophers of the medieval period fell sadly short because they left in place debilitating elements of the old "medieval synthesis." And he will show how that failure has prevented the new synthesis that he thinks necessary, a synthesis that is relevant to contemporary conditions.

This volume further solidifies Dewey's place as dialogue partner among philosophers living and working in our time. He anticipates, for example, by some fifty years Bruno Latour's well-known remark that "We have never been modern." What Latour meant was that modern philosophy split the human and social sciences off from the natural sciences in ways that maintained an old substance-ontology that seeks to know the essential nature of things. What our contemporary situation calls for instead, he suggested, is a functionalist approach that seeks to know what things do, that is, how things behave, and therefore how what is undesirable can be intelligently managed. Moreover, modern philosophy fostered discontinuities such as the split between a self-sufficient, culture-free nature, on one side, and a domain of culturally enmeshed human beings, on the other. What is needed now, in his view, is an account in which that split is healed—in which nature is treated as culture and human beings are understood as involved in the cutting edge of an evolving nature. In other words, we have never been modern because we, like the so-called "moderns," have never escaped the orbit of the "premoderns."

All of this, of course, is more or less what Dewey was saying some five decades earlier, and what he clearly articulates in the manuscript we now know as *Unmodern Philosophy and Modern Philosophy*. In this volume Dewey shows the way to a new philosophy, a philosophy that is not only relevant to but very much needed in our current situation. It is a philosophy that places ethics, social and political philosophy, and aesthetics at the center of philosophical discourse. It is an approach to philosophy that, were it to be embraced, would change forever the type of problems that are debated in professional journals and the ways that philosophy is taught in the class-room. It is presented here in this volume, and we are indebted to Phillip Deen for bringing it out of the archives into the light of day.

Larry A. Hickman
Center for Dewey Studies
Southern Illinois University Carbondale

Acknowledgments

On a personal level, I would first like to thank John J. McDermott of Texas A&M University and Larry Hickman and Tom Alexander of Southern Illinois University Carbondale for spurring and sustaining my interest in Dewey's thought. In addition, I thank the staff of the Center for Dewey Studies both for their invaluable work in keeping Dewey's legacy alive and for their assistance with this project. The staff of Southern Illinois University at Carbondale's Special Collections Research Center were essential in providing the manuscripts and aiding me when I came to visit. John Shook and the Center for Inquiry allowed me to get this project off the ground by providing a residential research position in the summer of 2009. And my thanks to the editors and readers of SIU Press for guiding me through the overwhelming task of getting Dewey's book out to the world.

Lastly, I want to acknowledge some of the countless ways that Wellesley College has aided me in this project—from providing a research grant and an assistant (Kristina Costa) who engaged in the trying work of transcribing Dewey's pages to giving me a place to teach and to turn the fractured manuscript into the present book. The bulk of that work was done over the 2009–10 academic year, one hundred years after Dewey was himself a visiting lecturer in Wellesley's department of philosophy and psychology. And, as I write these words, it is seventy years to the day since Dewey came to campus to speak on "Man and the Sciences," arguing that science is an active, imaginative and social enterprise and one necessary to fight the threat of totalitarianism. Wellesley College, my colleagues in the department of philosophy and the impressive young women who come here all continue to honor Dewey's commitment to practical intelligence and intelligent practice.

Phillip Deen

Wellesley, Massachusetts

May 2010

Introduction

On the occasion of his ninetieth birthday, John Dewey was interviewed by the *New York Times*. In that interview, he promised to write a book that was to be "the summation of his philosophical beliefs through the years." It seemed that Dewey had completed such a book, but that the manuscript had been lost. Displaying the equanimity that he was known for, he was inconsolable for two days and then "simply started to write again." Viewing it as an opportunity to write an even better book, he optimistically claimed, "You know, in a way this has given me new ideas, starting over fresh again. I think I have better ideas now" (Fine 1949). As Dewey scholars know, the book never appeared. They have been left to pine for it and speculate on its contents ever since Joseph Ratner wrote, in his editor's introduction to Dewey's reintroduction to *Experience and Nature*, "The unfinished introduction projected a grand design—a philosophical interpretation of the history of Western man. Dewey's original intention was to write such a book after he finished the introduction" (LW 1:329). In 1959, many of Dewey's friends gathered together to commemorate his 100th birthday, trade stories, and discuss his thought and character. In the course of their conversation, Corliss Lamont expressed his dismay that Dewey had never written one text encapsulating his philosophy. He continued, "I understand that toward the end of his life, he did start work on such a book and had finished about three-quarters of it." Of the manuscript's loss, Lamont could only say, "I think it was a tragedy" (Lamont 1959, 50–51). I am happy to write that the original manuscript has now been recovered. Though far from a perfect specimen and not precisely what Ratner and Lamont had thought, we have the opportunity to read the first "new" book by John Dewey in sixty years.

This introduction will do three things. The first is to recount the history of the manuscript and its recovery. The second is to summarize its contents, including Dewey's history of modern philosophy, when philosophy failed by collapsing into epistemology, and what a truly modern theory of knowing would require. The second section also draws out the philosophical framework imbuing the book, which Dewey called "cultural naturalism," and argues that this work cashes out Dewey's provocative claim from the reintroduction to *Experience and Nature* that, rather than using the term *experience*, he should have used *culture* all along. The last task is to present what I take to be the underlying project—to come to terms with modernity and the related task to develop a critical theory of culture.

History of the Manuscript

In its eight-year life, Dewey's manuscript underwent radical change, but the changes were foreshadowed from the beginning. Its earliest mention is in 1939 in a letter to Joseph Ratner. Originally entitled *The Philosophic Science*—or, in one later outline, *A Science Became*—Dewey meant to write a popular text on the relation between philosophy, science, and common sense. However, it immediately got away from him: "It isn't taking the shape I anticipated and intended—but more that of a cultural interpretation in terms of modern philosophy[.] . . . I am not trying to do anything except to indicate how, given the state of culture, philosophy took the course it has taken—from that point of view it is a justification instead of an adverse criticism. The damn thing involves a sort of philosophy of modern history[.]" Including a rough outline, he marked out a tripartite structure: an introduction, a set of problems such as "Problem of Knowledge—Method" and "Nature and Man—Subject & Object, etc." and a third part on "Solutions." The letter concludes with a bit of dramatic irony with the words, "But I'm afraid I've laid out too big a job" (1939.02.13, 07028).

His frustration at "the damn thing" would continue throughout. Beginning work in the summer of 1939 at his Hubbards retreat and continuing in Key West, he would write a year later that both pieces were "neither any good and I doubt if this is going to be" (1940.01.22, 09497). By February of 1941, he was on his third attempt at the book, claiming to have "a better start, but only a start" (1941.02.20, 07067). This start included three chapters on "The Continuing Life of Philosophy," "Conflict within Philosophy" and "The Conflict becomes Confusion," none of which have survived.

But something seems to have changed soon after. The recovered manuscripts run from the summer of 1941 to late 1942 (with, in one case, a revision in 1943) and mark a time of concentrated thought and effort. At time of war, "philosophy didn't seem to have much place in this hell of a world, but I got started in May and have kept at it more or less ever since, something of an escape; the book—if it ever is one—is rather different from anything I have done before—general philosophic theory—more of the 'I'm telling you' type and less argument" (1941.07.29, 09748; see also 1941.12.10, 13300). He began working in earnest and with a clearer sense of the final product. To Corinne Chisholm Frost he wrote,

The leading idea is that the problems and the different philosophies (attempts at solution) of modern times have their source in the strains or tensions produced by the (relative) dissolution of the medieval synthesis. . . . I'm trying something different from what I've done before and I have no idea how it is going to come out. I want to show that the confusion and chaos of so much of modern life is due first to the emergence of the new forces, Protestantism, Nationalism, democracy, industrial revolution, new physics etc. from out the medieval synthesis and secondly to the fact that many of the fundamental ideas of the old synthesis were not discarded but were carried over into the systems that attempt a new philosophical formulations, and thereby has prevented the development of a synthesis which actually corresponds to the vital conditions and forces of the present (1941.06.28, 09404).

By January of 1942, he claimed to have "an idea which will work out, which none of the earlier ones did—there is no straight-out 'modern' philosophy, that is conceived in modern terms of what is modern but an inconsistent mixture of old and new" (1942.01.23, 13074). In large part, this is precisely what he would go on to write.

Alternation between optimism and pessimism would continue. At one time, he would tell Arthur Bentley that he has made significant progress on issues of epistemology, human nature and individualism, the roots of modern thought in the Greek-medieval, and the completion of chapters nine and ten of the recovered manuscript (1942.03.19, 15220). He would also come up with a new title: *Unmodern Philosophy and Modern Philosophy* (1942.05.01, 13310). It is during this period of optimism running from mid-1941 through 1942 that Dewey wrote the manuscript that we have now. But, three years later, the book would reappear in his correspondence only for Dewey to tell Bentley, with whom he was writing *Knowing and the Known*, "I don't know whether I ever told you that twice I have started to write a 'social' interpretation of the history of philosophers—if not of philosophy. I accumulated a lot of mss but it never would jell. When we get this job done maybe I'll go back to it" (1945.02.14, 15410).

Of course, he did not get back to it and the manuscript went missing. Once the manuscript was gone, and with Joseph Ratner encouraging him to use the material from the reintroduction to *Experience and Nature* as the basis for going forward, Dewey hoped to begin his book on modern philosophy anew. Though he considered co-authoring with Ratner, and Ratner gladly accepted, it never came about (1949.07.11, 07254; 1949.07.16, 07256; 1949.07.18, 07258).

But let us turn to the part that is most intriguing—how did the text disappear, and how has it reappeared? In both cases, the answer is rather mundane. While Dewey's life may have spanned the period from the Civil War to the detonation of the thermonuclear bomb, the great mystery of what happened to his manuscript on modern philosophy comes down to whether, on a fateful day in 1947, Dewey left it in a cab or, if not, whether he left it on the sidewalk for someone to take it.

There are various accounts of the loss, but they tell largely the same story. To Raymond Dixon, Dewey wrote, "I put all my correspondence with the Philosophical Library in a briefcase, together with some typewritten chapters of a book I was working on in, which I lost on our motor trip in return from Nova Scotia—my own carelessness of course" (1947.10.11, 14441). The *New York Times* interview mentioned above claims that it was "because of an error of a subordinate while traveling." Corliss Lamont and Roberta Dewey told the same story: the Deweys had returned from their Nova Scotia cabin one summer to their apartment in New York. Leaving their bags for the doorman and taking the elevator up, Dewey suddenly realized that he had left his briefcase in the cab. The briefcase, they learned, had been removed from the cab but disappeared soon after (Lamont 1959, 50). This story was repeated by Roberta Dewey seven years after John's death. Upon the Deweys' return to New York after closing their Nova Scotia cabin, the doormen who unloaded the car waited for them to go upstairs before transferring everything—only the briefcase did not make it. "As John Dewey believed only in facts and there [were] no facts in this disappearance, only assumptions, it cannot be definitely stated that this manuscript was stolen that night" (1959.09.14, 17930). Though Dewey would not speculate, Roberta was happy to, noting that some boys had recently been caught committing similar crimes in the neighborhood.

So how do we have the present manuscript? The short answer is that it was among the Dewey Papers in the Special Collections at Southern Illinois University, catalogued and waiting for decades to be rediscovered. Archivists at the Special Collections Research Center believe that the manuscript was included in the original collection. The more difficult question is how it made it into the Dewey Papers at all. Each document had been catalogued by Jo Ann Boydston, the esteemed editor-in-chief of the *Collected Works of John Dewey*. However, in personal correspondence with me, Dr. Boydston recalled some of the chapter titles but had no other recollection of the manuscripts.

As for where it was before it appeared in the Special Collections, there are at least four theories. The first is that Joseph Ratner had it. Dewey frequently gave early chapters to him for comment. Ratner, a noted packrat, may have contributed the chapters to the Dewey Papers. This is possible, since his contributions to the collection were extensive. However, it does not explain why, in 1949, Ratner commiserated with Dewey over the loss of the manuscript and encouraged him to begin again (1949.07.06, 07255). Perhaps he simply forgot that he had them. Nor does it account for the fact that the manuscript was catalogued as part of the Dewey Papers, rather than Ratner's. The second theory is that Roberta Dewey had it. Shortly after Dewey's passing, George Dykhuizen asked her, "Have you investigated farther the manuscript which you uncovered in Nova Scotia and which you think may be the one believed to be lost?" (1952.10.01, 13674). In other words, the manuscript might not have been stolen, but left behind in Nova Scotia. We do not know if Roberta ever confirmed her suspicions. Her 1959 comments would indicate that she did not. Third, it is possible that the full manuscript was not lost, as Dewey indicated above that only a few chapters were in the briefcase. It may be that the legend of a missing manuscript, rather than missing chapters, was too tempting and spread falsely through the Dewey community. But why would Dewey speak so often as if the entire manuscript had been lost? Lastly, it is possible that Dewey lost the final draft, and what we have now is an assortment of earlier drafts. But, again, that does not explain why Dewey and Ratner spoke as if the entire thing had been lost and it was necessary to begin again. Dewey's correspondence also indicates that his work on the manuscript dried up after the burst of activity between 1941 and 1942—the period during which the extant manuscripts were written.

In short, it is presently a mystery how a manuscript thought to be lost by everyone, including the author, should reappear in the archives. Perhaps Dewey's "grand design—a philosophical interpretation of the history of Western man"—was never truly lost, only incomplete and forgotten somewhere among Dewey's papers. It would be ironic, after years of speculation on its content and the theft, if we were to discover that the manuscript had been waiting for us all along. Though we would be left to wonder, "What was *actually* in that briefcase . . . ?"

Dewey's Cultural History of Philosophy

In what was likely a journalistic flourish to make the story more tragic than it already was, the *New York Times* reporter claimed that the manuscript was complete as of 1945. Dewey's correspondence belies that claim. Dewey originally intended the text to have three parts—historical, theoretical, and practical. No such "practical" section seems to have been written. Furthermore, the latest and most complete outline we have shows the tripartite structure to have disappeared over time. Nevertheless, there still appear to be missing sections. For example, we have no manuscript numbered as chapter 5. And, despite the frequent appearance of social, political, and economic issues in the earlier chapters, they are typically intriguing promissory notes rather than sustained discussions. To recall one amusing example, Dewey concludes some notes for chapter 11 with this one to himself: "Something about freedom—somewhere" (Folder 54/3). In short, Dewey never completed the book he had hoped to write.

Nor is the manuscript pristine. At one extreme, roughly half of the chapters were written in one session and have survived as continuous manuscripts, lacking only the occasional page. At the opposite extreme, "The Search for Salvation" and "The Present Problem of Knowledge" were broken into dozens of pieces, sometimes even into isolated pages. Between the two, "Wandering between Two Worlds" and "Experience as Life Function" were joined together from separate but substantial drafts. Given these facts, it is truly amazing that the extant text is so cohesive in style, content, and argument. (For a full discussion of the condition of the manuscript and the editorial principles and judgments underlying the final product, see the Editor's Introduction.)

It has been remarked that there are no radical breaks in Dewey's work like we might find in Heidegger's or Wittgenstein's. As such, *Unmodern Philosophy and Modern Philosophy* discusses familiar Deweyan topics and themes. In this text, Dewey has rewritten and improved *Reconstruction in Philosophy* (with shades of *The Quest for Certainty*). It shares the semi-popular writing style, begins his account in premodern mythmaking and the way that modern philosophy unfortunately continues to carry on antiquated modes of thought, argues that conceptual dichotomies are outworn by the advent of science, and concludes with the social and moral upshot. That Dewey would argue that we have not fully understood and accepted the consequences of the scientific-technological revolution, particularly as it regards human values, is no surprise. This is arguably the central theme of Dewey's body of work. And, of course, he offers historical accounts in other works.

As Dewey's texts differ not in basic concepts but in detail and emphasis, we must then ask what subtle shades *Unmodern Philosophy* provides. But, in analyzing what does make it unique, we could take many routes. It is possible to evaluate Dewey's historical account, to compare the book against contemporary works such as the reintroduction to *Experience and Nature* or *Knowing and the Known*, or to examine it as an ontology of events, a functionalized psychology, or a theory of technological inquiry. It is each of these things and more. In the following presentation of Dewey's argument, I will approach it through the category of culture. In that vein, I will present both Dewey's cultural history of philosophy and the philosophical framework embodied in it—cultural naturalism.

It is well known that Dewey came to question the use of the term *experience* and hoped to replace it with *culture*. This was striking, given that it is hard to find a word closer to Dewey's heart than *experience*. It stands with *democracy, education, and inquiry* to form Dewey's final vocabulary. In the reintroduction to *Experience and Nature*, a book he came to believe should have been titled *Culture and Nature*, he presents this new term as an extension, not a rejection, of *experience*.

> "Experience" is a word used to designate, in a summary fashion, the complex of all which is distinctly human. . . . "Culture" includes the material and the ideal in their reciprocal interrelationships and (in marked contrast with the prevailing use of "experience") "culture" designates, also in their reciprocal interconnections, that immense diversity of human affairs, interests, concerns, values which compartmentalists pigeonhole under "religion," "morals," "aesthetics," "politics,' 'economics,' etc., etc. (LW 1: 331, 363; see also LW 1: 42).

Unfortunately, the reintroduction breaks off before Dewey gives a detailed discussion of what he meant by culture. But it is clear that it is a term inclusive of the whole range of human association. Revealing Hegel's "permanent deposit" in his thought, Dewey makes culture play the role of *Geist*, forming the most inclusive category within which various regions of human life interact. "We are given to thinking of society in large and vague ways. We should forget 'society' and think of law, industry, religion, medicine, politics, art, education, philosophy—and think of them in the plural." We may conceptually separate social phenomena into the economic, political, and moral, but they are all aspects of "one subject matter, highly complex and diversified" (LW 5: 120; Dewey 1927). By turning to "culture," Dewey once again hoped to escape the inherited dualisms and divisions that had brought down *experience, practice*, and a host of other terms.

Because it arises from a complex social world, philosophy must avoid any monistic approach to social phenomena. By *monistic* Dewey meant any theory that makes one phase of culture so central that the others are not necessary to explain social phenomena. He singled out Marxism and the British classical school for making economic theory the sole consideration, contemporary historians for doing the same with politics, social Darwinists for reducing everything to power, and clergymen and newspapers for proposing a simple moral reformation as the response to social problems. The relation between cultural spheres is dialectical in the sense that the groups are mutually dependent and no one of them is the ultimate foundation of the others. For example, Dewey's critique of ecclesiastical groups such as the medieval Church was not that they failed to address genuine human needs, but that a group that should serve spiritual needs also sought to control economic relations, the family, and the government. With Dewey's central concept and broad approach in mind, let us turn to his cultural history of philosophy.

The final text is divided into two parts, corresponding to the two conjuncts in the title. The first part, comprising chapters 1 through 7, traces the rise of modern philosophy and the epistemological problem that forms its core. Ironically, the purpose of this genealogy is to show how deeply "unmodern" modern philosophy is. The second part is not historical but prospective. In chapters 8 through 14, Dewey begins an account of a truly modern philosophy, one that overcomes the epistemological problem of relating *subject* and *object* by functionalizing and naturalizing the process of knowing. Let us survey each chapter in turn.

In "Philosophy and the Conflict of Beliefs," Dewey approaches philosophy as an anthropologist. He begins with prephilosophical cultures that nevertheless still told stories about their natural and cultural environment. They distinguished the ordinary from the extraordinary, lucky from unlucky, sacred from common. Desiring safety, they sought out means of control but, lacking developed science, they relied on animistic forces to protect and console themselves. Philosophy then began in myth and culture, but we should not think that it has escaped. Even today, philosophy arises in response to the clash of novel experience and inherited tradition. Unlike science, which, Dewey states, aspires to eliminate the social factor, philosophy delves into it. The cultural approach is therefore more inclusive than the merely scientific:

> Philosophy has to take account of scientific conclusions. . . . Yet philosophy takes them not as isolated, complete and final in themselves, but in the context of other beliefs, moral, political, religious, economic and aesthetic. . . . To hold that the conflict must be resolved exclusively in terms of scientific beliefs is as one sided as it is to hold that it must be resolved in terms of traditional religious beliefs. For neither of these beliefs exhausts the field of experience. (000)

Philosophy sets scientific inquiry into a broader cultural context while simultaneously—one hopes—taking up its methods.

"The Story of Nature" presents the birth of two ideas concerning the nature of Nature. Dewey lauds the Greeks for an easy, native ability to balance the natural and the human. They saw before them an ordered, natural world but were not hidebound by the priestly class into abandoning artistry, imagination, and novelty. Repeating the assertion that philosophy must be understood in response to its social medium, Dewey asserts that two competing stories of Nature arose out of two crafts: the agricultural and the mechanical. The agrarian class saw nature as a process of immanent growth arising from a seed and eventuating in some fixed end or limit.

Individual things were defined by their inclusion under a fixed type. For the industrial class, purpose is imposed from without by the artisan. Elements do not grow of their own internal principles, but are manipulated according to the principles of mixture and separation.

In chapter 3, "The Discovery of Rational Discourse," Dewey recounts the transition from narrative to philosophy that was achieved in ancient Greece. Stories of nature, presumed to give Adamic representation of the world, came into conflict externally as societies interacted or internally as they lost cohesion. The very capacity of language to represent came into question. The logic of inquiry was born when philosophers asked how rational discourse about nature was possible. Tracing the course running from the sophists through Socrates and Plato and ending in Aristotle, Dewey argues that the philosophical response to social disintegration was to assert that rational discourse requires an object of common understanding and intent—a world. For Plato, this shared object that would ground knowledge and thereby reintegrate society was the supernatural Idea, the basis of political craft. Aristotle, however, severed the internal connection between knowledge and social action since they unite only in contemplation. Aristotle subsumes worldly action to immanent ends working themselves out. According to Dewey, this conclusion was inevitable because the Greeks lacked a valid logic of inquiry. They were able to reconcile discourse with its object, the world, only because the forms of Greek discourse had been imposed on nature beforehand. Their logic of definition and classification lacked the methodological and physical tools needed to develop a true logic of discovery, experimentation, or inquiry.

Following this account of the ancient world, we have the fragmentary chapter on the medieval period, "The Search for Salvation." The defining project of medieval thought was to fashion an escape from this world of political turmoil out of Aristotle's theory of Being, the Hebraic godhead, and Roman natural law theory. These abstractions were synthesized and given emotional and institutional form in the Church. The Church achieved the seemingly impossible—a unity of theory and practice in a hierarchical society ordered according to the revealed will of God. Greek naturalism was supernaturalized. Dewey ends this part of his history by turning us toward the moderns, their debt to the idea of natural law, and the need to study modern science as part of a broader cultural movement.

"From Cosmic Nature to Human Nature" begins Dewey's four-chapter discussion of modern philosophy. Rebelling against the stifling medieval synthesis embodied in the Church, modern thinkers made human nature take the place of the cosmic order but overcompensated with an intuitive, introspective method that replicated the supernatural separation of mind from nature. For all its flaws, the ancient model was still a form of naturalism. The supernaturalism of the medieval period had split human nature from nature. The moderns rejected the dichotomy only to reverse it. Descartes and Locke, as the prototypically modern thinkers, did not overcome the split between the human and the natural but disagreed over whether to prioritize that which is internal to human nature or external to it. What began as the practical, human problem ossified into a metaphysical and epistemological one. Given a split between nature and human nature, the epistemological question was inevitable.

With modern philosophy, the question was not "*How* is rational discourse about nature possible?" but "*Is* knowledge possible?" It was no longer a matter of the logic of inquiry but of epistemology. In "Wandering between Two Worlds," the blame for epistemology again falls on the antiquated inheritance bequeathed by the Greek-medieval period. Dewey shows that the interminable debate between empiricists and rationalists effaces what they share—faculty psychology, a split between the internal and external, and beliefs in certain knowledge resting on first principles, universal laws, substances, and "the given." The result is fruitless arguments over "indubitable" truth not open to examination. Meanwhile, principles and data within scientific practice have their authority solely because of their function within inquiry, not because of temporal or ontological priority. Just as science was making rapid advances in the attainment of knowledge, philosophy was asking whether knowledge was possible at all.

"The Present Problem of Knowledge," a critical chapter for Dewey's cultural naturalism, consummates Dewey's genealogy of modern philosophy. He highlights modern philosophy's preoccupation with finding a method to secure certain knowledge and the resulting isolation of knowing from broader human concerns. The philosophical tradition has treated the problem of knowledge in the abstract when inquiry is actually a matter of concrete events. What constitutes a fact or a problem depends on the state of a culture and its tensions. To be a naturalist is to understand knowledge as an event, as a "knowledging," and method must begin from events-in-connection. "To say that man is in the natural world is then a way of saying that all events big or little that are or that can be characterized as human occur in connection with events investigated in other branches of inquiry, and are to be themselves investigated with any and all aids supplied by knowledge of these other events" (144). Inquiry is one cultural event pursued by particular groups, one event in relation to others.

As societies change over time, the problem of knowledge changes as well. Philosophy has historically distinguished between Truth revealed by Reason and belief attained by culturally embedded inquiry. The proper contrast is between culturally embedded groups that are hidebound by tradition and those that are reflective. The moral, religious, and aesthetic aspects of culture are dominated by groups invested in the ancient-medieval tradition, pushing out more reflective ones. Sadly, the scientific community—one highly refined group dedicated to reflective inquiry—has been given free rein to study nature but excluded from human concerns, broadly conceived. But the division of the of the natural from the human, as has been shown by Dewey's account so far, is itself an event with its own history and is not inevitable. The task going forward is to cultivate habits, mores, and institutions that integrate science's practices, making them one cultural sphere in transaction with the others.

Having set out his cultural history of modern philosophy in order to show how unmodern it is, Dewey turns to a constructive account of a genuinely modern philosophy in part 2. Specifically, he attempts to replace epistemology with a functionalized, naturalized account of knowing. After a short prefatory chapter, Dewey proceeds by overcoming a series of outworn philosophical dualisms.

Dewey's intention in "The Supreme Human Art" is to acknowledge the progressive element of modern philosophy—its concern to bring experience into the light of critical inquiry. "This direction of advance is conveyed, at least by contrast, by the general sense of writers modern in tenor that there was something hidden and occult in the older views. Stated in positive words, there was a sincere and energetic effort to get things out into the open, into the public air and light of day where they are open to inspection on equal terms by any and all who are properly equipped" (169). Berkeley's elimination of Lockean substance, for example, was an attempt to eliminate any occult forces operating behind events. However, Dewey quickly turns back to a critique, noting the failure of Hume, Kant, and contemporary idealists and realists to escape the quest for certainty, the split between inner and outer, and the prioritization of an immaterial Mind.

Chapter 9, "Things and Persons," identifies the first of five false dualisms. A naturalized account of personhood has been delayed because of ancient, medieval, and modern deposits. The Greek-medieval image of the nonphysical and immortal soul, the modern epistemological, knowing subject, and the liberal, asocial political individual all resulted from an image of personhood not rooted in transactional behavior. True to his genetic method, Dewey understands individuals to be unique histories or temporal continuities of behavior. Individuals, in turn, become persons when they take up social roles and the moral esteem or blame that comes in fulfilling them. Models of personhood rooted in intuitive self-awareness thereby have problems explaining knowledge of other persons and fail to recognize the affective, natural, and cultural interactions that make personhood and self-awareness possible. Things and persons then arise from the same material distinguished by the ways they function within cultural practice.

Chapter 10, "Mind and Body," functionalizes the operations of mind as minding, attending, or intending within an ongoing continuity of activity. They mark the redirection of energies, not the imposition of an external stimulus or internal will. Knowing is not passive observation, but disciplined observation and experimentation. Focusing on the supposed dichotomy of sensation and reflection, Dewey argues that the former marks a breach of habit or anticipation and the latter is the redirection of activity inward as the organism prepares a future course of overt action. Sensations are events, not isolated qualities (which are only had after discrimination and analysis). The second section, drawn from a separate manuscript, functionalizes the distinction between the empirical and the rational. The chapter concludes with a striking section in which Dewey openly describes knowing as a mode of technology. Knowledge could be the technology that regulates other technologies (commonly understood as tools) were it not for the fact that they are now governed by conflicting, unintelligent customs and institutions. Sadly, technology is claimed to be unable to produce new ends and reduced to mere instrumentality, the process of transforming materials into products is forgotten, and we are left with philosophical attempts to explain the "mystery" of how refined ideals come to be.

Making explicit use of the technological model of knowing, in "The Practical and the Theoretical," Dewey counters the historical, socially instituted, and stultifying denigration of practice and corresponding elevation of pure theory. The idea of theory as pure science is retained, but by making it an aspect of practice. The theoretical is functionalized to mean "having that quality or role played by theory within scientific practice." Practice is often reduced to the merely "practical," that which is subservient to some desired end. But inquiry is not practical when it serves an end external to itself, for pure science is committed to a process, not an outcome. Science is liberal and, as liberal, the practice includes reflection on ends. Instrumental action is not truly purposive action. The latter effects a continuous course in pursuit of some end-in-view. The theoretical is the hypothetical, the positing of general facts that lead us toward existential reconstruction of situations. Theory is then that phase of practice wherein habitual interaction is frustrated and energy turns inward to consider both ends and means and, thereby, to prepare the way for future activity. But, as practice is inherently moral, it is also aesthetic. Reflection may be enjoyed in itself through disinterested curiosity or reverie. Reflection, overt action, and even contemplation are then phases of a larger, ongoing whole.

Underlying the dichotomy of the practical and theoretical is that stated in the title of the next chapter, "The Material and the Ideal." Dewey contends that culture is a whole whose integrated parts are discriminated for the purposes of inquiry. Objects or events, whether they are chairs or religious rites, are embodied meanings. The material is distinguished from the non-material world of knowledge, value, and social organization in the analysis of culture, but such separation is not inherent. *Material* in functionalized to mean "relevant or germane to present inquiry," as when something is dismissed as "immaterial." Typically, we take one aspect of how an event transpires, hypostatize it, and make it the event's essential meaning.

In "Nature and Human Nature," Dewey recalls elements of "From Cosmic Nature to Human Nature" and regrets that modern philosophy overlooked an opportunity to overcome its Greek-medieval inheritance. He returns to the question of why humanism and naturalism came to be opposed. As the moderns turned toward human nature, they understood it in isolation from its social context. An unhealthy and egocentric individualism arose. Dewey sees this as part of the elimination, in the physical sciences, of moral ends from nature. Of course, he attributes this elimination to our Greek-medieval tradition's elevation of the secure and unchanging. Had philosophers been truly modern, they could have asked *why* it was that the elimination of ends produced rapid progress in the natural sciences. They could have then engaged in a fruitful discussion of the relations between various aspects of experience—the scientific, the esthetic, the moral—but they did not.

"'Experience as Life-Function" is the last extant chapter and serendipitously summarizes much of the preceding chapters. Dewey points toward a general theory of experience, postulating that experience is the process of living itself, that such living is a series of sociocultural events, that any psychological theory must begin from such social behavior and, lastly, that a theory of experience is a means to criticism and improvement of that behavior. In defense of these postulates, he argues that social interaction is the ground of meaning. We begin always and already within a meaningful whole. Out of this whole, we may distinguish organic from environmental, or epistemic from esthetic and practical, but these are always functional distinctions, not typological. All activity, including the scientific, is practical and forward-looking just as it is always capable of immediate esthetic appreciation. Whether a particular event is primarily a matter of truth, morality, or art is then a matter of situation and emphasis. In short, philosophy must make culture both its subject matter and its central analytical category. With that, the manuscript breaks off.

Because I have repeatedly highlighted the centrality of culture, it is important to note that culture is itself natural. There is no breach between culture and nature. As noted in Dewey's *Logic: The Theory of Inquiry*, the matrix of life is both biological and cultural (LW 12: Chs. 2–3). Were Dewey to elevate and isolate culture as the realm of human concerns above nature, he would have only repeated the error of unmodern philosophy. The isolation of the human—the realm of values, ends, theory, mind, personhood, etc.—from the natural is precisely the problem. Their separation was overcome in the natural sciences by Darwin. The lesson now needs to be extended to all other areas of human interest. This fact applies equally well to contemporary philosophers at one extreme who would reduce mind to the neurochemical operations of the brain and to others, like Dewey's late admirer Richard Rorty, who would reduce nature (insofar as it is meaningful) to culture. Natural inquiry is not, for Dewey, simply a type of literature oriented toward solidarity. As he had done in so many other areas of inquiry, Dewey showed that the solution to an outworn dualism is not to reverse and preserve it, but to overcome it by seeing it from a broader perspective. Once culture has flowered from nature, we may not uproot it.

Unfortunately, Dewey's presentation of a naturalized theory of knowing and its relation to the modern era is incomplete. Though we cannot be certain where Dewey intended to go next, there are scattered clues. Throughout the manuscript, he offers promissory notes indicating chapters to come, as when he points forward to discussions of economics or the relation between the individual and the social. In the late outline, he sketches some implications of experience for philosophy—that it offers a corrective to both philosophical dualisms and the cultural conflicts underneath them. He asks: "What is the general value of a philosophy theory of experience in the sense elicited in previous chapters? . . . Isolations and exaggerations. Genetic-functional view affords tested means of criticizing and correcting—since as expressed in philosophy they represent formulations of those in actual social life-experience, serve indirectly as indication of courses to be followed, policies to be adopted, socio-moral" (Special Collections folder 61/21). Dewey had hoped not only to provide an account of the cultural origins of philosophy, but also to engage the present culture and address its felt needs, tensions, and contradictions. As always, philosophy ultimately must concern itself with the problems of humanity.

Modernity and the Need for a Critical Theory of Culture

Because the surviving manuscript is incomplete, it is understandable that we might wonder what would have come next. Having surveyed the content of Dewey's history of unmodern and modern philosophy, I now turn to other texts written contemporaneously with the present one in search of clues. Looking to other texts, we find hints of Dewey's "grand design" promised by Ratner.[1] Dewey explicitly argued that the dualisms dividing modern philosophy express deeper cultural tensions. This is true not only of the ancients, medievals, and moderns, but also of philosophers today. The cultural contradictions of modernity live on and, Dewey argued, we still have not come to grips with them. The project was clearly still on his mind after the manuscript's disappearance, as shown when Dewey wrote in his 1948 reintroduction to *Reconstruction in Philosophy*: "[W]hat is called "modern" is as yet unformed, inchoate. Its confused strife and its unstable uncertainties reflect the mixture of an old and a new that are incompatible. The genuinely modern has still to be brought into existence" (MW 12: 273). In that spirit, I present Dewey's account of the broken modern period and his call for a critical and reconstructive theory of culture.

John Patrick Diggins has accused Dewey of ignoring the challenges posed by modernity. Diggins voiced a series of criticisms of Dewey's theory, including charges of an unfounded faith in scientific progress, a dismissal of the past, a failure to acknowledge the tragic irrationality of human experience, and an inability to appreciate the limits of knowledge under modernity. But what really galls him is the belief that the pragmatist does not suffer over the new age. Diggins shares Dewey's belief that, with the advent of the modern era, philosophy's dream of certain knowledge of the Absolute is impossible. However, he dismisses Dewey's naturalized reconstruction of underlying existential contradictions as an optimistic pre-postmodernism (Diggins 1994).[2]

Dewey has similarly been accused of offering no deep theory of culture. Perhaps the sharpest criticism came from the Frankfurt School, which argued that pragmatism is structurally unable to support a robust critique of basic social structures. In its supposed reduction of Truth to efficiency, any critique that it might muster collapses into the dominant ideology of late capitalism (Lukacs 1971, 188, 195; Adorno 1973, 373; Horkheimer 1972). This criticism was anticipated by Bertrand Russell and Lewis Mumford in

---

1. Some relevant works are "Introduction to the 1948 Reprint of Reconstruction in Philosophy" (MW 12: 256–77); "Objectivism-Subjectivism of Modern Philosophy" (LW 14: 189–200); "How Is Mind to Be Known?" (LW 15: 27–33); "Between Two Worlds" (LW 17: 451–65); "The Future of Philosophy" (LW 17: 466–70); "Modern Philosophy" (LW 16: 407–19) which is mentioned in Dewey's correspondence (1947.01.17, 13529); "Liberating the Social Scientist" (Special Collections folder 55/4); and "Philosophy and the Conflict of Beliefs" (folder 61/23).

2. For a systematic response to Diggins's portrayal of Dewey, see Eldridge 1998, 185–94. Contra Diggins, Thelma Lavine has argued that "Among the classical American philosophers—Royce, Peirce, James, Dewey and Mead—only Dewey perceived the axial significance of the conflicting philosophical frameworks that had emerged in the modern era; it was Dewey who devoted his lifelong career to exploring the multifactoral causes, the consequences for social practice, and the prospects for mediation and reconciliation of the philosophical contestations of modernity" (Lavine 1998, 217).

their contention that pragmatism was the philosophical expression of the Gilded Age and celebrated hubris and materialism (Russell 1922; Mumford 1926). Blending Weberian sociology and a deep knowledge of the pragmatic thought, C. Wright Mills argued that Dewey lacks an account of political action, that action that involves entrenched power structures and the value-decisions that underlie them (Mills 1964).

Even as sympathetic an author as Robert Westbrook, whose *John Dewey and American Democracy* emphasizes Dewey's role as a public intellectual, believes he lacks any comprehensive social theory. Referring to his *Logic*, Westbrook writes: "This neglect of the social context of inquiry points, I think, to a curious feature of Dewey's philosophy generally, which I am hard-pressed to explain. Although he was always insisting on the primacy of the social, Dewey really did not have a whole lot to say that could in any strict sense be termed social theory" (Westbrook 2005, 185; see also Wolfe 1998, 204). While Charles Frankel points out Dewey's abiding concern with social issues and goes so far as to write that his philosophy "was nothing if it was not, in its entirety, a social philosophy," he goes on to argue that a great failing of Dewey's thought is that he did not actually have a social theory, as traditionally understood (Frankel 1977, 6).[3]

If Dewey were part of some other philosophical tradition, then the absence of a critical social theory would not be as serious a problem. If he were a mystic, turning away from the world to contemplate the Godhead, or a positivist who builds from atomic facts unchanged by social context, then he would not be compelled to develop a broad theory. But Cornel West correctly notes that Dewey makes a basic claim that "social practices—contingent, power-laden, structured social practices—lie at the very center of knowledge." If pragmatism does not address basic structures and cultural conflicts, then it faces what West calls the "political critique of pragmatism"—that it has an "inadequate grasp of the complex operations of power, principally owing to a reluctance to take traditions of historical sociology and social theory seriously" (West 1999, 278; 1993, 135). It would be a tragic irony if pragmatism turns us toward culture only to have nothing compelling to say about it.

However, Dewey affirmed the need for a critical theory and gives it explicit direction—it must come to grasp the meaning and conditions of modernity. In an unpublished fragment written soon after the disappearance of the manuscript, we find Dewey stating the problem posed by the rise of modernity:

---

3. I do not mean to ignore the valuable contributions made to pragmatic social theory. To note only a few, they include Campbell 1992; Campbell 1995; Lewis and Smith 1980; Rucker 1969; Kloppenberg 1986; Purcell 1973; Joas 1993; Joas 1996; Habermas 1985.

The "moral" to be educed is that the primary business of moral theory, now and doubtless for a long time to come, is to forward the formation of a system of Mores or institutional customs which are sufficiently in balance with one another to give support and direction to vast and in-choate common life which has suddenly, unexpectedly, as if by a kind of fate come to replace the small, isolated and fairly tight communities of the past (Dewey 1948).

As shown in "Wandering between Two Worlds," Dewey believed modernity to have a quality of its own. It did not mark simply the current era, but was the institution of a new meaning to *experience*. In the broad meaning of the word, modern experience was a new relation between one human being and another and between human beings and nature. The innovations of Machiavelli in politics, Galileo and Copernicus in physics, and Luther in religion each displayed this shift into the modern age. Its defining quality is a breakdown of traditional stability and the institution of a commitment to the unknown, to the future.

Modernity was ushered in by the scientific-technological-industrial revolution. Technoscience has transformed virtually all aspects of culture.

It can be confidently affirmed that every aspect, content, structure and phase of human life has been radically changed, directly or indirectly, for weal or woe, by proliferating and accelerating industrial-technological revolutions. For example: they have changed the structure of family life, the status of women, the relations of the sexes, of parents and children; education has been changed in every respect, quantitatively and qualita-tively; vast populations have been urbanized, imposing new occupations and new ways of life; transportation and communication have been revo-lutionized, with incalculable human consequences; intra-national and international relations, friendly and hostile, cooperative and competitive have been multiplied and intensified; local and world-wide class and race problems have been generated or exacerbated. (LW 1: 358)

Should we think that Dewey was naïve about the level of disruption and disaster now possible because of modern invention, he also notes that "Over-shadowing it all, the industrial-technological revolutions are largely, if not wholly, responsible for two world wars in one generation and the threat of another of ultimate destructiveness" (LW 1: 358).

This book details a modern philosophy riven by a series of conceptual dualisms between mind and body, practical and theoretical, material and ideal, etc. When philosophy treats these dualisms in the abstract it ignores the underlying conflicts that lead us to conceptualize the world in this way. Dewey argued that

> the dualisms which are the staple of modern philosophy are, in the first place, reflections, mirrorings, of clashes, cleavages in the cultural life of the West; and . . . these splits and divisions are manifestations of the impact of new movements in science, industry, the arts generally, in religion and political organization upon institutions having deep roots in the past. The new movements gave a profound shock to established institutions, but they did not overthrow them (LW 16: 407).

Take for example the private sphere, a concept Dewey indicates he was to discuss further in the manuscript. It is not enough to simply note the rise of appeals to personal conscience and its rights between the fifteenth and the eighteenth centuries. "[T]he idea of a purely private area of consciousness, where whatever goes on has no external consequences, was in the first instance a product of institutional change, political and ecclesiastic[.]" And these changes could not have occurred "until social mobility and heterogeneity had brought about initiation and invention in technological matters and industry, and until secular pursuits had become formidable rivals to church and state" (LW 2: 267). The private sphere is a system of social relations, but one that has effaced its social character behind the abstract dispute between the Individual and Society.

As the whole of *Unmodern Philosophy and Modern Philosophy* testifies, change in material conditions does not necessarily manifest in changes in beliefs, ideals, traditions, and institutions. Our beliefs and institutions were developed when scarcity was a central concern, nature was a constant source of fear, and economic production was primarily the work of individuals. The industrial revolution changed all that. Though modern philosophy is seemingly marked by a corresponding disruption of traditional standards of truth, beauty, and rightness, Dewey contended that the underlying beliefs and their legitimization have remained rooted in a premodern world. Modern technoscience does not seek correspondence to a fixed reality, but sets elements of experience in relation to one another in the interest of improved future conduct. It is post-Darwinian, rejecting fixed ends and essences and turning to context, relation, and experiment. However, philosophers still use categories developed during the search for the immutable—even those positivist and realist philosophers who believe themselves to be truly scientific.

In the short term, the resilience of beliefs under new circumstances serves a valuable function. Our generally accepted, largely unreflective norms for behavior provide guidance and stability. They prevent the chaos that would accompany a collapse of tradition. Such "cultural lag" allows people to deal with new conditions without overwhelming confusion and dislocation.

However, in the long term, the conflict between traditional legitimacy and modern material conditions eventually does produce such dislocation. Problems arise when the culture is in disarray, the conditions for action are new, and traditional understanding of what is to be done no longer holds.

Parallel to the distinction between traditional and reflective groups made in "The Present Problem of Knowledge," Dewey distinguished between customary and reflective morality in the 1932 *Ethics*. Customary morality holds in stable, homogeneous cultures. There is no need for a critique of institutions, as they are sufficient to felt needs. "When social life is stable, when custom rules, the problems of morals have to do with the adjustments which individuals make to the institutions in which they live, rather than with the quality of the institutions themselves." Our mores and institutions hardly become an object for reflection at all. Moral theory is the product of reflective cultures, under conditions that no longer fit our expectation or ability to control. "When social life is in a state of flux, moral issues cease to gather exclusively about personal conformity and deviation. They centre in the value of social arrangements, of laws, of inherited traditions that have crystallized into institutions, in changes that are desirable. Institutions lose their quasi-sacredness and are objects of moral questioning. We now live in such a period" (LW 7: 314–15, 318). Attention shifts from how we may live up to our social roles and obligations to determining exactly what they are. Like the ancient Greeks, medievals, and moderns, we are forced to confront novel experience against the background of received customs and mores.

As recently as the turn of the twentieth century, Dewey believed it was possible to still speak of the world as our home. Responding to a passage from Royce that defined the role of philosophy as elaborating upon our basic feeling of law and comfort, Dewey countered that, though it may once have been possible to assume this feeling, it is not possible any more. Philosophy's task is not to simply articulate the world's apparent reasonableness, but to try to piece it together. It must look for "ways to make the world more one of worth and significance, more homelike, in fact" (LW 15: 169).

We need a theory that begins from the disarray of modern life. "We do not philosophize—that is to say, we do not construct theories—about our customs and habits and institutions until some sort of difficulty or obstruction raises questions in our minds about the ways in which we have been carrying out our group activities. It is always the social institution which precedes the theory; not the theory which precedes the institution" (Dewey 1919–20, 45). Positivist social science makes the mistake of thinking that its categories arise outside of particular circumstances and historical precedents. Instead, norms and institutions must be developed from within current practice, as fractured as it might be.

Under the fractured conditions of modernity—where new material conditions brought about by the industrial technological revolution are in conflict with the superstructure of traditional norms—philosophy is in danger of being ideology. "Until mankind has managed to develop a moderately unified or cohering set of institutional customs, moral theory is bound to remain either controversial, half-hearted and half-minded, or else, more or less in desperation a recourse to some dogma called 'science,' in support of the claim of some particular institution to rule the moral beliefs and practices of mankind" (Dewey 1948, n.p.)

"Modern" philosophy may claim to be scientific and universal, but invariably represents the interests of some particular institution or other. Inquiry is restricted by the institutions through which it works.

> Scientific method affects the conditions of life only through the medium of institutions to which scientific inquiry is *not* applied; to what the consequences of science *might* be were they so applied; such inquiry might hope to have some role, to play some part, in development of attitudes in the community that are liberal, well-tested, and grounded in fact (LW 15: 158).

The splits between ideal and material, value and fact, means and ends, and profit and use—the very conceptual divisions treated in the second part of this book—are not present in scientific practice on its own, but reflect institutionalized social divisions. Scientific inquiry, if it is not to become ideology, must be viewed through the category of culture.

Therefore, one condition for alleviating cultural conflicts is to free social inquiry itself from it ancient-medieval inheritance, allowing it to become a naturalistic, reflective and critical theory of culture. A running theme in Dewey's work is that social inquiry needs a revolution in method akin to the one that physical science underwent during the last few centuries. The scientific temper may have had success in the natural world, but the study of humankind is severely lacking. One sign of the immaturity of social inquiry is that its subject-matter is so fractured. Politics, art, economics, and jurisprudence are assigned to separate disciplines, each with its own methods and assumptions. When inquirers do not recognize that the varied facets of associated life are connected, then they cut off the means to alleviate the underlying conflicts. Social theory needs to realize that "one of the prime problems today is to show that human material in its full scope is now the proper subject-matter of philosophy" (LW 16: 417–18). Until then, it will work within its institutional divisions, using conceptual tools that reflect but do not critique the social conflicts that are properly its main concern.

Social theory is itself a product of social practice and is bound up in it, with all of the associated structures, customs, and shortcomings. Part of a critique of cultural conflicts must then be an identification and critique of the ways that inquiry into culture is itself distorted by them. "The important work is to make evident the social conditions—economic, political, moral and religious—which have restricted scientific inquiry" (LW 15: 167). Inquiry into culture must analyze those vested interests that have something to gain by shielding human concerns, economic arrangements, and customary values from genuine scientific inquiry.

Once the unscientific limitations placed on inquiry are removed, it may reflect on values. In his "Liberating the Social Scientist," Dewey surveyed recent works by Daniel Bell, Nathan Glazer, and Karl Polanyi in the sociology of sociology itself. What these researchers found was that social inquiry accepted basic social categories of "what is" and then simply set out to describe it, without regard for larger social concerns. But larger social issues are "necessarily and inevitably an integral part of the subject matter of inquiry" (LW 15: 226).[4] To separate *is* from *ought* is to concede questions of value to the status quo. Studies of means or power alone are not the whole of social science. What to give attention to is a choice on the part of the scientist, one often backed by powerful institutional interests.

As social inquiry must concern itself with values, it must also analyze and develop institutions. To complete the fragment quoted earlier on the business of moral theory, "The first work to be done is to inquire into the conditions which have brought about the disintegration of Mores that is now the marked feature of the human scene. . . . [T]he development of such unified institutional ways of living is now precisely the basic and all-inclusive problem and task of mankind" (Dewey 1948, n.p.). The reconstruction of modernity is both dependent upon the application of inquiry and a condition for that inquiry. A critical theory of culture was not only a part of Dewey's thought, it was an immanent, necessary one.

There is, of course, going to be a great deal of resistance to the use of science to develop new norms and institutions for a modern society, especially when scientific inquiry has played a large role in breaking down traditional authority. But Dewey believed that it was our only option. "A culture which permits science to destroy traditional values but which distrusts its power to create new ones is a culture which is destroying itself" (LW 13: 172). It is hard to argue that science does not determine the material relations of the modern world. We no longer rely on intuition or divine authority to determine how to set prices for goods, to cure disease or otherwise investigate

---

4. In a letter to Sidney Hook, Dewey remarked that he was compelled to rewrite "Liberating the Social Scientist" because the original draft was too influenced by the book on modern philosophy (1947.04.01, 13160). A substantial fragment of that early draft is found in Folder 55/4 of the Dewey Papers.

the natural world. The only question is whether we find the means to live democratically in the methods of scientific-technological inquiry, or stubbornly hold on to the traditional values that are bound to fade away.

By learning from the experimental attitude of the physical sciences, social inquiry could reconstruct its outworn institutions. Dewey directed social inquiry to take up the experimental method, which attends to the situation, calls out responses, measures them in practice, and then evaluates both ideals and consequences against the new, reconstructed situation. In the broadest terms, a Deweyan theory of culture would develop a culture's immanent values, look to consequences, and adopt an organic model. Let us turn briefly to each.

First, ideals are developed out of the material of shared life. Dewey rejected the belief, held by both positivists and absolutists, that values are external to inquiry. Science is instead shot-through with values. The question is whether they are immanent to inquiry or if they are imposed from outside. As critical theory must work from within the immanent valuations of a culture, "criticism is then equivalent to taking the standpoint of another social group, actual or possible, having other habits of praise-blame and other systems of rights-obligations" (MW 15: 238). The theorist evaluates the needs intrinsic to a group by its interaction with other cultural interests. Of particular importance, the critical theorist, though working from the material of present groups' valuations, is not bound to the precise belief systems of any one of them. If the intrinsic principles of shared life are not met by present culture, they may still be used to critique from the perspective of their future fulfillment.

> A social criterion must (1) express the intrinsic defining principle of human associations as they actually exist, but (2) in such a form that the idea or principle may be contrasted with existent concrete forms. Certain conditions have to be fulfilled in order that they may be a social group at all; these traits, abstracted, define society. This definition becomes a criterion when actual phenomena are compared with it to see how fully they realize or express it. Taken empirically, an ideal represents an actual tendency projected to its *limit*. Thus an ideal of society represents the tendencies that define actual societies carried to their limit. (MW 15: 238–39; see also LW 12: 493).

The norms that direct social theory must arise from within the practices of the culture and, when idealized, provide a critical vantage point.

Theory must also be consequentialist. In that vein, Dewey believed that the test of meaning and value is the set of conceivable consequences that an idea would have on the world. Ultimately, the measure of any social program is to be found in how it allows a society to address its problems and reconstruct conditions for the better. The fact is that inquiry modifies the world and, if we are to evaluate it, then it must be on the basis of those existential changes. Dewey believed that when making values final and intrinsic, we remove them from scrutiny. If they are not public, then there is no way to measure another individual's claim to truth. The door is open to ideology when subjective preferences are made absolute.

Let us apply this point to social inquiry in particular. It is only by locating concepts within social practice that they are accessible to inquiry. Intrinsic values cannot be adjudicated, but

> If we recognize that these conflicting standards express conflicting customs and aspirations, then we're bound to go back to these social forces and subject them to careful observation and tracing of consequences. In the observable results in social practice we find a common measure by which to choose among them, and at least introduce a reasonable element into what is otherwise an irrational clash of prejudices. (Dewey 1927, n.p.)

Timeless assertions of final values reflect prior social conditions. Therefore, if we are to resolve seemingly intractable moral conflicts, we must transform the concrete conditions underlying the conflict of abstract values. The judgments of social inquiry are judgments of practice and are inherently directed toward the transformation of a problematic situation.

Lastly, social inquiry must be holistic. As discussed in the last section, culture is a complex of equally significant facets of culture. Those who would make any one of these facets foundational—be they economic determinists waiting for the inevitable revolution or moralists calling for a change of heart to restore the nation—have made a grave error. For "isolating any one factor, no matter how strong its workings at a given time, is fatal to understanding and to intelligent action" (LW 14: 79).

Dewey was often criticized for his seeming unwillingness to offer specific proposals. This reflects his commitment to contingency and to democratic method. He does not offer an absolute condemnation or affirmation of a particular ideal except in its relation to its concrete consequences for other ideals. Dewey did not offer fixed goods; instead, he placed the emphasis on the means by which we evaluate any particular good in light of others. This upsets the possibility that we may ever establish an unchanging hierarchy of values. For this reason, he argued for the fundamental ideals of communication and growth. The ideal is that of the organic community that reconciles individual freedom and their social roles. In such a community, individuals share in one another's lives without alienation, and inquiry is undistorted by external forces such as the desire for profit. The only permanent good is the commitment to further inquiry. It is a method that is normatively justified, not any particular end or outcome of inquiry.

The critique and reconstruction of social structures is joined closely to the self-realization of the individual. Because Dewey did not leave us with any final substantive end, he left us with an emphasis on character. The best hope of a society is to produce individuals that refuse to block the path of inquiry. The reflective and holistic character of social theory must be integrated into individual lives. Economic processes and the political structures that guide them must take the development of each person as their goal. "Democracy has many meanings, but if it has a moral meaning, it is found in resolving that the supreme test of all political institutions and industrial arrangements shall be in the contribution they make to the all-around growth of every member of society" (MW 12: 187). We live our entire lives in association. We are members of churches, social groups, nations, families, etc. The question is then one of whether or not these associations allow us to develop into sensitive, self-determined, and productive people. Dewey's notoriety in educational theory may lead us to believe that he placed exclusive emphasis on the school as the agent of moral development. However, Dewey took the school to work in concert with other institutions. In fact, he went so far as to say that this educative function, broadly understood, is the true measure of any social institution (LW 5: 102).[5]

Because our democratic institutions are grounded on an outworn, "modern" liberalism, they are not well prepared to accept the collapse of these underlying theories and the change in material life. The complex set of relations that Dewey termed *culture* has become fractured and dislocated. The task is to determine how democratic ideals can be reconstituted and institutionalized throughout culture. The choice is then between a social environment that is the result of chance and tradition, or one guided by intelligence.

> When theories of values do not afford intellectual assistance in framing ideas and beliefs about values that are adequate to direct action, the gap must be filled by other means. If intelligent method is lacking, prejudice, the pressure of immediate circumstance, self-interest and class-interest, traditional customs, institutions of accidental historic origin, are *not* lacking, and they tend to take the place of intelligence (LW 4: 211–212).

This shines through in *Freedom and Culture*, published shortly before Dewey began work on *Unmodern Philosophy*. In that book, the driving concern is to upset the notion that the desire for political freedom was inborn in human nature and the inevitable *telos* of human history. Rather, the rise of

---

5. See also MW 9: 7, 9. In addition, see Dewey's argument that wants are made effective demands by social arrangements like the market (Hook 1926, 19).

totalitarianism had revealed that political liberty is not a given and must have roots in a larger whole—democratic culture. The desire for equal liberty is a permanent possibility within human nature, but so is the will to dominate. Those who would pursue democratic ends must then understand how to cultivate the democratic possibilities within human nature. They must attend not only to politics, but also to economics, natural science, the arts, and morality. Each is primordial and each must be understood as part of a complex of mutually influential and mutually dependent forces. "This complex of conditions which taxes the terms upon which human beings associate and live together is summed up in the word *Culture*" (LW 14: 67). By Dewey's account, totalitarianism is a retreat from the fact of modernity, an attempt to resolve all cultural questions through the creation of an all-encompassing blueprint. Democratic culture, in contrast, confronts and incorporates the lessons of modern science and culture (LW 17: 469).

It might seem that, in discussing the contradictions of modernity and the need for a critical theory of culture, we have strayed from the content of the book in your hands. We have not. Dewey may have written a cultural history of philosophy, but it is clear that he did not intend it to be of historical interest only. Historical works may be strategic interventions into present problems. Like his student John Herman Randall, Dewey understood history as the long process of humans attempting to resolve deep cultural tensions both against a backdrop of sedimented habits, customs, and institutions and with an eye to ever-evolving cultural ideals. History and philosophy (as disciplines) begin from the facts of cultural tension and change, and it is their function to maintain continuity, to synthesize the novel into the perennial when possible. And when this is not possible—as when the Western tradition must escape aspects of its Greek-medieval inheritance—it is the job of thought to propose new ideals, to find a new home for old ideals, and to develop more intelligent practices. For both Dewey and Randall, the central task of thought in our era is to incorporate the changes brought about by the scientific-technological revolution; specifically, to understand knowledge not as immediate, but as mediate and functional, always embedded in ongoing historical processes.

Dewey and Randall also shared a critical historiography. All histories are selective. Facts are relevant only to the inquiry at hand. This is not to say that history is whatever we make it, but that the historian is always swept forward by an evolving tradition in which the present leads us to alter what we take to be the critical precedents. In good pragmatic fashion, ever-developing consequences change the meaning of the original event. So our past depends on our image of the present and future. As Randall puts it, "The historian's choice of a principle of selection necessarily involves a certain choice of 'allegiance,' and act of 'faith' in one kind of future rather than another" (1958, 44).

And Dewey has definitely provided a selective history of Western philosophy. We should then ask what faith shaped Dewey's history. As always, it is his hope for a more humane, reflective, and democratic community. Dewey's call to recognize the breakdown of the promises of the Enlightenment was as severe or revolutionary a statement of the problem of modernity as those of his critics mentioned at the beginning of this section.[6] For example, like the Frankfurt School, he saw a connection between the darker side of modernity and totalitarianism. Too often, people feel that they are not part of a meaningful whole. Absent any genuine connection, people will find a way to belong. When, for example, social theory begins from the dichotomy of the individual versus society, it uses a conceptual tool that hampers the search for truth and limits our ability to critique the breakdown of community. By setting *individuality* in an abstract or conceptual opposition to totalitarianism, we overlook an important point—totalitarianism is itself an expression of atomic individualism. "This seemingly sudden *out*break of totalitarian collectivism was in fact the breaking *through* the surface, into overt manifestation, of underlying phases of the previous individualism" (LW 15: 215; see also MW 8: 421–46; Dewey 1946). When modern social conditions both produce this alienation and skew the analytic tools that we use to diagnose it, then it is exceedingly difficult to produce a better, more homelike world.

The purpose of a critical theory of culture is then to institute new customs that are appropriate to modern conditions, to integrate lost individuals into a democratic community. As Dewey believed that the scientific and technological revolution has opened up the possibility to finally institute a democratic culture, it must now actualize that possibility in the institutions, character, and customs of the people. The history befitting the needs of our present is one that explains the sources of our failure to apply the methods of open inquiry to ethics, society, and politics. In reconstructing Dewey's lost text, we find the remains of one last attempt to explain the history of a present burdened by an outworn inheritance and to offer cultural naturalism as a way forward.

Works Cited

Adorno, Theodor. 1973. *Negative Dialectics* trans. E. B. Ashton. New York: Continuum Press.

Campbell, James. 1992. *The Community Reconstructs: The Meaning of Pragmatic Social Thought.* Champaign-Urbana: University of Illinois Press.

6. As I would, Terry Hoy argues that Dewey understands the contradictions of modernity in a similar manner as the Frankfurt School. They share a critique that the "genuine possibility for intersubjectively shared human community has been betrayed by the ascendancy of a technical-instrumental reason pervading the political, social and administrative structure of society" (Hoy 1998, 21).

———. 1995. *Understanding Dewey.* Chicago: Open Court Press.

Dewey, John. 1919–20. *Lectures in China, 1919–1920.* Robert W. Clopton and Tsuin-Chen Ou, eds. Honolulu: University of Hawaii Press.

———. 1927. "Social Philosophy." Folder 65/7, John Dewey Papers, Special Collections, Southern Illinois University Carbondale.

———. 1946. "Miami Lecture." Folder 54/8, John Dewey Papers, Special Collections, Southern Illinois University Carbondale.

———. 1948. "Morals and Custom: A Study of the Relation of Natural Science and Morals." Folder 55/12, John Dewey Papers, Special Collections, Southern Illinois University Carbondale.

———. 1969–91. *The Collected Works of John Dewey, 1882–1953,* Carbondale: Southern Illinois University Press.

———. 1999–2004. *The Correspondence of John Dewey.* Carbondale: Southern Illinois University Press

Dickstein, Morris, ed. 1998. *The Revival of Pragmatism: New Essays on Social Thought, Law and Culture.* Durham, NC: Duke University Press.

Diggins., John Patrick. 1994. *The Promise of Pragmatism: Modernism and the Crisis of Knowledge and Authority.* Chicago: University of Chicago Press.

Eldridge, Michael. 1998. *Transforming Experience: John Dewey's Cultural Instrumentalism.* Nashville: Vanderbilt University Press.

Fine, Benjamin. 1949. "John Dewey at 90 Gets $90,000 Gift." *New York Times,* October 19.

Frankel, Charles. 1977. "John Dewey's Social Philosophy." In *New Studies in the Philosophy of John Dewey,* ed. Steven Cahn. Hanover, N.H.: University Press of New England.

Habermas, Jürgen. 1985. *The Theory of Communicative Action.* 2 vols. Boston: Beacon Press.

Hook, Sidney. 1926. "Notes on Dewey's Political Theory." Folder 65, John Dewey Papers, Special Collections, Southern Illinois University Carbondale.

Horkheimer, Max. 1972. *Critical Theory.* Trans. Matthew J. O'Connell. New York: Continuum Press.

Hoy, Terry. 1998. *The Political Philosophy of John Dewey: Towards a Constructive Renewal.* New York: Praeger Publishing.

Joas, Hans. 1993. *Pragmatism and Social Theory.* Chicago: University of Chicago Press.

———. 1996. *The Creativity of Action.* Chicago: University of Chicago Press.

Kloppenberg, James T. 1986. *Uncertain Victory: Social Progressivism in European and American Thought, 1870–1920.* New York: Oxford University Press.

Lamont, Corliss, ed. 1959. *Dialogue on John Dewey.* New York: Horizon Press.

Lavine, Thelma. 1998. "The Contemporary Significance of the American Philosophical Tradition: Lockean and Redemptive." In *Reading Dewey: Interpretations for a Postmodern Generation,* ed. Larry Hickman, 217–30. Bloomington: Indiana University Press.

Lewis, J. David, and Richard Smith. 1980. *American Sociology and Pragmatism: Mead, Chicago Sociology and Symbolic Interactionism.* Chicago: University of Chicago Press.

Lukacs, Georg. 1971. *History and Class Consciousness: Studies in Marxist Dialectics.* Trans. Rodney Livingstone. Cambridge: MIT Press.

Mills, C. Wright. 1964. *Sociology and Pragmatism: Higher Learning in America*. New York: Paine Whitman Publishers.

Mumford, Lewis. 1926. *The Golden Day: A Study in American Experience and Culture*. New York: Horace Liveright.

Purcell, Edward. 1973. *The Crisis of Democratic Theory*. Lexington: University Press of Kentucky.

Randall, John Herman. 1958. *Nature and Historical Experience: Essays in Naturalism and the Theory of History*. New York: Columbia University Press.

Rucker, Darnell. 1969. *The Chicago Pragmatists*. Minneapolis: University of Minnesota Press.

Russell, Bertrand. 1922. "As a Radical European Sees It." *Freeman* 4 (March 8, 1922): 608–10.

West, Cornel. 1993. "The Limits of Neopragmatism. " In *Keeping Faith: Philosophy and Race in America*. 135–41. London: Routledge.

———. 1999. "The Political Intellectual" *The Cornel West Reader*. New York: Basic Civitas Books.

Westbrook, Robert. 2005. *Democratic Hope: Pragmatism and the Politics of Truth*. Ithaca, N.Y.: Cornell University Press.

———. 1991. *John Dewey and American Democracy*. Ithaca, N.Y.: Cornell University Press.

Wolfe, Alan. 1998. "The Missing Pragmatic Revival in American Social Science." In Dickstein 1998, pp. 199–206.

Editor's Notes

In editing a manuscript of 160,000 words broken into hundreds of fragments, and one written in many drafts over at least three years as part
of a constantly evolving project, I have made countless judgment calls.
When his project began, Dewey intended to write a work on common sense,
science, and philosophy. It quickly turned into a cultural history of modern
philosophy. The text that is presented here reflects an attempt to faithfully represent an object in transition between these two points, but unlike
either. Ideally, I would have completed the book exactly as he imagined
it. But despite my best effort to divine Dewey's intent, between the many
reformulations of his project and the desirability of including as much of
the material as possible, that ultimately proved impossible. Chapters have
been reordered when necessary and separate documents joined by theme.
Were another to edit this volume, I have no doubt that the result would be
a different book (within limits). The purpose of these editor's notes is then
to make my judgments explicit so that they might be examined, tested, and
corrected by fellow members of the scholarly community of inquiry.

Misspellings and obvious typos have been corrected silently, without
comment. Likewise, nonsubstantive and clearly intended words such as *to*
or *the* have been inserted where needed and punctuation corrected in the
interest of clarity. Otherwise, Dewey's language has not been updated to
reflect current usage. For example, *clew* has not been replaced with *clue*.
All italicizations are Dewey's.

Insertions or changes by the editor, including missing words where the intention is unclear, pencil revisions, and words that run off the page, are enclosed
in brackets. These include any editorial footnotes. When possible, citations
have been provided. Where the word could not be inferred, [*illeg.*] is added.

Every effort has been made to group manuscripts as they are found
in SIU's Special Collection folders rather than draw from the 800 pages
of manuscripts freely. This approach has its strengths and weaknesses.
The original archivists collected papers according to Dewey's notations in
the upper-left corners of his manuscripts indicating the chapter number.

Materials marked "VII" would be grouped together with "vii," and so on. However, what Dewey believed would be in a particular chapter changed as the project evolved. For example, what was chapter 7 at one time would be moved forward and, according to the next outline, become chapter 4. Then, when setting about to write what he now conceived to be chapter 7, he would mark the new and unrelated material with "vii." This problem is compounded by Dewey's tendency to believe, at one point or another, that everything regarding the "unmodernity" of modern philosophy would appear in chapter 7—at least three chapters bore that number, just as there are three chapters 11. The result was that many discontinuous texts which inconsistently spoke to the same themes were gathered together as they were entered into the Dewey Papers. This would seem to provide a compelling argument for disregarding the Special Collection folder groupings and exercising my own judgment—organizing the manuscripts to provide for the clearest possible argument or narrative. The danger in this approach is that, given the number of fragments and the freedom to combine them as I please, the result would reflect my thoughts rather than Dewey's. Clarity and argumentative force would come as the price of infidelity. So, when possible, manuscript grouping has been retained even at the expense of some repetition or argumentative discontinuity. That said, it was necessary in some cases to divide material from a single folder into separate chapters or to compile a chapter from multiple folders. I detail when that has been done later in these Editor's Notes.

Ellipses have been introduced to mark the beginning of a new fragment within the same Special Collections folder. This may indicate either pages missing from a continuous manuscript or simply the joining of isolated fragments. Dewey would often take multiple runs at a chapter and, of these many attempts, we may have fragments with overlapping page numbers. For example, five of the manuscripts constituting "Mind and Body" were numbered 1–8, 14–40, 7–20, 31–38, and 22–41. They are all from the same folder, but they do not constitute one continuous text. Section breaks have been introduced to mark the beginning of material from another folder. For example, since "The Discovery of Rational Discourse" is drawn entirely from folder 53/17, only ellipses are present. However, "The Present Problem of Knowledge" is composed of manuscripts from four folders divided into five sections, so roman-numbered breaks are inserted. Finally, in a few cases where a particularly interesting passage from another folder was too short to warrant its own section, I added it as a footnote in an appropriate place. Unlike ellipses and section breaks, double-space breaks are Dewey's own.

The reader must take great care to remember that, as this book is composed of a fragmented, incomplete, and evolving work, internal references are not always to be trusted. Unfortunately, the order and content of chapters changed drastically throughout the project. Dewey refers back to chapters that have been lost and forward to chapters that were never written. Or, even worse, he would refer forward *and* backward to the same point as the chapter was being written and he reimagined its placement. He often refers to "the last point," "in the previous chapter," or "the compelling part of the task" when, because pages have been lost, the "point," "chapter" or "task" is not necessarily what precedes that particular text. This problem is so pervasive I was tempted to insert footnotes reminding the reader whenever one of these occurred, but out of fear that they would be distracting, I have not.

Though the best effort has been made to order the text according to Dewey's internal references, it is simply impossible for all such references to find their referent. Some referents are missing while, in other cases, references directly contradict. For example, the manuscript for "Nature and Human Nature" was numbered XIII, while "Experience as Life-Function" was numbered XI. Despite this fact, I have reversed the order on the basis of Dewey's claim in "Nature and Human Nature" that "the position that all psychological phenomena are transformations of biological phenomena, which transformations are effected under the influence of sociological or cultural conditions is, however a matter for later discussion." This would place it before "Experience as Life-Function." However, a footnote in "The Practical and the Theoretical" reads: "The indispensable role played by social-cultural conditions in formation of habitual responses is dealt with in the next chapter." This would imply that "Experience as Life-Function" would immediately follow "The Practical and the Theoretical." It is not possible to satisfy both, unless "Nature and Human Nature" were moved to before "The Practical and the Theoretical." Such a move would, in turn, confront the fact that the latter must, because of internal references, follow "Mind and Body." And so on. Similarly, there is sufficient textual support to arrange the material in "From Cosmic Nature to Human Nature," "Wandering between Two Worlds," and "The Present Problem of Knowledge" in a number of permutations.

I have included as much of the manuscript as possible. At times, this will result in repetition as Dewey worked ideas over in various drafts. This is most notable in "The Present Problem of Philosophy" and "Wandering between Two Worlds." Dewey wrote a few outlines, for both individual chapters and the overall project. This edition has hewed most closely to the latest one, found in folder 61/20 of the SIU Special Collections. That is not to say that it has been followed strictly. Chapters such as "From Cosmic Nature to Human Nature," originally intended to be chapter 7, do not appear in the latest outline. Nevertheless, it has been included here. Nor do chapters written early such as "Things and Persons" or "Mind and Body." Dewey did indicate that he wanted to include discussions of "individuals" and of "psychology," and these discussions could fall under these headings, but those specific chapters have not been mentioned.

I conclude these editor's notes with information on each chapter. With the exception of chapters 7 and 14, all chapter titles are Dewey's.

1. "Philosophy and the Conflict of Beliefs"—Folder 53/16 of the Dewey Papers at the Special Collection Research Center at Southern Illinois University at Carbondale. As the first seven pages of the manuscript have not survived, the intended title of this chapter is unknown. An early chapter 1 was titled "The Continuing Life of Philosophy" in Dewey's letter to Joseph Ratner (1941.02.21, 07068), but there is reason to believe that the chapter of that name has not survived. In the later outline in folder 61/12, he called the first chapter "Philosophy, Past and ??." The chosen title is from the manuscript in folder 61/23. Though tempted to integrate that manuscript into chapter 1, I was not sufficiently confident that it was part of the book, though it is close in theme and was grouped with the other manuscripts.

2. "The Story of Nature"—Folder 61/12.

3. "The Discovery of Rational Discourse"—Folder 53/17. Dewey wrote this chapter's introduction at least three times. He first typed four pages. Unsatisfied with the first two pages, he scratched them out and hand-wrote four pages on the backs of the originals. Apparently not satisfied with the rewrite, he then wrote four pages on fresh sheets of paper. The two scratched out pages have been replaced with the final handwritten version.

4. "The Search for Salvation"—This is the most fragmented chapter of all, composed of loose fragments from "The Search for Salvation (61/15)," "Chapter ii (61/13)" and "The Discovery of Rational Discourse" (53/17). Dewey makes clear throughout the manuscript and various outlines that he intended an analysis of the way that ancient categories and assumptions regarding natural philosophy were retained in supernatural form in the medieval period. Sadly, much of that material has been lost. Because the remaining fragments are so short and scattered, I have not isolated each folder's contents into its own section, as I have done throughout most of the book. Instead, in the interest of clarity and flow, I have blended them together.

5. "From Cosmic Nature to Human Nature"—Folder 54/1. Rather than break up the continuous manuscript, I have included relevant material from other manuscripts as footnotes. In the late outline, Dewey indicated that he wanted to have a chapter on "Individual" to discuss the turn inward, but it is not clear whether this was to be that chapter. This chapter also shares themes with "Nature and Human Nature," but that manuscript must come at the end and therefore could not be incorporated into chapter 5.

6. "Wandering between Two Worlds"—The three sections are drawn from separate manuscripts. Section I: Folder 53/18; II: 54/6, dated April–May 7, 1940; III: 61/13. The chapter suffers from repetition. The first and second sections make the same arguments but with different emphases. Although in an earlier version I attempted to weave these two sections together in the interest of continuity and economy, ultimately, I left them separate in the interest of fidelity to the original manuscripts. Regarding the chapter's order: Internal references in "From Cosmic Nature to Human Nature" appear to refer to material from section II, which would indicate that "Wandering" precedes "Cosmic Nature." However, references in section I refer back to "Cosmic Nature." The apparent contradiction could be resolved in two ways: (1) separate the two sections and make section II into its own chapter, preceding "Cosmic Nature"; or (2) keep the two sections in this chapter and merely acknowledge the possible problem in a footnote. I have chosen the latter approach. In Section III, Dewey refers to the chapter as "Philosophy out of Gear"—the only time, so far as I can tell, that he used that title.

7. "The Present Problem of Knowledge"—The five sections are drawn from four different manuscripts. Section I: Folder 61/16; II: 54/1; III: 53/12, dated June–December 1941; IV: 53/15, revised September 28–October 7, 1942; V: 54/1. This chapter title is not Dewey's. The opening section is titled "Modern Philosophy as Systematic Reduplication" and it was tempting to use that for the chapter title. However, that title would be more fitting for the preceding chapters. The title I have provided better reflects the chapter's central concern.

8. "The Supreme Human Art"—Section I: Folder 53/15; II: 53/12. This chapter and the previous one make use of "The Supreme Human Art" (53/15). This is one of the most fractured of the extant texts, second only to those on the medieval period comprising chapter 4. Besides a ragged manuscript and a broad split between discussions of science and language, it is evident that Dewey made repeated attempts to write it—for example, there are seven extant pages 6.

9. "Things and Persons"—Folder 54/2, dated October 1942. A complete manuscript is mentioned in Dewey's letter to Arthur F. Bentley (1942.03.19, 15220).

10. "Mind and Body"—Section I: Folder 54/5, dated October 1942; II: 54/3 "The Empirical and the Rational"; III: 54/5. A complete manuscript named "mind and matter" is also mentioned in Dewey's 1942 letter to Arthur Bentley (1942.03.19, 15220). The insertion of section II was a difficult decision. The text is from a substantial manuscript described as "chapter XI," that Dewey may have intended to follow "Mind and Body." However, mutual references between "Mind and Body" and "The Practical and Theoretical"

give compelling evidence that they are contiguous. It was also tempting to place "The Empirical and the Rational" after "The Practical and the Theoretical," but its content does not fit well there and mutual references make it clear that "The Material and the Ideal" is to follow immediately afterward. The choice ultimately was between cutting it entirely and placing it within "Mind and Body." I did the latter.

11. "The Practical and the Theoretical"—Section I: Folder 54/3 "The Practical and the Theoretical"; II: 54/5.

12. "The Material and the Ideal"—Folder 53/13, dated September 26, 1941. This chapter was originally titled "XII—The Material and the Ideal," similar to the dichotomous titles of the other chapters. However, in a late outline, Dewey changed the title and chapter order. He indicated that he intended to rename it "Material and Economics" and move it forward to follow "Language" and precede "Individual." I have chosen to keep its original title and location since Dewey never got around to revising it—as the mutual references between this chapter and "The Practical and the Theoretical" show.

13. "Nature and Human Nature"—Folder 61/21.

14. "Experience as Life-Function"—Section I: Folder 61/17, II: 61/19, III: 61/18, IV: 61/19. This title is not Dewey's. I chose it on the basis of the chapter's content, Jo Ann Boydston's thumbnail description while cataloguing the manuscript, and Dewey's sketch of the chapter in the late outline (61/20).

PART ONE

I. Philosophy and the Conflict of Beliefs

Man is a teller of tales, a spreader of reports. He tells his story in every medium; by the spoken work, by pantomime and drama, in carvings in wood and stone, in rite and cult, in memorial and monument. His beliefs are social beliefs; they are of import because of this fact. Moreover, beliefs are serially as well as contemporaneously told and shared. They become traditions, and there are no traces of any form of mankind so primitive as not to reveal him possessed of traditions. Of other animals we find bones; associated with the remains of the human body are always objects that are symbols of common beliefs.

When groups having different traditional beliefs come into close intercourse with one another, there is a shock which makes belief an object of attentive observation. Philosophies have always flourished in such periods. Consider, for example, the time of the sophists; the conflux of different Mediterranean civilizations when Rome was mistress; the definition of Christian dogmas against threatening heresies; the period called the renascence. There is another type of conflict and of beliefs, and one even more important in recent centuries. Science has given us new ways of reaching beliefs about nature, and these newer and not as yet acclimatized beliefs do not harmonize with the older beliefs transmitted from Roman-Hellenistic civilization and from the Middle Ages. The story of these conflicts of special traditions with one another, and of novel beliefs in conflict with those of tradition, forms the theme of this series of addresses. This chapter is given to discussion of the background of beliefs out of which philosophy arose.

A philosopher deals with the beliefs which are characteristic of the culture of the society in which he lives. Philosophy as it proceeds piles up its own special traditions and, in consequence, a philosopher, especially for the last century and a half, is distracted. He has to keep one eye on living contemporary beliefs and the other on beliefs embodied in the tradition of prior great systems. The outcome is rarely a solid stereoscopic vision. The confusion of thought which reflects the actual state of the social world to-day is increased by this special source of confusion. The fact that Greek thought was not so troubled, that it reflected a native culture developing on its own heath, and growing so rapidly and spontaneously that men thought in terms of living problems rather than in those of results reached in prior reflection, is perhaps the chief reason for the perennial attractiveness of Greek thought.

It presents a freshness, naïveté and directness which we in vain would emulate. Before Greek reflection on beliefs arose there were, however, bodies of beliefs already in existence, and these formed its material. The story of early Greek thought is already being rewritten in the light of its gradual emergence from this body of beliefs. I am no specialist in this field and shall not detain you with any account of the special background of Greek philosophy as that is being imaginatively reconstructed by the efforts of anthropologist, archeologist, historian, and philologist. What concerns us is rather certain traits of all pre-philosophic beliefs, traits which form the common matrix out of which emerged all the world's philosophies, Asiatic as well as European. In turning to this cultural background of belief, I shall of necessity repeat things which are more or less commonplaces. But if philosophy is a study of society with respect to its fundamental and transmitted beliefs, and if there is a time when these beliefs had not yet been complicated and sophisticated by the result of prior intellectual criticism and organization, the conclusions of the anthropologist provides priceless data for the study of the origin and course of philosophy itself.

One universal trait of the untried beliefs of mankind is the distinction drawn in them between the ordinary and the extraordinary. Mankind is conspicuously sensitive to the difference between the prosaic expected run of events and that which by contrast is weird, uncanny, mysterious, beyond expectation, and beyond control by means of the appliances and procedures by which the ordinary run of events is administered. The two realms may be said to mark out by way of anticipation what are later called the natural and the supernatural. But we should miss the point of the difference in primitive beliefs if we read into them the connotations which these words have for us. The two realms of the usual and the extraordinary overlapped and blended; they were inextricably mixed. There was no sharp division between heaven and earth so that the differences between the mysterious and the commonplace might be referred to separated sources or realms. God and the world were not so distinguished that one set of affairs belonged to God's sphere as the supernatural, and the other to the natural world. Much less did the distinction correspond to that now drawn between the material and the spiritual. Spirit as the breath of life was what we should now term natural and in many of its phenomena was regular enough, free from anything mysterious. Things we now call physical were, on the other hand, the scene of all sorts of strange happenings as well as of the uniformities which made possible the routine of the arts. In this aspect, they testified to the presence of spirits or at least of some occult power which had to be placated or approached with unusual ceremony and which, when so approached, might become a powerful and inexplicable addition to the capacities of the one who got into rapport with it. In short, the distinction between the usual and regular and the queer and mysterious was one which cut across all our present classifications.

While I cannot cite explicit authority from an anthropologist for the statement that this generic distinction includes two species within itself, the lucky and the unlucky on one side and the holy and the profane on the other, I think no violence is done their reports by this mode of statement. We shall, however, misunderstand the import of the distinction of things into the holy and the non-holy if we think of the holy in terms of present associations. The term is quite free from moral significance; in its physical signification, its indication of power, it has a sinister side. Whatever is holy is fraught with danger; it is not to be casually approached. It is taboo. Whatever is unusually charged with danger, whatever emits from itself the injunction *"noli me tangere,"* is holy. Nor should the distinction between the lucky and the holy be taken to denote a sharp division. On the contrary, good fortune or conspicuous success in life was dependent upon the right approach to mysterious power, and to its favor in imparting to the suppliant some of its own extraordinary endowment. On the other hand, any object commonplace in itself which stands in intimate emotional association with happy issue out of some uncertain crisis is likely to have causal responsibility for the resulting good fortune attributed to it, and thus to come within the range of the holy.

In spite of the fact that the same object may fall into the categories of both the lucky and the sacred, since both may fall within the area of that which arouses amazement and the sense of mystery, there is a functional difference between the two categories. That which is pre-eminently blessed or fortunate may be an object of awe but also a means to be used. It may be manipulated to bring about the desired good fortune. It finds special material embodiment for itself in a stone, tree, the things contained in a medicine man's kit, or even in a day of the week, in connection perhaps with some phase of the moon, a day which is then a holy-day, and on its way to become, with secularization, a holiday. Divinations, spells, or incantations, usually in possession of a special class who owns objects having mysterious power, are the means of manipulation. That which is holy may not have, however, any such definite localization. It may be a spirit which comes and goes at its own volition, or it may be some animated natural force, like sun or wind. In any case it is approached in [an][1] attitude of subjection, not of

---

1. [Replacing "allenis."]

manipulation, with prior fastings. The aim may be to obtain some favor which will bring fortune, but the personal disposition with which approach is made is that of submission not of command and use. Thus the distinction between the two divisions of the extraordinary, the lucky and the holy with their opposites, holds with respect to the personal attitude involved. Neither classification is made on an intellectual basis. In this respect again it differs *toto coelo* from the distinction now drawn between natural and supernatural. The root of the difference is one found in immediate emotional and imaginative experience. In some cases, the experience is one expressed in rites and ceremonies which divine the course of events or bend them to a favorable issue of fortune. In other cases, the experience is one expressed in subjection, supplication, propitiation and sacrifice, communion and alliance. How far the difference is connected with the distinction sometimes drawn between magic and religion may be left undecided. But at all events, it militates against any sharp division between the two.

Safety is the primary human demand. There are other pressing needs of course. There are demands for food and sustenance; for reproduction; of children for care and nurture; there are urgent aggressive tendencies. Out of these grow all sorts of derived interests in invention, manipulation, construction, combat, decoration and display. But the need for security, the demand for assurance of favorable outcome, runs through all of them and cuts across all interests and occupations. They come to naught, they are worse than vanity and vexation, unless there is hope of conducting them to a successful issue. Now security depends upon some measure of control over environing conditions. The crises in which the event of failure or success was precarious and action was perilous, were numerous and compelling in early life. It might be a matter of illness or wound, of child-birth or death, of the catamenial flow of women, of war with a hostile group, of a swift current where rocks beset the frail canoe, a hunt, obtaining an adequate harvest, of achieving honor and respect among fellow men. Moreover, the tools and techniques of the matter of fact arts were so undeveloped, so much at the mercy of untoward forces which they did not control, that even they had to be buttressed by association with the "supernatural" to guarantee their issue.

As the drowning man grasps at a straw, so any man caught in deep peril and all pervasive uncertainty grasps in his imagination at anything which promises security of the future. Since primitive man did not possess the instruments and the technology of command of natural energies, opportunities for experiencing the extraordinary and uncanny were omnipresent, and search for means of alliance with supernal potencies never-ceasing. Man possessed, indeed, certain efficacious tools and certain habits of skill which took care of routine cases in uniform matter-of-fact ways; consonant with these habits there developed matter-of-fact beliefs. But since the confined area of the reasonably regular and assured was set within a much wider territory of the precarious and perilous, and since forces resonating from the latter were continuously invading the unprotected boundary of ordinary acts and occupations, matter-of-fact beliefs were a dim nucleus about which I appended the vast penumbra of beliefs about the "supernatural." The ordinary occupation, making or using a weapon or bowl or mat, sowing and gathering grain, was associated with supernatural belief and action.

Familiarity is said to breed contempt; familiar control and use certainly generated the sentiment of equality, of being on a level with surrounding conditions. Primitive man had his occasions for elation and superiority, just as he had his orgies, revels and triumphs. But he never attained that condition of secure control wherein familiarity bred a permanent feeling of contempt for the things of his environment, or even one of equality. The uncertain was always just around the corner. Deference to the unknown, desire for propitiation, the need of support from powers beyond, tempered his life. Consequently man's beliefs with regard to the ordinary, his matter-of-fact beliefs, those akin in kind to our scientific beliefs, stood upon a lower plane, occupied a lower status, than those of a religious and symbolic character. It might seem quite superfluous to point out that the holy and sacred had a prestige, a value, that was not possessed by the secular and ordinary. That difference is with us still a matter of course. But when we recall that the insane and epileptic were once thought to be divinely afflicted or obsessed, that disease was thought to be of external and uncanny origin, we are reminded that the factors on the basis of which we draw the distinction between the superior worth of the holy in contrast with the worldly (largely a moral basis) did not operate in early days. If we substitute such terms as the extraordinary and the ordinary, the eccentric and the normal, the uncertain and the regular, we at once see that the distinction into higher and lower values is by [no] means intrinsically given.

We approach here the bearing of our discussion upon philosophy viewed as organization and criticism of pre-existing beliefs. The points that have been mentioned, the division of beliefs into those concerned with matter-of-fact things and with mysterious powers, the dependence of the former upon the latter and their much inferior rank, left their profound impress upon the early course of philosophizing. The beliefs in question were widely shared; they were the subject of tradition and of special care to effect their transmission; they had to do with things of highest emotional value and practical importance. It is then, we may confidently assert, antecedently probable that philosophy should find its final problems set by the contrast and connections of the two modes of belief, and should derive its cues from those of higher worth. The content of the beliefs varied immensely. Careful and informed anthropologists have about surrendered the old attempt to find a single and universal content for the religious beliefs of all primitive peoples, contenting themselves with the unity and universality of emotionalized imaginative experience. Content varied with local environment, with diffusion from other groups, with conditions which although more or less accidental in origin got embedded in tradition. These differences do not concern us here, though it is of utmost import for the hardly as yet commenced comparative study of the course taken by philosophies in China and India in their contrast with the European tradition.

The fact that this very diversity of content is connected with social differences is, however, of great significance for philosophy. It testifies to the extent to which the material in which the extraordinary emotional experience took on intellectual form was patterned after social interests and relationships. I cannot follow the school of Durkheim in holding that the social group is the prototype of the worshipped gods, being the reality symbolized in all religious rites and beliefs. But we are on safer ground when we suggest that the material, by means of which the experience of the weird and uncanny assumed imaginative shape and report, must have been in close affiliation with the organization and affairs of social groups. For it is psychologically necessary that imagination, even the most fantastic, draw its material from somewhere. And what more available source is there than the prevailing modes of association with others, since these are in any case the objects of most constant attention and interest, the direct sources of personal [weal] and woe, and the medium through which intercourse with the physical environment is for the most part mediated? It is doubtless possible to push too far the hypothesis that the content of beliefs about divine beings and forces were modeled upon the patterns directly supplied by group life. We know that borrowings from neighbors played a great part, and we may surmise that personal observations of natural objects and forces played their part. But to become a part of traditional belief, these borrowings and observations had to be acceptable to a group: and there is plenty of evidence that they would be accepted in proportion as they were assimilable to existing patterns of social interest and occupation. Nothing is more remarkable than the ease and extent of diffusion among primitive peoples, save the immunity and resistance displayed to all that was basically alien to dominant social patterns.

The role of already extant social material in giving form to beliefs is so obviously necessary to incorporation of belief [within] tradition that it need not be dwelt upon. Its significance for philosophy may, however, be pointed out. In his attitude and method, a philosopher was marked out from his fellow artist, the poet. The latter repeated and rounded out the stories and legends characteristic of his group, thus giving them a new source of appeal. The philosopher, bringing reflective thought to bear, stood further aloof; he was almost of necessity a somewhat suspect character. He was tolerated in the degree his fellows could recognize, in spite of novelty of form, material congenial to the spirit of their own lives. This social factor in the beliefs which he adapted and made over not only was a condition of acceptability, but it gave his work solid content; it afforded protection against mere private speculativeness and intellectual eccentricity. It furnished, to use the current term, objectivity to his ideas. His originality was displayed in the way he dealt with his material, not in supplying the material. Without the element of social content, the philosopher would have been both without an audience and without meaty and weighty subject-matter.

This general idea has a special application in a field which is somewhat technical, but which should, I think, be mentioned. Tylor advanced the idea that all forms of religion arose from and centered in a belief in souls or spirits present in any worshipped natural object or natural force in such a way that presence of spirit furnished the thing or force in question with its peculiar potency and constituted it the recipient of religious attention. This theory, called animism, has had wide general vogue. The essence of religious belief, that which is behind worship, supplication, rite, cult, and myth is, according to this view, the attribution to sun, moon, mountain, river or plant, animal, stone or whatever of a soul like unto the human soul, and possessed therefore of similar likes, and dislikes, loves and hates, purposes and desires, which are however exercised in more mobile, hidden, and powerful ways than human souls are capable of. As Tylor put it: "It seems as though the conception of a human soul when once attained to by man, served as type or model on which he framed not only his ideas of other souls of a lower grade, but also his ideas of spiritual beings in general, from the tiniest elf that sports in the long grass up to the heavenly Creator and Rule of the world, the Great Spirit."[2] As the doings of the human body are initiated or carried on by its indwelling soul, so the operations of all parts of nature are executed by their souls.

I am not concerned to deny some elements involved in this theory. Dreams may well have suggested the idea of a double of the human form, mobile, tenuous, and capable of deeds like those of the human body but magnified in scale and intensity. And worship of spirits of ancestors and of sun, moon, and other objects has undoubtedly played a considerable role in many aspects of many religions. But these admissions are far from embodying the full force of the animistic theory. The notion of a bodily double, composed of highly thinned matter and gifted with unusual powers of movement, is far from

---

2. Tylor, *Primitive Culture*, II, p. 109. [Tylor, Edward Burnett. *Primitive Culture* (1871) volume II, p. 110.]

being the idea of soul or spirit required by the theory. The latter demands a conception of this double as peculiarly physical in nature, as a centre of will, desire, intent, and emotions, as something marked off from the gross physical body by possession of peculiar attributes, similar to those which later psychology ascribed to "mind" or "consciousness." The supposition that primitive man had this notion before he had religious beliefs, beliefs involving the "supernatural," is highly dubious.

The doubts spring from facts known to anthropologists and from psychological considerations. I confine myself to the latter, as those relevant to our purpose. Is it possible to suppose that primitive man, in that early stage wherein some religious belief demonstrably exists, had attained a definite notion of any coherent psychical unity, the centre of thought, emotion, desire and will, a notion so definite that he could clothe or ensoul the bodily double with it, and then project it into things? The supposition that such a thing is possible is itself a reflection of a fairly recent introspective psychology which assumed that the soul or consciousness furnished intuitive and immediate awareness of its own states and acts. In other words, the theory reads back into primitive belief the outcome of a highly sophisticated subjective doctrine. An analogy may perhaps make the point clearer. Evidently men could not conceive divine beings as kings until they had some experience of the rule of monarchs in their own social life; they could not conceive of the gods as operating according to a scheme of laws until laws had attained a certain degree of consolidated structure in their own social organization. Similarly, they could not conceive of the operations of natural objects as worked by an immanent spirit until in their own experience they had attained to the notion of a single unified psychical centre and power, possessed of specified qualities and abilities. Now what is here asserted is that this latter notion is not [as] primitive as religious belief and [creed], but marks the attainment, even when the idea is entertained in a rudimentary form, of a definite type of culture and of social organization.[3]

---

3. [From folder 53/16, p. 24: Now this is just what did *not* happen in Greek thought. We may be reasonably sure that even when personification and ensouling of objects and natural forces most ran riot, they never formed the whole story. The persons and souls never had the independence and stability which is attributed to them in some forms of modern thought. They were set in a context of underlying social and cosmic conditions which was still more stable and ultimate and which upon the whole ruled them instead of being at the mercy of their personal desires and purposes. The idea of the unity and stability of the soul and person is a distinctly modern idea. In early beliefs which were most given to employment of psychical personifications, there were still many souls in the same person, and these were given to startling transformations. "To return to our main problem: how does primitive man conceive the ego? It may at once be said that one thing he has never done: he has never fallen into the error of thinking of it as a unified whole or of regarding it as static. For him it has always been a dynamic entity, possessed of so many constituents that even the thinker has been unable to fuse them into one unit." [Paul] Radin, *Primitive Man as Philosopher* (1957), p. 259. Again,

What men naturally observe and study is behavior, behavior of persons and of things. What most interests them, in their native estate, is the bearing of behavior upon wellbeing, consequences of harm and benefit, not necessarily of a narrow egoistic kind but with respect to their possessions, the members of their family, their clan or tribe. A distinction which is drawn very early is that between favorable and unfavorable behavior; that which assists, supports, promotes and that which hinders, opposes, destroys—the friendly and the hostile. We say the wind is gentle, the sky angry. We also say that such sayings are metaphorical. But there is no evidence that they are of necessity any more or any less metaphorical with us than they are with the savage. The tendency to move toward a certain consequence is indicated—precisely as when things were first called sweet it was meant they brought agreeable experience in their train. After the notion of definite and fairly unified psychical centre had arisen, such qualifications of things might be "rationalized" by attributing gentle or angry behavior to a "soul." It is absurd, however, to suppose that a full-fledged notion of personal and psychical identity came first. That men read the natural phenomena which seriously affected their welfare and fortune in language borrowed from familiar forms of personal behavior is infinitely more probable than that they set out with a notion of distinctively psychical states and acts which they first attached to their bodily double and then projected into nature.

That primitive man early arrived at the notion of breath, vapor, a shadowy form or film and conceived it as having life and motion of a lively and subtle kind, is quite probable. This was undoubtedly the substratum of the idea of soul or spirit. But it is a long way from such an idea to distinctively emotional, intellectual and volitional traits, organized into a persistent and unified psychical centre, such as later came to be connected with the notion of soul and spirit. To suppose that because savages have the first idea they necessarily have the second is to fuse together a primitive idea and one derived from a much later development of reflective self-consciousness. Instead of its being true that favor and aid was sought because some natural object or power was first conceived of as psychical, it is much more likely to be true that the habit of supplicating assistance from the mysterious potencies with which man was surrounded was one reason why, in the course of time, these powers were endowed with some kind of personality. For this ascription could not occur until men had attained in their own experience to a definite notion of personality. To account for the origin and growth of

---

speaking of the Maori: "The nature of the impingement of individual upon individual and of the individual upon the external world is utterly different from anything a Western European can possibly imagine. The medley of combinations and permutations it would permit is quite bewildering." Ibid., p. 264.]

this notion is by no means easy; perhaps it is impossible as yet. But of two considerations we may be antecedently sure. The notion was derived from modes of behavior which were outwardly observable, modes of observed behavior which were of interest and concern because they affected welfare. And the derivation could not come about until the life of a social group had reached a point in which personal character, in its moral qualities, counted for something so distinctive that it was forced upon recognition. It is safe to say that personal moral identity and unity was attributed to a few outstanding persons long before the great mass of ordinary, undistinguished persons were thought of as "souls" in any other sense than that of having material doubles in shadows and vapory films. It is even possible that the generalization was not made in Europe until after Christianity had made itself felt. We know for example that it was a matter of warm debate in Christian circles whether women had souls.

The tenor of the preceding discussion may leave the impression that it is especially concerned with the origin and nature of religious beliefs. Such is not the intention however. Consideration of specifically religious beliefs is incidental to the theme of the beliefs about the world (including man) which formed the given subject-matter of philosophy when the latter manifested itself. We return to this theme, bringing with us whatever enlightenment and store of ideas the previous discussion may have afforded.

It is sometimes said that the effect of philosophy is to make man morally and intellectually at home in his world: to reveal the universe as something congenial to man's highest and truest aspirations. Of the beliefs which are the background of philosophy, it may at least be asserted that they are means of providing a working adaptation of human attitudes to whatever is most profoundly stirring in the environment. They arise in crises of extreme emotional unsettlement. They operate to bridge over the disturbing break between the acts and plans of men and the mysterious forces which decide their issue. They exhibit the sense of a threatening discord and conflict and the yearning for the restoration of harmony. The harmony is attained by varying ratios of attitudes of subjection and compliance and of utilization of favors obtained. Man achieves unity partly by yielding and accommodating and in part by employing their gift of extraordinary powers which is the reward of discipline in abasement, supplication and sacrifice in order to coerce the course of events. Rapport with mysterious potencies effects alliance with them, incorporation of them. The effect is both an exalted sense of harmony and peace so intense that "peace" does not designate tranquil repose, and also of power to command events otherwise intractable. Philosophies have accordingly been doctrines both of consolation and reconciliation and of control. Sometimes, when the environment natural and social is adverse, the element of consolation has been uppermost; sometimes that of power and domination. Never has there been a philosophy which did not show a trace of both aspects; they are the passive and the active sides of the same experience. Philosophies of peace and refuge have at least also been methods of securing control of one's own desires when administrative direction of the external environment seemed most hopeless. Never has control been so adequate that the men who advanced philosophies of command of nature or of the supernatural have not been obliged to console themselves with anticipations of a harmony not yet attained to.

Unreflective and philosophic beliefs alike reveal the fundamental predicament of man. In part the world in which he lives is favorable and benign; without some measure of this support he could not continue to exist. But in part the universe has impinged upon man to his undoing and frustration. In moments of highest security peril is still imminent; pride goes before a fall, and prosperity is a warning.

Tension between the reinforcement which the world, natural or supernatural, affords and the menace of withdrawal of its support is the universal state of man. When man most relies in his action upon knowledge and insight he acts also in ignorance and at his peril. This tension displays itself spontaneously in pathos, humor and tragedy; it is the stimulus to belief in what lies beyond the senses, and philosophy, working with the material provided by unreflective beliefs, is its reflective expression. If men lived in a world wholly made for them, unremittingly favorable to the satisfaction of their desires and the execution of their purposes and ambitions, neither religion nor philosophy would have any reason for coming into being.

All fundamental beliefs are bound to reflect this double and ambiguous relation of the life of man to the world in which he lives, yielding a sense of support, communion, and alliance and a sense of invasion, subjection, and frustration. The material involved in the beliefs that reflect this sense of opposite relations will vary enormously according as the favorable or adverse phase is uppermost. It will vary also according to the means of defense and direction that are under human control at different ages and in diverse places. We cannot understand the content of primitive beliefs until we have thought away the vast store of appliances, technological and intellectual, by which we today avert and mitigate the adverse impact of the world upon our interests and destiny. Most of what we now attribute to our own ignorance or inexpertness and which we strive to overcome by taking better thought, by improving our arts of understanding and management, was once assigned directly to the operation of occult forces, uncontrollable by any normal means. The converse is true. Success that we attribute to our knowledge and skill was attributed to the grace of overshadowing potencies.

When the state of affairs had reached a sufficient degree of stable order in the arts and in social organization, philosophy as attempt at organization of beliefs arose. In this attempt, those factors of tradition which made explicit the elements of union and reinforcement between man and the universe were seized upon as constituting the truly normal or natural. The problem was to account for the untoward and adverse factors. Some comprehensive and basic principle of unity being postulated, the philosophic problem was, *par excellence*, so to describe it that deviations and frustrations might be accounted for. It is difficult to imagine the rise of any attempt to penetrate below the outer shell of beliefs and to organize their inner meanings, excepting where there is an experience and a social regime in which order and harmony have reached a certain preponderance.

Some phases of Indian philosophy may seem to contradict this statement. For they appear to reflect a dominant sense of insecurity, evil, and unsettlement in the actual state of affairs. But even here, the special office of philosophy is to enforce the idea of an underlying unity as a principle of harmony between man and the universal reality and to show how an abiding sense of unity with it may be achieved. Nevertheless in making the statement, it was the origin of philosophy in Greece that was pre-eminently in mind. When philosophy began its career there, the state of affairs represented a remarkable combination of stability and freedom. The Greeks attained to a significant equilibrium, even if a comparatively short lived one, of their customs and aims with the natural world. Upon the whole they felt neither hopelessly below nature, overwhelmed by it, nor elated with supremacy over it. Rather they were one with it and with themselves. Their own lives were sufficiently ordered and organized so that it was not a hopeless undertaking to organize their beliefs. Yet the capacity of the human mind to entertain incompatible beliefs at the same time is immense. The traditions upon which and with which they worked contained many and varied elements. In consequence, different thinkers, even within the same group, having a rich store to draw upon, seized upon different elements as clues that led to the unifying principle. Diversity soon led to rivalry. Competition, mutual attack and defense, became a force in the development of philosophic theories—a fact also notably exemplified in India and China. Intellectual opposition and conflict are an integral part of our philosophic heritage and they will not cease unless mankind arrives at a dull monotone of custom and tradition.

It is time however to gather together and summarize our conclusions in their definitive bearings upon philosophy. The outstanding result may be most readily stated negatively. The notion that a philosophy arises in purely individual excogitations upon existences and truths which nakedly and directly confront a thinker is an absurd legend. Theoretical reflection arises in a social medium. The conflicts and discrepancies within the traditions of a social group, or between them and newly forming beliefs, are the occasion of philosophizing. The philosopher's problems come to him in this context, no matter for how remote from it is the language, the technical vocabulary, in which his speculations are finally recorded. In addition that *with* which he thinks, as well as that about which he thinks, what we loosely denominate his mind, comes from some [portion] of the beliefs of the social medium. He casts his imaginations in material drawn from tradition and from the peculiar context of his day and place.

These considerations draw an ineffaceable line between the intellectual enterprises respectively anything named science and philosophy. I do not mean that science dispenses or can dispense with tradition and other socially instituted resources. No thinking being can do so and still have left to think upon or with. But science employs its socially originated material as a resource, as instrumentalities and capital, in inquiry into a realm taken to be just what it is apart from the intervention of social attitudes. Time generally reveals indeed a considerable amount of illusion in the supposition that prior science has been dealing with material pure from social adulteration. But the presence of this illusory element does not affect the ideal of science; as it progresses, it develops a technique and a symbolism for the purpose of discounting the socially contributed factor, of reducing it to a minimum. Philosophy, on the other hand, is pre-eminently occupied with precisely this intervening factor. It is at home when engaged in criticizing, evaluating, clearing up, and systematizing socially conditioned beliefs.

This fact, as we noticed at the outset, is made a ground of reproach and disparagement by opponents of philosophy. It is resentfully denied to be a fact by many, perhaps most, philosophers who find it an abdication of philosophy from its high estate, disloyalty to its fine office. The question of fact, like any matter of fact, is not one to be argued about, but is a matter for observation. Suffice it to say that the history of philosophy *looks* as if it were a fact. What otherwise is the point of discriminating philosophies as Occidental and Oriental? Of dividing European thought into ancient, medieval and modern? Or subdividing ancient philosophy as that of Ionian and Italian colonies, of Athens and of Hellenistic syncretism? What have these divisions and those of Patristic, scholastic, renascence thought to do with a revelation of ultimate truth unmediated by social conditions marked by characteristic troubles, needs and aspirations? To say that we have now escaped from implication in the social predicament and are to be coldly impersonal and "scientific" is at least but a prophecy; it is for the future to verify the prediction, or to discover in present philosophy the same mirroring of human beliefs that draw upon the social medium which we so clearly find in its past history.

The demand that philosophy should be *at* one with science is justified. But to be one with it is quite a different matter from being at one with it. Philosophy has to take account of scientific conclusions; it should not contain anything at variance with them as far as they are authentically scientific. It should utilize them positively. But this conception is entirely consistent with what has been said. For these conclusions, in their general trend and application, are an important part of the social beliefs with which philosophy is concerned. Yet philosophy takes them not as isolated, complete and final in themselves, but in the context of other beliefs, moral, political, religious, economic and aesthetic. Indeed, the apparent conflict that exists between some conclusions of science and some of the more cherished non-scientific beliefs sets one of the most urgent problems of present philosophizing. To hold that the conflict must be resolved exclusively in terms of scientific beliefs is as one sided as it is to hold that it must be resolved in terms of traditional religious beliefs. For neither of these beliefs exhausts the field of experience.

It is even more true, if possible, that philosophy must be at one with science in its intellectual attitude and procedures than in its conclusions. A man does not gain new mental faculties when he turns philosopher, nor does he come into possession of some unique faculty not used in other forms of inquiry. He has the common powers of observation, imagination, guessing, calculation, testing of hypotheses, shared by all. As far as science displays a model of the most effective way of using these capacities his methods should conform. Subject-matter, not distinctive intellectual organs, differentiate philosophy from science. This different subject-matter however makes a decided difference in the *use* to which methods generically similar are put. For philosophy is concerned with the methods in their humane bearing rather than with applying them directly in further inquiry into the subject-matter of the natural sciences. How do they impinge upon collective mental disposition? What do they import in the way of reconstruction of habits of belief in religious, moral and political affairs? After he has adopted the scientific attitude as a matter of course in his own methods, these questions still remain as part of the problem of a philosopher.

James cites from [Cite missing]. I should like to paraphrase this saying: The sickliest way in which a student of philosophy can approach his subject-matter is that of a search for ultimate impersonal revelation of truth. It does not need saying that he is to prefer truth to falsity; to be on his guard against prejudice and partisanship, to be open to truth from whatever source it comes. Unless he can achieve this attitude he will never make a philosopher.

But these traits define his moral attitude, not the subject-matter he deals with. That remains the predicaments, troubles, evils and goods, aspirations, failures and achievements of men in their associated activities as they are reflected in the beliefs that express equally their tested convictions and their desires, purposes, and policies. Let a student approach this subject-matter in a spirit which is constantly sensitive to indications of this sort, constantly sympathetic and constantly eager for illumination of his sympathy, and he will find the study of philosophy immensely rewarding, even in those fields which at first sight seem bristling with technicalities and aridly remote from the well-springs of desire and imagination. Let him seek for an authoritative final solution in terms of absolute truths of all questions raised, and he will come, I fear, to the end of his road either a disillusioned skeptic or a slave to some partisan dogma. If he maintains a sympathetic fidelity to the human interests expressed in various vocabularies in philosophies, he will find as he ventures to enter upon independent reflection, that he has enough to occupy his thought and imagination, as well as his heart, in critical valuation of traditional beliefs as they connect with the life of his own day; enough to do in following the suggestions he thus derives into forms capable of communication to his fellow [men].[4]

---

4. [The manuscript ends here, but a separate fragment speaks to Dewey's historical interest in this book: "[T]he attempt of history is to tell a story in which different temporal events are taken out of their apparent independence and isolation and are woven into strands of continuity. History itself as long as it is confined to history does not pass judgment in the way of evaluation of events of right and wrong, good or bad, though as history it is obliged to record the fate of various movements in the sense of telling where actually, historically temporally they came out, what they led up to in success or failure with respect to their own intent or trend. Consequently I have not attempted in [these] chapters which follow critical evaluation of the various movements—those interested in my estimate of their respective values will find it in some of my other writings but not here. The conclusions even of the final chapter regarding what seems to be the indications of the direction in which philosophy can go forward from the present in dealing with the problems presented in earlier chapters may be interpreted as historical in import."]

II. The Story of Nature

Just why the history of philosophic speculation in Europe began in the Ionian colonies of Greece in the sixth century before our era, it is impossible to say, but we may surmise. It was a period of universal intellectual ferment in Asia. By a remarkable coincidence—perhaps more than a coincidence—the same age witnessed the beginnings of new ways of thinking in both India and China. The colonies preserved the Hellenic tradition intact and yet the loosening of the ties that bound colonies to the mainland may well have made it easier to view tradition with greater detachment. Intercourse with Egypt and with the rest of Asia Minor broadened the horizon: there came into view a number of diverse stories of the origin and nature of the world. The Greeks were a sea-faring people, and a variety of natural phenomena were brought before their extraordinarily keen powers of observation. While the fine arts did not flourish in Ionia as they later did in Athens, the Greek mind was plastic. Harmonious and measured composition of the scene and material of their experiences was native to its genius. The fragments of the early philosophers that remain certainly testify to acute interest in astronomic, geographical, and meteorological phenomena; the fact that [treat]ment of these phenomena by Ionian wise men has always been considered to belong to the record of philosophy rather than of mythology is evidence that they interpreted their observations in a way which was imaginatively free and at the same time was ordered, composed.

Of one thing we may be sure. As compared with their neighbors and with many of their successors, Greek life was never priest-ridden. Their storied legends and their religious beliefs, their cosmogonies and system of deities, had long been taken out of the hands of medicine men and priests. The Greeks were unique in the fact that the guardianship and report of these tales passed over into the keeping of literary artists. The Homeric poems rather than any ecclesiastically controlled documents formed the scriptures of Hellas. It is impossible to exaggerate the importance of this liberation. It was not what mathematicians call a sufficient condition of the rise of philosophy, but it was a necessary condition—a *sine qua non*. To conceive of the gods and divine things in poetic terms, in artistic imagery, is already to have taken the first step in free theorizing; once it occurs, the rest is easy. Further steps were rendered almost inevitable, we [*illeg.*] suppose, because of the nature of the literary record. In it the gods of Olympus were humanized, while the life and destiny of [men] were intimately associated with divine things poetically rather than dogmatically conceived. The old gap between the extraordinary and the usual was not eliminated but as it came to be thought of it was liberalized and humanized. The gods were like men, only almost perfect in enjoyment and in power to form and execute their purposes—always the trait most prized by the Greeks. Since their purposes were like those of men, and since the purposes of men in Greek communities were reasonably ordered, being emancipated from eccentric fantasy and inordinate desire, the literary version eliminated gross superstition and immoderate imaginings. These undoubtedly persisted in folk-lore and in popular rite and cult. But in the literary tradition, thinkers found material and stimulus to an imaginative telling of the story of Nature which would not violate the requirements of a humane reason.

There was animism aplenty in the background. But it was not an animism of the sort with which the theory of Tylor has made us familiar. The account of the gods and divine things given by the poets is not one in which spooks and ghosts do extraordinary and unaccountable things, but one in which gods who are animated by the same purposes and passions as men, only in exalted and idealized form, do the same sort of things and prize the same excellencies as do men. In their quasi-humanization, they were still close to the powers of nature and they were thought of in most intimate connection with the latter. But observation and the arts had advanced to a point where regularity and order, rather than inexplicable chance and mystery, were seen to be the chief traits of natural forces. The sun, the procession of the heavens and the seasons, the growth of plants and animals, contained a divine animation, but they expressed measure and loss. The gods with all their passionate desires were compelled to observe an overruling order. Although their amours, deceptions, and violence were later made the object of severe moral condemnation, yet there were limits which even the gods could transgress only at their peril.

Thus the office of the philosophers was to tell the story of nature in a language which to them was naturalistic, a tale of those orderly transformations of fire, air, or water in which were contained all the phenomena which especially held their attentive observations. Yet the natural force whose course they related was not materialistic in a modern sense. Nature was still animated as in the older tradition; in technical language, the philosophers were hylozoists. Water, air, fire, whatever element was seized upon, was living, active, self-moving; the diversified phenomena of nature were its own self-initiated and self-executed transformations. Animated nature held matter and mind, soul and body, suspended in solution. The story was naturalistic, but since that whose story was related was alive, the tale was epic and dramatic.

A great charm of early Greek thought is its union of free and bold imagination with detailed observation of natural processes. Thinkers cut the ties which bound them to the letter of old traditions with no seeming consciousness of what they were doing, almost as if they had never heard of the old legends. They, however, made the severance graciously, because in departing from the letter they conserved the spirit of tradition. They organized its scattered members into a living whole. They accomplished spontaneously what most later philosophers have done laboriously. For all philosophy as reflection upon existing beliefs operates both destructively and constructively. To organize beliefs, a philosophy must reject and select. It must disintegrate and dissolve before it can crystallize in a new precipitate. Sometimes one phase is dominant, sometimes the other; sometimes criticism is the main task, sometimes an organization which justifies. A self-conscious generation is embarrassed by being aware of its work, whether apologetic or disintegrative. The early Greeks engaged in both offices simultaneously and naïvely. We are not reminded in reading the fragments which have come to us of either a justificatory nor a destructive intent. Imagination rose freely upon its own wings, but in the atmosphere of natural phenomena.[1]

Aristotle says in his *Metaphysics*: "The ancients have handed down from remote antiquity the tradition in mythical form that the heavenly bodies are gods and that the divine encompasses the whole natural world. Other things are a later addition in mythical words, designed for persuasion of the multitude, and because of expedience, including the maintenance of social institutions."[2] However much Aristotle may have been in historical error regarding the origin of the things he took to be superstitiously added, his statement applies in full force to the beliefs which the early Ionic philosophers took for granted. It is remarkable how easily they sloughed off as irrelevant accretions the mass of legends and stories, a mass that in association with rite and cult of purification, appeasement and fertilization we well know persisted among the populace and that reappeared later among philosophers themselves when the time was overripe with social decay. But

1. [Dewey indicated that he may have wanted to cut this paragraph.]

2. [Aristotle, *Metaphysics* 12.8,1074b1–5. The W. D. Ross translation reads as follows: "Our forefathers in the most remote ages have handed down to their posterity a tradition, in the form of a myth, that these [heavenly] bodies are gods and that the divine encloses the whole of nature. The rest of the tradition has been added later in mythical form with a view to the persuasion of the multitude and to its legal and utilitarian expediency."]

even more significant is the fact that they seized the essence of the tradition; the forces which rule nature are divine and they encompass man, his works and his environment. Water, air, fire, number, and measure are different modes of naming the divine principle that encompasses and runs through all things, and that so rules their changes that particular things which exist and particular events which happen are both from it and within it. We may, we indeed must, regard these thinkers as the heralds of an onmoving host of inquirers into the secrets of nature; as concerned to deal in a rational manner with the matter-of-fact beliefs which were transmitted to them from Babylon and Egypt as well as from their own acute observations of sea and land. But they were philosophers also, and they were philosophers in virtue of the fact that they extracted from the mass of detailed legends, myths, and traditional tales a precious essence—belief in a single, all-encompassing, and all-ruling principle, the divine: a rational distillation even though it bears the marks of its origin in what Gilbert Murray well calls the uncharted, the extraordinary and uncanny.[3]

Such a work was not the deed of a day. Before the philosophers wrote and taught, poets had far advanced the operation of generalization and consolidation. As they told the story of the origin, development and vicissitudes of gods and men, they effected a work of generalization and consolidation. Cosmogonies and theogonies were rife. It is an old saying that Socrates brought philosophy down from the sky to earth and man. But the earlier philosophies accomplished an even greater task. They brought the beliefs which were the stuff of which cosmogonies were woven, down from remote time and places from the weird, strange and far-away to the heavens, the sea and the earth with which men are even now surrounded. At the same time, they retained as a principle of cosmic unity and governance the idea of surpassing and encompassing divinity. Thus was the idea of nature conceived, and thus was the tribe of observers and speculators upon the ways of nature begot.

There has been an acute controversy as to the meaning of Nature in early Greek thought, a dispute as to whether it means the birth and growth of things, the attempt to bring the multiplicity of changes into a single coherent story, or whether it means an underlying substance, something permanent under and above all change. The Greek *phusis*, like our word nature, that is also associated with natal and nativity, signified both birth and an inherent and unchanging structure which causes things to be of the kind they are. Fortunately for our purposes, we do not need to pass judgment between the two interpretations. Nature, *phusis*, the object of the philosopher's love,

---

3. [Dewey may be thinking of Gilbert Murray's "Saturnia Regna" from *The Five Stages of Greek Religion* (1925).]

soon came to denote both these things, whichever came first. Yet we must protest against reading into "Nature" as the object of early philosophic study the connotations which now cling to the word "substance." The right word is Principle, *archê*, rather than substance. And in using this word, we must further avoid certain significations now associated with it. We must consider principle both as primary and as rule: we must recall the connection of principle with Prince as well as with law of, say, the multiplication table. That is, we must take the term dynamically, as the force which brought about the changes and transformations of things, as well as intellectually in the sense of a theory which explains these changes. Both of these significations are far removed from the now usual connotation of "substance." *Archê* may have signified the permanent, but it was that permanently and unremittingly in operation, not something abidingly at rest, save as a moving cycle taken as a whole *is* rest. We may call it unchanging, but only in the sense that it was exemplified in all changes as in Protean forms.

Nature as a scene of transformations that display order, rule, even in [its] seemingly wildest alterations, is the theme of Greek thought. Sensitivity to change is a peculiar characteristic of Greek observation of human life and the natural environment. Greek thought is separated from the entire modern tradition by absence of the idea of creation and a creator. Creation in the sense of making as the poet makes, of producing as the artist and artisan produce, as plants and animals beget offspring, yes; but the producing and making is itself a natural event in an encompassing unity of operations, and operates with and upon a material already at hand. The gods themselves, immortal and imperishable as they are in comparison with man, once came into being and have a limit set by fate to their existence. They came from that whole which the philosophers called Nature and to it they shall return in their due season. Fire, air, water, mobile and generative, assuming many forms in their cycles, figure as the symbols of the ultimate principle or archê. The Greeks needed no one to tell them that mountains were part of the flux of things; they never took solid rock as a principle of explanation in their story of the universe.

Their sensitiveness to ceaseless change was not mitigated by their interpretation of the scene of human life. As is said in a drama of Euripides, "All is change, to and fro; the life of man shifts in endless wandering."[4] The story told by Herodotus of what Solon says in his interview with Croesus is typical of Greek thought and is summed up in the proverb: "Count no man happy till after death; till the natural end has come, no tale can be told." "We must look," as Solon said to Croesus, "to the conclusion of every matter and

---

4. [Perhaps "change succeeds to change, and man's life veers and shifts in endless restlessness" from Euripides, *Hyppolitus*.]

see how it shall *end*."[5] So Semonides: "We know nothing of how heaven will bring each thing to accomplishment,"[6] similarly Theognis: "No man knows whether his work will come to a good or a bad end."[7] Corresponding to this acute sense of the uncertain course of any change was a firm sense that all things in the world and in life have their "end," a final limit which cannot be avoided or overpassed. That excess, or passing beyond set bounds, was the one unforgivable sin of *hybris*, I hardly need remind you. "When a man's own feet are running to destruction, heaven also lends them speed." To the same effect is the pervasive sense of destiny, of that principle of measure by which all beings have their allotted career in place and time, in order that proportion and measure may everywhere rule. That sense of measure, of the mean proportional which governs Greek art is everywhere expressed until the period of dissolution in Greek thought.

Archê, as the encompassing and ruling principle, was thus one with the setting of bounds, limits, by which the due measure of the whole is preserved. This principle in its exercise of this [illeg.] function was conceived after a time in Greek philosophy as Intellect, Reason, *Nous*. But as we must avoid the suggestion of creation, in the Jewish-Christian sense, in connection with Greek thought, so we must steer clear of thinking of Reason in modern terms, or as something which introduced order and harmony from without. The order of things *is* reason. It is frequently remarked that the Greeks had no word that corresponds to our "personality." Neither did they have a single word for what we call "consciousness," and much less did they connect reason with the idea of selfhood, the ego, or with consciousness. Events in their changes observe a limit; they move toward a final work as their limiting close, and this character *is* Rationality. Even as late as Plato, "mind" as something marked by conscious purpose and desire, is set lower in the scale than measure, and with Aristotle "consciousness" in God is rather the possessed cognitive enjoyment of Being than the Being itself, an enjoyment incident to perfection of Being.

If we turn from these general considerations to philosophy proper, we find we have the key to its constant problem. Modern thought is so preoccupied with the question of the relation of subject and object, in knowing and in action, that it is at once a relief and a perplexity to find that question conspicuous by its absence in Greek thought. Its problem was the relation of the abiding principle to the concrete scene of actual transformations. The problem is not overt in the earliest speculators; they are so busy giving an account of the single and enduring principle in terms of the changes it

5. [Herodotus, *Histories* 1.32.]

6. [Source unknown.]

7. [Theognis, *Elegiac Poems*, 1.135.]

underwent and undertook to see any problem. This naïve estate soon gave way, however, to a formulation of what had been tacitly involved. From this time on, specifically after the conflict of the Eleatic and Heraclitean traditions set in, all systems of philosophy are versions of some attempted harmonization of identity and differencing, the one and other, the many, of being and non-being, of generation and decay in their connection with the principle which brought them about and which was itself subject neither to birth nor decay. Mechanical atoms and the void, qualitative seeds and their intermixtures, Nominal Ideas and phenomenal existences, Actuality and Potentiality, Essence and Matter are the technical symbols in the proffered solutions.

Details do not concern our survey. I wish rather to indicate the two broad streams which issued after a time from the genial essays to tell the story of alterations and transformations which composed the epic of nature. And at this point we recur to our underlying theme: The influence of the social medium. Of the two divergent streams one [*illeg.*] rise in the land and the other in the shop. The older tradition was that associated with agriculture, with man as tiller of the soil, with which may be combined man as navigator of the seas, since agrarian and sailor alike are in most direct and constant contact with the great forces of nature. The newer social fact, giving rise to a new view of nature, was the development of the manual arts, the deliberate and technical reshaping of natural materials by use of natural energies.

Let me first point to a common phrase in the two conflicting ways of envisaging nature. That Greek thought was the story of Nature as an embracing whole, operating according to principle in all its varied changes, a story in which traditional beliefs were revised in the light of new observations; has been stated. What set men on the search which ended with the discovery of Nature and inquiry into the nature *of* Nature? We can only guess, but it is not a guess that the search undertaken was not an unconditioned ebullition. It had its causes somewhere in the social situation which confronted the Greeks. And if we render our guess as to its cause in sufficiently general terms, we may at least come upon something significantly suggestive. Greek life even in the colonies was rich, free, and diversified beyond that found elsewhere. At the same time, it was extraordinarily unstable.[8] The arts, fine, mechanical, and social, were highly developed. But political harmony and enduring consistency of political policies and institutions were notoriously beyond Greek achievement. Men began by thinking of the order of the polis, the unity and stability maintained with the city-walls, as the type of order. Beyond the neighborhood of the city began the wild. Within peace and regularity, law; without, the lawless, the irregular. Anything might and

---

8. [Dewey bracketed the remainder of the paragraph]

did occur in the wild. Attachment to the familiar and dread of the unknown conspired to make the city the model of order, decorum, and security. But as political life became a scene of factional life, of revolution and insecurity, and as a sense of uniform cycles in natural phenomena grew up, the situation was reversed. The pattern of regularity was sought for in the structure and behavior of the heavens and the kosmos.

Disturbance of social customs and traditions has always been the occasion of demand for some settled objective order which may serve as a norm. The concept of nature has assumed many and diverse forms during the last twenty-five hundred years; its one constant element has been the idea of something stable and regular which might serve as a model and standard for institution of [illeg.] order in human affairs. Thus it was with the contrast of natural and positive law (*Jus*) in the Roman Empire, a conception which controlled legal and moral thought for a thousand years: thus it was in the eighteenth century when the changing state of Europe stood in contrast with the uniformity of natural phenomena revealed in the great scientific development of the seventeenth century. Amid all the divergent conceptions of Nature, there has always been as its core the conviction of an objective order and system which, as it stands in contrast with a breakdown in traditional principles of guidance and a disintegration of the customs upon which men had previously relied, might serve as a directive rule and a firm rock of refuge.

Seen in this light, the contempt poured by Eleatic, Heraclitean, by Empedocles, Democritus and Plato upon popular beliefs is noteworthy. The tendency is summarized in Plato's assertion that the public itself is the great misleader and corrupter. This conviction is the obverse side of the conviction that the discovery of the character of the all-encompassing and governing principle, or *archê*, is a moral and social necessity, because insight into it is the source of all illumination and all control, collective and individual, in human affairs—"Nature" was but a name for the original and abiding regulative force, the force generative of all particular changes and yet setting limits to their shifting movement. Nature is the native, the inherent and abiding, and also the normal, the pattern of regularity, the base-line from which to measure deviations. Hence it gave the directive law for human striving and achievement. The reports of the earliest thinkers are so fragmentary that they give the impression of purely theoretical inquiry into natural phenomena. But it is safe to infer that intellectual speculation more and more took on a definite practical import in its function in supplying the rule of social life and individual conduct. The Greeks never once called men wise, *sophoi*, merely because they knew facts. The idea that the regulative and encompassing principle which is Nature is the divine of necessity carried with it the idea of a norm for life. Within a generation or two, the records of the Ionic and Italian wise men, incomplete as they are, explicitly display an employment of whatever conception of Nature was reached as the determinate principle of right social organization and of righteous conduct.

Gilbert Murray remarks that "it is a canon of religious study that the gods reflect the social state, past or present."[9] It should also be a canon for the study of early philosophy that the generalization and consolidations found in it are a reflection of the social state. The outstanding characteristic of Greek culture in the period under consideration, along with political disturbance and factionalism, was the growth of the arts to the point of self-consciousness, that is, to the point wherein they demanded and received reflective attention. The arts of medicine, drama, navigation, artisanship, gymnastics, war, speech-making, political control and administration were gradually liberated from subjection to routine ancestral custom. Now among the arts the sharpest contrast, but as to their own in procedure and as to their social setting, was between the agrarian and the mechanical. The former had to do with living, growing things; the latter with making objects by means of reshaping of materials. This contrast showed itself in philosophy, at first vaguely, then with definiteness. The outcome was the formulation of two opposed ideas of Nature: on one hand, the organic, vital, spiritualistic; and on the other, the mechanical, two views that have persisted in one form or another throughout the whole subsequent philosophical tradition.

The carrying over of the distinction between the arts into reflective thought is, to my mind, the key to understanding the earlier natural philosophy of the Greeks. At all events, I shall accept this idea as a working hypothesis and shall attempt to use it as a clew in interpreting the course of that philosophy. Let us start, then, with the supposition that some thinkers viewed Nature and constructed their notion of it as the governing and encompassing principle on the model of observation of characters which inevitably impress themselves upon the minds of those viewing natural forces form the standpoint of agrarian practice. The student can then compare the conclusions that follow from the supposition with the main traits of early Greek philosophy.

(1) One thing which could not escape attention is growth from original germs, seeds, roots. The fact of such growth proves that the original elements are endued with life, with power of self-movement and development from within. Growth moreover follows a certain uniform course; seeds pass regularly through a succession of stages. Growth has a natural limit and close, an end, as well as a natural beginning. The whole movement is internally regulated so as to attain the end of maturity, or the full grown plant an animal. From this then issue more seeds to that the cycle is repeated

---

9. [Gilbert Murray, *The Five Stages of Greek Religion* (1925), 46.]

in endless succession. If this notion is generalized by extension to the total course of events constituting the universe, it leads to the search for some primitive element containing within itself generative force, and exhibiting a cycle of regular transformations that move toward a fixed goal, whereupon the cycle is reversed, the mature fruit being the author of germs or roots which again enact the drama of growth. The net conclusion is that Nature is possessed of life, self-movement, and self-governance and teleological operation—that is, direction of change toward a fixed and predestined end.

(2) Growth involves interaction of elements qualitative in nature and qualitatively opposites of each other. All growth is between extremes which are opposed; life brings on death and death is the source of new life; the matured form and the undeveloped primitive. And the process also takes place by means of a union of opposites. In animal reproduction, there is union of an active male and a passive female; so in Nature there is interaction of the fructifying energy of heaven with the receptivity of the earth; the course of the seasons, the cycle of movements of sun and moon, the alternation of day and night, all exemplify a moving rhythm generated by intermingling of opposites, one active, the other passive. Right and left, up and down, the propitious and sinister, odd and even, the one and the many, wet and dry, cold and hot, heavy and light, the mobile and stationary, the rule of tyrant and populace, the existence in the city of the prosperous and the needy, are the opposed qualitative elements whose union and interaction determines the course of events. Anyone who thought in symbols derived from the agrarian tradition was committed to characterizing nature in terms of a drama worked by qualitative opposites. One or other factor, the active or the passive, the energizing or the receptive, might dominate a particular stage of the resulting combination. But measure and limits, determinate beginning and close, orderly cyclical movement, overruled the changing incidents and composed them into a whole so that their story could be told.

(3) The regularity of the life-cycle of plants and animals is manifest in the constant reproduction of life forms having like properties. Seminal germs breed true; from corn comes corn, chicks from the egg of the hen; oaks from acorns; human beings from human seed. Fidelity to type holds of nature amid her seemingly most varied and irregular changes. Water subjected to heat generates vapor, air, which moves upward; subjected to cold it condenses and moves downward. Water reveals its dual potency also in the fact that it leaves behind it a sedimentary deposit of earth when it evaporates. From the mid-sky of tenuous vapor descend the showers which replenish the waters and vivify vegetation. Living growth is a process of aggregation, expansion, of enlargement; death is a process of dispersion, disintegration, contraction and separation. The endless generation, growth,

decay and dissolution of plants and animals that nevertheless assume constant and ever-repeated types is thus paralleled by the ceaseless origins, sequences of qualitative unions and separations of all the changes that form the spectacle of nature. All alike are expressions of the breeding true to type, the running true to form, which regulates all natural vicissitudes. The enduring qualitative character of the seminal elements rules all processes and operations and endows their products with community of form, with recurrently exemplified permanent natures. All things thus have generic characters in virtue of which they are what they are, and are nameable, identifiable and distinguishable, knowable. Transition is no mere flux, for the flux is regulated by type forms in consequence of which every cycle of change is closed in forms which are fixed and recurrent.

(4) Hence all things fell into species and kinds. The existence of inclusive families is such a marked trait of plant and animal life that it cannot escape recognition. The primary concept of natural relationship is that of kinship—of kinds. The smaller and more immediate family is in turn part of a large family, the tribe and race. Within the family all are related by a participation in a single and including nature. The individual passes; the kind, the family, endures. Apart from membership, apart from comprehension within his own kind, the individual is impotent, an outlaw, an accident. Since families are parts of large families, there is a hierarchy of kinds; and kinds are the most stable and significant the more inclusive they are. Moreover, since the seminal generative nature is qualitative in character, families, kinds, species are definitely marked off from one another by fixed qualities. They are mutually exclusive of one another even when all are included in a more comprehensive genus. Each has its allotted place and its apportioned properties. Measure rules here; the horse has not the properties of the dog; the bull not those of the pig. Mixed and intermediate forms are monstrous, transitory indications of disturbance and upheaval in the order of fixed and distinct kinds which nature truly is. So every natural element, fire, earth, air and water, light and heavy, warm and cold, wet and dry, mobile and set, has its own proper place and motion. Each is after its own kind and its abiding dwelling place with others of its kind. The scene of nature is the spectacle of constant change because it, like all living things, exhibits a union of opposites. The change is nevertheless one that manifests order because of the restless desire of each thing to be at home with its own kind. The endless panorama of orderly change makes the conflict and the resolution of the opposed tendencies of growth between opposites and by union of opposites, and of stable, unchanging kinds.

The conception of Nature's nature framed on the pattern of the industrial arts is as unlike as may well be. Supposing we here take as our working hypothesis the supposition that some city-bred people, expropriated perhaps from land-ownership, and familiar with the operations of manufacturing— in its literal sense—and with trade and exchange, attempt to derive from this mode of experience the symbols in which to read the book of nature. How will they conceive it? Making, constructing, not growth, provides the pattern and clew. Making involves an external power acting on material, not an internal source and inner directive principle of change.

(1) Hence the roots or ultimates are conceived of as elements of composition, rather than as seminal. At first, following presumably the lead of different materials worked upon, they are thought of as qualitatively differentiated, though there may be only a few qualities and a multitude of elements. But reflection makes it evident that materials are workable not in virtue of being wet or dry, hot or cold, but rather in virtue of their texture and grain. Clay, marble, wood, leather, fibers of wool, linen, and reed lend themselves to manipulation and reshaping in virtue of properties of density, of hardness and softness, of degrees of mobility in virtue of [which] they may be stretched, hammered, molded, twisted. Artisans must early have learned to think of heat as a means of softening, rendering things fluid or at least more malleable; of wetness as that which caused things to be more pliable; of cold as that which hardened things into shape. In this way, qualities cease to be ultimate differences; they are subordinated to shape. The difference between air and vapor, oil, water and wines, rocks and boards is taken to be one of degrees of tenuity and density, of remoteness and closeness of the same elements, rather than a qualitative difference belonging to elements themselves. Thus heterogeneity of quality was subordinated to homogeneity of structural elements. When nature was read by means of such symbols, an atomic theory naturally arose. The elements were small solid chunks, like each other in stuff, differentiated by position and perhaps by size and shape and differences in density—itself a difference in spatial relation. Any *intrinsic* mobility they might possess was conceived after the analogy of bodies falling in space, and hence a matter of weight and figure, not of quality, all other movements were due to being pushed or pulled by other like elements and their aggregations: there was no internal movement directing them to a predestined end.

(2) Hence the process of change is one wholly of aggregation and separation in space. There is no generation, no growth—save change in size and texture—and not decay and death. The ultimate elements are impenetrable and indestructible solids, that is, these are the last units of divisibility and the first of composition. Transformation is change of form in the external sense in which form signifies only shape, a matter of space occupancy. What seems to be birth, growth, and death are but cases of rarefaction and

condensation; that is, of coming closer together and moving further apart on the part of ultimate units too small to be seen—save perhaps in the motes dancing in the sunshine. Hence it is absurd to ascribe an end, a closing period, to a series of such changes. Such an apparent consummation is but a temporary equilibrium in the thrust and pull of bodies on each other; it is a pause, a truce, not a goal. Since the reshaping of things comes from without, it is absurd to ascribe to natural elements a tendency toward some particular outcome; compound things are inherently indifferent to the form they happen to take on; that being a matter of external aggregation and separation. Anything which can be called soul is a mode of finer and more mobile unseverable, or indivisible, elements. The properties of the same are just those belonging to extremely fine and mobile particles.

(3) Science does not then consist of the ordering of things into kinds according to their distinctive properties, and of defining each kind according to the other kinds which it includes and excludes. Knowledge is rather insight into the formula of mixture and separation. It is like a prescription or recipe, which tells a physician or cook, or metal worker, how much of each stuff to select and how to compound it with suitable quantities of other stuffs. To the artisan, knowledge is knowing *how*: knowing with what material to start and in what quantity or dose, and in what order to proceed from the simple to the compound. The "end" is nothing intrinsic towards which the whole process of change immanently tends so that in knowing it we alone understand the beginning and the process of change. It is simply the more composite and it is known or understood by knowing the elements out of which it is composed and the manner of their composition, composition being always a matter of spatial conjunction. Generalize this view and we get to the atomism of original elements that cannot be severed, or that are indivisible, out of which as the primitive originals, all things are formed by processes of spatial segregation and aggregation. The theory of the process of knowledge conforms to this theory of its object. The artisan depends upon sense perception of materials and spatial changes. Sense perception, the norm of all knowledge, is itself a mechanical process of receiving fine mobile films or "images" of things and of their proper admixture within the fine elements that form the mind. Sense perception gives, therefore, true knowledge in the degree in which it recognizes figures, shapes, and motions: color, sound, smell, etc., being only their confused and, as it were, conventional compound.

(4) To the artisan, then, ends are external and externally initiated. Plan, design, corresponding to the idea of what it is he wishes to shape, weapon, jar, building, statue, mat or basket, is important, but it is brought to bear externally, through his own operations upon the material. The harvest, the fruit, to the agronomist, is the natural consummation of intrinsic processes

of growth. Nature, sun, rain, soil and wind do or undo the work, according to the measure and proportion they observe and exceed. His own task is wholly auxiliary; he has primarily to note and conform to the operations of nature itself. And everything turns upon their own outcome or end. To the artisan, original elements, that from and by which, is all important, for they determine the results which can be effected. The question of what for, to what end, determines his own acts, but not the structure and properties of what he works with. To the farmer, on the other hand, it is congenial to think of all natural forces as existing within and for the sake of the fruits, whether of achievement or frustration, they bring about. The real beginning is with the perfected or mature form from which issue the seeds of more growths. It is natural for the one to think of natural elements as indifferent and even recalcitrant, needing to be bent by human intervention to use and enjoyment. To the other it is natural to think of natural process as themselves bent upon the fruit which gives meaning and value to them, normally an end of use and enjoyment, but one of tragedy and catastrophe when operative nature is troubled and offended.

Two general remarks are needed to complete the sketch. The agricultural tradition is the older. Thinkers who refined and generalized the material of its belief were in closest contact with the underlying hopes, fears, activities and outlook of mankind. Manufacturing, reshaping things, is relatively an innovation. It had no such deep roots in the past; no such intimate association with the desire of men to be in harmony with nature. The art of agriculture is a natural art, so closely does it conform with large scale phenomena of nature. The artisan's art is an *artificial* art; it seems to coerce nature and subject it to a foreign yoke. It is no cause for surprise then that the matter of the classic philosophic tradition was drawn from the spiritualistic and teleological beliefs about nature, and that the materialistic and mechanistic view was never more than an uncongenial heresy.

Prestige from social conditions attached moreover to the agricultural tradition. The farmer as a worker, a tiller of the soil and bearer of burdens, occupied a low enough status. But owners of the soil, those rooted in it and flourishing when it flourished, were the aristocrats of the ancient world. They were natural lords in peace and natural chieftains in war. They made up the immemorially old families, descended mayhap from heroes and semi-divinities. The artisans on the other hand were socially ignored if not actually despised and disenfranchised. They were the proletariat. In some cases, at least they were not only not citizens but not natives. They were remnants of a conquered group or were settlers attracted by prospect of work and wage. It is interesting to note that when social philosophies came to be articulate, framed, this contrast was also mirrored. The dominant or classic philosophy held political order and organization to be the work of nature, divine and embracing all secure goods. The other school held that political organization was something made, manufactured like a pot or a house, by human beings for human advantage and utilities, the result of external forces brought to bear upon the relations of indivisible ultimate units so as to effect by means of aggregation and composition something of profit to the units. To one, justice was by nature; to the other, it was by convention.

Proof of the hypothesis which has been propounded is out of the question in any stringent sense of proof. Something less than proof but approximating it might be obtained by applying the method in detail to the fragments of the Pre-Socratics which have come down to us. As they stand, they surely offer a challenge to the student. If adoption of the point of view of two great strains of belief from which thinkers selected material and obtained direction brings light and order to the story, it will be as much as can be expected in [the] test of any hypothesis. But time forbids entering upon this detailed interpretation. We shall conclude, then, with calling to mind some antecedently probable considerations, of the same general nature as those with which we set out.

Let it be noted in the first place that some hypothesis as a method of interpretation is imperatively called for. The alternative is not between that advanced and an antiquarian and philosophical study that is content to terminate with information as to just what was said by Thales, Anaximander, Anaximenes, Pythagoras, Heraclitus, Parmenides, Empedocles and the rest of them. Such studies are necessary; but they end with material that still needs to be understood, not with understanding. Consequently the reasonableness of the supposition advanced will look quite different to one who contrasts it with some other explanatory theory of the course taken by early philosophy and to one who contrasts it with no theory at all, since he rests upon the informational data as if they were final. The relative voice, the absence of any rival method of interpretation may then give that which has been said a claim to benevolent hearing.

There are certain conditions which any principle of interpretation must fulfill. Those who accept the Hegelian theory that the history of philosophy is an immanent self-enclosed dialectic unfolding of ultimate truth are exempt from considering the relation which the course of philosophic thought bears to the environments in which it has taken on divergent forms. Other students of the mutations and career of philosophy are committed to the notion that philosophies are modes of intellectual *response* to the social media within which they arise. To be acquainted with what has been said by persons philosophical, even in the most accurate and careful way possible, is not enough. To a student of philosophy, such acquaintance is but preliminary. We cannot know any scheme of thought as a response unless we take into account what *it was a response to*. Context gives gestures their meanings; they are idle movements in the air unless we know their occasion and intent, and these are found outside themselves.

I sometimes have a feeling that writers on the history of philosophy bring to their task a conception of mind and mental activity which would be promptly and emphatically repudiated if it were made articulate. They write as if the mind of the philosopher, empty of prepossessions derived from tradition and uninspired by any humane interest of their [environment] were confronted by the universe at large, uncolored by any local properties and untempered by any temporal preoccupations: and as if the mind then proceeded, by direct intercourse in general with the universe in general, to bring forth a system. Not thus can the situation be conceived. The philosopher is first and last a human being with his own intellectual and emotional habits who is involved in a concrete scene having its own color of tradition; its own occupations and dominant desires; its own overhanging problems and preferred ways of meeting them. His intellectual response is a function of these two variables. A *contemporary* philosopher, the student of [*illeg.*] comes to his work, protected and perhaps muffled by an immense intervening apparatus. He carries in his head a vast body of distinctions previously made, of problems already formulated, of solutions formulated ready to hand. He can think if he will in terms of categories and systems already provided. The two variables, himself as a thinker and the cultural material thought about, are insofar technalized, if I may venture the word, for him in advance. The mind is removed from contact with the vital traditions and movement of the time and place, and the material thought about is not the existent scene but ideas and doctrines previously distilled from a great variety of other such scenes. But this is just the situation which did not exist for early thinkers, for example in Ionia and the Italian colonies, then in Athens. Personal vision and interest and the immediate scene counted instead.

Consequently, if he is to be intelligent, the student should find out what body of traditional beliefs was alive and active in forming the mind of the philosopher, and that he should reconstruct the environment sufficiently to know what problems its needs imposed upon the thinker, and what direction it gave to the imaginings it evoked. These considerations reach deeper than the particular interpretation which I have offered. But even in its too bare outline it may approach sufficiently near the truth to guide the student in his own interpretations. What is important is not the exact truth of the hypothesis offered but the recognition of the underlying conditions of philosophy. If they are recognized, this particular hypothesis may in due course receive correction, confirmation or displacement by a better one.

The hypothesis in short may be taken as an illustration of the sort of study philosophy calls out when it is viewed as a response to the social situations in which the life of the individual thinker is set. If it serves this purpose, I should be glad to see it replaced by whatever more apt and penetrating theory may be devised. Meantime, the attempt on the part of students to give filling to the blanks left in the outline presented may be of service in that most fascinating of all human studies, the endeavor of man to come to intellectual terms with the world in which he lives.

III. The Discovery of Rational Discourse

The earliest philosophies were stories of nature. As Homer told the story of the Trojan War and the wanderings of Odysseus, so Thales and the others recounted the epic of the doings and works of nature, relating the movements, strifes, and return home of the elements that formed its *dramatis personae*. They told the tale boldly and naively, not questioning the capacity to compose the actions of nature into a single coherent story. The different tales disagreed, however; they competed with one another for listeners and for credence. This scene of conflict gradually and piecemeal brought about a shift of attention. Instead of devoting themselves wholly to the outward scene, the story-tellers began to ask about the worth of the witnesses of the scene. Was the eye or the ear the more to be trusted? Or did both eye and ear bear false testimony and was thought the only witness to be relied upon?

The transfer of attention from that whose story was told to the story itself did not amount, however, to a distinct change in the subject-matter of philosophy till the geographical focus of thought shifted from the colonies to Greece. The great, the classic, movement of ancient philosophy originated in this transfer. Mankind has always used language to give accounts, reports, or things, and has been for the most part totally unaware that there was anything extraordinary involved in the enterprise. Speech was treated as if it inevitably fitted the things talked about as a glove conforms to the hand. The mind assumed without thinking about it that language is the natural and appropriate vestment in which things and thought inevitably clothe themselves. The voice of man was treated as if it were the voice of things—the significance and order of things made articulate. With the development of generalized but rival stories of nature, this assumption became a problem: it was something to be examined and explained. How can it be that language embraces the truth and reality of things? How especially can it mirror transparently the true being and full scope of the universe itself? As long as language only reported episodes here and there, the question did not force itself upon the mind. But when it ventured to undertake telling the story of nature as a whole, it was inevitable that the question should sooner or later be raised. To give an account *of* nature is also to account *for* its phenomena. Logos or language can report, it would seem, the cosmic scheme only if it has its own *logos*, its own rationale. Thus Athenian philosophy really centered on this problem: How is rational discourse possible? How is it that the structure of discourse about nature is possible, to tell the story of nature, that is, give a report and account of it which is faithful? This discovery of the existence and importance of rational discourse masked an intellectual revolution. It turned thought from the physics of nature to its inherent logic. The outcome was the discovery of intellectual method. The word "logic" is significant. It means both speech and thought which is rational in procedure, which is really *thought* and not mere incoherent fancy. The word "dialectic" is equally significant. This is akin to "dialogue"; it is intellectual intercourse, the regulated change and development of ideas which results in understanding and hence in agreement, in unity of mind. Both logic and dialectic signify, in short, rational discourse. At the end when men turned again from logic to physics, the result was that physics became metaphysics. Nature was not merely physical; it was the embodiment of logical forms and structures, and knowledge of them was much more important than was acquaintance with material elements and processes. The latter entered into science only as they fitted into the logical or rational framework of nature.

While the revolution occurred at Athens, there was a transition period which is named the period of the Sophists—literally the wise men. Basil Gildersleeve used to say that the nearest English counterpart to the Greek *sophoi* was the word "professor"—with a certain malicious stress on *professing*. Mahaffy calls them peripatetic journalists; Gomperz says they were half-professors and half-journalistic publicists. Instruction of children remained traditional in Greece; innovations were confined to the education of adults with especial reference to young men just emerging into full citizenship. The sophists professed to teach "virtue." At least, that is the English word which is more often employed in translation. It is misleading, however, unless we strip it of moralistic implications. "Excellence" comes nearer the idea, with some emphasis upon the idea of excelling, surpassing. Trained skill and power of achievement, with the social recognition and esteem they command, is perhaps as near the meaning as we can get. A passage from Gomperz is worth quoting in full. "The time had come when undisciplined empiricism had more and more to give way to the rule of art. There was hardly an aspect of life which remained unaffected by that tendency. What was not reformed was codified, and both processes went almost hand in hand. A profusion of text-books was poured forth; all the business of mankind, from cooking a dinner to painting a picture, from going on a walk to waging a war, was guided by rules and wherever possible reduced to rules."[1]

We shall not go far wrong if we conceive the sophists as the leaders in this reduction of all the arts of life to rules and principles, and especially as the purveyors and disseminators of the codes which were the result. Medicine, diet, tactics, training of horses, music, painting, architecture, phonics, language, literary exposition and criticism, stage management, agriculture, were all so treated. As the movement reached Athens, the civic arts were more and more emphasized. Persuasion by means of speech was at the heat of public life, both in politics and in litigation. The arts of oratory and rhetoric emerged and those who taught them promised, as the fruit of their teaching, success and eminence in public life. To us, familiar as we are with all kinds of hand-books and encyclopedias, the movement may not seem very important. But in its place and epoch it marked what was hardly less than a revolution. The arts had been learned by apprenticeship in actual practice, learning by doing. In all the civic arts, such education had signified the most intimate identification with the traditions and habits of one's own community. Now it was asserted that these things could be learned theoretically; by mastering principles and rules abstracted from the onerous discipline of practical exercises. It was assumed that even in law and politics, these principles were capable of intellectual formulations of a general sort, independently of gradual saturation with the traditions of the local community. It is no wonder that the conservatives saw in these professions a menace, a disloyalty, while others welcomed them as the promise of the emancipation of the arts from routine experiences, and the earnest [promise] of the rule of life by reason.

Athens was the flower and the fruit of all that was most valuable in Hellenic culture. Inevitably the travelling wise men were drawn to Athens and there their teaching left its permanent impress. There is truth in the conventional treatment according to which Greek philosophy is divided into great periods, the Pre-Socratic and the Post-Socratic, the sophists being treated as a transition, an interlude. The sophists gradually shifted the centre of attention and interest from the Nature philosophy of Ionia and Italy to the humanistic philosophy which flourished later in Athens. However, they accomplished this shift piece-meal and as it were casually, without explicit consideration of the effect of the change upon man's ideas and ideals about himself and his relation to his fellows. In Athens the tremendous impact of the old Nature philosophy upon human conduct and social institutions came to consciousness. The easy profession of the sophists to teach wisdom about this, that and the other thing, so as to impart skilled ability or virtue in the

---

1. [Theodor Gomperz. *Greek Thinkers—A History of Ancient Philosophy* (1906), vol. 1, p. 386.]

various occupations which dealt with the things in question, was converted by Socrates into the most tremendous and difficult of all problems: What is wisdom? What is teaching and learning? What is virtue? Can it be known and cannot it be taught? It is quite likely that Plato's picture of the antagonism of Socrates to the travelling wise men and teachers is exaggerated, as it is sure that he exaggerated for his own purposes their disintegrating and corrupting influence. But that he accused them on the ground that they took their pay for making men better and wiser is quite possible. At all events, Socrates took the profession of communication of wisdom and trained excellence in the pursuits of life seriously. He apprehended its all-engrossing importance for the conduct of life; it was no technical and professional affair, but it was of revolutionary import for the purposes and undertakings of the city-state and the individual. The more insistent and blatant the professions of the ability to impart wisdom and virtue in its train, the more urgent, then, became the question as to the nature of communication, of wisdom, of virtue.

It is dramatically, and probably biographically, certain that Socrates professed ignorance not knowledge, the love of wisdom, or philosophy, not its possession. It is also certain that when he conversed with others he found them also ignorant while they had a conceit of necessary knowledge which he was free from. This general ignorance, including as it did ignorance of the state of ignorance, defined the mission of Socrates, and his ardent and relentless apostleship in striving to convince his fellow citizens of their lack of wisdom in all the important matters where they were sure they already possessed it, presumably accounts for his death. For the effort to develop a sense of ignorance—answering to the conviction of sin in evangelical Christian circles—and of the need for unremitting search for wisdom, whose possession was the condition of conversion to a new life, was an attack on tradition more fundamental than that in which any Sophist engaged. It was a complete challenge to existing customs, institutions and beliefs; naturally, they avenged themselves.

Socrates plied his mission by means of conversation; as everybody knows he left not a single written word behind, nor, if we trust Plato rather than Zenophon, did he either lecture or preach. Dialogue not monologue was his forte, to the end that a mutual confession of ignorance having been reached, a cooperative search for wisdom might ensue. This fact is of immense significance. It supplies corroboration of the statement that the great Athenian revolution in philosophy turned from discussing nature and giving an account of it to the examination of the nature and procedure of discussion and report. Discourse as the means of telling a wisdom already possessed had to be converted into a means of arriving at the possibility of effecting such a truth.

. . .

A free rendering of the surmises about the Socratic method or logic to which the accounts of Plato entitle us would run somewhat as follows. The conflicts of belief and opinion among men are a reflection of division and lack of integration in social institutions themselves. It is impossible to have a unified and stable city-state until there is one mind among its members. The state of personal ignorance on the part of those who professed wisdom and virtue was a symbol of the uncertain foundation of social life and conduct. Conflict and opposition of beliefs is, however, complete evidence of an underlying unity which must be discovered. Men do not disagree as long as they are talking about different things; they can differ only as they intend and purport to refer to the same thing. This discovery puts the common estate of division and conflict in belief and conduct in a new light. It reveals that division is due to lack of understanding; that understanding *is* agreement, harmony, for it indicates knowledge of common and shared intent. Induction is at least the process of eliciting the fact of the being of such an object of common intent, an object somehow contained in whatever obscure way in the minds of all, or all it could not be intended or meant by all. Definition is the statement of the nature of the ulterior common or universal object so that it is clearly grasped and capable of definite retention. The object sought for is not only an object common, below all differences of belief, to those who discourse together, but it is common to a number of cases, to all the cases to which a common name may be appropriately applied in discourse. Not only do Socrates and these with whom he is conversing intend the same thing when they say justice, if their words have any meaning at all, but all the various acts which may properly be called just participate in the same object.

The implications of the Socratic position developed by Plato form the basis of the classic tradition in European philosophy. But before we deal with the Platonic elaboration (which may have been trenched upon in what has just been attributed to Socrates) we must note the utter superficiality of a once usual method of interpreting the Platonic Ideas. It has been said *ad nauseam* that Plato's basic error consisted in taking words for things, or at least in taking the generalized ideas at which men psychologically arrived, for real and independent object, the supreme realities in fact. It is true that Socrates set out from an examination of rational discourse and in that sense occupied himself with language. But Socrates paid language the compliment of supposing that it meant something beyond itself, that it was an embodiment of knowledge or at least of something taken to be knowledge. The objective intent of language involved to him a community of intended reference on the part of different minds as a precondition of any intelligible discourse, and a joint sharing on the part of many things and acts in a common nature or kind of being. Either all just acts share and exemplify the same nature or they are all called just in the same accidental and irrational way in which the same sound, spelled rain, rein or reign, is applied to different things. Not the hypostatizing of words but the conviction that discourse is rational and reasoned only as it *means* something objective which is the ground of understanding and agreement among men and which is the only justified or objective basis of all distinctions, classifications and generalizations made in our ideas is the method of Socratic logic. He and Plato after him may have misconceived the intrinsic character of this objective bond of union between things and minds. But to make this admission is not to denigrate the fact that he undertook precisely the task which his modern critics so glibly slip over: an examination of the possibility, nature and conditions of validity of discourse that deals in an intelligently consistent way with the realities involved in all beliefs. If we put it in modern terms, remembering that all thinking involves the use of symbols, and signs, of language in its broadest sense, we may assert that Socrates was the first to ask: What is the nature of thinking when it reaches or purports to reach its goal: the truth about things? It is not too much to say that European civilization since his day has been differentiated from other cultures by its belief in its possession of [an] orderly intellectual method for stating and reaching [the] truth about things. This belief, hallucinatory or sound, we owe to the work of the Socratic school.

Lack of time forbids consideration of all but one of the schools of philosophy formed by professed disciples of Socrates. Plato is the follower whose works remain in any adequate representation and he is the disciple whose influence has transcended all the rest. At his hands, the common object of discourse and intent, and of a whole group of related things, became the ultimate reality, "the Idea," an enduring form or structure of an indefinite number of changing existences, scattered in space and time, the object of all inquiry and the goal of all learning, the seat of all ultimate authority, the basis of all agreement and harmony in human conduct, personal and collective, and hence the model and pattern of all intelligent endeavor, individual and social. Plato did much more, however, than elaborate the logical suggestions he got from Socrates. The latter, as far as we can judge, was indifferent and possibly opposed to physical inquiries. Man was the intellectual concern of man; nature was but a setting for his conduct, to be used and enjoyed, or if needs must be, to be endured and suffered. With Plato the setting ceased to be an external theater of only esthetic and practical import. It was intrinsically implicated in the life of man, or rather the life and destiny of man were intimately involved with the nature of Nature. But in terms of historic development, he attempted a synthesis of earlier philosophies of Nature with the logical and ethical-political ideas he derived from Socrates. His comprehensive and dramatic vision in which logic was elevated to a metaphysics, the latter united with cosmology, and both with anthropology, ethics, and politics, has as it were defined the office of European philosophy since his day and created a model which is the admiration and the despair of successive generations of philosophers.

That Plato instituted a world of reality beyond and above Nature as Nature had been conceived of up to his day is notorious. This fact makes him the progenitor of the mystic strain in the Neoplatonists of Alexandria and the fountainhead of all transcendental philosophies since his day. The common or universal objects of Socrates, possibly restricted by the latter to ethical matters like justice, courage and other concerns of high human excellence, were extended to include the ultimate and stable reality and goal of knowledge in all matters. They were stable and hence eternal; they alone could be said to *be* in the full sense of the word, since change is alteration, or othering, and to be other than being is to be mutable and to participate in defect, non-being. The world of natural phenomena, in which of course are included all physical existences, is one of coming into and passing out of being, rather than of being proper. In man however there is reason which is in the literal sense supra-natural and supra-psychical, the direct reflex of eternal archetypal Forms of Being. and capable, by means of disciplines of which mathematics and dialectic are the chief intellectual modes, of being so elicited and emancipated, that it may behold the Ideas directly, and through its realized participation in them be taught to bring into subjection and harmony all of man's nature which in itself is unstable, irregular, and divisive. This personal harmonization is, however, the counterpart of a city-state which is ruled by those having had insight into and communion with the ultimate Forms of Being, which are therefore the patterns to which law and administration must conform. The regulation of the state, including education according to natural capacity, regulation of economic and sexual relations, censorship of literature and the arts, the use of gymnastic to secure the natural medium of a harmonized soul, and legislation is identical with the rule among men of possessed wisdom.

The "transcendentalism" of Plato is thus widely different in effect from that which has obtained in other forms of so-called *a priori* thought. No matter how intense may be Plato's appreciation of the esthetic intuition of ultimate Forms of Being, his political interest is never long in abeyance. There is put in the mouth of Socrates in his speech of defense against his accusers, a story which is most significant for Plato. Socrates, having been told by the Delphic oracle that he was the wisest of Athenians, and knowing his own ignorance, commenced his career of cross-examination of his fellows. With respect to his search for possessors of wisdom, they are divided into three classes. The poets know many fine and noble things especially regarding conduct. But since they do not know how they know, or why the things they say are so, they have not wisdom. The craftsmen know well the things relating to their own procedures, but they are not judges of the end or good of what they do, and they imagine that they are judges of all sorts of matters which lie beyond their special expertness. As for the politicians, they know neither ends nor means; they have but the semblance of knowledge. The implied corollary, an implication made explicit in other dialogues, is the need of an art which will combine the insight into ends or goods which the poets have in an intuitive, inspired way with the kind of knowledge of materials and techniques involved in their realization that artisans have in their lesser matters, which is then brought to bear upon the conduct and organization of the city-state. This royal or legislative art is the operative expression of the knowledge of true Being in its relation to Becoming which is the goal of philosophy, a knowledge to which dialectic is the supreme contributory art. Plato's conviction that knowledge and action are one does not fail him at any point in the scale of insight. As sensation is to appetitive action, or belief ungrounded in reason is to accustomed behavior, so is true wisdom to conduct which controls or rules in the interest of the harmonious whole. Ecstatic vision of the ultimate forms of Being, obtained when the lover of wisdom ascends out of the cave of semblances, is but antecedent to the return of the philosopher into the world of phenomena that conduct therein may be organized and regulated in the light of the eternal archetypes of reality. In a word, Plato was profoundly moved by the threatened factional disintegration and strife of Athenian life and conceived of attained wisdom as the only possible basis of its integration and stable governance.

The aspiration was doomed to defeat; there is evidence that Plato himself was not over-hopeful. But he never parted with his conviction that with respect to the stable organization of the state, it was adoption of his scheme or nothing. The speedy event was the loss of Athenian independence and political integrity. In this sense, Plato's system was surely utopian. But the situation as he saw it defines the nature of the "transcendental" character of his philosophic system. The existing social instability and chaos could not be reformed from within; patterns and energizing force from without were required. The patterns and the *puo sto*, the leverage, of political integration had to come from without, from something beyond and above the natural scene. Anything else signified that the blind could lead the blind; the diseased and deformed generate health and beauty; the changing produce the enduring; the unstable and divided give birth to order and harmony.

Plato may have erred. But at least for well over a millennium of years Europe trod the path he marked out. A corrupt and fallen world could be organized and ruled only by principles drawn from a supernatural realm of Being. It is, at all events, not for those who accept the traditional Christian theology to rail at Plato's metaphysics. Special revelation was substituted for the disciplined reason of Plato, but the conception of the relation of the natural to the transcendent is the same in both systems. The modern Platonist, he who accepts the intuition of essences apart from existence, may reject the Christian scheme as well as the Platonic idea of philosophy as the supreme political art. But in so doing he only repeats in himself acceptance of the modern tradition of an egoistic individualism of mind, and adopts also that isolation of knowledge from action which demarcates modern thought from Platonic assertions of their indivisible union.

The activity of the Sophists had created the sense of two outstanding and allied problems. Some of them had taught the subordination of art to nature, while others had proclaimed the supremacy of the arts over nature. In this difference they doubtless got their cues from the split among the earlier natural philosophers between those who derived their patterns of interpretation from agriculture, conforming itself to the course and cycles of nature, and those who were impressed by the power of the statesmen's arts to utilize and control natural materials and processes for human needs and purposes. The other problem they bequeathed to Athenian thought was the relation of nature and *nomos*, human custom, convention. Are language, social organization and law, morals, by nature, or by *nomos*? If the latter, is *nomos* itself a matter of enactment and decree or of convention and compact become customary and second nature?

Our hasty outline sketch requires at least some further content drawn from Plato's attitude toward these questions. His answer to the first determines his cosmology. Nature is itself a divine art and human art is an imitation of this divine art. Between the realm of ultimate Forms of Being, the Ideas, and the world of phenomena stands a demiurge, a divine artisan, who shapes passive and inert matter according to patterns, geometrical and arithmetical, by means of which matter imitates or reproduces as best it may the supernal ideas; at the same time, the phenomena thus shaped are, in accordance with the generalized animistic tradition, ensouled with a living world spirit, so that movement is imparted to them. Thus Plato, treating nature as a work of divine art, strove to reconcile the two opposed traditions.

His solution of the problem of Nature versus *Nomos* was similar. His analysis of the arts which had already been achieved proved to him that they were successful because the artisan in the first place acknowledged the different forms which matter exhibited in various materials and adapted his work to them. In the second place, the arts have or rather are, *technê*. That is, they involve a serial order of processes or a technique in which by progressive steps the raw material is converted into the complete matured form which is the proper and good end of the art. This technique also copies the order of natural sequential operations. In the third place, the arts are graded in scale of excellence in the degree in which they observe and embody principles of number and measure, degenerating into pseudo-arts as they fail to respect arithmetical and geometrical designs.

The political art is the legislative art: that is the art of the control and rule of life, social and individual. It deals with the whole, and its model and norms must be sought in the very nature of things. Hence it is in contrast with the lesser arts which are possessed of a kind of knowledge low in degree but fitting the material, ends, and processes involved. The politicians and would -be rulers are, as we have seen, the most pretentiously ignorant of all men. Hence existing *Nomos*, the whole prevailing body of customs and institutions, is as it stands a chaotic conglomerate. In it, blind custom and arbitrary enactment intermingle. A true *Nomos*, a just political system and regime, waits upon that development of a ruling supreme art which is the counterpart of attained wisdom. The ideal *Nomos* would exist according to and by Nature. It would involve knowledge of raw material—in this case, human nature and its native potentialities—knowledge of a technique that would by graded serial operations bring them to full fruition, each according to its natural capacity and fitness (the technique of education of which this legislation is a part), and above all knowledge of the final and supreme end, the ultimate and comprehensive good. In this last respect *Nomos*, or institutions, are according to and by something above Nature. By this road would Plato harmonize in a more inclusive system the two conflicting social and moral traditions.

Aristotle was the thinker who gave that form to the critical systematization of beliefs which was destined to prevail in the final and Christian synthesis of the thirteenth century. He was a disciple of Plato but a disciple with a decided difference. The dissolution of Greek social life had gone so far that there was no longer the question of the Platonic heroic endeavor for revolutionary reform. Even if such had not been the case, Aristotle's temperament and interest led him in another direction. We must never forget in any study of Plato his passionate conviction of the union of knowledge and action. That conviction left Aristotle more than cold. Reason and knowledge were indeed of utmost importance in the moral and political conduct, but they operated there, as it were, by the way, incidentally. The essential function of reason is to know, to grasp the truth in and of itself. There is indeed a unity of knowing and action, but the action which properly corresponds to thought is a purely theoretic activity; it is self-sufficient and complete in itself. The idea that it should pass on into practical activity would imply that it was not self-sufficient and final, that it *needs* something beyond itself or is inherently defective, imperfect. From Aristotle, subsequent philosophizing inherits the tradition of the isolation of knowledge from practice and the superiority of self-inclusive, self-revolving intellectual contemplation to any form of practical dealing with things, moral and political as well as physical.

Aristotle also broke away from his teacher in another important respect. Where Plato was mathematically inclined, Aristotle was a naturalist. If the idea suggested in the last hour is correct, he may be said to have elevated the agricultural tradition that [*illeg.*] to the Nth power. He was a physician rather than a physicist. His favorite studies were those which we now call biological; he studied political constitutions as he studied animals' structures and functions. They were something to be distinguished, defined and classified. States were also "by nature" since man is a naturally political animal. Plato's thought was dominated by examination of the arts, the arts actually in existence but pre-eminently by the thought of the supreme art, which did not exist, save in his own tentative designs. Aristotle took all of his clues from the life-history of living things, and read Nature in symbols thus obtained. He continued and organized the philosophy based on what we have called the agrarian tradition, so much so that it was hardly possible not to anticipate some of the terms of the fruition it attained at his hands in the account of it already given.

The empirical sober strain in Aristotle in its contrast with the transcendental strain of Plato has to be understood in connection with these two distinctions. Having no concern with the problem of moral and political revolution, he had no need for transcendent Forms of Being. As one concerned with knowing as an end itself, it sufficed to study natural existence as concretion of Forms of Being in things. Hence his constant polemic against Plato, in metaphysics, cosmology, logic, morals and politics, for holding to Forms separate from actual natural existence. Hence his "realism" as distinguished from that idealism which in Plato it is so difficult to discriminate from utopianism. If Forms are already in things, imparting to them their structure and regulating their capacities, it suffices to elicit and define them and systematize things in accord with them. Nature is conceived as a whole of many kinds in which everything is done and produced by internal and intrinsic self-movement. It operates like art, but in the arts the movement which shapes things and the end to which they are shaped are supplied from without, by human action and design, as the sculptor carves out the marble block and the carpenter erects a house. In Nature the end, the design or form and the movement toward the complete realization are immanent in nature. Conceiving the structure and operation of nature after the model supplied by the arts, there is no need for the Platonic demiurge or intervening architect and builder. The well-known Aristotelian four "causes" or principles thus represent Nature framed after the pattern of the factors of art. There is material or stuff, that which is shaped; there is impact and impartation of energy from without the particular stuff, but within the course of Nature; there is form, or the particular design and arrangement of parts which distinguishes articles made from one another and makes each to be what it is; there is the completed outcome, the finished and final form to which everything within the scope of the specific kind tends to move, the complete manifestation of the form which constitutes the essential reality of each kind of thing.

With this phase of natural existence, derived from the Platonic tradition but installed within nature, Aristotle combined factors derived from the qualitative and vital school of the earlier physiologers. The material substratum or stuff consists of original qualities of hot-cold, light-heavy, dry-moist, which combine in various combinations and permutations to form the four elements of earth, air, fire and water. The error of the early naturalists consisted in taking these original elements to be the whole of nature. In reality they are but the "material" basis, and even then they express not bare matter but matter formed or informed by the qualitative essences which are grasped by sense knowledge. They are related to the entire nature of things as the leather of the shoemaker, the wood of the carpenter, are related to their finished, complete product. In reference to this complete nature or reality they are potentialities. Unlike the stuff of the artisan, however, when movement is imparted to them, they change of themselves in the direction of their complete form or end, which is the reason, the why, of their existence. Therefore they are truly known, rationally understood, only in their terminal and fulfilling forms. For they alone are the actualities of which the "nature" of the physiologers was but the potentiality. Nature is then teleological through and through. As the scholastic put it, Nature does nothing in vain; everything strives under the direction of its internally regulative form to a completion which gives it its rationale and which forms its true, because complete or perfect, nature. The designs or patterned arrangements of characteristic forms of objects are of material elements; these are not imparted by an external mind, as most moderns have conceived design and purpose but are the regulative structure of things controlling change. The latter is but the movement in which original elements as potential and material realize their own fullness of being.

The philosophy of Aristotle thus brings to an organized consummation the elements dispersed throughout earlier systems of thought; in his own language, it is an actualization of all of which they are the potencies—with the sole omission of the mechanical atomic philosophy which of course could have entered into his scheme only to destroy its symmetry. Nature is conceived after the analogy of the origin, growth and development of living creatures; a rounded out statement of the suggestions drawn by the early thinkers from experiences of living creatures. The moral conviction of Socrates as to the supremacy of ends and the control of conduct was freed from its distinctively ethical significance so that ends were naturalized in objects, each after its kind, as the actuality to which all change of material elements was directed. The Platonic Forms of Being as the ultimate reality of all phenomena and the goal of all true insight were joined with the material elements drawn from natural philosophy to furnish the inherent constitution of all things. The ever-present problem of the enduring and the changing was solved by the idea of a rhythmic alternation of actions in which the actual moves the potential toward its own actualization or fulfilled perfection as the oak bears acorns and endows them with the potency, under congenial conditions, to change into more oaks. Everything in heaven, the air, and on the waters and earth were fitted into the comprehensive cosmic scheme.

It remains to formulate explicitly some of the points touched upon. (1) The true individual is the species or kind. Nature consists of many kinds of things, each having its *own* immutable form of essential nature. As various oaks are the diversification in spatial and temporal existence of the enduring oak-type and pattern, which rules the material elements and causes change to take on a determinate movement toward a mature exemplification of itself, so all things which are born, grow and pass away are not the complete individuals they seem to be to sense, but are, when truly known or to the eye of rational understanding, but partial members of the real whole or complete individual, the substance which is the species. Except as parts of the species they have in themselves no more reality than has form or essence without actual embodiment. What sense takes to be complete individuals or wholes are in reality only parts, that is particulars. Their inclusion into the eternal and immutable kind or species confers upon them their reality and renders objects of knowledge. This principle holds good of human beings as of other things. The organized social whole, in whatever variety the state exists, comprehends particular human creatures in themselves and is the substance of their being. It is hardly necessary to point out how this conception lent itself in later ages to the uses of Church and Empire, or to the rationalistic schemes in which the whole is always more than an assemblage of parts. It may be worth noting, however, that long after astronomy and physics had departed from the Aristotelian tradition, the doctrine of the immutability and supremacy of species and their typical forms persisted in zoology and botany. It was not seriously challenged until the appearance of Darwin's work, whose very title *The Origin of Species* was a challenge to the entire Aristotelian tradition.

(2) Kinds or species as the ultimate substances of which particular things are partial expressions form a graded hierarchy. The lowest place is occupied by things which are most material, that is, things in which ready mutability, movement between opposites, shows that potentialities are relatively more conspicuous than actuality. The highest place is occupied by God, the pure intelligence which is pure actuality. Next in order of being and worth comes the heavenly firmament, composed of the highest, the most ethereal, qualities, and marking its close approximation to pure actuality by its eternal circular movement. To fill out the scheme would be to retell the astronomy, cosmology and physics of Aristotle. It is pertinent, however, to indicate how the scheme enabled him to place man in his relation with nature. He occupies a mid-station. As a vital creature he is an actualization of the potentialities of plant and animal life and hence functions as a nutritive and mobile-sentient being. He also has the potentiality of reason; when this potentiality is actualized through contact with the Forms of objects, there is rational insight and understanding. In so far, man attaining to real or pure theoretical knowledge is like the divine pure activity. Thus man shares in the two realms; his soul is the complete or perfected activity or entelechy of the body, and shares in the vicissitudes of physical existence. As sharing in reason actualized in adequate knowledge, he is like God above matter and the contingencies of change. Thus Aristotle was able to give a naturalistic account of psychical life including the ordinary discursive operations of the intellect, while holding that his natural endowment was, in the case of those attaining pure knowledge, but a stepping stone to that self-enclosed complete rational activity in which nature attains its own culminating reality. This activity constitutes a bliss different in quality from that which man can possess in his participation in physical and social conditions. Strange as it would have seemed to Aristotle, if he could have anticipated the future, this idea became in Christian theology the intellectual basis of distinction between the bliss of supernaturally induced salvation and all natural goods of whatever sort, just as his glorification of the theoretical life became the basis of assertion of the superiority of the monastic life of meditation upon divine things over the pursuits of the regular clergy.

Dante's reference to Aristotle as "the master of those who know" is familiar.[2] Measured by capacity to organize into a close-knit system the scientific beliefs of his own day, including those relating to a wide diversity of political forms, and the results of his own acute and indefatigable researches, to

---

2. [Dante, *Inferno*, canto 5.]

combine the conclusions with a cognate metaphysics and logic while making room for a purified version of what was most reasonable in Greek religion, he deserved the title. His logic is a perfect reflection of the constitution of nature as he saw it, the structure of the syllogism as the model of true knowledge corresponds with the concretion of universal forms with particulars. Perfectly sensible knowledge is the actualization, through an organic body, of the sensible forms of objects; rational knowledge is the actualization, mediated by perceptual knowledge, of rational and final forms. Knowledge is wholly realistic in mode but wholly "idealistic in content in its highest reaches, because the subject-matter is itself that order and harmony of Being which constitutes Reason or Nous."[3] "Experience," the body of undergoings and actions, connected with the living organism, is a ladder by means of which forms are gradually elicited from their seeming submergence in matter, and are then defined and classified. Experience has its place, but in the end lifts man to a realm beyond itself. Given the standpoint of Aristotle, which was that of a critical sifting and organization of what was most significant in Greek civilization, justice is done to everything; for everything has its due place provided for it in the complete system.

The qualification is, however, a pregnant and perhaps an ominous one, given the subject-matter of Greek life by which he was of necessity restricted. If I am correct in my hypothesis employed in interpretation of this classic period of Greek thought, the movement was essentially a discovery and formulation of rational discourse and its implications. In such discourse, what the Greeks currently said about the world and themselves, said in word, in institutions and in art, was made reasonable, coherent. But the subject-matter was still the material of discourse. It was just stated that logic corresponded exactly to the ontological and cosmological structure of Nature. It was a logic of the syllogism of classification and definition, because Nature was a realm of fixed species hierarchically ordered in which a series of forms provided essential Being. But if the whole enterprise rested on the world of discourse, if it was but a systematization of the material already current in discourse, then what actually happened was that Nature was compelled to fit the framework of discourse. The harmony of logic with Nature signifies that Nature had first been saturated with a logic which corresponded to the forms and material of Greek discourse. At no point did the system escape from the limitations set. The world and life had developed and taken on certain meanings characteristic of Greek culture and these were expressed in a flexible and exact manner in Greek syntax. It was a wonderful feat to explore the content of Greek culture and to reflect it in an artistically composed intellectual whole. I do not doubt that that culture was a genuine foreground

---

3. [Cite unknown.]

of Nature in a particular perspective. But to expand its dimensions until it was equated with the universe is another story. Taken in connection with other perspectives, the Greek, rich and varied as it was, suffered from too [many] defects to stand such inflation. The state of invention and technology rendered any adequate experimental analysis of nature impossible. The best that can be done under such conditions [is to] organize and define critically what is already believed, and the body of existing beliefs in absence of any technique of systematic discovery had of necessity developed accidentally and causally. Aristotle himself was a competent observer; in general the Greeks were exceedingly acute observers. But they were compelled to take things in gross, as they presented themselves in the medium of the unaided habits and of custom. Thus while Aristotle made discoveries, he had no logic of discovery but only one of classification and definition of already existing material. Free reason rather than authority was the ideal of Aristotle reflecting the spirit of Greece itself. But a logic of classification and definition of given material in contrast with a logic of authority is just the method which meets the requirements of any would-be spiritual authority, and the time came when Aristotle's logic was adapted to this purpose. It was a strange and alien use of it, but there was nothing in its makeup to forbid the use.

Viewed from another perspective, any philosophy which seized upon and held true to the spirit of the classic tradition was recommitted to a certain disregard of experience. Nothing could be further from the truth than the notion that Greek thought was an *a priori* spinning out of *a priori* notions. Even [when] it was most speculative, it built with the suggestions which came to it from actually observed material physical and social. One might even say that the chief defects of Greek science are due to the fact that it stuck so closely to ideas which imaged the scene present in sense perception and custom. For because of absence of proper technology of instruments and processes, inquiries could not penetrate behind the surface screen; the minute and subtle operations of natural energies wholly escaped them. The most the reflective observer could do was to form direct and casual material into a picture which gave esthetic delight to compose an ordered story whose plot and heroes were patterned after ordinary sense-observation. In a true sense, the Greeks were too little, not too much devoted to sense perception; the effort of Plato to introduce mathematical calculations did not bear fruits for almost two thousand years. Only in the sixteenth century did scientific inquirers begin successfully to challenge the reports sense makes about the world.

The derogation of experience did not signify then lack of respect for sense-perception as the fount of ideas, the source of theories. Leibniz's saying that there is nothing in the intellect which had not first been in sense is true of Greek natural philosophy. The malady is deeper and graver. In modern science, the ideas suggested in perceptual experience are but hypotheses, points of view, initiators of new calculations that are to terminate in new experimental observations and revisions of old interpretations. They are temporary avenues of escape from the otherwise overwhelming pressure of immediate local and temporal circumstance, while flight away from the immediate scene is the instrumentality of return to it equipped with powers of discovery of what was previously hidden and covert. To the Greeks, to Aristotle, the ideas suggested by the immediate scene were rational in themselves and so final. They were culminating, complete in themselves; it remained only to organize and refine and define them. They were not used to create new and bettered experience of the same things by which they were suggested; they were not methodological and technological tools whose application to the scene of experience would control and enrich its course and content. They were to be contemplatively enjoyed, not to be used.

The discovery that ideas may be enjoyed, that they may be employed to reach new ideas, that this growth of ideas through union and fission may be regulated by orderly method, that this operation is the source of a new delight, was a discovery the value of which cannot be overestimated. It involved emancipation of thought and the creation of a new distinctive occupation: that of knowing. But the ultimate measure of value lies in a factor which was left tacit, unrevealed and unused: the possibility of an objective test and revision of the ideas which entered into the operation. When it is said that classic thought hypostatized ideas and intellect, the saying is to be understood to signify that precisely the testing and remaking of ideas by application in instituting new discoveries and controls of natural processes was not incorporated into the scheme.

Thus the world of experience and the realm of reason and understanding dwelt in a state of feudal inferiority and superiority. One was forever below, the other eternally above. The lower was necessary in order to ascend to the higher, but once the ascent was made intellect abode in the higher realm. They were congenial and cognate; only base practical needs compelled an excursion of return to the lower world of experience, of partiality and change, and whenever the pressure of practical need permitted the spirit again rose to live in the realm in which it was free and unfettered. It was of the essence of the scheme that mind, spirit, could not employ its congenial insight as a means for directing the course of change, and for ameliorating the impact of its hard and course material on life. Each was forever fixed in its own determinate character. Animated versions to the contemplative theory of knowledge and to the complete isolation of theory from practice are sometimes taken to signify insensitiveness to the charms of the leisurely and meditative life and a devotion to mere activity for its own sake. This criticism misses the point. There is no involved disparagement of contemplation and no love of action. What is objected to is the complete separation of the realm of actual experience from that of reason and thought. Exemption of the conclusions of thought from responsibility to application in directing and enriching experience, whatever it may indicate regarding the ultimate validity of such conclusions, signifies that experience must be left what it was: crude, blind, the sport of accident, changing only through catastrophe and revolution, or through the efforts of that not contemptible body of persons—politicians, industrialists and financiers—who are interested chiefly only in those changes in its make-up and course which are turned to their own ledger account of profit. Action is introduced not as an end worthy in itself but as the only means by which the results of mind and spirit can be incorporated in the common stream of human experience. The discovery of discourse as a realm of meanings was the undying contribution of Greek philosophers. But its discovery in the movement of history is but antecedent to a reorganization of experience into a better and fuller medium of manifest and communicated meanings.

The experimental method could hardly have arisen in any case until there were at hand the tools and technique of an analysis of objects which would reveal things not present to the eye or ear, and until the things of the industrial arts had ceased to be matters of contempt. But the logic of Aristotle, the logic of definition and classification, which lifted men out of experience into a self-enclosed and self-sufficient realm of reason, operated to perpetuate and consecrate the conditions out of which it grew. Not till the sixteenth and seventeenth centuries was mankind enabled to strike out upon a new path.

IV. The Search for Salvation

T he fate of the Aristotelian philosophy is as dramatic as is that of the Greek civilization it mirrored. It is a splendid consummation; after it comes dispersion and degeneration, until, at last, it rose to new life in the twelfth and thirteenth centuries of our era as the animating spirit of Christian theology, as truly a renascence as that we are accustomed to calling by the latter name. Not that Aristotelianism immediately died; on the contrary, it remained as a school of teaching and study. But its almost professional or professorial character is testified to by the fact that Aristotelianism was not until the later revival a living and active intellectual presence in the sense in which Neoplatonism, Stoicism or even Epicureanism directed the thoughts and aspirations of men. Antiquity displays no great figure who perpetuated Aristotelianism as a gospel of salvation in a troubled time, when mankind was devoted to the search for redemption. This fact is of utmost significance in understanding both Aristotle and the troubled age which set in. Aristotle was too much a representative of all that was best in Greece to make an appeal in the Hellenistic world with its chaotic and tentative syncretism of Greek, Oriental and Roman elements. He was too soberly temperate, too much interested in Nature as an object of reasoned study.

. . .

Gilbert Murray brought the penetrating designation "Failure of Nerve" to bear upon the larger or human Frame of Reference, the climate in which opinions were formed in the centuries immediately preceding and following the Christian era. Patristic Philosophy as well as Neoplatonic philosophy has to be placed in this setting. The search for salvation, out of this world, was the pervading quest. Differences of schools, however great with respect to one another, are of minor significance in comparison with what they had in common; the sense of the present world as something to be escaped from. Rome and Alexandria represent the polar opposites of this particular one world. The problem of unity, of wholeness in the Platonic civi-moral sense, was not even an academic problem. Actual condition of social life, including political organization, forbade indulgence in social utopias in connection with *this* world, while in Patristic philosophy they obtained a supernaturally guaranteed locus in the next and heavenly world. The net outcome was the formation, with Rome as its center, of a new philosophic frame of reference. The ethical frame was dominant but upon a ground that differs radically from that of the Platonic vision of an ordered civic organization of life.

The foundation of the three Schools, Skeptic, Epicurean and Stoic that characterized the Roman period was agreement and coalition of private individuals of a voluntary, self-chosen, non-political sort. The Schools were such in much more than an intellectually scholastic sense. They were also schools of discipline in cultivation of a like-mindedness as the one and only secure basis of communal [life]. Until the time of Constantine, this is as true of the Christian community-sect as of those already mentioned, in spite of the great difference made by looking forward to a second coming which would put an end to the existing transitory miserable regime.

It would be going far beyond the record to say that the combined or net outcome of the various school of this period was the entrance of the element called individualistic or "subjective" into the main current of belief. But it is not too much to say that the conditions prevailing during this period provided the negative condition of the later explicit formulation of subjectivism. Civic and political organization was no longer one of intimate connections. It was definitely jural and external to the daily lives of those who were in a legal sense citizens of an Empire that was a "state" but in no sense a community or even a "nation" in its modern sense. Impingement of this situation on intellectual attitudes was not only the separation of moral from political and legal, but also drawing a line between that regarded as *external* and that taken to be *internal*—the forerunning preparation for the later separation of "subjective" and "objective."

Specifically this situation, centering at Rome, was a decisive factor in that fusion of systematic Latin externalism in politics and law with the Alexandrian system according to which the supreme task of philosophy was to direct man up from the existing troubled and insecure world of sense and appetite up to a vision of sure [bliss] which was super-rational as well as supersensuous since it involved the merging completely of the beholder with that beheld in an ecstatic mystical vision. The official theological philosophy of the Roman Christian Church developed through a union of these polar opposites, Platonism, mixed with Neoplatonism, furnished the "spiritual" super-moral frame of reference while the Roman contribution supplied the formulated justification of the Church as an Institution.

The influence of the Stoic School went deep. It also spread widely and in so many diverse directions that it is easier to underestimate than to exaggerate its extent.

. . .

The cosmos of the Stoics was one in which the moral was the natural and the natural was the moral. It gave to men of good will a sure support and direction in even the worst of troubles: seen in the light of its order, the evils fall into place within a necessary total order. The solution of the problem of evil was so heroic, so much a matter of stern manhood, that only strong and noble spirits could rally to it.

The Roman departure from Greek moral thought was extreme. Greek moral beliefs are based through and through upon the supreme place of Ends. In current terms of moral theory, they were rooted in the principle of Good, not of Law, which at most and best was instrumental to the Good as end. In Latin thought, the idea of Law was supreme. Natural law states what is in the eternal order and what should be in the temporal order of the world. Moreover *Jus* as a collective name for the whole system of obligations and rights was connected much more intimately, than merely etymologically, with *Jubere*, to *command*. Man's business is loyal obedience to fulfill the law of his own being not as his but as the very law of things. Because the moral law was "natural," the very law of things, it was not arbitrary but rational. The radical change from the Greek way of seeing and understanding brought with it a similar change also in the view taken of Reason. It parted with the quality of theoretic insight, to be attained by following the road of understanding and enlightenment. It retained that element of *ratio*, of proportion and harmony, that traditionally attends reason, but it became at the hands of the Stoics the harmony of man with the order of nature not that harmony of things which is the Greek cosmos.

It would be impossible to overstate the influence exerted by the view of natural law throughout the course of subsequent human history.

. . .

The commands or "orders" to which we as human beings are subject is, in this concept of law of Nature, expression of that which is normal and "natural" in the constitution of the system of things in which we live. Christian theological philosophy has no difficulty in adapting principles of Latin origin and Stoic formulation to its own ends. The laws of God and the laws of a natural or normal state of affairs are one and the same. They are inherently rational and inherently subordinate to the Good as the end towards which all things normally move (the Greek aspect) as well as in respect to authoritative commands—the Roman aspect.

. . .

It is not as philosophies that philosophic doctrines have exerted public influence. Those who interpret the range of such influence from the standpoint of the technical and professional formulation in its own terms are right in their light estimate of the importance of philosophic systems. But as far as the entire consequence of philosophy in human affairs is measured on this basis, the conclusion reached is profoundly erroneous. The case of Stoicism is in point. Its influence in subsequent history has been immense. But [this] occurred indirectly through infiltration to jurisprudence, politics, religion and theology. And no one can say that the influence exerted by lawyers, statesmen and priests has been slight. And what was just said about Stoicism is true on a large scale about the philosophies of the great Greek masters, Plato and Aristotle. If we look at their writings for just what they are, as systems produced under certain specific conditions at certain dates, we should, I think, be compelled to say that their force did not long outlast the lives of their authors. But we look at them as formulations of widely felt human problems and movements and as indirectly reflected back into those movements, the story is very different.

It is in the medium of the rise of Christianity that these two Greek thinkers have endured till at the present day they are still of vital consequence in the lives of great numbers who are wholly innocent of any technical knowledge of the men and their work. The emotional and imaginative qualities of religious faiths do not need to be expatiated upon. Nor, I suppose, is it needful to dwell at length upon the fact that human beings in mass or collectively form their beliefs in that medium rather than in that which we rather pompously call that of the intellect. The thing which is enduringly effective, however, is the existence of a social institution as the source, bearer, nurse, and administrator of the imaginative and emotional appeals. Apart from backing of this sort, emotion is fickle and imagination errant if not fantastic. More particularly, it is through the Roman Catholic Church that the ideas of Plato and Aristotle effectively entered the culture of the western world until they live on in man's interpretation and understanding of what they do and what they believe at the present time.

Through its absorption into a religious faith that was enforced in a comprehensive institutional medium, a particular philosophical system entered in an intimate and vital way into every day human belief. And when the word "belief" is here used it must be understood to include intense emotional and volitional responses; in fact to include them in a way in which they quite overshadowed belief in its cold and comparatively neutral "intellectual" sense. In this way a philosophic system which otherwise would have appealed

only to a small elite, and to them only [through] prolonged specialized training, became so transformed as to be an integral part of all the attitudes and
interests which were habitually taken and entertained by the multitude of
human beings whom philosophy would never have reached if it had been
represented in its own terms. Aristotelianism redivivus was clothed with
religious concern which covered all the interests of this life and that extended into an eternity of bliss and woe in another life in another world.

Platonic, Aristotelian, and Stoic philosophies had all of them in different
ways clothed the natural world with human and moral traits. As has been
previously indicated, this clothing was what rendered the natural world
a *cosmos* in its original sense. It is sometimes said that the chief object of
philosophy is to construe the universe in which man lives in a way which
exhibits its congeniality with the deepest and highest aspirations of man.
Whether or not the philosophers of old Europe deliberately undertook this
task, the philosophies they produced presented a picture and scheme of
things in which physical events and structures were enclosed in a framework
of esthetic and supra-civic moral values. And what is even more significant
(since it was these traits which conferred upon the schemes in question the
status of *philosophy*), the fusion of the natural and the moral was presented
as based upon a rational foundation and as a matter of the very highest
form of science.

. . .

Certain doctrines, which otherwise were of interest simply to a small
band of professional philosophers, were clothed with flesh and blood.[1] Operating as an authoritative social institution, the Church effected that complete
fusion of abstract cosmological and ontological speculations with concrete
historical details which was referred to in another connection. Because of
the institutional position of the Church, this amalgam of a science of nature,
metaphysics, and history became completely interwoven with the beliefs
about the origin, nature and destiny of mankind which regulated daily life
in all aspects and details. If supposed events of Hebraic and subsequent
history had not been so completely and intricately woven together with the
strands derived from Greek philosophers into a single texture of life, there
is no reason to suppose that the philosophies of Plato and Aristotle would
have been more or other than what they are now when their doctrines are
taught to university students as an interesting chapter in the history of
technical philosophy speculation.

---

1. It goes without saying that I am here engaging in considerable historic foreshortening.
It took some time before the teachings of St. Thomas, based upon those of Aristotle, won a
victory over the doctrines of other Schoolmen and became the official dogmas of the Church.

In fact, the classic tradition came to life by taking on the flesh and blood of unremitting daily moral discipline, inspiring and exciting imaginative presentation through the arts, and intense emotional appeal through the claim of controlling everlasting bliss and agony.

. . .

The metaphysical philosophy of Alexandria, roughly subsumed under the title "Neo-Platonism," had an aim that may be called practical and moral, even though from its own standpoint things moral had a rather [low] rank in the ordered scale of being. This aim marked a development, with Oriental coloring, of that aspect of Plato according to which science and philosophy are properly means of ascent to direct intuition of absolute Being, an intuition that goes beyond knowledge because involving direct participation in the nature of the divine and accordingly brought with it purification of the soul from all earthly dross and sharing in a bliss so ecstatic as to be ineffable—a kind of knowledge if that word be of a higher order than understanding and comprehension. This strain of philosophy was accordingly at the other pole from that of the schools that developed under the influence of Rome. However, Christian communities and congregations originated in the Orient and were steeped in the Oriental way of belief and yet were organized into an institution in the shadow of the early Roman Empire. The Patristic phase of theological philosophy drew freely and at will upon both Greek and Roman sources, the Church as an administrative and legislative institution, comparable to Rome itself, serving as the cement which held together elements that were inherently alien.

The fact that it was the Church which brought together "theoretical" and "practical" attitudes and movements, which otherwise were splitting off and going their own ways, is a fact of utmost importance for the subsequent story of philosophy. Extraneous events of the kind called accidental played a part in producing the conditions on account of which the philosophers of the Church came to regard Aristotle as the "master of those who know" and who framed Christian theology as far as possible upon the model provided by the system of Aristotle. But in comparison with intrinsic reasons, these extraneous affairs are of no very great account. They were occasions rather than causes of the development that occurred. Of the reasons which I have called intrinsic, I shall mention two. One of them is that the "realistic" strain in Aristotle's theory of knowledge lent itself to provision of the claims of the Church to ultimate and complete authority in all matters of belief having moral-religious implications and consequences. Platonic identification of ultimate Being with Reason could easily be used, and was used, to justify giving rationality in man a degree of freedom that was dangerous to the institutional dogmas of the Church—a freedom which promoted heresy and schism. The philosophy of Aristotle, on the contrary, subordinated reason to Being. Under European conditions of, say, the twelfth century, the clergy formed the one trained intellectual class. It controlled all educational policies and practices. The Church was the home of all the arts and the guardian of all lore transmitted from antiquity. It was the evident symbol of that which had Being, which truly existed. As the authoritative exponent of that which truly has Being, the realistic conservatism of Aristotle supplied the instrumentalities that were need for formulation of doctrines that seemed to justify the supremacy of "authority" over "Reason" showing the intrinsic rationality of "authority."

The other cause to be mentioned operated more directly. The Church, at its height, that is during the eleventh through the thirteenth centuries, could with good reason claim to be catholic—that is, universal, as far as western Europe was concerned—and the rest of the globe did not then count in western Europe. The genius of Aristotle was universal. There was no branch or phase of knowledge and of human conduct that he had not touched and touched in ways that brought it into system with other branches and phases. There seemed to be a preestablished harmony of divine origin between the opportunity and the need for systematic all-comprehensive formulation of all phases of knowledge and life, firmly rooted in an ontology which was one with theology, and the synoptic scope of the philosophical activities of Aristotle.

The net outcome was an accomplishing, for the time being, of a complete equilibrium of the theoretical and the practical aspects of philosophy. When historical conditions are taken into account there is nothing surprising, still less paradoxical, in the fact that this was brought about upon the basis of a doctrine of the complete supremacy of the "theoretical." In his own time, Aristotle was outside the current of events that substituted empire for the city-state. He was a spectator engaged in beholding from without the sweep of events. His philosophy was that of spectatorship, such participation as occurred being dictated from the side of Being. But in medieval culture, philosophy was a formulation of the tenets and dogmas of an institution and of an institution that possessed chief disciplinary power—so readily confused with authority—in all matters of belief as well as of other forms of behavior.

More than one historian of philosophy has suggested that the status of theological philosophers in the Middle Ages is of a kind that realized the dream of Plato about a community in which philosophers would be rulers. As far as the two faces of philosophy are concerned, it may be said that the earthly representatives of supernal standards and absolute truth were in charge of the most important social affairs. In the Platonic scheme, only a comparatively small number, at the apex of the community, were in direct possession of the truth. There were those under them who had a working substitute, right opinion or belief, consisting of teachings accepted upon the authority of those above them, and through them as media finding its way down to the masses whose virtue was to obey. Medieval "faith" answers this description. It was primarily a matter of humble acceptance of a system of truths which as such were of a theoretical or doctrinal nature. But the acceptance provided the moral code by which to live—and die. Representatives of monastic orders were the spiritual elite. The philosopher-theologians, the Schoolmen, were monks. Parish priests occupied a lower place; for them the practical side of philosophy was preeminent. St. Thomas Aquinas formulated and justified this doctrine by citing Aristotle as to the intrinsic superiority of the "theoretical" over the "practical" life.

One particular illustration of combination of the supremacy of the "theoretical" with respect to the few and of the "practical" for the multitude is worth notice. Greek theories of morals were based upon rational insight into Ends which were the Goods for the sake of which things exist. The quality of Roman moral theory is illustrated by the fact that it never got away from association of *jus* with *jubeo*, command. If we speak in terms of alleged (but nonexistent) faculties, Will occupied in the Latin scheme the place held by Reason in the Greek. Now the Church adopted, for the masses, the Roman view. The working administration of moral discipline, especially through the Confessional as a condition of receipt of the Sacraments, was based upon a systematic elaboration of the Ten Commandments of the Old Testament. Command and obedience were the regulative ideals. But for those who rose to the philosophical plane, the official view became such as to retain the Greek view [intact]. Moral laws are inherently rational. They come to us as commands in that in Supreme Being, Reason and Will are one.

The present discussion is not concerned with the special causes which broke into and largely destroyed the equilibrium of the "theoretical" and the "practical" which marked the medieval consummation.

. . .

But Christian theology made central a doctrine not taught by Aristotle— one in fact contrary to his teaching. The "efficient causation" or creation was attributed to God. In this sense, *universali* are prior to and outside of things in space and time—that if, of all created things. They are *now* within them. But that is because "*universalis ante res*" were first in the eternal pure Intellect of God as ultimate beings, his "spiritual" nature serving to emphasize the sense of the immaterial and ideal nature of the essences and forms that make things to be *what* they are, though the action of God is the cause of their being at all. The cosmology of Plato is freely drawn upon to provide the supernatural background required by the theology of Christianity, Aristotle then being the "natural" philosopher of the medieval Church—his insistence of the priority of Being to Reason being a safeguard against the heresies that the Platonic supremacy of reason so easily generated.

The way in which classic theological philosophy dealt with the problem of evil provides a more striking example of the ease with which the categories of the real and ideal can be manipulated in discourse. Medieval philosophy is ultra-Platonic in assertion of the evils and corruptions of existing things in their present state. The assertion was perhaps not so much one of direct sensitiveness as in the case of Plato. The latter wanted power and authority and could not obtain them. The theologians of the Middle Ages were organs of the organization which possessed both power and moral authority. And in spite of many conditions that strike most people today as horrible, the minor artists of the period seem to have derived much more joy from their occupations than do the mass of factory workers today. These two matters are not relevant logically to the present theme. They may stand as symbols of the fact that the doctrines of theological theology, before the rise of some phases of Protestantism, were to combine, as far as formal statement goes, the view that the world is corrupt through and through with doctrines of an institutional order that rendered living in that world a reasonably comfortable affair.

The world and man are not, as with Plato, originally and inherently defective. They came pure from the Creator; perfect, as far as anything finite can be. They were corrupted beyond anything recognized by Plato by the sin of our first parents. As in the Platonic scheme, the evils which exist can be overcome only as existing things are laid hold of by perfect Being which is outside, above and beyond. The Platonic scheme suffered, however from an inner contradiction. Plato could make no provision save accident for the intervention that was required if there was to be unified and total social order. Even if knowledge of it was attained, even if love of wisdom succeeded in achieving its goal of wisdom, there remained the problem of putting wisdom into effect. Plato could only suggest that a legislator and ruler might be born who was also a philosopher. It is not surprising that later philosophy which came under the influence of Plato, or Neoplatonism, extracted exclusively from the writings of Plato that part of his doctrine that had to do with the discipline that would result in a direct vision of Being in which all trace of the earthly and lower would be annihilated.

But according to medieval theological philosophy, God as perfect and all-powerful Being had by an act of grace provided sure means for recovery in this world form the moral evils of original sin and corruption and in a future world of complete and triumphant restoration of a kingdom[.]

. . .

Certain defining traits of the medieval philosophical pattern were bequeathed to later generations, persisting in writers who rejected, from one cause and another, its entire institutional framework. In a discussion that went into historical detail it would be necessary to speak of the revival of Stoic cosmology, or rather of the enduring influence it exerted in a new application. This cosmology owed its popular hold to the fact that it completely fused—confused if you please—physical, rational and moral categories. This fusion makes no great demand on abstraction and it accords with the human desire for what is and what ought to be to coincide. It had a greater influence upon Fathers of the Church who said things which crystallized in "The Law of Nature" than theologians admitted—even to themselves. Because of the new turn taken in the seventeenth century of astronomy and physics, it took on a new meaning. Laws of nature became intermediary between the Laws of God and the laws of man. They possessed on their own account the "universality" which was the mark of reason in the classic tradition; they were transparently and directly open to human reason; they could be referred to God, but to God's reason, not his will save as that was a manifestation of reason. The older meaning was in time projected into the generalizations that resulted from scientific inquiry. Laws of nature became natural as opposed to supernatural but without losing the elevation and dignity proper to them in their earlier sense. In so far, they had an ideal quality identified with the properties they possessed as statements of "reality." Although a law is but fact viewed with respect to its generality, a certain penumbra of awe still hangs about laws of nature in popular esteem while facts are bare.

A distinction between natural and positive law came down to the seventeenth century from Roman antiquity through scholastic formulations. The former was fixed and eternal; the standard of justice and rightful authority. In the later period it took on a new face and function. The change in conditions that was proceeding apace required both extensive criticism of old customs and institutions and construction of new standards and rules to meet new conditions. While the *De Jure Belli et Pacis*[2] was directed primarily at a formulation of rules of action to be observed between nations, where positive law was (and still mostly is) absent it is almost impossible to exaggerate its influence upon moral and political philosophy, especially in Germany. Sociality as the bond of union and of peace was an expression of nature, universal and rational in nature. Through the medium of a succession of teachers in Germany, largely in faculties of law where Stoic ideas were still powerful, but including men like Leibniz, the idea came to

2. [Hugo Grotius, *On the Laws of War and Peace* (1625).]

Kant in full maturity. In spite of his "critical" doubts, it supplied by union with the standpoint of Newton's philosophy of nature the substantial core of his teaching, Hume and Rousseau operating as ferments to alter its form and color.

It thus came about that the Platonic distinction of noumena, the ideal world which is also that which is ultimately real, and the world of phenomena, which is urgently that in which we immediately live, was repeated in a new form. To Newton himself physical laws were not physical in the present sense of the word. He had no occasion, moreover, to question the old belief that mathematical principles were of themselves and directly principles of things in their existence.

. . .

Because the medieval Church employed Greek cosmology and Greek metaphysics as its intellectual tool and the weapon of achieving an all-inclusive synthesis, the Greek philosophy as an amalgam of the Platonic and the Aristotelian in which the former supplied, upon the whole, the substance and the latter the form and technique, is also an intimate and vital constituent of contemporary culture so that the reference which is made to it in these pages is anything but antiquarian.

From a technically philosophical point of view, the outstanding trait—the all but miraculous feature—of the medieval synthesis is that it adopted the essential naturalism of the cosmic formulations of Aristotle and then fitted it into a super-natural system in which it was made to take a subordinate but still indispensably necessary place. The same sort of thing happened upon the side of method of statement. The medieval synthesis in its most highly integrated form, and the form finally officially sanctioned, taught that principles which are fundamental and ultimate are so far above human reason that they are possessed by human beings only by virtue of supernatural revelation and are capable of being retained in their purity only through the intervention of a supernaturally founded and directed institution. Nevertheless when the revelation is once made it is possible as well as desirable to show that its contents are in accord with reason.

If the union of Greek naturalism and Jewish-Christian supernatural had not actually taken place and maintained itself in theological philosophy and in institutional practical for centuries, it would have been asserted in advance to be inherently impossible.

. . .

These features of the Christian scheme [the sending of his only Son as a sacrificial offering, and the establishment of a divinely guided institution as the continuing intermediary between man and God][3] are familiar to all reared under the influence of its teachings. If some of its essential features no longer have much vitality even among those who call themselves Christians, save "fundamentalists," and yet western culture still calls itself Christian, that fact is both an integral part of the change from medieval to modern culture and the ground of many of the confusions and conflicts out of which arise, if not directly, many of the issues with which modern philosophy has been occupied. The change, one which goes within the churches as well as outside, by the generic if vague name of "liberalism," was directly precipitated by the revolutionary transformation of natural science that has been going on steadily since the sixteenth century. But social changes which have rendered morally shocking principles that once were taken to be morally fundamental have probably played the larger part in toning down and relegating to the background in most Protestant circles theological doctrines which once formed the very structure of Christian doctrine.

It is not many years ago that the most conspicuous aspect of the break of modern with medieval culture focused in what was called the "conflict of science with religion" or "the warfare of science and theology." In the medieval period, astronomy, physics, biology, the teachings inherited from secular antiquity that constituted interpretations of history, were so completely entangled with moral-religious views that an attempt to change the former was treated by the Church as an attack upon the latter. The sciences, as we now understand them, had to struggle against powerfully entrenched institutions of church and state to get a hearing.

· · ·

The idea that the change which took place from the methods and subject matter of Greek-medieval natural philosophy or science to the standpoint, methods and conclusions of modern science is just an affair of abandoning error and accepting truth is too crude to have received explicit statement. Nevertheless there is much philosophic in the treatment given to the rise and growth of modern science which comes close to being on a par with this notion. On the negative side, there is the rather conspicuous failure to develop, up to the present day, the treatment which offers the one intelligent alternative to the crudity in question. For that alternative is an account of the change in science as a part of the changes that were going on in general cultural conditions. More or less has been said about the effect of the new science upon industry, politics, the fine arts, upon the whole range of human intercourse and communication. But it has to be admitted that very

---

3. [The bracketed clause was inserted by the editor from material in the preceding incomplete sentence.]

little has been done as yet in writing the story of modern science in terms of these cultural conditions as *its* generating source.

On the positive side, philosophers themselves set the fashion of speaking of the new scientific movement as if its main problem were the liberation of something called mind or intellect from the distorting and benumbing influence of the complex of existing conditions to which today the name *culture* is applied. They wrote as if once this emancipation were accomplished, the intellect in virtue of its own nature would enter upon the path that leads from darkness into light. Most decidedly they did *not* write as if the problem were one of effecting the general transformation of culture (of which science was one part) which could bring along with it a revolution in science.

The common assumption seems to have been that since medieval culture had been dominated by a religious-theological outlook and interest, and since the customs and the official authorities who represented this domination were actively opposed to the new movement, it followed, a virtually self-evident matter, that the one thing needed was the emancipation of mind from all outside influence whatever. This attitude was equivalent to the view that mind, intellect, or whatever name was used to designate the knowing agency, was a separate and independent order of Being. And philosophers who allied themselves with the newer movement lost no time in writing as if the cause of the new science and proclamation of the necessity of emancipating intellect from everything that impeded and diverted it from operating in accord with its own separate and independent being were one and the same thing. The attacks made upon the standpoint, method and conclusions of the new science by representatives of established institutional usages confirmed this view. They were but the other side of the same cultural picture. They too treated "reason" as if it were a separate and independent kind of being. Only in their case, it was a power which if it were unleashed from subjection to external authority would be morally dangerous in a supreme degree:—a view which persisted in the sinister meaning later given to "free-thinking."

Declaration of the independence and self-sufficiency of [the] knowing mind thus made definite sense, provided it had been taken for what it was— namely a cultural event occurring at a time of cultural crisis. For in that case "mind, intellect, reason" would have been only shorthand names for the whole complex of extensive cultural conditions that were operating to bring into existence a new view of nature and new ways of dealing with it, practically and cognitively, on behalf of a new type of cultural interest and concern.

V. From Cosmic Nature to Human Nature

The trend of modern philosophy is now under steady fire on the ground of its one-sided subjective character. The criticism is [all] the more significant because it is directed against an attitude which was regarded by the very philosophers who are now attacked as the ground of their authorized claim to a hearing—the discovery of the principle which not only formed the distinguishing trait of the modern over against the medieval and ancient but which made modern times synonymous with a time of unlimited opportunity, of expanding promise and unending progress. It is important, however, to note that the writings which are now assailed are a blend of two constituents which have no necessary connection with one another, so that the particular postulate now under fire as being subjective is in fact a striking example of the thesis that the traits which are genuinely new have been formulated in terms of old beliefs with which they are at war, instead of in their own terms.

The positive factor is a sense of human power of initiation, invention, discovery, energy, daring in enterprise, a sense so new as to be revolutionary in effect. It expressed itself in a magnification of human resources by which forces and events could be brought under ever-increasing control. It was not just the idea of the possibility of control by human beings in behalf of the welfare of mankind which was new. For the idea derived its drive and poignancy from the fact that the things in question were those which had been supposed to be natural and inevitable in just the sense in which earthquakes are natural and inevitable. Magnification of the power of human nature took place in contrast with a prior magnification of the overruling power of cosmic nature. The latter was a formulated reflection of customs and institutions that determined actual relations and transactions [and] that was employed to "explain" (i.e. justify) the status quo. The contrast was a struggle against habits and traditions so long and so thoroughly established that they now claimed to speak with the authority of Nature—and of Nature's God.

In other words, the conflict between the new and the old was not just an intellectual controversy. In order to make headway, the new sense of the power of human nature over the course of events had to meet institutions hoary with age invested with the emotional associations, awe of which had gathered about them in uncounted years. Just because established customs and institutions claimed to be necessary manifestations of cosmic nature, the representatives of the new forces that were stirring felt compelled to represent them as products of ignorance, superstition and sloth—of, in short, the less developed and least desirable traits of human nature. In their desire to free the human power they were struggling to emancipate from any responsibility for conditions they found to be oppressive and evil, the agents of the new movement carried the proclamation of emancipation from subjection to cosmic nature to a point in which human nature was set over against everything else in nature as a separate and independent authority, finding its apt formulation in the doctrine of the "sovereignty of the individual."

Reaction against the practical absorption of human nature within cosmic nature, an absorption which tended to paralyze initiative and restrict discovery, took the form of the doctrine of an equally one-sided supremacy of human nature to be realized in fact by setting it over against cosmic nature as a power so aloof as to be independent in its operations. That the magnification of human nature which followed took the form of glorification of what was called "the individual," the self, the *ego*, and that mind and everything mental was described in terms of powers attributed to the individual in question is another affair, and one which did not have the direct social and practical background, source and authority which belonged to the playing-up of the newly discovered potentialities of human beings. So far as there was a direct practical origin of the conversion of the constituents of human nature, in distinction from absolutistic or socially irresponsible cosmic nature, it sprang from the fact that after all the power of custom and institutions, as strong in matters of belief, including those of "science" as of other concerns, had to be challenged by this man and that man who, in the very process of challenging, acted without the sanction of that which was publicly established and, indeed, against the latter.[1]

---

1. [From folder (53/15): "[Belief in] such a thing in existence as intellect, mind, reason, mental faculties or powers, wholly apart from the customs, occupations, traditions and concerns of a given society at a given time and place (that, indeed, the latter are factors which have to be eliminated as corrupting and deadening forces if "intellect" is to take its own proper course) is one of the constituents of the heritage from the old which caused philosophy in the seventeenth and later centuries to take the course it followed. At first sight it may seem paradoxical to say that reaction against the established and dominant tradition was a main factor in causing representatives of the new science to assert with especial emphasis and definiteness one of the basic components of that tradition. But these men needed a *pou sto* to give them base for leverage in attacking the old and winning converts to the new. There is then nothing surprising in the fact that instead of regarding a particular tradition and a particular set of institutions and social requirements as the foe, they thought such things

But as far as philosophical formulations of the new movement were concerned, the matter was far from beginning and ending at this point. The powers and capacities belonging to human nature in its differentiation from cosmic nature were not just referred to "individuals" in the sense in which *private* may be properly distinguished from public, and the socially singular from the socially incorporated; that which was called "individual," and thereby in effect the human generally, was interpreted and described in terms borrowed from the ancient theories of mind, the mental, psychical, spiritual, which has been taken up into Christian theology and which through the Church had found their way into the popular culture of the Western world. Because of this latter influence, the practical, the essentially moral and social, operation of this and that daring pioneer in breaking away from old custom and from accepted tradition, which was the legitimate heart of modern individualism as a *social* manifestation, was transformed into a metaphysical doctrine of the inherent constitution of human beings.

The next chapter will be given to discussion of this distortion of the factor which was practically and socially important, a distortion constituting the truly obnoxious feature in "subjectivism," and which is a distortion because it sprang from infusion of alien elements which were powerful because of historic conditions, not because of anything belonging to the practical movement. It is not an easy matter to separate even for purposes of discussion the genuine and vital factor of the new movement from the philosophical formulation it underwent because of adventitious cultural conditions. The difficulty is increased because the intellectual formulations were so used in justifying and propagating the new movement against its powerful foes that they were taken up into the movement as a going social concern and were so absorbed into the latter as to seem to be an integral part of it. I may cite as an illustration the use made by law-courts of certain aspects of the "individualistic" theoretical formulation to support and advance certain industrial and business policies of vast social import. I do not think it can be doubted that for the most part the judges supposed they were enunciating propositions that were so embedded in the facts with which the courts were dealing as to be inherent in them. Since during the eighteenth and nineteenth centuries the theoretical interpretations involved profoundly affected popular usage of such words as *self, person, individual* (and hence by contrast the word *social*), it was comparatively easy for judges to suppose they were only making explicit important significations bound up with occurrence of the

---

were the enemy *per se*, and hence put the idea of pure mind, knower, consciousness inherently equipped with direct and self-sufficient organs of arriving at truth over against tradition and custom as the source of darkness, ignorance, error and failure to adopt and employ the methods which put science on the road in which steady fructifying advance was assured."]

events they were in fact shaping and canalizing in a given social direction, instead of merely expounding, as they supposed, something already there.

In lieu of something better, I shall start the discussion by quoting two sentences from Adam Smith. For while they slant in a particular theoretical direction, they are, in their own context, reasonably neutral as well as non-technical. "Every man is by nature first and principally recommended to his own care. . . . Every man, therefore, is much more deeply interested in whatever concerns himself than in what concerns any other man."[2] And if this is true in the case of specified "other men," some of whom may be very close to one, it is all the more true when it is a matter of personal concern over against concern for mankind generally or an indefinite collection of other men. When these words are placed in another context than that in which their author put them, there is nothing new about them. In a certain traditional context, the words express the ruling principle of the *natural* man in his distinction from, and opposition to the *moral* man. In that context, they are the commonplace of the morally regrettable selfish aspect of human nature. Their function in the system of Smith is just the opposite, and it is in this opposite sense that they are indicative of the new movement. For according to Smith each man in carrying on and regulating the affairs of his daily life is "led by an invisible hand to promote an end which was no part of his intention"—namely, the public good, in fact, he thereby promotes this end much more effectively than if he had consciously aimed at the public good. The desire, innate in each man, to better his own condition is the means by which society as a whole, mankind in general, makes sure progress. The principle condemned as immoral becomes, when intelligently pursued (and it is the interest of each one to be intelligent), the source of social harmony as well as of social progress.

I pass from these remarks of Smith's to a much more generalized statement of his contemporary, David Hume. The latter wrote, "It is evident that all the sciences have a relation, greater or less, to human nature; and that however wide one may seem to run from it, they still return back by one passage or another. . . . Here is the only expedient by which we can hope for success in our philosophical researches—to leave the tedious lingering method we have hitherto followed; and instead of taking now and then a castle or a village on the frontier, to march up to the capital and center of these sciences, to human nature itself; which being once masters of we may everywhere else hope for an easy victory. In pretending then to explain the principles of human nature, we in effect propose a complete system of all the sciences built upon a foundation almost entirely new and the only one upon which they can be built."[3]

---

2. [Adam Smith, *The Theory of the Moral Sentiments* (1759), pt. 6, sec. 2, ch. 1.]

3. [David Hume, *A Treatise of Human Nature* (1739), introduction, xix.]

The sweep of Hume's proposal as compared with that of Smith is evident. The passage sets forth an aim as ambitiously comprehensive as is expressed in the systems of Bacon or Descartes, and this in spite of Hume's well deserved standing as the leading skeptic of modern philosophy. The causes which deflected Hume from the constructive task he here proposed into negative channels lie outside the scope of our present discussion, save as they are indications of traits in his theory of human nature which effectually prevented it from serving as the foundation of a complete system of all the sciences. But, nevertheless, the idea that human nature is "the capital and center" of all scientific knowledge is a striking expression of what I have called the transfer of concern and activity from cosmic to human nature. That the discovery of human nature was profoundly affected by views inherited from the classic Greek-medieval tradition to such an extent that it was even more a discovery of the implications of old views about mind and the self than it was a discovery of "human nature itself" is no cause of astonishment when we consider how deeply that tradition was embedded in the education given by the institutional customs of European culture.

The distortions thus introduced will, however, be ignored for the present. The positive practical tendency, no matter how badly deflected its theoretical formulations, was in the direction of a new freedom, the kind of freedom that proceeds from ability to control the conditions under which life goes on. Transfer of the seat of power and authority from cosmic nature metaphysically and theologically understood to human nature was equivalent to a proclamation of that initiation and control of changes in the estate of mankind had passed from a nature in which man was so absorbed as to be virtually its subject and slave to a nature which was within human jurisdiction and administration—since it was in fact human nature itself. The counterpart of this liberation of human affairs from subjection to an order of nature which was metaphysically and theologically settled and set was the belief that the chief cause of social evils, of injurious social inequality, oppression, enforced submission to uncontrollable events and consequent stagnation, was the millennial-old failure to understand and grasp the powers that constitute human nature. The failure was equivalent to the domination of mankind by ignorance and superstition. The new attitude was, accordingly, the inauguration of a new age, the age of enlightenment, of freedom and progress.[4]

---

4. [From (54/1): "As the Seventeenth Century was the century *par excellence* of cosmic nature, with its all-comprehensive systems (like those of Descartes, Leibniz, Spinoza, Hobbes and Newton), so the Eighteenth Century was as definitely that of human nature. The varied aspects of the Enlightenment, the *Éclair-issement*, the *Aufklaerung*, were its characteristic expression. And they all betoken the discovery of man." Dewey appended a footnote reading: "While Locke wrote in the latter part of the seventeenth century he ushered in the controlling

The change was nothing short of a revolutionary one—especially in view of identification of the "natural" state of human nature as that of corruption and moral impotency. It is usual today to hear from press and well as pulpit and platform that the sense of the infinite worth of human personality is a product of the Christian faith. Since one essential consideration is omitted the saying is definitely misleading. The point that is left out or suppressed is that "infinite worth" was subscribed to human beings by historic Christianity in a strictly supernatural context and only in that connection. As such, as just human beings, nothing is more degraded and more powerless for good than mankind. As a matter of fact, belief in the worth and the power of human beings with respect to their own human nature is the product of convergence of a number of factors of a secular kind. It applies even today only to the doctrines of churches that are of the "liberal" type. To ascribe the belief to the Christian religion is to do fundamental injustice to the Christian scheme of sin and salvation. In order to grasp the attitude taken by the Churches, Catholic and Protestant alike, to human nature it is not necessary to go to the sayings of the Fathers about the condition of women, or the assertions of the lost and to-be-damned condition of infants ardently asserted by Protestant divines. Belief that it is inherently "lost" and incapable of accomplishing anything but evil inheres in the very doctrine of man's sinful condition requiring redemption through supernatural external intervention. Without this article of faith, there is nothing peculiar in Christian doctrine. Since the significance of the "subjectivism" (and "individualism") of modern action and thought cannot be understood unless we realize how radically new was faith in the power of human beings, it is needful to grasp the historic contrast in its full force.

For this purpose I shall cite the interpretation given by the official philosopher of the Roman Church, St. Thomas Aquinas, of the injunction "Love thy neighbor as thyself."[5] The principle underlying what is expressed in this

---

ideas of the eighteenth century. Pope's declaration that "the proper study of mankind is Man" might well be put at the head of every chapter of histories of philosophy when dealing with the eighteenth century."]

5. [Dewey left a blank space in which, one may assume, he meant to supply the appropriate quote. It is possible that he was referring to Aquinas's *On the Perfection of the Spiritual Life*, ch. 2: "For what we should primarily love out of charity is the supreme good that makes us happy, namely God, while secondarily we should love our neighbor out of charity, with whom we are joined in a certain social bond, in the participation of happiness; hence we should love in our neighbor out of charity in reference to a mutual attainment of beatitude. And the Lord showed this order of the precepts of charity in Mat 22:37–39, saying, "You shall love the Lord your God with all your heart, and with all your soul, and with all your mind. This is the great and first commandment. And a second is like it, You shall love your neighbor as yourself." Therefore the perfection of the spiritual life consists first and principally in the love of God; hence the Lord, speaking to Abraham, says, "I am God Almighty; walk before me, and be perfect" (Gen 17:1)."]

theological discussion is a constant one in this particular traditional institution. It is still applied directly to present social and political problems. Consider, for example, the following from G. K Chesterton, written about the prospect of democracy in the United States: "As far as that democracy becomes or remains *Catholic* and Christian, that democracy will remain democratic.... Men will more and more realize that there is no meaning in democracy if there is no meaning in anything and that *there is no meaning in anything if the universe has not a center of significance and an authority that is the author of our rights.*"[6]

The implication of the passage is evident. There is nothing in human beings and their human relations to one another and to the world in which human beings live which provides a ground for respect of men and women and their rights. Human nature has to be referred to the super-natural, and to it as taught and enforced by a particular historic institution claiming supernatural origin and authority to justify its title to decent and fair regard and treatment.

That the new attitude in its intellectual aspect of formulated tenets of philosophy was in fact a reflection of large-scale social tendencies so that the new ideas at most were but intermediate intervening episodes in the larger process of social change was overlooked because of the almost intoxicating sense of the novelty of the ideas as ideas. Both the ideas and the practical movements they inspired were taken to be manifestations of powers of human nature which were so native, or original, and inherent that they had to be isolated from and be set in opposition to all other natural powers and events. The fact that social conditions had themselves reached a state of dissolution of old forms and of their re-forming into new habitual ways of living was lost from view in the stress of urgency to hasten the destruction of the old. Deliberate and systematic attack upon the old conceals from recognition the fact that the new forces were themselves the manifestation of general social conditions.[7] The result was the subjectivism and individualism of philosophical theory and of ethics, politics, and economics.

---

6. *What I Saw in America.* Italics not in original text; in connection with the last sentence it is to be noted that the only interpretation of "Christian" which is admitted is that of the Catholic Church, with *its* record of respect for human rights in their human capacity.

7. The way in which the rise of new science and the new philosophy of knowledge and social relationships was bound up with such things as the rise of new modes of technology, with transition from feudalism to the early stage of capitalist industry, with new geographical explorations, discoveries and settlements, and the new opportunities and resources thereby supplied, is only now beginning to receive adequate attention. When the story is adequately told, there will not be any longer any ground for the notion that the new sense of the traits which are called "individual" was anything but a manifestation of the changes that were taking place in socio-cultural conditions. When that fact is understood, there will follow a great alteration in philosophical theory. For the grounds for setting the individual, the self, subject, mind and consciousness over against the rest of nature will have been destroyed.

. . .

"Mind" became personal. When the evidence of mind was found in nature, it was because God, a personal Mind, had put them there. When the ancient piety was retained concerning science, it found a new mode of expression. In discovering the laws of nature, human minds were thinking God's thoughts after him. No language is or could be more revealing than the identification of *mind with the self*, with the *Ego* or *I*. Descartes and Berkeley both use the expression "mind or the self." The assumed equivalence is the more revealing because no attempt is made to justify it by argument. It was taken to be a matter of course taken for granted that was evident on its face. Yet any proof would have seemed more monstrous to, say, an Athenian philosopher. The self identification would have been too extreme an assertion of intellectual anarchy, a denial of even the semblance of knowledge, to have appealed to the most iconoclastic of sophists.

These remarks apply particularly to the philosophers who were engaged in promoting the new science. But the fact that self and mind could be identified in a matter of course indicates that popular attitudes had already undergone a great change; or, stating the matter in general terms, what was going on in science was also going on in other interests and changing the attitudes of men who had no particular concern with the revolution in natural science. The extent to which Protestants in early days asserted the right of private judgment, and direct illumination of human beings by God, is usually much exaggerated. But revolt against an institution which had regulated the actions and beliefs of men for centuries involved shifting in the centre of authority in the direction of capacities inhering in individuals. Rebellion against long established institutional answers and claims was taking place also in politics and industry. Industrial and political changes weakened first the force and then the rightful legitimacy of custom and tradition. This weakening was the practical equivalent of a strengthening of initiative, invention, vigor, enterprise as intrinsic properties of human nature. When men began to bargain between themselves to fix the price of goods, wages of labor, rates of interest, and finally the rent of land, something happened which went much further than an alteration in an isolated field or that is disposed of by calling it the decline of feudalism and the rise of capitalism. It was a shift from rule by custom to recognition of the power inhering in human desire, intention, judgment and choice. And, as happens regularly when a power is sufficiently established to be recognized as a power, it is put forward as a rightful claim. The most direct means of justifying the new economic activities and capacities as rights was to hold that they inhered in the very structure of human nature, so that denial of them was denial of the intrinsic worth and dignity of human nature.[8] As far as politics is concerned, it is not necessary to wait until the theory of popular government and democracy was explicitly formulated in order to find an illustration.[9]

. . .

As was said earlier in this discussion, it is not possible to disentangle the genuinely new and fruitful factor in what I would call the discovery of *human nature* as a potential means of directing the human career emancipated from submergence in the cosmic scheme from the formulations it received in terms of ideas that have no place except in terms of the old tradition. This statement applies to the quotations which have been made. It applies to such an extent that in order to make clearer what is what by the value newly attributed to human nature and by the thesis that this new estimate is the distinguishing trait of what is genuinely modern in the philosophies that have appeared since the sixteenth century, I shall now introduce an emphasis which is not found in the passages cited. The things which are fundamentally characteristic are the following. (1) The conviction that man's career and destiny are much more in his own power, are less fatalistically dependent upon a nature of which he is, metaphysically and cosmologically, an incidental product, than had been supposed in past ages. (2) The basis of translating this possibility into an actuality was institution and use of a new method of knowing, a method so different from that which had given birth to what was traditionally called science that it demanded a radically new departure, a new start. This start could be had

---

8. The change was registered in social philosophy marked by the revolutionary transfer in the seat of natural law and natural rights from cosmic to human nature, a matter which is discussed in a later chapter. [No such chapter appears to be extant.]

9. [From folder (53/15): "There was another factor that combined with that just stated to create the problem of knowing as it has been dealt with by modern philosophy. This was the rise of individualism in politics, industry, and Protestantism. The *private* character of the mental states (which were the only means of knowing the physical world was set over against them) might be viewed as a factor in the epistemological problem as that has just been stated. But it may be doubted whether the sense of their intrinsically private character would have been so especially acute had it not been for the rise of individualism. It is noteworthy that both Descartes and Berkeley speak of the mind *or* self. It is the more noteworthy because they make the identification in an incidental way as if it were something that could be taken for granted and that needed no justification. Yet it is safe to say that such an idea would not even have been understood, much less accepted, in either Greek or medieval philosophy.

Independently of the rise of individualism in other quarters, the conditions under which the new science arose promoted its rise in the intellectual class. For the old beliefs were institutionalized to such an extent that new conceptions were in effect a revolt against established intellectual and moral authority. At the present time, the individual investigator is backed up by an extensive body of ascertained facts and principles and the methods he employs have the sanction of successful use as well as of the practical utilities that have arisen from application of what has been found out. Pioneers in the new science were in the opposite condition. From the standpoint of scientific orthodoxy they were heretics. Nothing is more natural than that they should appeal to the powers of the individual mind freed from the benumbing influence of tradition, custom and institutions that claimed authority over belief."]

only by recognizing that the initiative in knowing and the operations constituting it exist in human nature: or, in the language of the period that "mind," "understanding," "intellect" have their seat in human nature and are under human direction. Attacks upon syllogistic method (characteristic of the "rationalism" of Descartes, as well as the "empiricism" of Locke), the struggle of scientific men to get free from theological preconceptions and commitments, the attempts to erect "reasonableness" into an ultimate criterion in religion, morals, jurisprudence and economics (no matter how divergently different schools might define "reason"), are manifestations of the new valuation put upon human nature. (3) The outcome contemplated, the end to which the revolutionary change in knowing tended, was what Bacon called the advancement of the human estate. The nature and extent of the change in the social order that was to result was envisaged with great difference in articulateness in British and continental thought—as has already been indicated. In the former it was usually explicitly held up to view; in the former [latter], it was made incidental, almost a by-product. At the same time, not much reading between lines is required to see that it was regarded as ultimately inevitable, although something to come about insensibly rather than by deliberate effort.

Some remarks are added as to the practical causes (as distinguished from causes derived from the old tradition) why human nature was thought of so largely in "individual" terms instead of generically. The key is suggested, if not definitely set forth, in the quotation from Locke about the chief cause of existing ignorance and error. If the latter are due to surrender of belief and assent to the "authority" of custom, it is obvious that breaking loose from what is currently accepted is the way out. The protest, the mutation of a new road, must proceed from one who sets himself against the control of belief exerted by the habitual trend of belief. Custom and firmly established institutions constitute what is "natural." Indeed, they provide the criterion of what is natural in the degree in which they have been so long established that they have acquired power which is identified with authority. Hence any move away from them is at once said to be contrary to nature or to the will of God. So far as this [state of] affairs prevails, all human beings alike are subject to that which envelops them. There is no occasion for marking out the difference, the apartness, the break, that constitutes a sense of the individual quality of any human being. As protest and revolt grew with respect to feudal political institutions, to the Church, to tradition, the latter were found oppressive and what they oppressed were the human beings who had the initiative and courage to break away—and this breaking away involved an active struggle, which was readily interpreted as a conflict of "individual" human nature against the "social"—that is, in fact, against human nature as it was institutionalized in set and rigid forms. The men of intellectual cast who were engaged in carrying on the attack against traditional science were those who were most conscious of this aspect of the struggle. They were the men who formulated the doctrine of the individual character of mind or understanding in its native and pure character over against the factitious properties it had acquired in the course of education and intercourse with others who have also surrendered their native "powers" of intellect. Locke puts in words an attitude characteristic of all who were engaged in breaking with any mode of established tradition when he said that in the process of education matters of custom were so insinuated that they were taken to be "principles," revered as of paramount and sacred authority, and hence "the great and unerring deciders of truth and falsity"[10] A worker in the scientific field today is not particularly aware of the "individual" quality of his work even when he introduced an innovation. For the methods and conclusions of science themselves constitute at the present time a well established tradition and the particular man who departs in some respect (even if it is as important a matter as the theory of relativity in contrast with Newtonian physics) has the support and "authority" of scientific tradition in so doing. His appeal is to methods which will enable any scientific worker who uses them to observe the facts which induced his innovation and thereby test the value of the new conclusion. Pioneers in new scientific lines had no such support three centuries ago; appeal to methods then recognized as authoritative would have been equivalent to ready-made condemnation.

It is, however, an error in interpretation of intellectual history to suppose that there was in the seventeenth or in the great part eighteenth and part of the nineteenth centuries anything approaching a thoroughgoing "individualism" or "subjectivism." That which prevented the development of this attitude, which indeed prevented those who identified the "self" or ego with mind from seeing the implications of their own position, is well illustrated in the case of Locke. It is expressed in his firm conviction that the powers of outer nature and of inner human nature and mind are pre-adapted to one another in the very constitution of the Nature which, under divine providence, includes them both in a scheme having a common design. The powers of material bodies acting upon the mind after all "produce therein those perceptions they are *ordained* and adapted to."[11]

Deism with its belief in overruling patterns of design is the implicit (and often the explicit) background of Locke's theory. I do not believe there is any doubt that the reason Locke did not take more seriously the "difficulty" involved in the view that if the sole objects of knowledge are ideas and relations between them, we have no way of knowing they "agree with" or "conform

---

10. [John Locke, *Essay Concerning Human Understanding* (1690), bk. 4, ch. 20, sec. 9.]
11. [Ibid., bk. 4, ch. 4, sec. 4]

to" external things or even that there are any such things was because his basic postulate after all was that of a harmony and agreement of powers designed and ordained by a supreme Being whose existence was a matter of rational demonstration. Leibniz introduced "pre-established harmony" as a *formulated* principle. But belief in such harmony was the very heart and life of "natural religion," of deism, and of the use made of design—the bridge by which science crossed over from the supernatural to the natural. Indeed, the explicit formulation of the idea by Leibniz and the use which he made of it was what exposed it to critical and hostile examination, no examination being needed as long as it operated as means of tacit control.

Locke abounds in such phrases as that "our complex ideas of substances, *being made* all of them in reference to things existing without us, and *intended* to be representations of substances as they really are, are no further real than as they are such combinations of simple ideas *as are really united and co-exist in things without us*."[12]

. . .

Locke's actuating purpose appears clearly when he says, "if we take a view of our ignorance, which being infinitely larger than our knowledge," it "may serve much to the quieting of disputes and improvement of *useful* knowledge if . . . we confine our thoughts within the contemplation of those things that are within the reach of our knowledge and launch not out in that abyss of darkness."[13]

If we contrast the attitude of Locke as expressed in these passages with such a saying as the following statement by Descartes, we shall perceive, I believe, the difference between what I have designated the respectively "practical" tenor of the philosophy of the first and the "theoretical" intent of the latter: "As all the sciences all together are nothing but the human intelligence, which always remains one and the same no matter what be the variety of the objects to which it applies itself, in as much as this variety changes its own nature no more than the diversity of objects upon which the sunshine changes *its* nature, there is *no need of confining the human mind within any limit*."[14] There is a point in dwelling upon this distinction far beyond labeling one type of philosophy practical and the other theoretical in spirit, interesting as it may be to know that one type of philosophy is chiefly concerned to show how a thoroughgoing reformation of science is to be effected while the other type is primarily concerned with the connection between the right kind of knowledge and human welfare.

---

12. [Ibid., bk. 2, ch. 30, sec. 5.]
13. [Ibid., bk. 4, ch. 3, sec. 22.]
14. [René Descartes, Rule 1 from *Rules for the Direction of the Mind* (1628), in vol. 1 of *The Philosophical Writings of Descartes* (Cambridge University Press, 1985)].

The wider end served by noting the distinction is the realization that a problem which appears to be the same problem when it is stated in general terms, like say "the problem of knowledge," has, in fact, different contents and directions according to the cultural situation in which it is bred and nourished. The systems of Descartes and Locke had, as was pointed out in the previous chapter,[15] important beliefs in common, since the both arose within a culture having the same generic moral-religious tradition and outlook. And with respect to specifically philosophic formulations, the intellectual leaders of the Continent and Great Britain had been educated during the medieval and post-medieval periods in universities speaking the same language and partaking in the same currents. But the success in Great Britain of the Protestant Revolt, the accomplishment of a political revolution in the direction of representative government, and the weakening of feudal institutions by the earlier rise of an industrial-trading class are marks of a culture in which the rise of the new science caused the problem of knowledge to take a specifically moral or "practical" turn. And the fact of the relatively prompt and easy triumph of Newton's natural philosophy in England proves that the new astronomy and physics did not produce the crisis nor have [they] yet [met] the enemies that mark their continental career. This fact is equivalent to the fact of less concern with the technically scientific or "theoretical" aspect of the problem of knowledge and greater concern with the problem of its effect upon other affairs of a more directly human nature. When Voltaire brought back from England a popular pocket edition of a combination of Newtonian natural philosophy and Lockean moral philosophy, conditions were so changed in France (conditions that culminated in the Revolution of 1789) that their amalgamation virtually swept official Cartesianism off the boards.

The point just mentioned serves to illustrate a matter to be borne of mind in every interpretation of modern philosophy. It was the fashion for a considerable period (the fashion has not completely passed away) to simplify the account given of the course of philosophy by setting up a continuous or unbroken line of descent. In England, unsolved problems and unexamined principles of Locke gave rise to the philosophy of Berkeley that in turn bred the philosophy of Hume. Meantime, upon the continent, different elements of the philosophy of Descartes were taken up and developed by Spinoza and Leibniz (to mention in each strain only the outstanding figures), whose work was carried on by Kant until he made acquaintance with Hume, Shaftesbury and other British writers, when he effected a union of the "rationalist" strain of the continent and the empiricist strain of England—thereby determining

---

15. [The previous chapter referred to here could be the manuscript now included as section 2 of chapter 6. See the editor's introduction for further information.]

(at least according to German accounts) the entire subsequent course of philosophy. This handy schematic account marks in general the sort of thing that happens when the story of philosophy is isolated from the general human story. And in particular, while there can be no doubt of the influence exercised by each of the men mentioned upon his successor, it completely neglects the fact that the direction taken by the influence is dialectical or logical only in appearance. In actuality, it was determined by a combination of the dominant preoccupations of the later philosophers (Berkeley for example being a Bishop) and change in social conditions. That is to say, in spite of the vast influence exerted by linguistic formulations which endure and so are contemporary, there is no philosophy of anything like the first rank in which vital contemporary conditions are not decisive as to the use made of the literary documents.

The substance of the foregoing is capable of being summed up in the statement that the first phase in discussion of the "problem of knowledge" consisted, along with attacks upon the Aristotelian and scholastic methods and conclusions (the defects of the latter being regarded as the necessary fruit of the methods that were officially sanctioned), of attempts to set forth in some detail the foundations and main features of a very different method, one consonant with the procedures and conclusions of the astronomy and physics that were undermining and replacing the old cosmology or natural philosophy. The fact that the first formulations of the new science dealt primarily with astronomical phenomena, that is to say with considerations most remote from human affairs, is doubly significant. On one hand, it shook the very foundations of the traditional world-picture of a bounded universe with this earth as its fixed centre, about which everything else moved or with reference to which other movements in the heavens were determined. In shaking these foundations, it had direct hostile impact upon the transformation wrought by medieval Christian philosophy in the natural philosophy (including the cosmic astronomical frame) it adopted from Aristotle. There is nothing more extraordinary in all human history than the conversion of the "theoretical" and morally neutral cosmology of Aristotle into a thoroughly morally planned and morally conducted drama, one moreover in which the naturalism of Aristotle was enclosed within a framework having supernatural action at its base and supernaturally determined eternal bliss of suffering at its apex. Hence, as I have previously remarked, the substitution of the Copernican for the Aristotelian-Ptolemaic astronomical system was in effect a moral crisis, not just a change in scientific subject matter.

On the other hand, the spatial (and later the temporal) remoteness of scientific subject matter, during the earlier stage of the new science, contributed mightily to the sense that the new science was concerned with an *"external"* world and that *human* affairs in all moral aspects and respects fall within another and an *"inner"* domain and order of existence. While the new science was revolutionary in effect, the men who pursued it and those who wrote in its defense and who tried to formulate its basis and principles were in no sense revolutionary in respect to the foundations in the constitution of man of morals. The more the old cosmological foundations of morals, of all that concerned the values and destiny of man, was displaced, the more explicit and systematic became the assertion of its inherent foundation in human nature. The more immediate technical result in philosophy was retention of the old terminology regarding the spirit, mind, or soul, and its powers, intellect, reason, understanding, imagination, sense-perception, minus the support they had received in the classic cosmological system as actualizations or what already has Being in the cosmic scheme of Nature and which exists potentially in the processes of the organic body. Through its faculties, mind set up in business for itself, so to speak. The enduring effect was to convert the problem of the *method* of knowledge that is scientific in nature into the problem of [whether] such a thing as knowledge is possible anyway. The earlier problem of method passed almost insensibly into what is known technically as the *epistemological* problem, and out of this problem with its premises of the inner and outer, that is, some kind of unique relation of mental or psychical and physical, subjective and objective, knowing self and world to be known, were spawned the systems definitely and explicitly characteristic of nineteenth century philosophies: Idealisms, rationalistic and empirical, objective and subjective, absolute and relative: Realisms, naïve, presentational, representative, dualistic, monistic, and occasionally pluralistic; phenomenalisms, positivisms, and agnosticisms.

In making the distinction between the earlier and the later period in philosophical handling of the problem of knowledge, I have no intention of denying or slurring over the fact that the germinal seeds (in some case already starting to sprout) are contained in the earlier statements. But these seeds are planted, as far as it concerns the intention of the philosopher gardeners, in a soil and climate in which the *existence* of knowledge is assumed; the problem is its source, nature and extent or limits. The historical "revolution" which Kant considered that he effected in its various "Critiques" consisted in conversion of these aspects of the question of proper method into the radical problem of how it is *possible* anyway.

In tracing the later form of the problem to those of its sources that are contained in the earlier form, I make no apology for recurring to Descartes and Locke. I have already discussed the Cartesian basic doctrine that "indubitable and certain" knowledge (from which all other forms of knowledge hang) can be found only within Mind, which in itself is inherently "spiritual"—that is, immaterial. It is a substance whose essence is *thinking*—note the retention and projection of two basic principles of the old metaphysical tradition, tied up with an identification of thinking with an *immediate* self-revealing activity, termed consciousness, which is wholly alien to the old tradition. This immaterial mind is located *in* a body; "location in" being a substitute for the older idea that mind (save in its highest form) is a function of an organic body—and yet a logical enough derivate in view of the medieval insistence upon an imperishable spirit. The immaterial mind is *simple* because immaterial and unextended. The body is completely material, and matter is also a substance, but its essence is *extension* and hence it is divisible and compoundable without limit.[16]

Now if we leave out the heritage of substance and essence, there is nothing merely arbitrary in the view put forward by Descartes as to the "external" world. It is a direct outcome of the new physical science as that was propounded by Galileo. In Descartes' own words, "The nature of matter or of body does not consist in its being hard or heavy or colored or something that affects our senses in any other way, but solely in the fact that it is a *substance* extended in length, depth, and breadth. . . . All the properties clearly known in it may be reduced to this one, that it can be divided or moved according to its parts."[17] Descartes carried generalization of this point of view further than did Galileo. The reason is simple. Descartes was early convinced of the great superiority of mathematics to all other natural sciences: In fact, it was the source and substance of whatever is necessary and certain in any statement of natural phenomena. It is in no way dependent upon any aid or support adventitious to mind itself. In consequence no science of the "external" world is possible unless the essence of the latter is such that mathematical determinations are directly applicable. The only developed and assured form of mathematics in his day was geometry. Descartes as a matter of course thought of geometry as the science of extension. His Eureka and Q.E.D. in the above sense followed at once. His invention of *analytic* geometry by uniting algebra—previously, as he says, of no practical use in science, being "confined to symbols as to be an obscure and confused art"— immensely extended and refined the availability of geometry for scientific

---

16. Descartes denies, quite consistently, that animals "think;" their operations [being] of the nature of machines, just as all physiological operations in man are strictly "mechanical."

17. "Properties" as well as "substance" has its traditional metaphysical-logical meaning in this passage. As he writes in another passage: "Everything else that can be attributed to body *presupposes* extension. . . . Figure cannot be understood save in an extended thing, nor motion except in extended space," figure and motion being "properties." [René Descartes, *Principles of Philosophy* (1644), pt. 2, sec. 4., in vol. 1 of *Philosophical Writings*; see note 14].

statement of natural phenomena, but confirmed instead of faltering the idea that their essence is extension.[18]

When we turn to Descartes's psychology or account of the "inner" substance we find, in the first place, that he retains intact the classic notion of its faculties with, of course, the shift from potentialities *to be* actualized by intercourse, with sensible and rational forms already in existence to "*powers*" in active operation on their own account.

In view of the orthodox education of Descartes in a Jesuit school, the casual evidences afforded in his writings of the weakened popular hold of scholastic philosophy are the more significant. He ridicules for example the old definition of movement in terms of potentiality in words that indicate the formula was already becoming almost unintelligible to one with any scientific training. *The* power is Rational Intelligence which is Thinking in its highest and purest form, and upon it "depends the knowledge of all other things, not reciprocally . . . But it is aided (and often hindered) with respect to knowledge of certain sorts of things by the senses and the imagination," which, however, are important as occasions for the exercise of pure thought, not as means of arriving at truth.[19] "The intellect alone is capable of conceiving truth."[20] The senses, as organs of the body, only receive physical images of things—not metaphorically as he takes pains to state but literally as wax receives the image or copy of a seal. That is, the body in its external form is "really" modified by the object in the same way the surface of the wax is modified. And his theory demands that this is as true when we perceive heat and cold, color or sound, as when we perceive hardness or roughness. Since modifications of extension are all that exists in the "external" world, the only impressions they can make are lines and figures—geometrical in nature. These forms (notice the complete range in the nature of forms) are enduringly impressed upon the imagination which is also corporeal in nature. The pure intellect is pure energy which is called sense when it is directed upon the impressions left by external figures upon sense organs and imagination when it operates to combine or otherwise manipulate images that are enduringly left in that part of the body which is their proper receptacle.

Later, eighteenth- and nineteenth-century ideas have been habitually read back into Descartes and Locke, making sensations and images mental

---

18. The invention by Leibniz and Newton of the calculus did not change the basic place of mathematical formulation. It displaced, however, "static" attributes, appropriate to extension, by "dynamic" ones. The category of energy and motion came to the fore. [René Descartes, *Discourse on the Method* (1637), pt. 2, in vol. 1 of *Philosophical Writings*; see note 14].

19. [Citation unclear. Perhaps a reference to the preface to the French edition of Descartes's *Principles of Philosophy* (1644).]

20. [Descartes, Rule 12 from *Rules for the Direction of the Mind* (1628), in vol. 1 of *Philosophical Writings*; see note 14].

or psychical occurrences. Hence the importance of noting their "inherent" physical character as directly produced by other physical bodies, only the "mental" event being the *actus purus* of Intellect in beholding them. The source of our errors consists in the fact that instead of awaiting the result of that inspection by the intellect which will give us a clear and distinct apprehension or idea, we permit ourselves to be moved by impulse and appetite and so give to confused and mixed ideas a degree of reality and truth they do not possess. Such qualities as colors, sounds, flavors, pains, hungers, thirsts, are none of them properties of bodies—since science finds only geometrical properties in body. They are "obscure and confused" ideas which are nevertheless lively and vivid. They testify to the fact that the self is closely conjoined with the body, not merely located in it like a pilot in a ship. And if we refrain from anything more than taking these qualities of sense to be helps which guide us in maintaining the body in existence and health—if, that is we treat color, sound, etc for precisely what they are, namely, as the feeling of thirst, we shall not in any way be deceived by them.

Descartes has a more difficult hurdle to get over. The certainty of mathematics is completely bound up with its being *within* intellect as a manifestation of its own energy. Yet his entire theory of physical knowledge, of material and external bodies, is based upon the idea of one-to-one correspondence between them and mathematical principles. It is often said that the attention given by Descartes to proof of the Being of God is just a product of his Catholic bringing-up and surroundings, if not a deliberate attempt to keep whenever he could within Orthodox bounds. But there can be no doubt of the place occupied by this proof in his whole system. It is his way of answering the difficulty just stated. It is probably that the failure of subsequent philosophers of the "rationalist" type, till the time of Kant, to raise the question of the ground of proof for applicability of mathematics to physical phenomena was the proof of the *"solvitur ambulando"*[21] type. The dependence of physics and astronomy upon mathematics and the success of mathematical formulation seemed to make it aside from the point to raise the question. When Descartes wrote, the successful application of mathematics was still in the future; his own specific attempts in that direction were not particularly fruitful.

The existence of God helped Descartes over more than one stile. On the face of matters, Descartes's solutions left him and his successors with three tough problems. All of them grew out of the sharp separation the complete split made between the knower and the world to be known. The cleavage and problem remained when opposition between two "substances" with contrary "essences" was attenuated (by attrition from events rather than by

21. [Meaning "solved by walking" or "solved by practical experiment."]

systematic intent) into two kinds of events, one physical and external and the other mental and internal. Knowledge of the world demanded that the latter order conform or correspond to the former. What is the significance of conformity in the case of two orders of existence so different that the defining traits of one are the exact opposite of those of the other order? And how shall we know when it is attained? How does the mental series of events know when it has got successfully outside of and beyond itself to grasp what is unqualifiedly unlike itself? Or more generally how can it do so at all, successfully or unsuccessfully—the problem of the so-called "transcendent reference" of knowledge. So-called "realistic" theories reduce, at bottom, to saying "Anyway it doesn't," with a variety of ingenious accounts of how it does so, and so-called "idealistic" theories amount to saying "It doesn't and all the better for that, since it is happier lot to live in a world which, like ourselves, is made of mental stuff than in a world of hard tough-grained inconsiderate material things."

The second problem was that which the followers of Descartes had to face most immediately. The body belongs to the "material" world. Yet knowledge of *particular* objects (even when they are regarded as special portions or figures of infinitely protracted extension) requires that images made on the sense organs at the surface of the body and collected in the imagination somehow reach and affect the mind, if only enough to remind the latter of their presence so as to supply an "occasion" for the mind's noting them. And phenomena of volition, which Descartes did not dream of doubting, prove that mind is capable of directing the efforts of the body. Here is the material whose enduring deposit was the question of the "relation of mind and body"—a problem in which all the difficulties connected with the general problem of the relation of an immaterial knower as subject and agent to a material external world got tied into a hard knot.

The third general problem may be stated in the words of Descartes himself. "I find in myself two quite different ideas of the sun. One of them has its origin in the senses, and is to be put in the class of those which come from *without*, by which it appears to me extremely small. The other is drawn from astronomical consideration, that is to say from certain notions born with me, or at least formed by myself in some way or other—by which it appears to me many times greater than the whole earth. Certainly these two ideas that I conceive of the sun cannot both be like the same sun."[22] As between the two suns, Descartes votes emphatically for the scientific sun, since the one which comes immediately from its appearance is the one least resembling the real sun. The problem of this particular reduplication is about as actual a

---

22. [René Descartes, "Meditation III," in *Meditations on First Philosophy* (1641), in vol. 1 of *Philosophical Writings*; see note 14].

theme as when Descartes formulated it. A philosophical text today is hardly reputable unless when it comes to discussion of the theory of knowledge it raises the question of whether the seen table, the solid and stable article at which we eat or put books and papers, or the table which is a swarming swirl of minute molecules, separated by what are relatively vast spaces, is the "real and true" table. Or if the question is not put in the form of superior "reality," we learn that philosophy must find some way of reconciling the two reals or, at all events, seemingly reals. In the case of Descartes, God, in all three of these instances, served as the *tertium quid* to bridge the gap so as to enable opposites to get along with one another.

The approach to knowledge from "without," as presented by Locke, is involved in the same problems with a reversed twist. He had to meet exactly the same difficulty that confronted Descartes although the source of the difficulty was so opposite as to evoke a different formulation. Locke *started* his account of knowledge with a world made of minute bodies having the qualities or, properly speaking, the powers of solidity[23]—extension, figure and mobility—in short, with the "physical" world of Newton's natural philosophy instead of with a system of mathematical "conceptions." These bodies, being in motion, affect motions in the human body which by means of the nerves are transmitted to the brain and there act upon the mind, treating "simple ideas" from which all our knowledge of external things is derived. "It is," he says, "the actual receiving of ideas from without that gives us notice of the existence of other things"—"other," that is, than [our] own existence which is intuitively known and that of God which is known by rational demonstration.[24] Locke with his usual candor remarks, "It is evident the mind knows not things immediately but only by the intervention of the ideas it has of them. Our knowledge therefore is real only as there is conformity between our ideas and the reality of things. But shall here be the criterion? How shall the mind, when it perceives nothing but its own ideas, know that they agree with things themselves?"[25] In this passage, there is found, as far as I am aware, the first explicit statement of what came later to be named the "epistemological" problem, whose discussion, while growing out of the earlier discussions of the right method of obtaining knowledge (in contrast with the wrong methods previously in use) gradually relegated

---

23. In one of his few direct criticisms of Descartes (from whose writings he said he first obtained his relish for philosophical reading, Oxford still teaching a scholasticized version of Aristotle) he attacks the Cartesian identification of matter with extension because of [the] omission of *solidity*, extension being an affair of space, which is continuous and immovable, and hence an "idea" as different from that of space as it from the idea of scarlet color—though neither can exist apart from extension.

24. [Locke, *Essay*, bk. 4, ch. 11, sec. 2.]

25. [Ibid., bk. 4, ch. 4, sec. 4.]

the question of methods to a secondary position[.] While Locke states the question frankly, not waiting to have it thrust upon him as an obnoxious logical consequence of his premises, there is no evidence that he took it very seriously. He remarks of it, quite moderately in view of the central place it came to occupy in later philosophical writings, that "it seems not to lack difficulty." But he does not begin to devote to it the space he gives either to the question of our knowledge of our own existence or of that of the existence of God. Although his special answer is of no great historic importance in comparison with the combination of his views and those of Descartes in fixing the course taken by later philosophy, we may note that we are certain of the existence of *something* without because of the existence of some simple ideas which "the mind can by no means make of itself" and which therefore "must necessarily be the product of things operating on the mind in the natural way."[26] While this fact only proves the existence of something external that acts upon us, the "practical" turn given by Locke to his system (a point discussed in the previous chapter) is used by him in conjunction with his rational assurance of the existence of God, to give us a reasonable (as distinct from rationally necessary) assurance of a certain act of conformity of our ideas within to things without. The perceptions within are so ordained and arranged by the Creator as to be adapted, and with a regularity that can be counted upon, to our needs. And our understanding being given to man not "barely for speculation but also for the conduct of his life,"[27] no reasonable creature will complain if he has the kind of knowledge that enables him to find his way about, so to speak, among the things of the external world, if the ideas they produce in him give him warning about what is useful to him and instruction as to what things are useful and how to use them. Hence Locke was not specially troubled by the fact that he believed that no matter "how far over human industry may advance useful and experimental philosophy in physical things, scientifical will still be out of our reach; because we want perfect and adequate ideas of those very bodies which are nearest us and most under our command."[28]

---

26. [Ibid.]

27. [Ibid., bk. 4, ch. 14, sec. 1.]

28. The reader who supposes that the problem and this method of solution are out of date in the twentieth century should note that a philosopher as "modern" as George Santayana still finds the problem as philosophically insistent as did Locke. Even more so in fact, since he takes it to be axiomatic that _____. And his solution by appeal to "animal faith" is that of Locke, minus the guarantee the latter has become of adaptation to our needs by a powerful and twice kindly disposed divine creator. The extraordinary force capable of being exercised by formulae when once they are established in custom is shown by the fact that just as Locke never asked how, upon the ground of his conclusion, anyone ever arrived at the premise (in this case Newtonian science) from which the conclusion is derived nor what would happen to the conclusion if the contradictory premises were dropped. So today discussions about

"*Scientifical*" knowledge having here its traditional sense of necessary and demonstrative.

It is futile even to mention the problem of knowledge which emerged from the writings of Descartes and Locke if it be not kept in mind that in some form or other its presentation was historically inescapable given the persistence of the old belief in an immaterial mind that is the subject and agent of knowing and the kind of a world to be known that offered itself as the proper subject matter of the new science of nature, in conjunction with perpetuation of the old basic tradition of the strict one-to-one correspondence of knowledge (if true) with "Reality" or Being. Or, put the other way around, given the introduction of a "physical" subject matter, as a set of entities that are stripped of all qualities save those of a completely indifferent homogeneous time, space, motion whose connections with one another and with man are wholly bare of anything like an end or purpose, side by side with *retention* of an unextended mind, immaterial knower (whether conceived as "substance," processes, or states making no difference to this problem), and someone or other was bound in time to raise the question of how the two could get along together. Those who raised the question were not more foolish than others. They were more acute or possessed a more sensitive intellectual consciousness. But, to repeat, the question grew to a mature and engrossing form out of an earlier condition in which it appeared as an incident of attempts to formulate a new method of knowledge that would be in line with the efforts of the new type of scientific inquiry, and not out of line with the rapidly growing interest in "natural" events at the expense or predominant interest in the supernatural. There is one important exception to be made with respect to the statement just made about elimination of purpose. It is true that it was eliminated in description and "explanation" of all particular phenomena, Descartes being explicit and thoroughgoing in admitting only "mechanical" accounts of the processes and structures of living creatures, including the human body, save when the latter was immediately and seemingly miraculously conjoined with the spiritual activities of mind as thinking substance. But as is indicated, for example, by Locke's reference to what God had ordained in adaptation to human needs, the old idea of overruling ends persisted in a highly generalized form after

---

knowledge still rest upon a presumed knowledge of physical things which act by means of a known organism, having a nervous system we also know about, upon a mind or consciousness to produce in it mental states so totally unlike the things which cause them that the existence and nature of the latter are problematic themes of philosophical discussion. Yet the reader who thinks that it is a sign of a kind of mania that philosophers do not try dropping one or the other of the two mutually contradictory positions may do well to ask if he does not accept them himself, though without taking the trouble to bring them into conjunction with another. [Ibid., bk. 4, ch. 3, sec. 26]

it ceased to be applicable and used in the case of specified phenomena. In this connection, certain expressions which Locke frequently uses are even more instructive than his special reference to adaptation. I refer to his use of such expressions as the "natural correspondence and connection" *some* of our ideas have with one another, conjoined to the statement that "it is the office and excellency of our reason to trace these, and to hold them together in that union and correspondence which is founded in their peculiar beings," or, as he puts the matter in less sweeping words, a "certain number of the simple ideas conveyed in by the senses *go constantly together.*"[29] I have in mind also such remarks as "Nature makes many particular things which do agree with one another in many sensible qualities, and probably too in their internal frame and constitution."[30] And at times he so forgets his official doctrine as to speak of one of the relations between ideas that constitutes knowledge as "coexistence or necessary connection." The passage in which the stronger sentence is found [is one] in which this kind of union, called *natural*, is put in contrast with another kind of connection said to be due wholly to "chance or custom" by which "ideas that are not in themselves at all akin" get knitted together so that [when] one appears its companion comes too. In this way "wrong" connections are built up between ideas that "in between themselves are loose and independent one of another"[31] and yet seem, because of custom, to have *real* correspondence with one another.

I believe that the honorific use of *nature* which is found in such remarks as these represents the deepest conviction of Locke, a conviction which upon the whole is more cause than effect of his reference to God as one who renders things fitted, suited, adapted to us. Were I to venture a guess as to why he was so little disturbed by the question which seems not to lack difficulty, it would be that his faith in Nature as an orderly and ordered whole is so profound that his theoretical proof that "ideas" are so simple and independent that there can be no necessary connections among these which are received from without although this mind's own workmanship may establish them among ideas that do not purport to conform to external things—as in the case of morals and mathematics. For it would be impossible, I think, to overstate the appeal and force of the word *Nature* through the latter part of the seventeenth century and practically the whole of the eighteenth. Natural reason, *il lume naturale*, natural law and natural religion had natural correspondence with one another. The picture that Newton presented of

---

29. [Ibid., bk. 2, ch. 23, sec. 5 and sec. 1.]
30. [Ibid., bk. 3, ch. 6, sec. 36.]
31. [Ibid., bk. 2, ch. 23, sec. 9.]

the solar system in the most emphatic and honorific sense of *system* made a profound effect upon [the] public imagination. Here as elsewhere, properties that had been the exclusive possession of the other world took up their habitat in this world minus the arbitrary character which had previously marked them. The earlier phase of the modern period was not marked by any sense of moral or "spiritual" loss because the new science had eliminated ends and qualities from the natural scene. On the contrary, there was an atmosphere of buoyant hope and a sense of release of powers that had been penned up—a sense that reached a climax in the "Enlightenment" of the eighteenth century. "Nature and Nature's God" were benevolently interfused. Leibniz put forward the formula of pre-established harmony. It was advanced nominally in order to deal with some of the technical difficulties that had been raised—such as the connection of mind and body—and in that particular capacity it had no great vogue. But the sense of a harmony that was so deeply established that it must have been pre-established was virtually universal in circles which were affected by the new ways of viewing nature.

I am not writing a history of "modern" philosophy and my account of what happened in philosophy during the two centuries or more after Descartes and Locke will be schematic as well as much foreshortened. The ordinary account of Locke reads back into him "subjective" ideas that are foreign to him. His "ideas" were not themselves mental states or mental processes. [They are] as he says over and over again "the immediate *objects*" of the mind in perceiving.[32] But his "ideas" were left in such an ambiguous position that when later philosophers gave their attention to the consequences of the new science instead of to exposition of its method they passed almost insensible into mentalistic existences, Descartes having prepared the way by statements which pointed directly to that conclusion. The point in which Locke's doctrine was the closest to that of Descartes became the decisive consideration for Locke's immediate successors.

This point is Locke's doctrine of intuitive knowledge of the existence of the self. The identity of the self or person, of the "I," is not in the least,

---

32. In his own words, "It stands for whatever is the object of the understanding when a man thinks" (that is when he is conscious or aware) and it is used "to express whatever is meant by phantasm, notion, species." These are scholastic names for the immediate subject of knowledge, "species" being the Latin translation of the form or *eidos* of Aristotle. There was nothing new in making it the "object" of thought. But treating it as the effect of a material body as its "efficient cause" was something which only the materialistic atomists of antiquity had ventured upon. It wasn't mental and it wasn't physical in the case of Locke. But neither had the form, *eidos*, or species been either mental or physical. Moreover "sensations" in the case of Locke are not mental; they are rather physiological; they become ideas when the power of perception is directed upon them.

according to Locke, an affair of the identity of a substance. It is "conscious-ness that makes everyone to be what he calls self" and "consciousness always accompanies thinking," since it is "impossible for anyone to perceive with-out perceiving that he does perceive."[33] What is called "personal identity" consists exclusively in having the same "consciousness" at different times and places, and this by definition is the same as perceiving or knowing that one has the same consciousness. In every case, simple ideas are the sole *material* knowledge but they are not themselves instances of knowledge, the latter being a matter of *relations* perceived to exist between ideas. But in the case of the sameness of consciousness at different times and places, the two terms of the relation are identical with each other thing. "When we see, hear, smell, taste, meditate, or will anything, we know that we do."[34] Here, as in the case of the Cartesian "I Doubt," there is a sheet anchor of absolute certainty. For instead of saying that the two related terms that constitute the knowledge are one and the same, we can say that in this case all relation is eliminated and in "consciousness" knower and knower are completely one. Locke himself utilizes this consideration only to show that we have a direct and intuitive knowledge of self. But given acceptance of the new notion that knowledge is a relation of the inner and the outer and given the retention of the old notions of the identification of knowledge with what is primary and indubitable and of the inherent correspondence of true or certain knowledge with "reality," we see Locke supplying to his predecessors an out-and-out "subjectivistic" standpoint and a starting-point in which *at* the very start there is no longer any "outer"—although *mirabale dictu* the "inner" remains with, if anything, an intensification of the properties it had when *inner* was defined in terms of opposition to "outer." And those who did not have the concern for a new science of the world that was mathematical throughout which Descartes had could readily discover in his views the necessity for taking the same starting point in every discussion regarding knowledge.[35]

As far, then, as concerns a highly abstract statement of the problem of knowledge, there is a certain justification for the conventional interpreta-tion according to which Berkeley simply eliminated some of the logical

33. [Ibid., bk. 2, ch. 27, sec. 10 and sec. 9.]

34. [Ibid., sec. 11.]

35. If, once more, it is supposed that this way of approach to the Problem of Knowledge and other philosophical issues (all of which are taken to depend upon the problem of knowledge) is outworn, I mention not just this and that contemporary philosopher, but the so-called phenomenological school now flourishing. For we are told that the way to obtain a "scien-tific" philosophy, binding on all thinkers, is to forget everything that is scientific including its method of inquiry, and make a "subjectivistic" or Cartesian approach, starting from the "pure consciousness of an individual knower." And as if in self-irony, it is said that such an approach is the only one free from all presuppositions—another example of the power exerted by familiarity.

inconsistencies from Locke's doctrine in his elimination of any material and outer substratum, being *perceived* and being *existence* being the same in every case and not just in that of the self while Hume continued the work of logical purification by eliminating also any mental substance underlying impressions and ideas (which, however, were not impressed by anything); reducing "self" to a Lockean train of "ideas," now mental and conscious "states" or "processes," in continual rapid flux. For the particular purpose in hand, I shall in any case ignore the significant differences that mark off the attitudes and writings of the three men. For what is pertinent here is the form taken by the problem of knowledge. For, no matter the proffered solution, the problem was taken as being set by a number of affairs which duplicated each other in a strange way in spite of being contraries of each other in constitution and stuff. There was the outer and physical world to be known and there was a mirror reflection of it in mind or in consciousness; the subjective and objective; the material and the immaterial; the mind and the body; the self and the world. Under the nurturing care of Kant, there even developed two selves, one "empirical" and hence "phenomenal" and the other "rational" and "noumenal." This doubling up furnished upon the side of the inner duplicate the subject matter of the science of psychology so as to correspond, by a kind of pre-established harmony the science of physics which dealt with the external edition of two-sided "Reality."[36] It had its own laws or uniformities discoverable by introspection or direct inspection, and hence could be treated quite conveniently without getting involved in [the] "epistemological" problem—which psychologists in their self-imposed scientific stand often regarded as "metaphysical" even though their occupation had no other foundation. Having been originally borrowed from epistemological philosophy after it had become established as "scientific," it was returned to philosophy as various philosophers could use its supposed subject matter, having standing as science, to formulate their own specific problems with a clear conscience.

---

36. [Dewey's note to self: "Quote James."]

VI. Wandering between Two Worlds

I

No verses of Matthew Arnold's are better known I suppose than that which describes modern man as "Wandering between two worlds, one dead / The other powerless to be born."[1] In an essay he puts the matter without the exaggeration of poetry in the following words: "Modern times find themselves with an immense body of institutions, established facts, accredited dogmas, customs and rules, which have come to us from times not modern. In this system their life has to be carried forward; yet they have a sense that their system is not of their own creation, and that it by no means corresponds exactly with the wants of their actual life; that, for them, it is customary, not rational. *The awakening of this sense is the awakening of the modern spirit.*"[2] I have taken the liberty of italicizing the words of the last sentence. I have done so because the sentence indicates, perhaps more definitely than their author intended, that "modern times" are inchoate in their modernity, so much so that the awakening of "the modern spirit" consists of a sense of discrepancy, of conflict, between the tendencies and requirements that are modern and the established institutions, customs, traditions, creeds, within which the tendencies that are modern are compelled to operate. Its sense is that of tension and confusion, rather than of something definitively going its own way on terms that are compatible with its own direction of movement. Were we to say that those who are dreaming live exclusively, in a sense, based on esteem for the past, we should have to say that those who live with a sense of definitely achieved present exist in a state of hallucination.

. . .

Given such conditions in general, it is reasonable to expect that philosophies which are produced in these conditions will reflect the state of inchoateness,

---

1. ["Stanzas from the Grande Chartreuse," in *Complete Prose Works of Matthew Arnold.,* ed. Robert Super (1960), 3:109.]
2. ["Heinrich Heine," in ibid., 3:112.]

confusion, and uncertainty. They are born of that state and they continue to share it. Even those who have no sympathy with the view of philosophy here put forward will be among the first to admit that modern systems as a collection—instead of some one system which is preferred—are more noteworthy for statements of problems than for conclusions expressing solutions that command any widespread assent. It is difficult to account for the number and diversity of systems that have appeared in the last three centuries, and for their controversial quality, if they are looked upon as engaged in a scientific study of "ultimate reality." It is a simple matter to account for these features if these philosophies are engaged in trying to disentangle, to lay hold of, and to formulate some facet or aspect of the existing confused scene, namely that particular one which is taken to point to the highway that leads to a goal of articulate coherent expression of what is genuinely modern in the new culture.

We are brought back to the reasons that render serious consideration of Greek and medieval philosophies and theologies pertinent to an appraisal of modern philosophies. The latter cannot be understood without taking into account the active operative presence within them of the "principles" that were formulated earlier. For, as a rule, the things to which the name *principles* is given are settled directions of attention and interest, ways of observing and describing that are so habitual and controlling that they regulate other observations because they are not themselves observed.

It has been said in previous discussions that if the doctrines of medieval theology be looked upon as if they were exclusively theoretical or "intellectual" statements and the conclusions of modern science be taken in the same way, or as technical, the conflict of science and theology would been comparatively episodic. It represents in fact a crisis because theological philosophy with its context of an institution that was "normative" for the arts, for education, for economic and political relations, as well as for moral discipline, had incorporated the science of nature into its own structure. It there formed the comprehensive frame of reference within which all doctrines and every variety of conduct were placed in order to pass upon their validity and fix their significance. When scientific subject matter moved outside the frame, the latter remained substantially intact with reference to humanist and moral matters. Its perpetuation directly affected the status of science. Because it was outside, it became a more or less separate and specialized affair. Science exerted an immense effect upon other aspects of modern culture. But the changes it has produced have occurred for the most [part] through the revolution it has wrought in industry, by being "applied." The *method* by which its conclusions have been reached has been narrowly restricted to so-called "external" and physical events. The field of distinctly humane concerns has been left, save incidentally, within the old frame of reference and subject to methods consonant with—because derived from—the old doctrines. The dualisms which are a dominant feature of modern philosophical systems are, fundamentally, expressions of the split within our culture between the "scientific" and the "moral." I know of no more convincing proof of this statement than the fact that industrial affairs in which, as just said, the influence of the new science has been almost without limit, are regarded by official economists as well as in popular estimate as "material" in the depreciated sense of *material* inherited from the old science, and a sense that places it in a "realm" separated from that which is assigned to morals and values—at least values of the kind that receives the honor of being named "intrinsic" in distinction from another kind disparaged by being called "extrinsic."

The previous chapter contained a number of examples of the confused mixture in "modern" attitudes and beliefs of the new and the old, a confusion due to insistence upon injecting into the new scientific outlook of old scientific formulations.[3] The injection deprived the latter of whatever virtue they had possessed in their own context while it infected and perverted the operative force of the new. I propose in this chapter to give a number of further instances of a more systematic, less incidental, sort.

I begin with the fact that the unquestioned assumption that underlies the classic scheme is that there is an exact one-to-one correspondence between knowledge (provided of course it *is* knowledge) and "reality," there being those different grades of sense, customary opinion, of knowledge, and necessary and universal rational knowledge in correspondence with different grades of change as absence of full Being or "Is-ness." There is hardly a modern system that has not retained the notion of the correspondence of knowledge in its proper sense with something named "reality." Even the attacks that were made about ancient metaphysics and ontology took, almost without exception, the course of holding that its error was in holding that kind of knowledge is accessible to our "finite minds," the conditions of *our* knowledge limiting the latter to "phenomena" in distinction from "things-in-themselves."

If those who were antagonistic to the older cosmological science accepted without demur one of the main propositions of the tradition of which this science is a part, one can readily infer the attitude taken by those who retained the idea that philosophy is a kind of supreme science since it is concerned to know ultimate reality. The classic tradition had, at least in the

---

3. [As pointed out in the Editor's Notes, internal references cannot always be trusted. When Dewey refers to a "previous chapter," we may not assume that he had the previous chapter of this volume in mind.]

case of Aristotle, placed the operations that constitute knowledge within the natural world which the operations were engaged in knowing. One may not rate highly the method by which this view was reached and supported, since it was bound up with the idea of rational forms and essences inherent in knowable things and knowledge as taking possession of them by a process of actualization of potentialities belonging to man as the kind of living creature which he is. But at all events, the potentialities and the processes of actualization were natural. If it had not been for the intervention of supra-naturalism, conclusions reached by the new natural knowledge might have utilized propositions of the psychology of Aristotle to develop a genuinely naturalistic account of knowing. Because of this intervention and the heritage of a knowing mind outside of the natural world which bequeathed the theory of knowledge, modern philosophies became a tortured wrestling with the problem of how an immaterial knowing "subject" could possibly know a world of "objects" defined by properties that were completely antithetical to those of knowing and the knower.

There is another illustration of a somewhat more technical nature of the unfortunate effect of the injection of the notion of an exact correspondence of knowledge and of "reality" as such. The depth of the infection of modern philosophy by this notion may be gathered not only by the vogue of "phenomenalism" (in the sense just stated) and of influential forms of the "positivist" doctrine but from the fact that an outstanding "problem" of modern philosophy has been to decide whether everyday perceptions or physical science is that which accords with reality; or if neither one is in strict correspondence, which gives the philosophical theory of knowledge the better clue to the nature of the "real." The impasse that resulted from these modes of approach has tended, of late, to change the form of the problem without affecting its substance. Any amount of ingenuity has been expended of late in attempts to reconcile the reports of sense perception with those of physics. The main preoccupation of the most influential philosophical school of Great Britain for a generation has been meticulous, so-called "analytic," efforts to show how the "objects" (so-called) of physics can be derived from, or shown to be consistent with "sense-data."

Since the time of Kant, the type of philosophy that arrogated for itself the title "critical" has had for its main problem that of determining the conditions under which knowledge is possible. Had it not been for the sad admixture of modern knowledge with pre-scientific doctrines, the only intelligible meaning of this question would have been an investigation of the constituting subject matter of existing knowledge to see how it had been arrived at and how the results of a critical examination of this kind might be employed to expedite further knowledge. The form actually taken in the formulation and discussion of the question "How is knowledge possible?" affords convincing proof that the theory of knowledge was tailored to fit prior assumptions that lie wholly outside what is known—but that lie all too much within our heritage from medievalism.

Students of philosophy are so familiar with efforts put forth, on the basis of prior assumptions about the nature of a knowing mind, consciousness, or whatever, to discover how knowledge of something completely different from itself is possible, that sheer familiarity has made the problem seem "natural" and even inevitable. They would be surprised and probably grieved if they were invited to examine the behavior of scientific men investigating, say, the cause of cancer or the field of electro-magnetic phenomena and by careful observation of *their* observations solve the question of how scientific knowledge is possible. But if such were tried, it would become clear that this sort of method provides the only way in which the meaning of such terms as "mind," "sense," "perception," etc., etc., can be determined, so that when, as at present, these terms are shoved under the entire discussion so they furnish its premises, it is clear that *they* are not the results of any scientific discussion. Yet they must come from somewhere. The hypothesis here propounded is that they come from those elements of the medieval worldview which were so tied up with basic moral-religious beliefs that they still have an almost iron grip upon us today, even though they have lost the support once afforded them by science.

I have stated the case so far from the side of unquestioned preconceptions about the "knowing subject" as fixing the conditions of statement and discussion of the question: How is knowledge possible? The arbitrariness of the question, when it is stated in terms of conditions established prior to and independently of any case of something actually known, appears equally evident when it is stated from the side of "reality" as the "object" at large with which the knowing "subject" at large is concerned. Were the subject matter which is relevant to the question and decisive as to its answer derived from the actual conduct or of behavior of the inquiry-type, it would be clear that the only intelligible sense that could be given the word "reality" would be that [which] depends on the results of competently conducted inquiry. Any such sense would be specific not in the form of a wholesale theory of "reality" at large. And by calling it specific, I mean that it would be precisely of the same order as that of the investigation of a monetary token by an expert to determine whether it is a *genuine* or a *counterfeit* promise to pay. The term "reality" as a term of universal scope has no place in a theory of knowledge that is grounded in the methods and conclusions of actual cases of knowledge. It has no place even as a specific term save as it stands for what is genuine in contrast with the spurious which has passed or is likely to pass for the genuine article, or for ascertained *fact* in distinction from a fiction that is current, or more reasonably from a view which has been tentatively entertained as a working hypothesis in lieu of definitive determination of fact.

From the standpoint of cultural history and "cultural lag," the fact that the philosophic question of knowledge has been posed in terms of conditions fixed beforehand is not as arbitrary as it is when it is looked at from the standpoint of the actual conduct of inquiries which yield knowledge. For in Greek-medieval science the theory that knowledge is an affair of direct and exact correspondence with "Reality" is more than pertinent; it is inherent. It follows directly from the kind of "naturalism" that is involved in the doctrine of Aristotle. Since human knowledge is an actualization of potentialities existing "by nature" or biologically in the human being as an organism, the actualization being effected by natural intercourse of the organism with events in which forms were immanent, it followed, almost truistically, that different grades of knowledge must stand in exact correspondence with the different grades of Being of the structure or constitution of nature. Since Being in its most complete sense is immutable, knowledge which is necessary and universal is of supreme rank; it alone is science. Mutable things find their proper manifestation in sense-perception, "empirical" knowledge and opinion, which stand in the same relation to the grades of being found in changing phenomena that science stands to immutable Being.

In this connection it is worthwhile to recur in a general fashion to the "naturalistic" character of the earlier psychology of knowledge that was illustrated in the previous chapter in the particular case of the meaning of the "potentialities" in its contrast with the doctrine of "faculties of mind" which was the modern edition of the doctrine. As was indicated earlier, medieval philosophers adhered "in principle" to the doctrine that man originally and by intention belongs in nature and, while at its head, is in harmony with its other components. Such a view has no room for the opposition of subject and object that has been at the bottom of most distinctively "modern" statements of the problem of knowledge. There is now according to the medieval view a deep-seated and all-embracing alienation of man from nature. But it is *moral*, not inherently metaphysical or cosmological. It was so profound and so pervasive that an extensive system of supernaturally initiated events was required to overcome it.

There can hardly be any doubt that this doctrine of the moral alienation of man from nature was such a controlling feature of medieval life in the impact of Church theology upon the mass of the people as to completely hide from view the official formulation with its Aristotelian slant. Thus it paved the way for assertion and general acceptance of that split between the natural world as the "object" of knowledge and man with respect to his endowment of knowing faculties, as agent of knowing which is formulated in the dualisms of modern philosophies.[4]

Another evidence of the "naturalism" (a kind of naturalism depending wholly of course upon a view of nature which conferred upon it the qualities most highly prized in human life) of the earlier view is found in the changed meaning of the word "physical." In the system of Aristotle it stood for everything in the constitution of nature which is affected with or is subject to change. From this point of view, psychical phenomena which are marked by change, as is notoriously the case with immediately perceived events, fall within the wider scope of the physical. They are of a different kind within the "physical" in that phenomena of living creatures, especially of animals, show a certain degree of self-movement, a property absent from inanimate changes. The change to the doctrine that the "mental" or generally the psychological is of radically different order from that of physics, subject to different categories and to be known by different methods, is another instance of the consequences resulting from the shift away from graded ranks of higher-lower to sharply marked divisions.

The new science with its denial of the inherently qualitative nature of the subjects of knowledge, its assertion of the homogeneity of spatial regions, periods of time and of motions, and its substitution of connections of changes for fixed forms and essences as the subject of knowledge, did away with the notion of grades of Being (Reality) and of grades in knowledge. The notion of necessary correspondence of the one with the other was then left in its most general and blank form. It is incredible, however, that it would have been left in the highly influential estate it holds in modern philosophy merely as a cosmological or scientific doctrine. Its entanglement in the medieval period with issues and beliefs of vast human moment, by means of its incorporation in morals and religion, is the only thing that explains why the old standpoint regarding knowledge did not silently and insensibly drop away in behalf of a theory of knowledge formed on the ground of actual knowledge.

The view that the highest mode of knowledge, namely "science," was an apprehension of the kind of being which is inherently fixed and immutable and therefore is necessary in form and universal in scope, had a further effect in the philosophical theories which were formed, an effect which is another example of "wandering between two worlds," or at least in a confused mixture of two different cultures and climates of belief. It is found in the perpetuation of the notion that *certainty* is a required character of anything

---

4. Incidentally, the rise of modern natural science intensified and sharpened the sense of the opposition of the natural and the supernatural. Miraculous occurrences were such a familiar part of medieval culture as to blur the distinction of natural and supernatural.

claiming to be knowledge in its full sense: And this in spite of the fact that the actual practices which yield the most authentic forms of knowledge of the natural world are stated with a *probability* coefficient.

The fact that Descartes stands as the founder of the continental school of philosophy which is called "rationalistic" and the British school which is called "empiristic," and the large part played in modern philosophy by the controversy between the two schools, has led writers on the history of philosophy to pass over lightly the agreement between the two philosophers upon a matter more fundamental in the construction of modern philosophical theories of knowledge than the difference between them. The conflict between their systems is a civil war not a foreign one. We do not need to depend upon Locke's one statement that "The first books which gave him a relish for philosophical reading were those of Descartes."[5] The basic and controlling premise they held in common was that the problem of knowledge is, at its roots, the problem of determining the conditions for the attainment of certainty, certainty absolute because without any qualifying possibility of doubt.

In the case of Descartes, convincing evidence on this point is found in the fact that he professes to set forth from a state of universal doubting of everything in a search for something inherently indubitable. We have in addition a number of statements of the most explicit kind. As Archimedes only needed a fixed and immovable point to move the globe, so it might be enough for him if he could find "barely one thing that is certain and indubitable." And to one who objected to the unnecessarily round-about course he took to establish his own existence, replied that that "thought" was the only one of his activities of which he was wholly certain in the sense of metaphysical certitude. While it is like painting the lily to quote special passages to prove how completely Descartes equated knowledge and certainty, the influence of mathematics upon Descartes and upon the subsequent "rationalist" Continental school makes it pertinent to note that after saying that "only those objects engage our attention to the sure and indubitable knowledge of which our mental powers seem adequate" and that "science in its entirety is true and evident cognition," he lays down as a basic rule "our inquiries should be directed ... to what we can clearly and perspicuously behold (intuit) and with certainty deduce." *Intuition*, he goes on to state, is "the undoubting conception which an unclouded and attentive mind gives us so readily and clearly that we are wholly freed from doubt about what we understand," since "it springs from the light of reason alone." Given these simple first truths,

---

5. As reported by Lady Ascham, and printed in Le Clerc's *Eloge*. For Locke is at one with Descartes in identifying knowledge with certainty, so that the whole problem of philosophy as to the right or proper method of knowledge

science or certain knowledge is constructed through *deduction*, which "is necessary inference from other facts known with certainty."[6]

Locke's emphatic insistence upon observation, in distinction from the Cartesian emphasis upon "conception" or rational principles that were from the beginning "in" the mind or "innate" (for in this view they constitute or *are* the mind), was without doubt reinforced if not occasioned by the Newtonian science with its assertion that all scientific principles have to subjected to test and verification by events that are perceptible. But it is equally true that Descartes found support for *his* view from appreciation of the part played and to be played by mathematics. Descartes permitted a genuine appreciation of the role of mathematics to be completely governed by an inherited identification of knowledge in its scientific form with what is "necessary" and by an inheritance of the old idea that only "reason" can grasp the necessary. His doctrine was [governed] by an editing that converted *necessity* into absolute certainty. It was a mixture of new and old in which substitution of mathematics for the syllogism was the new element and retention of "reason" and necessity the old.

In an analogous fashion, the Lockean idea of the importance of observation was a genuine reflection of the new science. But the identification of knowledge with certainty led him to identify observation with what he called "experience," the latter consisting of "simple ideas," which were forced willy-nilly upon the mind from "without"; and which were therefore the necessary "materials" of knowledge. Being necessary, being what the mind could not help having, they were the only legitimate elements of knowledge as over against vain opinions formed "within" and hence lacking the warrant of coercion by the world of "real" things without. The existence of something *within* and something else *without* was the unquestioned assumption of Descartes and of Locke alike. They differed in that Descartes found the source and guaranty of certainty within while Locke found it without.

In spite of the extreme antithesis conventional interpretations have set up between Descartes and Locke, the theories of both are under the domination of a psychology of faculties or mental powers derived from ancient doctrines—a domination so complete that it precluded, for one as for the other, the construction of a straightforward theory of knowledge. The difference is that Descartes endowed these powers with a content of their own, while Locke held that the "powers" are empty and blank of themselves and

---

6. [Rules 2 and 3 in René Descartes, *Rules for the Direction of the Mind* (1628). The English quotation can be found in *The Philosophical Writings of Descartes*, vol. 1 (Cambridge University Press, 1985): 10, 13.

have to derive their material, as has just been said, from "without."[7] Hence his attack upon innate ideas, and hence his theory of simple ideas.

Striking evidence of the hold of earlier doctrines upon Locke is found in thoroughly eulogistic statements about reason. Descartes wrote that "good sense" (which he identified with the *lumae naturale* of reason) is the most widely distributed of all things, equal in all normal human beings and capable, *when directed by right method*, of discriminating infallibly (with certainty) what is true and what is false. But it was Locke who wrote, "Every man carries about with him a touchstone, if he will make use of it, to distinguish substantial gold from superficial glitterings, truth from appearances. This touchstone . . . is from natural reason."[8] And again he wrote, "Reason is natural revelation, whereby the eternal father of light and fountain of all knowledge, communicates to mankind that portion of truth he laid within the reach of their natural faculties."[9] In fact, in the popular sense of the word rationalist, Locke was more completely rationalistic than Descartes. For the latter excerpted "revealed" truths, while Locke held that doctrines purporting to come from on high must submit to judgment at the bar of reason. Moreover, Locke held that while natural knowledge is not capable of certainty, morals and mathematics are equally capable of attaining necessary and infallible truths since they are products of the "workmanship of the understanding." Ideas about the "outside" are "ectypes;" they have to conform to their "external" models. Moral and mathematical ideas are "archetypal." "Real things are no further concerned, or intended to be meant by mathematical propositions than as things really agree to those archetypes in mind."[10] And in the next paragraph Locke goes on to say that moral knowledge is capable of the same certainty as mathematical, since our moral ideas are also archetypal.[11]

---

7. The importance attached by Locke to "powers," within and without (an importance overlooked in most current interpretations) affords instructive evidence of the transitional condition held by science in his day. His theory, for example, of what he called secondary qualities is a theory of *powers* exercised by primary qualities. Only later were they transformed into "mental" phenomena. Locke's actual position is stated as follows: Just as the properties of Newtonian atoms, namely size, figure, solidity and motion are "generally allowed to be called powers," so colors, sounds, qualities of hot and of cold are in fact powers in things which so as "to comply with the common way of speaking I call qualities, but for distinction secondary qualities." [*Essay Concerning Human Understanding* (1690), bk. 2, ch. 8, sec. 10.]

8. [John Locke, *Of the Conduct of the Understanding* (1706), sec. 3.]

9. [Locke, *Essay*, bk. 4, ch. 19, sec. 4]

10. [Ibid., bk. 4, ch. 4, sec. 6.]

11. It would be a great mistake to infer from the fact that Descartes and Locke are sixteenth-seventeenth century authors, that identification of knowledge with certainty has now ceased to exert influence upon the "problem" and theory of knowledge. It would be easy to cite passages from contemporaries of philosophical repute holding that mathematics is the only subject deserving the name of science, because it alone deals with subject matter and "objects" that

The identification of knowledge with certainty runs through his entire *Essay Concerning the Human Understanding.* I quote one typical passage. "Sometimes the mind perceives the agreement or disagreement of two ideas immediately by themselves, without the intervention of any other . . . In this the mind is at no pains of proving or examining but perceives the truth, as the eye doth light, only being directed towards it. . . . This kind of knowledge is the clearest and most certain that human frailty is capable of. This part of knowledge is irresistible, and, like bright sunshine, forces itself immediately to be perceived as soon as ever the mind turns its view that way; and leaves no room for hesitation, doubt, or examination . . . it is upon this intuition that depends all the certainty and evidence of all our knowledge. . . . This intuition is necessary in all of the connection of the intermediate ideas, without which we cannot attain knowledge and certainty."[12] And in view of Descartes' insistence upon the view that the only certainty we can *directly* attain (hence that upon which all knowledge of the "external" world depends) is furnished by our thoughts within so far as they proceed from thinking itself without any contribution from without, it is interesting to note that Locke is in agreement, as far as *general* knowledge is concerned. In his own words "For all general knowledge lies only in our own thoughts, and consists barely in the contemplation of our own abstract ideas."[13]

The Cartesian emphasis upon the necessity of beginning with "simple" ideas, since they alone are so clear and distinct as to be free from the possibility of doubt, is manifest in the following statement of Locke's: "There is nothing can be plainer to a man than the clear and distinct perception he has of those simply ideas which, being each in itself compounded, contains in itself nothing but one uniform appearance or conception in the mind and is not distinguishable into different ideas."[14] In the total story of modern philosophy, this element of agreement is more important than the difference between them as to the source of ideas so simple as to be indubitable foundations, important as was this latter split within the mainstream.

The preconception that a theory of knowledge must be framed on the foundation provided by *first truths* as premises is so closely bound up with identification of knowledge with that which cannot be doubted as to be a part or aspect of the latter doctrine.

---

are inherently their own nature. And a favorite topic of discussion among those who regard themselves as positivists and officially antimetaphysical is the "problem" of the justification for *induction*. The underlying assumption is that it *ought* to be a variety of *deduction*, since only the latter reaches necessary conclusions!

12. [Locke, *Essay,* bk. 4, ch. 2, sec. 1.]

13. [Ibid., bk. 4, ch, 6, sec. 13.]

14. [Ibid., bk. 2, ch, 2, sec. 1.]

. . .

The managers of institutions, political, ecclesiastic, industrial, make a business of express formulation and teaching of an attitude which has its roots in the desire of human beings for security, for something unshakeable to fall back upon. Widespread popular acceptance of the idea is the source of a large part of their "authority." What is *back* of us is backing, support or authorization. Myths of the Garden of Eden, the Golden Age and the quasi-mythical notion of the Good Old Times are evidences of the human propensity to attach superiority to what is supposed to come first. Most "reform" movements have justified themselves on the round that they are merely striving to recover an earlier and purer state of things by stripping away accretions that later grew up, and have corrupted the original pure state. Philosophical formulations of the inherent priority in rank and in claims for recognition of something supposed to be "first" proceed from a pretty deep-seated human attitude; one, moreover, which has been exploited, cashed in upon and confirmed by ruling powers that wished to have the added power that comes from belief in legitimate authority. Just as one meaning of "natural" is that which is familiar and customary, so another meaning (embedded in the word itself) is that which is native, innate, and the road from this signification to the natural and the "normal" and from the norm to the normative, the regulative, is an easy one to travel. The upholders of a laissez-faire economic regime in the appeal to natural laws, that of "supply and demand" for example, had their course made ready for them by theologians and by philosophers who repeated their doctrines stripped of supernatural reference.

In fact, belief in the supremacy of first principles so abounds at the present time that what I have just been saying will seem to many to be expatiating upon the obvious. There is, however, a reason why I have given so many sentences to this point. It provides a striking example of the extent to which the instruction that is derivable from present day science is governed, even nullified, by beliefs formed in pre-scientific conditions. For if one derives his theory of knowledge from facts obtained by observation of the conduct of actual knowing—and of course if not actual it is not observable—one does not find a trace of support for the identification of knowledge with certainty nor yet for the doctrine of the primacy of "first" principles.

Mathematicians have been led to abandon the doctrine that axioms and definitions are "self-evident truths." They have been led to this abandonment by the development of mathematics, not as a result from any outside dogma. Postulates have taken the place of old-fashioned axioms—as far as scientific standing is concerned. And the import and validity of postulates is decided by what *follows* from them, in other words, by that which in comparison is *last*. If this is true in the case of mathematics, we can anticipate what we shall find when we turn to physical knowledge. What Locke significantly, if unwittingly, called the "pains of examining" everywhere rules. What comes at the close of an investigation has a better standing as knowledge than that which was available when the inquiry began. Although what counts at the beginning of a given inquiry has a certain priority, which is not merely chronological, yet in connection with the continuum of inquiry, it has a terminal position in reference to previous scientific investigations. And, moreover, it is subject to confirmation and to revision in the course of the very inquiry over which it exerts regulative capacity. The very word *hypothesis* has changed its signification because of the development of science. In Descartes, Spinoza, Leibniz (as has recently been pointed out) it retains the Platonic sense. It is a truth which stands under other truths and which supports them. The latter are secondary because derived. They are primary because known directly by intellectual intuition. In the actual conduct of natural knowing, an hypothesis is as indispensable as it was in the old teaching. But it is a *working* principle to guide observation and experiment, and it is tested, confirmed, overthrown, modified, by the conclusions reached in the inquiries in which it functions. The subject-matter to which the name *data* is given have also to be searched for with pains. What appears to be such at the beginning, or to be "given" outright at the outset, is known to contain much that in fact is not fit to serve save as raw material, requiring it to be experimentally analyzed and more or less transformed and to be measured before it enters the scientific picture.

There is no fact more convincingly testified to by the history of science than that acceptance of first principles as fixed truths to which all derived ideas must confirm has operated as a clog and obstacle. There are many philosophers and theologians who still argue for the necessity of some higher form of knowledge just because of the absence of that which is inherently indubitable within the field of scientific knowledge—even though among themselves there is an unfortunate lack of agreement and mutual certainty as to just *what* truths constitute this higher knowledge based on first and ultimate "principles." In view of the contrast between progressive attainment of agreement and of conclusions settled enough (if not absolutely certain) to [go] ahead upon with increased agreement and increase[d] future operating capital in science and the enduring unsettlement and controversy in the field of "higher" knowledge, there is something ironical in the attacks that are made upon natural science for its absence of pretension to final certainties. It would seem to be more advantageous to possess a method self-rectifying in use than to own "absolute" truths that not only get in the way of fruitful inquiry but that are denied by some schools with the same dogmatic fervor they are asserted by others. In spite of the fact that a theory of knowledge based upon the actual practice or conduct of knowing would hold that knowledge is a going concern in which conclusions are much more important than premises (since they determined the premises of subsequent inquiries) and *last* things in the sense of consequences, outcomes of inquiry, more important than first, as far as philosophical formulations are concerned we are hardly as yet even wandering between two worlds. With comparatively few exceptions we are still living in the old world. In morals, in particular, the belief still prevails that the sole alternative to anarchy and chaos is acceptance of standards and rules given at the beginning.

Because of his insistence upon the view that in morals all ideas and judgments must be tested by consequences, the fact that John Stuart Mill retained the old view in his general theory of knowledge is the more striking evidence of the grip maintained by the old theory—a case even more striking because of the sincerity with which he believed himself to be thoroughly empirical. He writes in his *Logic* about one hundred years ago as follows: "Truths are known to us in two ways; some are known directly and of themselves; some through the medium of other truths. The former are the subject of Intuition, or Consciousness; the latter of inference. The truths known by Intuition are the original premises from which all others are inferred. Our assent to the conclusion being grounded on the truth of the premises, we could never arrive at any knowledge by reasoning, unless something could be known antecedently to all reasoning."[15] Probably the most interesting thing about this passage is that Mill makes no attempt to justify it; it was the common doctrine of all schools and could be taken for granted. Differences of a serious kind existed, and Mill stood on one ground, that which he supposed was "empirical." But the differences did not have to do with the necessity for truths "known directly and of themselves." It concerned the question whether they came from reason or from sense-perception. Mill's account of the task he set himself in his *Logic* is in line with the passage just quoted as far as identification of knowledge and certainty is concerned. He regarded "inductive logic" as the theory of methods employed in the sciences and of it he wrote, "The business of inductive logic is to provide rules and models (such as the syllogism and its rules are for ratiocination) to which if inductive arguments conform, these arguments are conclusive, and not otherwise." And later, when claiming that the rules or canons of

---

15. There is a technical definition of reasoning according to which the last sentence is strict tautology. But Mill uses "ratiocination" not *reasoning* in that connection. The latter word he uses as synonymous with inference and with everything he calls "induction." [See J. S. Mill, *A System of Logic, Ratiocinative and Inductive* (1843), vol. 1, sec. 4, introduction.]

"induction" are concerned with *proof*, he speaks of "the need for a test for induction, similar to the syllogistic test for ratiocination."[16]

As I have remarked, the *Logic* was written almost one hundred years ago. It might be thought, then, that the type of doctrine he presents moved far into the background since that time. But its basic idea still flourishes in a multitude of forms although it may be stated from a different angle. For example, as "modern" a writer as Bertrand Russell has argued that [blank space] is not possible without *a priori* principles which are taken to be true "directly and of themselves." The idea that principles which have a certain regulatory effect upon inquiry and inference present conclusions derived from past inquiry, and are tested and better in the consequences resulting from further inquiries, seems to him to evince a regrettable indifference to truth.[17]

A closely allied admixture of the old and the new is found in the notion which has general currency about the meaning of law in science. I do not refer to anything as crass as the idea that "laws" *govern* phenomena, although that notion still has considerable popular following.

Indeed, it undoubtedly served a transitional purpose at one time. Then forms and essences were expelled as occult and laws took the place they had held; a certain fusion of the Stoic Law of Nature and the Christian idea of a Creator who ruled nature by the inherently universal principles of Reason helped protect the representatives of the new science from even more intense charges of impiety. "Nature" and its laws operated a while as Vice Regent for the Divine Being who was ceasing to engage as directly and miraculously in the course of events as had been done earlier.

But what I have in mind here is the projection into the idea of law of the old idea of the universal and the necessary as inherent marks of anything that deserves to be called science. In the actual conduct of science as that [which] is an observable affair, a law is a formulation of *general* fact—general in two respects. One of them is the range of the fact as an extensive system of spatial-temporal connections. The other sense of general as applied to fact is regularity of recurrence under stated conditions capable of pretty

---

16. [Ibid., vol. 1, ch. 9, fn 85 and sec. 6.]

17. Incidentally, it may be remarked that his special ground for asserting the necessity for truths intuitively known is an idea about experience which is another case of injection of ideas that arose when modern science was in its infancy. Experience is undoubtedly an ambiguous word. But the only ground upon which it can be defined, as Mr. Russell has defined [it], is uncritical acceptance of a seventeenth century [definition], which is none the worse merely because it [was] stated in that century, but which needs criticism because it was formed by a strange amalgam of Newtonian physical ideas with ideas about the "mind" as the organ of knowing inherited from medieval theological philosophy.

exact specification. That some subject matters are inherently necessary and others are only contingent and that only the former are fit and proper for scientific knowledge is not a doctrine that commends itself today to scientific men when they are engaged in pursuit of their special occupation. It is the common postulate that all events are capable of being formulated in scientific terms, though practical obstacles stand in the way of achieving this formulation in many cases. When an event is discovered that is an exception to a regularity which had previously been taken as a law, it is no longer regarded as out of the domain of scientific knowledge. It is welcomed as an occasion for further inquiries which will extend and refine formulations previously made.

But it is an old story that there is often divergence between speech-behavior and other kinds of behavior. Scientific men as well as professed philosophers often talk in a way that continues the ancient tradition of assigning a higher status to law than to fact. Examination of reports upon the nature of science in general will bear out the following statement: "The scientific rationalist . . . is firmly convinced that he is antimetaphysical. He sets 'fact' and not principles at the beginning. But it is a historical fact that in all metaphysics principles have been able to fulfill their assigned role only by being *at once homogeneous with facts and superior to them in dignity*."[18] And he has no difficulty in showing how professed non-metaphysical writers have adopted this anomalous position. The idea that laws "rule" facts may be abandoned. But it persists in the belief that laws are *above* and *over* facts at least in the matter of dignity. In general, the attenuated form of the old view of entities which are necessary and universal in virtue of their essential nature, is that they regard what they have found out as a pre-existent *unity*, when actually (as far, that is, as the work of science is concerned) it represents a *unification* which has been accomplished, not different, with respect to a deliberately effected unification, from that found in a well-constructed work of literary art—though very different in intent and subject matter.

One of the most striking cases of confusion resulting from admixture of old and new is found in the matter already mentioned in another context: the substitution in science of connection of changes for the immutable—of events for "substances." Everything considered, it is not surprising that for a long time substitution was a half-hearted affair. Newton's minute "bodies" or particles of matter might be in constant motion but they had the properties traditionally assigned to substances. They were ultimate and indivisible and as far as their structural properties were concerned they were as fixed

18. Georgio de Santillana, "The Development of Rationalism and Empiricism," *International Encyclopedia of Unified Science*, vol. 2, no. 8, p. 43. Italics not in original text.

as was an Aristotelian substance. Our imagination was so imbued with his view that even now the contrary view which is accepted in every competent mathematical formulation offers almost insuperable obstacles to naturalization in ordinary ways of looking at things.

An enduring illustration is found in what occurred in the case of the doctrine of "evolution" and development. In its face it is a doctrine about changes and of continual change. But it has been a common notion that no theory of growth had a scientific standing unless it could be shown that the series of changes constituting it were held in strict subjection to and over-ruling of "law"—which was fixed as every reputable law must be. The idea of evolution came into "modern" philosophy by a metaphysical route to solve a metaphysical problem. To Leibniz, evolution is an unfolding from within of what is already there in a wrapped up form or an "involved" state. It is accordingly opposite to changes effected from without; the latter accordingly lack the serial properties which are characteristic of the changes of living forms. Many features of the doctrine of Leibniz have dropped out by the wayside. But in popular opinion "evolution" is still thought of as occurring from one fixed point to another fixed point. For a time, interpretation of changes in terms of "evolution" was thought to guarantee, under the title of *progress*, their general inherently positive value, as in the earlier doctrine change was identified with deterioration save as kept within bounds that are fixed. Karl Marx, Auguste Comte, Herbert Spencer (and the anthropologist, Morgan) have little in common in their special doctrines. But they agree with one another and with the ancient teaching in one fundamental respect. They do not believe that the series of changes to which the name "development" or "evolution" is given is capable of scientific treatment unless there is either a series of fixed uniform changes or else some general "law" regulating the order in which changes occur.

Belief in a kind of superiority in what is taken to come first has even invaded, under the interpretation given as "genetic method," the treatment of history. Existing customs and institutions have been supposed to be explained when they are carried back in time until they can be traced to some aboriginal state of affairs. This procedure repeats, in reverse, the course taken by those who took fixed ends to be the measure of the "reality" knowledge was supposed to be in search of. Both doctrines overlook the fact that *first, last, intermediate, original* and *final* are words that have no meaning save in reference to a stretch of spatial-temporal events, which is selected and demarcated as subject matter of a particular inquiry. When "origins" are given absolute or detached status, we may be sure, no matter what the display of scientific techniques, of a confusing, mystifying projection of an old standpoint into what purports to be scientific in the modern sense.

The foregoing illustrations are largely taken from material which is technically philosophical. In so far they are more important as symptomatic registration of general conditions than for their own direct effect. Before speaking of the definitely non-technical human aspects of our cultural estate as one of "an immense body of institutions, accredited dogmas, customs and rules" which are out of accord with the conditions of our actual life, I shall mention one instance of borderline quality. "Causation" is a theme that is the subject of long-continued examination in philosophical literature. But it also enters into popular judgment of every aspect of our behavior—legal, moral, political, economic. Popular ideas about freedom and accountability are tied up with it. In the domain of religious beliefs, it is enough to refer to The First Cause. Now in spite of philosophical criticisms of the identification of causation with the action of some specified "force" and continued attempts to state it as a connection of serially ordered events, the idea of the primacy in the sense of superiority, of "cause" in contrast to what "effect" stands for, is the prevailing idea. For example, the considerations embodied in the title Darwin gave one of his books, *The Descent of Man*, aroused an intense antagonism just because giving chronological priority to some "lower" form of life has seemed to many people to be in effect a denial of the "reality" of all traits which are distinctly human—a reduction of them to the level of "reality" of say the anthropoid apes, which by the same logic are then reduced to the level of the properties found in the primeval slime. And in a case that presents the attitude just mentioned in a generalized form, we find bitter hostility to any form of philosophic naturalism, even on the part of those who nominally disavow acceptance of supernaturalism, which is based upon the notion that naturalism automatically, *ipso facto* so to say, reduces the *humanly* natural to whatever the opponent happens to regard as occupying the "lowest" and most contemptible place in the natural world. This procedure is so lacking in sense of and for fact that it testifies to the grip of a pre-scientific view—a grip, in many cases, which has not been loosened by undergoing the discipline of philosophic study. And examination will disclose the existence of an entire class of professed moralists who make a habitual practice of denying the validity of the values presented by ordinary affairs until they have been referred to a "higher" source or authorship quite aside to the events the values in question directly qualify.

These last sentences may be used to introduce discussion of the attitude and method that still is in command of inquiry into events having a marked social-moral quality. I have already remarked upon the prevalence of the habit of falling back upon some immanent, inherent, or intrinsic nature or essence when it is a question of describing, analyzing, or "explaining" events designated *moral*. In the case of affairs that have come, to a reasonable degree, under the jurisdiction of scientific method, it is widely recognized that this mode of treatment consists of saying the same thing over twice, first in a particular concrete form and then in a vaguely general form, and taking the loose general statement as the ground that accounts for the actual fact. Not so in moral judgments and theories.

For example, men are taken to do what they do because they are "bad," while the conduct of others is accounted for on the ground of their inherently virtuous natures. It is probable that the particular hypostatization that bears the name of "sin" and "man's sinful nature" does not now have the "explanatory efficacy" once attributed to it. But the old idea of an inherent depravity has been contemporaneously revived in a more refined garb as an explanation of the troubled state of the world, pointing by a reverse stroke to the only possible exit from social ills. And [during] a time of tragic stress, the idea uses a response that gives it new vitality: a fact which throws considerable light upon the states of affairs in the middle ages when the idea held general sway—and this in spite of the chorus of voices now singing of the idyllic character of the medieval period.

If it is objected that the illustrations I have given are so crude as not to be typical of the now widely taken attitude toward the method of dealing with socio-moral affairs, I would reply that their very crassness makes the more conspicuous reduplication of an event into a vague shadow or ghost of itself which is then employed to "explain" the event having actual body. A more refined example, and what should be a more convincing one, is supplied by the response that is awakened to the suggestion that events in the moral field be treated by a method analogous (making allowance of course in detail for modifications methods always undergo in adaptation to special subject matters) to that in accepted use in the physical field: Namely, inquiry into conditions and consequences, or, stating the matter with more accuracy, determination of the extensive temporal-spatial event of which the deed or character in question is a short-span component. For if there is anything made evident by the operations which constitute inquiry in the physical field, it is that what is directly accessible is so fragmentary that patient search (equipped with instrumentalities of art to supplement eye, touch, ear) is imperatively demanded to arrive at an event that will stand up as such throughout continued inquiry.[19] Nonetheless, any attempt to employ this type of method in the case of moral inquiry is very generally condemned as a

19. It seems to me very likely that in a time when there was neither the material nor the mathematical equipment that is required in order to carry on this kind of search and to report its results, a feeling for the need was back of the distinction that was made between the "real" and the "apparent."

denial of what is morally distinctive and significant and an attempt [is made] to replace it by something of a different order. If we contrast the distance that lies between a formulation of, say, light in mathematical physics and the words that have to be used to describe the light by which we see when we read and move about with what happens when an attempt is made in dealing with moral phenomena (and to a great extent the same is true with respect to psychological phenomena), to move even a short span away, we may begin to appreciate how completely (or almost completely) the attitude taken in understanding the former is still under the control of habits formed in the pre-scientific era. It is not even a question of moving directly into the use of a method that is scientific in its broad sense. It took centuries to naturalize even to the present degree, the new method in physical matters, and it will take much longer to effect a reasonable degree of naturalization in dealing with events classed in the moral category. The point I am here making concerns a much more modest affair: the possibility of obtaining a moderately impartial hearing for the possibility and desirability of movement in the direction indicated.

If we leave the domain of social theory and enter that of overt social practice we shall find much more extensive and convincing evidence in respect to the point that [we are] making. In fact, it is so abundant that it would take more than a paragraph or two, more than a chapter of a single volume to rehearse it. I content myself at this place with mention of one case: Our accustomed and pretty well established methods of punishment, and, more generally, our usual attitude toward criminality. For it is a blend of sentimentality, of desire to get "bad" men out of sight so as to forget them as far as possible, and of a revengeful disposition dressed out as "retributive justice"—with here and there a genuine effort to study generating conditions and the consequences of this and that method of penalization—in short, to take the longer and wider view which is the heart of what bears the name "science."

The human aspect of wandering not so much *between* two worlds as *in* two worlds, taking our direction now from a chart of *that* world and now from a chart of this one, is reflected in philosophy rather than caused by the latter. Modern philosophies are more significant as an exposition of symptoms than as a diagnosis or prognosis. Nonetheless, while the admixture of new and old of which modern systems are composed plays a part in perpetuating the old, it would not be modern in even a noteworthy chronological sense unless it also pointed up and sharpened our sensitivity of response to what is new. I recur to the statement quoted at the beginning of this chapter. "The awakening of this sense namely, the sense of the discord between an immense body of inherited institutions and attitudes and the needs that arise out of the new condition and needs of life—is the awakening of the modern spirit" —its awakening, not its achievement, its mature manifestation, nor even its confident movement in a world whose roads direct its forward steps.[20] As far as there is admitted truth in the words of Matthew Arnold, it would be un- reasonable to expect our philosophies to be far in advance of the times which produce them. That philosophies from the time of Bacon and Descartes to the present have done much to awaken and spread the sense that defines the modern spirit is charged against them by the intellectual representatives and apologists of the old order. Eliminate from the accusation the implication of a heretical falling off, due to willful and sinful pride, and the charge brings with it an element of positive accrediting. But a processing of awakening has being awake for its goal. If the goal is not reached when sufficient time has elapsed, there is reason to doubt the genuineness of the arousal.

II

The problem of knowledge in its widest and deepest sense is a moral prob- lem, understanding by "moral" the question of human values as far as they are capable of being forwarded and expanded, retarded and frustrated, by deliberate human conduct.[21] The philosophic problem of knowledge thus concerns the place and function of what is known (or is supposed to be known at a given time) in a given social order—including the problem both of its function as it operates at the time and potential values which critical examination of the existing situation in knowledge it might sustain were certain social changes to be made. This statement is probably too general. For the most part, needed enlargement and illustration will come in the course of further discussion. But we may be reasonably sure in [illeg.] the question of what knowledge does and does not do in society is in any case a question of how it interacts with the other main interests that actuate a given social order: namely, the arts, fine and technological, law and government, industry and the economical phase of social life, the [illeg.] daily intercourse and intercommunications that [illeg.] the current religious beliefs.

The idea as to the philosophical problem of knowledge which has been just set forth is anything but the one that is usually presented. Yet the fact is not inconsistent with the view just presented. For the question of this difference of the place and the work of knowledge in a given social culture faces two ways. It concerns what a given community esteems in the way of

---

20. [Dewey has not repeated the Arnold quote from the beginning of this chapter, but only paraphrased it.]

21. [It will become clear to the reader that this section repeats many of the arguments from section I. The original manuscripts with their different emphases have not been blended together.]

knowledge and the order of value in which it prizes different modes or kinds of knowledge, this being [*illeg.*] the relative amounts of energy it expends in securing one of them, the methods it employs in acquiring and distributing knowledge. If, for example, a given socio-cultural order believes that reason, as a special and transcendent faculty, is the source of the knowledge that is supreme in value, the theory of knowledge it generates and supports will be different from that of a society which, like that of the European Middle Ages, holds that the highest and most indispensable knowledge is had only through supernatural revelation—and if there were a society in practice that held to experimental observation as the means of authentic knowledge, it would develop quite another view of the problem of knowledge and its proper solution.

These remarks are definitely applicable to the notion about the nature of the problem of knowledge which prevails at the present time in philosophical circles. It reflects and expresses the beliefs and attitudes that arose in the period when "science" as it is now carried on practically was in its infancy; when it formed such a radically new departure that its representatives were in constant conflict with the agencies which upheld what had been accepted as science for centuries and which exercises immense institutional authority. To the defects caused by the immature state of the new methods and results of science were added irrelevancies and exaggerations occasioned by the warfare it was obliged to wage in order to get a chance to live. The net result was that the problem of knowledge was formulated as the problem of the *possibility*, origin and nature of knowledge *in general, at large, ueberhaupt* as what will be called in what follows the *epistemological* problem, in which it was assumed that a solution had to be found for the possibility of knowledge *in general* before the conclusions reached in dealing with special matters by methods actually practiced by competent inquirers could be accepted as knowledge.

That the problem of knowledge, conceived and stated in such terms, took on a very different form from that which would now be reached if it were framed on the basis of careful examination of the best methods actually employed by competent and trained investigators in mathematics, astronomy, physics, chemistry, etc., and on the ground of conclusions reached and validated in these inquiries hardly requires argument for its support. It is a consideration which directly suggests that we can separate the broad and comprehensive social and moral problem from a problem which is necessarily included within although upon its face it is narrower and more technical: Namely, the problem of what is knowledge in terms of its claims and credentials as *knowledge*, a problem to be approached and dealt with in terms of the methods actually employed in reaching conclusions that are accepted because of the authenticated competency of the methods of inquiry and test employed in obtaining them. The immediate task of the next chapters is, accordingly, to point out the harmful heritage from the pre-scientific age (pre-scientific as judged from present practices accepted as scientific) which still affects serious discussions in the field of the philosophy of knowledge; to show the contrasting considerations that would form the content of a theory of knowledge framed on the ground of the present freed from the incubus of an outworn but still influential past, and then show the effect of this change upon a number of the fundamental special themes and issues of our present backward philosophy.

Those men who formulated the new views about knowledge and the way to attain it took over from the traditional and institutionally sanctioned doctrine, the belief that knowledge in its emphatic and highest form is identical with certainty. They not only did not dream of questioning the necessity for this assimilation, but assailed traditional methods on the ground that the certainty they yielded was but specious; they claimed for the methods they were presenting a vastly superior capacity for achieving results that could not be questioned. They would have put themselves out of the running before the race started if they had taken any other stand. Descartes and Locke are universally regarded as the initiators of the two most influential schools of the modern philosophical theory of knowledge. I begin this phase of my discussion then with showing that they both entertained the same idea of the basic problem of philosophy—namely, that it is the attainment of certainty, and that the difference between them, out of which grew the opposition of the so-called "rationalistic" and "empiricist" schools, was the division of opinion as to the way in which certainty could be attained.

It is significant that Descartes began both his *Rules for the Direction of Mind* and his *Discourse on the Method of Rightly Conducting the Reason and Seeking for Truth in the Sciences* by going through the form of doubting all that he had previously believed and what others currently accepted as truth in the sciences.

. . .

As over against mere opinion and conjecture, everything is open and aboveboard at every step of the way—from original simple elements up to the most complex system. It is no wonder "clear" and "distinct" are favorite words of Descartes.

Assimilation of the signification of the word *knowledge* to that of complete *certainty* is still so current that to many persons the substance of the foregoing will seem a matter of common sense, though they may differ as to definitions of intuition and deduction. While, however, Descartes took his cue from mathematics, especially geometry, he was far from taking mathematical principles as the basic premises of ultimate science—which in accord with tradition he held to be philosophy. For philosophy, that is for science in its most fundamental, comprehensive and assured form, that which remains unassailable by any doubt, even when one is skeptical about mathematical propositions is *Thought* (*cogitatio, pensee*) as manifestation of Mind. For doubting is a form of thought and though one doubt everything else he cannot doubt he is doubting. Hence his famous *Cogito, ergo sum*—an expression in which "*ergo*" does not have the force of inference from one to the other but signifies the direct, and hence indubitable identity of mind, thought and the self, since the very essence of the *ego*, of the self, is to *think*. Descartes says, "By thought (*cogitatio*) I understand all that of which we are conscious as operating within us." It includes, he goes on to say, imagination and feeling as well as intellect. *"Thought is a word that covers everything which exists within us in such a way that we are immediately conscious of it."*[22]

The idea that the one thing directly *known*, i.e., certain, is mental in nature made a complete break with the Greek-medieval tradition. It introduced such an entirely new note into philosophy that it is quite common to call Descartes the founder of modern philosophy. Since in physical science he followed Galileo in holding that its subject matter is properly definable only in terms of geometrical figures and motions which are alterations in purely spatial relations and figures, he may justly be regarded as the fountainhead of modern philosophy as far as the latter's preoccupation with the problem of the *possibility of knowledge* is concerned. For if a mental order of existence is all which is intuitively and hence certainly known, the problem of how there can be any passage from it to the physical order of existence, which is a radically different kind of Being, has to be faced. Descartes supposed that he could resolve this problem by means of a distinction between different kinds of thought, different acts and states of mind, this distinction being guaranteed by intuitive consciousness precisely because it was a difference in *thoughts*.

For some of these thoughts are manifestations of Pure Intellect or Reason—another belief taken over without critical examination from his established philosophical tradition. For to say that a thing resided in or proceeded from *pure* intellect signified that it was free from dependence upon and admixture with anything of an adventitious and foreign source. Hence *these* thoughts were intrinsically different from those they were affected by or were dependent upon any factor or condition external to mind itself. Thoughts of this kind Descartes called *conceptions*, while imaginations [and] sense-perceptions were affected by an alien element. Hence "the *sciences*

---

22. [René Descartes, "Reply to Objections II, Arguments Demonstrating the Existence of God and the Distinction between Soul and Body, Drawn Up in Geometrical Fashion" in *Meditations on First Philosophy* (1641), in vol. 2 of *Philosophical Writings*, 113; see note 6].

altogether are nothing but the human intelligence, which always remains one and the same, no matter what the variety of the subjects to which it directs itself," so that, as he says, "Nothing diverts us more from the truth than directing our efforts [of knowing] toward particular ends instead of turning them upon this single universal end."[23] The meat of the position is in the conclusion that the first thing to be known is the Intellect itself . . . since upon it depends the knowledge of all other things, and not reciprocally. And "As regards the power to conceive a truth, it appears to me that I have that power from no other source than my own nature."[24]

These sentences, especially the latter one, may be read, when they are taken out of their technical doctrinal context, as a magnificently sweeping expression of confidence in the human capacity to attain truth. It may be read with the significance it gains when it is put in opposition to trust in custom, external political and ecclesiastical authority, and to abject enslavement to all that attempts to keep human powers from active development of their own potentialities. Viewed in this aspect, the words are a striking mark of the revolt against the medieval heritage that was going on in so many aspects of human life. But in its technical doctrinal context, the statements are a re-affirmation of the sufficiency of rational intuition and deduction to attain truth without the aid of "experience" or any observation which involved the use of the senses or any other bodily organs.

All scientific truth, all truth not of a supernatural order, was inherent in the intellect. It was native, "innate." When a critic objected to calling "rational" truths *innate*, Descartes replied that all he meant by the term was that the thoughts, which were *conceptions*, were called innate because they proceeded solely from "a faculty of thinking which is within me." In reply to another objection, however, he goes even further, saying that *all* ideas, even those about material things and those in which the senses take part, are innate, being made by the mind's own thinking. For material things, including sense organs and brain, can "only transmit to mind occasions for forming ideas."[25]

What has been said does not cover, however, the entire solution which Descartes supplied to the problem of how knowledge can possibly cross the gulf that existed, according to him, between the only kind of Being that is capable of being directly known, namely the mental, and the physical or material

---

23. [Rule 1 from Descartes, *Rules,* in vol. 1 of *Philosophical Writings*; see note 6.]

24. [René Descartes, "Meditation III," in *Meditations on First Philosophy* (1641), in vol. 2 of *Philosophical Writings*; see note 6.]

25. The student of the history of philosophy will recall how the Cartesian theory of knowledge caused the "problem" of the relation of "mind and body" to become an inseparable part of the epistemological problem. [Possibly from "Comments on a Certain Broadsheet" (1647) in vol. 1 of *Philosophical Writings*, 304; see note 6.]

order of Being which is radically unlike. In fact his emphasis upon conceptions and perceptions as products or manifestations of mind is but an emphatic expression of that problem. Descartes pointed out that all mathematical principles (conceptions) have to do with measurable and proportionate "orders" or relations. Hence they have for their subject matter only [the] properties [of] figure, size, extent and solidity defined as three-dimensional form. He also was a pioneer in that phase of modern physics which substituted mathematical relationships for syllogistic ones as the sole material of intuition and deduction in physical science. Hence *the* problem of the philosophic theory of the possibility of physical science was the question how we can be certain that mathematical truths, which are products of the inherent constitution of mind, are applicable to a realm of Being which is wholly "external," since non-mental. The concern of Descartes to prove the existence of God has sometimes been said to have been the result of Descartes's desire not to get into trouble with the Church, the case of Galileo being sufficiently fresh in his mind to cause him to suppress publication of his main physical treatise. But in fact his concern with this proof grew directly and profoundly out of the general problem of getting over a mental order of Being to a physical one. For the consideration upon which his demonstration rested was that there is *one* idea (conception) which by its own inherent nature carries with it the fact of existence beyond the idea: namely, the conception of God. This instance of reference beyond itself he then employed as evidence of the possibility of the same kind of "external" reference in the case of mathematical conceptions, for the nature of God is such that it is impossible he should deceive us in a matter of such fundamental importance as the foundation upon which rests our knowledge of the natural world.

. . .

Locke holds that the only completely indubitable elements are those the mind receives from *without* and that it receives in such a coercive manner that mind cannot help taking them for just what they are. The difference is great. But here too the conflict is of the nature of civil warfare. For both proceed on the assumption that there are two orders of existence, one internal and mental, the other external and material, and that knowledge is some kind of a transaction between them. The difference between the two philosophers concerns the *direction* in which the transaction occurs, from within to without or the reverse.

Accordingly, Locke assails the doctrine of the innate with a vigor equal to that of Descartes in insisting upon it. The mind, he says, is originally a piece of blank paper void of all characters, and all the materials of reason and knowledge are received from without. Locke holds that any other view

abolishes checks and tests that should control the mind in reaching its beliefs. It encourages and sanctions the all too human tendency to take whatever beliefs the mind forms, no matter how extravagant, as true provided
they are congenial. Belief that some ideas are innate protects them from
all examination; hence, as Locke pointed out, the doctrine of innate ideas
appealed greatly to potentates of church and state who desire to support
the power they wielded with the moral authority that belonged to truths so
final that they could not be questioned.

To the process by which all materials of knowledge were received from
without, Locke gave the name "experience." In making "experience" the
ultimate test for the certainty of the materials which the powers of mind
elaborated into knowledge and judgments (Locke's name for beliefs that fell
short of knowledge or certainty but that were worthy of acceptance), he was
insisting, then, that in knowledge, as distinct from fancy, mere opinion, sheer
dogma, etc., the mind added nothing and took away nothing, but followed
faithfully the lead that the real world forced upon it. Because of the extent
to which later developments of the movement initiated by Locke have been
read back into Locke himself, it is necessary to add two further statements
to protect his idea of experience from misconception. One is that while
Locke insisted that all the *materials* of knowledge were given mind from "the
external world," the fact that mind was an empty chamber, a blank piece of
paper, was not meant to deprive it of actual *powers*. On the contrary, *power*
may be said to be the prime "category" of Locke with respect both to "external things" and the mind within. But although the powers were within,
there was no immediate or direct knowledge of them in that capacity. Their
operations had to affect the mind and leave impressions upon it exactly as
did the operations of the powers constituting external objects. In Locke's
own words, "The operations of our minds within us, *as it is employed about
the ideas it had got*, furnish the understanding with another set of ideas."[26]
Hence Locke called the source of our knowledge of the existence of "powers"
or faculties of perceiving, remembering, doubting, willing or reasoning *inner
sense*, as distinct from outer sense, since it was through the impressions by
the powers made on mind, that we know them. The other remark is that
the impressions made by outer and inner powers were not themselves ideas.
And this statement holds equally when the word "sensations" is substituted
for "impressions." In and of themselves they are *bodily*. They become ideas
and the materials of knowledge, only when the power (called perception by
Locke) is turned upon them. As he wrote, "Whatever alterations are made
in the body, if they reach not the mind; whatever impressions are made
on the outward parts, if they are not taken notice of within; there is no

26. [Locke, *Essay*, bk. 2, ch. 1, sec. 4.]

perception."[27] As truly as in the case of Descartes, the physical or bodily excitation is but an occasion. Operation of powers, external and internal, are necessary causal conditions of the existence of ideas as the material of knowledge. But Locke's ideas are *objects* of mind, not its *states*. And "experience" did not consist of ideas, much less of mental states. It was, to repeat, a name for the fact that all the materials of knowledge, even of the mind's knowledge of itself, were coercively supplied from without.

What stands out with respect to the theories of both of these men, traditionally the heads of the two most important schools of modern philosophical thought, is that both framed their accounts of knowledge on the basis of and in the terms of certain premises that were assumed to be necessary and that were supposed to condition knowledge in advance. Both believed in a relation between *inner* and *outer* (later more technically called "subjective" and "objective") that conditioned knowledge, and both supposed that knowing was carried on by a mind, intellect, understanding, which had peculiar possessions of its own. The fact that they and their followers, who regarded themselves as spokesmen for radically new departures in scientific methods and conclusions, thought of the problem of knowledge in terms of fixed antecedent assumptions to which the theory of knowledge had to be accommodated is the chief reason why modern philosophy represents such a confused union of elements which conflict with one another, being drawn as they were from antique traditions on one side and from a new movement that was still inchoate on the other.

Later we shall be compelled to touch upon a number of the unreal problems that depended upon the attempts to frame a theory of knowledge on the basis of assumptions that were incompatible with the procedures by which authentic knowledge was actually and progressively obtained. For the present, discussion is confined to the assumption that knowledge and indubitable certainty are so completely one that the basic problem of knowledge concerns attaining certainty as to what is certain. For while Descartes and Locke agreed in the assumption of their identity, it is more than ironically significant that what Descartes thought was most certain, certain inner and innate "conceptions," was to Locke more than doubtful since it was not totally devoid of proof but the source of infectious error, while Descartes, in advance, regarded the senses, upon which Locke relied for indubitable subject matter, as conditions which had so misled men that giving them any function whatever in knowledge had been the chief historic obstacle to development of sound scientific method!

I shall not stop here to argue that such complete disagreement in content within complete agreement in form is of itself strong indication of something

---

27. [Ibid., bk. 2, ch. 9, sec. 3.]

radically wrong in the premise. Turning abruptly to the actual practice of knowing as it is exemplified in the methods that determine present day science, we find that there is no claim to absolute certainty and infallibility for any conclusion while it is held that *probability*, which is the mark of every scientific conclusion, is capable of pretty definite measurement so that conclusions, reached by acknowledged methods, have that security which enables them to be acted upon with confidence that the result of acting upon them will be either to confirm them or to detect any error lurking in them—thereby in either case attaining a higher probability co-efficient. A phrase that is in common use, *practical* or *moral* certainty, describes the actual goal of scientific practice, over against the alleged inherent *theoretical* certainty of the traditional theory of knowledge. At the same time, the methods employed in the practice of knowing are such that they prevent hasty jumping in given cases to the belief that this goal has been completely attained in those cases.

Failure to distinguish between working security, which is a temporal and progressive matter, and theoretical certainty, which is absolute, non-temporal and fixed, is a very common ailment. The burden of the antique tradition is that without absolute, self-warranted certainty there is no firm anchorage anywhere but only endless, aimless drifting. Its influence is so great that many persons, even those who are not outwardly adherents of the old faith, will think that change from knowledge which is intrinsically certain in and of itself to knowledge which is of some order of *probability*, even though it be tempered and measured and of a kind to be self-correcting (instead of self-*evident*) is a change in the wrong direction. They will not see the humor in the remark of a clerical representative of the old philosophy who declaimed as to the terrible state we should be in if we had only the same assurance in morals that we have in physics and chemistry!

However, those who are not pre-committed will be willing to look at the matter in the context of what I called the inclusive and human philosophical problem of knowledge. When the matter is looked at in this context, it is clear that belief in the inherent absolute certainty of truths, a kind of certainty that places them outside of criticism or even examination, that confers upon them authoritative claim to impose themselves, is the very essence of dogmatism, the fortress in which every class, set or sect that desires to control the beliefs of others takes refuge. The assumption first presents itself in an innocent guise. It offers itself usually in the guise of the "axioms" of Euclidian geometry with the prestige that long attached to that subject as the very model of truly *scientific* knowledge. Then it is but a short step to the principle as a social and moral one.

At the time in which I am writing—the early forties, there is a definite organized attempt to lead men to believe that the basic source of the ills from which the world now suffers is the heretical departure of mankind from unquestioning credence in certain inherently certain truths. But when the terms in which the endeavor is formulated are subjected to examination, it is always found that the particular truths involved are those represented and presented by a particular historic institution. The plea that is being made is essentially a *political* one although it is offered as a metaphysical or "theological" principle which sets forth the fundamental precondition of all intellectual and moral stability.

There are determinate or specific causes for the many ills mankind is suffering from at present. In all matters in which use of scientific method is current, there is no attempt to "explain" events that take place by reference to general forces, say, electricity, heat, light. Events are described and accounted for in terms of their spatial-temporal connections with other events. "Principles," laws, are formulations of these connections as they are ascertained by means of repeated and carefully checked investigations. Were I to say that the confusion and conflict which is now so rife a feature of social life, domestic and international, is produced by the adherence of groups having great economic and political power to codes or principles which must be accepted without examination or qualification, I should come close to reverting to the pre-scientific belief in merely general forces and superior governing laws. But one is within the bounds of concrete observable fact when one points out (i) that different groups, classes, sects, etc., hold to and insist upon ultimate first principles of radically different tenors and tenets, and (ii) that assertion of their inherent and absolute truth stands brutally in the way of discussion, negotiation, compromise. The remaining alternative method is appeal to strife with victory to the stronger. The supposed conflict between truth on one side and willful error and ignorance on the other turns into a physical struggle.

In short, continued acceptance and assertion of the doctrine of first principles, true in themselves and hence the standards by reference to which all other claimants to truth must be measured *is a specific and concrete condition* contributing to production of the present scene of confusion and conflict *in so far* as it (i) promotes loyalty to ends and methods that are held, because of their own inherent nature, to be incapable of comparison, mutual adjustment and modification; and in so far as it (ii) prevents the use of the scientific method of search for other concrete causal conditions that have generated evils from which present society suffers and stands in the way of the corresponding search for concrete testable methods of overcoming these ills. If one examines the instances in which some progress has been verifiably made, whether in industrial technologies, in medicine, law, penology, psychiatry or whatever, one finds that the progress is uniformly marked by getting away from wholesale generalities through continual introduction of the method of ever finer and finer distinctions. In morals and politics, i.e., in the field of the more basic human relationships, adherence to the doctrine of truths that are inherently absolutely certain and that are the criteria by which all other beliefs are to be tested with respect to *their truth*, blocks the road to use of the method by which progress has been ensured in other fields. Instead of questions of more and less, we have issues generated because of stark irreconcilable opposition or contrariness.

What has just been said falls within the scope of what I have called the inclusive philosophical problem concerning what is known and the method of knowing the place occupied and the function exercised in the broad field of human interests. The identification of knowledge with certainty raises questions also within the included problem as to the nature of its knowledge in its own structure. The influence exerted by geometry upon Greek formulation of logical theory is well known. Geometry achieved scientific form when physics, chemistry and biology were hardly in their infancy; the propositions of Euclid still appear in school-texts with little change when statements made at the same period about physical matters would now be cited, if at all, only as examples of speculations that are almost grotesque. The model that geometry set for logic as the theory of knowledge was definite. Begin with a few simple definitions and self-evident truths and proceed by orderly steps that follow necessarily from what is given at the outset to more and more complex propositions until the entire field has been exhaustively covered. The net result as far as the general theory of knowledge is concerned was to establish the conclusions reached by the doctrine that inferential or mediating reason depend for acceptance as *true* upon principles or premises that were given complete and readymade at the outset. Association of the word *principle* with that which comes *first* is now blurred and vaporous. It was once intrinsic and necessary. That which was first in knowledge was primary and that which was primary was chief; it ruled every conclusion that had a claim upon belief as the *prince* ruled his subjects. First principles being first were not merely *at* the beginning but they constituted the very beginning of things and all else was secondary and derived.

. . .

[T]he attempt to locate the unquestionable (and for that reason the source and guarantor of all else claiming to be knowledge) in something that is *first* has influenced in a thoroughgoing way the entire allegedly "modern" theory of knowledge, as is made manifest in the assumption which is common to the views of both Descartes and Locke. For the conflict that exists between the two schools which took their origin from these two men concerns the nature of that which is first, conceptions provided from "within" or impressions made from "without." Unless they had agreed in the assumption that what is "first" is that from which all *knowledge reached through inquiries* depended for its certainty, and hence its right to be termed *knowledge*, there would not have been the conflict which has actually marked the course of the modern philosophic theory of knowledge.

Certain factors in the operations which constitute actual or working scientific procedure and which yield the conclusions that have scientific standing respectively were called "conceptions" and "sensations" (impressions). Their presence was acknowledged by the Cartesian and the Lockean schools alike. It was assumed by both schools that any sound theory of knowledge must be formulated in terms that were accommodated from the very start to views about "conceptions" and "sensations;" these viewers, moreover, not being derived from any observation of the operations by which knowledge was actually obtained but were nevertheless assumed to be conditions which antecedently determined the process of knowing.[28] The question of what meaning, if any, can be given these terms on the basis of observation of operations that yield tested authentic conclusions, is one which is best discussed in connection with that aspect of the historical theory of knowledge that constitutes the conflict of "rationalism" (so-called) with "empiricism" so-called. That aspect of modern philosophy is so important that it deserves a chapter of its own. What can be affirmed here is that the "rationalist" or Cartesian school never critically examined what it called "conceptions" as the first truths from which all else in the way of knowledge followed and that the "empiricist" or Lockeian school never subjected what it called sensations or impressions to any such investigation. The only topic discussed was which one had primacy, or firstness, and the account that was rendered of each, the description or definition which resulted, was determined by the answer given to the question of primacy. If "sensations" were first, conceptions were copies or compounds.[29] If "conceptions" were first, sensations were negligible and irrelevant as far as the problem of true knowledge is concerned, save as they tended by their "practical" urgency to distract [the] mind and thereby presented a formidable obstacle to adoption of the right method of knowing. They were, according at least to Descartes, of the nature of these bodily appetites which prevent, unless they are deliberately

---

28. In fact, they were of course an uncriticized inheritance from Greek-medieval metaphysics.

29. This statement does not hold unqualifiedly of Locke himself. According to him mathematical and moral "conceptions" were the "workmanship of the understanding," and had the status of *archetypes* that were standards by which actual existences could and in some cases should be judged.

kept in subjection, reason from accomplishing its proper work. And while the Aristotelian-medieval view was able by means of its doctrine of forms and of actualization of what was potential to treat sense-perception as an implicit carrier of rational forms and thereby subscribe, speciously, to the doctrine that there was nothing in the intellect that had not previously been in sense, the demonstration by modern physics that "forms" were occult and its substitution of "efficient" for final causes compelled modern "rationalist" thought to take an inherently disparaging view of sense-perception. For it placed the latter in inherent opposition and conflict with "conceptions" while in Greek-medieval doctrine, sense-perception was an enemy of rational intellect only when it tried to usurp the function of control.

The conflict which has been waged in modern philosophy between those who believed they spoke on behalf of truths ascertained and tested in experience and those who believed they upheld the claims of rationality against hostile and degrading forces, is an illustration of what was remarked earlier about the confusion engendered and the loss suffered because of acceptance of supposed inherently certain principles. For truths which claim acceptance because they are inherently indubitable cannot be subjected to the examination and criticism whose result might be removal of misunderstanding and promotion of cooperation where conflict had been the rule. Sheer contrariness and stark, undisguised warfare were bound to issue. Discussion is accordingly brought back to the effect exercised upon the course of modern philosophy by uncritical adoption of the ancient-medieval identification of knowledge and certainty in its contrast with the theory of knowledge that would be framed if the working procedures of science were employed as that which furnishes the material and the pattern for a theory of knowledge. There are many sciences in existence, from the A of Astronomy and Anthropology through the alphabet to the Z of Zoology. To my mind it is indisputable that if their methods and their conclusions, instead of preconceptions derived from Greek-medieval philosophy, had been used as the groundwork of a theory of knowledge, the latter would now have consistency and clearness instead of being a scene of interminable conflict.

Let us consider, for example, what would be the accepted doctrine in this case about first and primary material, whether in respect to "conceptions" or "perceptions" so called. There would be no controversy about the important place and office of general principles nor of the fact that they possess a certain firstness and a certain authority with respect to undertaking and carrying on new inquiries. For it would also be evident that these principles have the authority they possess because they are the tested outcome of long-continued previous inquiries. With respect to what has been done previously they occupy a last position; with respect to what is still taking place they are first. Neither statement tells the entire truth nor do both of them added together save as it is clearly recognized that knowledge is a *going concern* so that whatever is found out or known is so much working capital to be invested in further enterprises of knowledge. When the generalizations or principles that have resulted from previous knowings are frozen and are taken as having final intellectual authority, then the inertia of sheer custom has laid its heaving hand upon inquiry. Further discoveries are not absolutely stopped. But they are confined to routine paths until a courageous new departure opens up new fields. Even the most adequately rested and certified "first principles" have in actual scientific knowing something of the quality of *hypothesis* still clinging to them, and this fact instead of being something to complain or mourn about is in actual practice stimulus to ever-renewed knowing.

Moreover, in spite of appeal of "philosophers" (better versed in tradition than in science) to mathematics in support of their doctrine of fixed and certain first truths, the development of mathematics gives a flat contradiction to a doctrine which, after all, only reflected an early stage of that science. The definitions and axioms with which a mathematical discipline sets out are *postulates*, not truths. And mathematics has developed by encouraging the greatest possible freedom in institution of working postulates. As proof note how geometries, based upon modification of the Euclidian "axiom" of parallels, not only have unquestioned scientific standing but have immensely widened the field of mathematical inquiry.

There are also in every science such things as primary data or primary data of observation that have a certain privileged position with respect to the state of the science and the undertaking of further investigations. No one acquainted with the sciences of astronomy, physics or biology would think of assigning equal rank as far as scientific value is concerned to all facts even though they are all equally actual. Some facts have a crucial position; their importance is strategic rather than tactical. And some data are, so to speak, *harder* than other data. In the given state of inquiry, with resources available at the time, we cannot go beyond them. But exactly as is the case with accepted generalizations, one is almost tempted to say even more than is the case with the latter, the primacy of facts of this sort is temporal and functional. If one surveys the history of a science, the problem of determining what events are data and what are not has been its outstanding difficulty. Perhaps more mistakes that stood in the way of progress of a science have been due to taking as data matters that were not data with respect to the problem under investigation—although they might be "facts" in the general sense of being observed occurrences. Sectioning and ranking of factual data is a scientific achievement. When the operations which make the achievement possible are neglected, a subject remains such a backward state that it is called a science mostly by courtesy.

From the standpoint of a doctrine of knowledge built on the foundation of observation of science as a going concern, such considerations as the foregoing are themselves primary in respect to that theory. As far as I can see, the only recourse to those who wish to maintain the doctrine of first and ultimate truths in its traditional form of that which is absolutely the source of any truth that marks other beliefs, is to speak contemptuously of the vale of what they disparagingly called "special" sciences, including the methods by which conclusions are obtained and tested. Their "merely" probable character is contrasted with the affirmations of metaphysics or theology which are said to constitute true and ultimate science because they are "first principles" and therefore indubitably certain. Thus we are taken back to the philosophy of the pre-scientific epoch, and into the region of interminable controversy and conflict—interminable because there is no possibility of discovering common ground in the case of opposed principles each of which claims absolute truth in itself.[30]

There are still philosophers who are aware of the radical change that has taken place in mathematics and who nevertheless are so under the influence of the Greek-medieval tradition that they regard mathematics as the only subject matter worthy of the name science. They manifest an attitude of irritation and exasperation because the "inductive" operations of the natural sciences [must] be reduced to or converted into the necessary "deductive" operations of pure mathematics. But at the same time they hold, as with their premises they are logically forced to do, that this mathematical subject matter has nothing whatever to do with any thing that exists, that takes place in space and time. They point with pride to the "pure" character of the subject matter of mathematics—*pure* because not sullied in any way by the grossness which clings to everything that exists in space-time.[31] Yet upon examination, it is clear that all this circuitous flight away from the world in which we live and behave and in which happens everything that does happen is motivated by unwillingness to accept, in the form of a theoretical or a generalized doctrine, the fact that is exhibited in every phase of the practice of knowing: The fact, namely, that *consequences, outcomes,*

---

30. The gulf separating the pre-scientific and the scientific attitude is well illustrated in the reversal of signification that has occurred in the word *hypothesis*. Plato uses the word frequently. But in his case it has its literal etymological signification. It is that which "stands under" all other conclusions as the foundation and support of the structure of knowledge.

31. The aspect of the doctrine of an intrinsic difference in kind in the scientific ranking of "merely" probably natural knowledge and certain metaphysical knowledge which depends upon perpetuation of the Greek-medieval view of the morally low status of everything "material" and physical is discussed in a later chapter.

conclusions of inquiry have, with respect to trusted claim to truth, a rank and status incomparably superior to that possessed by antecedents, first and beginning materials. And, to return to one aspect of the inclusive human philosophical theory of knowledge, it is not seen that recognition of the superiority of consequences over antecedents is an enduring stimulus and inspiration to continued and continual search, while the effect of the other is to encourage lazy and dogmatic quiescence, since what is truly important is already in our possession, and further search and discoveries can yield at best only results of secondary and technical ("material") import.

III

Returning now to the historic survey. We find that the incompatibilities mentioned arose consequently from retention of medieval habits and dispositions, religion and morals, and in the method and conclusions of all subjects concerned with distinctively human life, and complete rejection of the medieval method in all matters concerned with the method and conclusion in all subjects concerned with the "natural" or physical world. In consequence, modern beliefs developed into much sharper dualisms than were characteristic of Greek philosophy and of medieval theoretical formulations—although not of medieval *practices* for the great mass, a fact that undoubtedly facilitated the development of the later sharply dualistic positions.[32] For classic philosophy formulated the distinction in terms of a hierarchical qualitative order in the scale of Being, in terms not of absolute divisions in kind. The Aristotelian technique for reaching this graded view of differences that were made absolute as a consequence of the revolution in natural science consisted of determinations on the basis of potentialities and actualities. Matter was the potentiality of which Mind was the actuality; the organic body as the potentiality of which soul (inherently a form of life and hence having the lower grade of vegetation and the higher grade of animal) was the actualized realization. This way of looking at, understanding and reporting the constitution of things was united with the view that the hen comes before the egg—that actuality is prior in order of things as well as in rank.

The scientific change (of which the names of Galileo and Newton are representative) was in effect if not openly an attack upon the cosmology

---

32. An example of what is involved in the last sentence of the text is that while for the small group of priests who were occupied with theological formulation, morals are based, in accord with classic Greek thought, upon reason (revelation being above reason but capable of rational formulation and justification), for all believers who of course were the great mass it was stated in terms of authoritative commandments of injunction and prohibition with sanctions of penalty and reward. If future life in another world of heaven and hell are taken into account, medieval theology was the author practically speaking of utilitarian ethics.

that was involved in the method and conclusions of Greek science, both as Greek and in its medieval version. It abandoned potentiality and actuality as working categories, substituting connections of things in space and time. It abandoned fixed *forms*, substituting up to practically the twentieth century, fixed laws expressing uniform relations in space and time. Except in the case of living things, it rejected the idea that science proceeded in terms of definition and classification resting upon fixity of species or kinds; and the work of Darwin and his followers in biology completed the repudiation in the case of living creatures including man. Continuity in processes of change became the accepted scientific alternative. It rejected qualitative diversity on behalf of differences that were scientifically stated as quantitative.[33]

But certain traits of the earlier philosophy were so deeply and pervasively embedded in everyday habits of life that (i) the old categories and method persisted in full force so as to decide the pattern of inquiry and belief in all moral and political subjects; that is to say, in all affairs and problems distinctively human, whether personal or collective. (2) Differences that had [been] treated as differences in grade of Being were converted, as has been already stated in terms of complete or absolute splits, of which the basic one was that between Man as Man and the Natural world. The basic interests and concerns of Man, humane and humanistic values in general were regarded as *extra*-natural, even when no longer openly viewed as *super*-natural, since nature and the natural were regarded as exclusively physical.

It is a commonplace of the history of philosophy that for centuries the problems that were regarded as typically philosophical were occupied with the search for solutions of dualisms of mind and matter, soul and body, subject and object, individual self as Ego and Social as some sort of connection with Others, the kind of connection being a basic "problem" of Moral and Political philosophy. They all sprang, in one way or another, with disturbances and shocks that expressed the result of the impact of the "natural science" upon established beliefs that were as deeply embedded in all other institutions as they were in language as the medium of communication and instruction. As has been already indicated, the "Warfare of Science with Religion" was but the most obvious and overt sign of the necessity for readjustments in all the different phases of human life and hence all phases of man's belief about himself and the world in which he lives.[34]

---

33. The nature of the change in physics in its significance for philosophers is discussed later [*illeg.*]. [Placement of footnote is unclear in original manuscript.]

34. I refer to my Gifford Lectures, published as *The Quest for Certainty* (NY 1929) especially Chs. II and III for a more detailed account of the nature of the conflict between the older "science" of Nature and the method and conclusions of accepted inquiries into natural events during and since the fifteenth century.

The net outcome of an historic survey is indicated in the title prefixed to this chapter: *Philosophy out of Gear.*[35] The needed readjustments as yet are arrested and inchoate. The main "problems" of modern philosophy have to be treated, if they are to be rendered intelligible, as formulations of failure to carry the application of the standpoint and methods proper to science—in its modern sense—all the way through. The most important affairs of life, those treated in the "social sciences" (or, better stated, in the inquiries and beliefs about the ends and means that are deeply involved in the traditions and institutions that the affairs of Man as Man) were formed prior to and hence apart from the rise of science as that is manifested in the physical science, the net result being that the *natural* world is regarded as physical or material in a sense that sharply marks off what is designated by those names from the human and moral. In consequence, we do not enjoy the benefits that would accrue from integrated organization of beliefs, either ancient or modern attitudes and dispositions.

---

35. [This is the only known time Dewey used this title. All other instances, including the latest outline, use the original title.]

VII. The Present Problem of Knowledge

I

On the surface the unity of modern philosophy is merely chronological. Systems are so diverse and conflicting, they breathe such a controversial air, that it looks to a casual observer as if about all they have in common is the centuries in which they appeared. If, however, one looks for unity in problems discussed rather than in the conclusions reached, one is more successful in the search. And underneath the common problem one finds common premises by which the problem was generated. The problem is the grounds, extent and limits, source and organs of Knowledge. The material of the common premises was supplied by one part of the factors that constitute the wandering between two worlds which has been mentioned. As the factors in question operated to set up the premises which made the problem of knowledge take the form it did take, they consisted of a union of belief-attitudes corresponding to the new natural science in its revolt against the classic-medieval cosmology with basic belief-attitudes that persisted actively in habits formed in the prescientific periods, habits that were incorporated in institutions clothed with high emotional values. Since the two components of the union determining the form taken by the problem of knowledge were in fact irrelevant, even opposed, to each other, there is no cause for surprise in the fact that the problem as stated led only to increasing confusion and the controversial diversity which marks the course of epistemological philosophy during recent centuries.

The most conspicuous feature of the philosophical writings of the sixteenth and seventeenth centuries is preoccupation with the question of the right method to be adopted in order to obtain dependable knowledge in a systematic and progressive way. In their positive aspect the new writings corresponded to the endeavors of the men who were engaged in creating a new cosmological science, beginning with astronomy. In their negative aspect, they were attacks upon the method of Aristotle—particularly in the degenerate state into which it had fallen in the later period of scholasticism but containing also a radical challenge to the entire account of the nature of knowledge and the method of attaining it given in actual fact by Aristotle himself.

The effective contribution by Francis Bacon to the advancement of the new science has often been exaggerated. But if his writings are looked at as a sign of the times, especially as to the growing discontent with traditional science and a sense of the necessity for a new and radical departure, it is hardly possible to overstate its significance. The antagonistic reference of his *Novum Organon* to Aristotle's account of knowledge and the method of science appears in its very title. In spite of the defects of the method he proposed—due largely to the fact that he did not break away from traditional doctrines as much in fact as in vehemence of assertion—his insistence that traditional science imposed human opinion, under the guise of logic, upon facts rather submitting it to fact, and his insistence that reversal of this attitude would result in human ability to command the powers of nature in a way that would usher in an era of invention and human progress was prophetic of the new science which even then was coming into existence.

A little later, Descartes contributed directly to promotion of the new science in his invention of analytic geometry. If his philosophical writings on method did not have the same good fortune to anything like the same extent, they certainly intensified the cultural ferment about method and stimulated scientific undertakings of a new type. The titles of his other writings testify to the preoccupation of the times with the problem of method. Aside from *Rules for the Direction of the Mind,* he wrote a tractate expressly on *Method.* Its full title is, accordingly, worth quoting. It reads, *"Discourse on the Method of rightly conducting the Reason and seeking Truth in the Sciences."* In addition to his *Essay on the Human Understanding,* which is in substance an account of the way in which knowledge comes naturally into existence and accordingly an account of the way in which it should be sought, Locke wrote a tractate on *The Conduct of the Understanding.* Spinoza supplemented his *Ethics,* which is a treatise on the source and worth of different kinds of knowledge, with an essay called *The Improvement of the Understanding.*

When the dates of these writings are compared with those of the men whose labors brought about the actual revolution which occurred in natural philosophy, something other than mere chronological coincidence is apparent. But what should also be evident is that the philosophical writers did not base their theories of knowledge upon an analysis of the way in which men of science proceeded in reaching their conclusions, but upon consideration derived from a very different source. They were of such an entirely different order that they finally led to formulation of *the* problem of knowledge in the following terms: How is knowledge possible anyway?

In other words, the more methods of obtaining scientific knowledge were perfected and the more the store of such knowledge was extended and refined, the more puzzling, philosophically, did it become that there could be any such thing anyway.

Volumes would not and could not prove more convincingly that the philosophical formulation and attempted solutions of issues arising in connection with knowledge were conducted on the basis of considerations that were wholly irrelevant to the consideration that governed the men who were carrying on the inquiries which yielded knowledge in actuality. More specifically, they proceeded on the basis of certain conditions prior to and independent of attainment of knowledge which had to be met and fulfilled before anything which was found out was entitled to be called knowledge. There is not a single philosophical discussion of the philosophical theory of knowledge during this entire period that even mentions the fact that those who wrote on the subject based their writings on the assumption that they were already in possession of knowledge which was absolutely certain: Namely, of the conditions outside of knowledge in the concrete which had to be satisfied in order that we might [ac]knowledge that the latter was knowledge in fact and truth.

The explanation of such an anomalous situation is found of course in historical considerations which were much more deeply and firmly rooted than were the specific conclusions and methods of the new science in the period in which it was still struggling for existence. It is instructive that even Newton's classic work bore the title *Mathematical Principles of Natural Philosophy*. The word *Physics* as the regularly accepted name for systematic knowledge of the natural world is hardly more than a generation old. In short, not only philosophers concerned with the general theory of knowledge but scientific inquirers themselves accepted till recently, at least in name, the classic view that philosophy is divided into three branches, Natural, Moral and Metaphysical.

Because of religious and theological influences, the theories of Greek philosophers about the soul, mind, spirit, intellect, sense and reason, had ceased to be just philosophical doctrines. They had become articles of popular belief whose hold with the populace, including the larger part of the clergy, was emotional and practical, institutional rather than intellectual, in quality. For such socio-cultural historical causes as these the philosophical theories of knowledge were constructed in terms of mind and its organs rather than in terms of methods observably employed in attaining what was known. I doubt if in the seventeenth, eighteenth and the greater part of the nineteenth centuries, it would not have seemed irrational to the point of absurdity to say that the treatment [ought] to be reversed and that views entertained about mind and about ways or "organs" of knowing had to be formulated in terms of what was actually known in the various branches of science, including the anthropological and cultural.

The following sentence was written by John Locke, but the point of view which controls it was the one that was commonly accepted in philosophy. "I thought the first step toward satisfying several inquiries the mind of man was very apt to run into, was to take a survey of our understanding, examine our own powers, and see to what things they were adapted."[1] And the sentence occurs in connection with a statement to the effect that it "was necessary to examine our own abilities and see what objects our understandings were or were not fitted to deal with."[2] The familiar fact that British philosophy is classified as "empirical," that it held that observation by means of the senses is the organ of agency that was intrinsically or "naturally" *fitted* to yield knowledge, while Continental philosophers put their trust in a faculty of reason, accounts for much of the controversial quality of modern philosophy. But even more important is the light it throws upon a contemporary extraneous historical and "social" generative cause of the philosophical version of the problem of knowledge: Extraneous and irrelevant, that is, to the actual practice and results of scientific knowing. I refer to the predominantly practical character of British philosophy in contrast with the general disavowal of anything but a theoretical and speculative intent or bearing on the part of Continental philosophers.

The position of Locke in this matter is typical as to the British position. What led him to examine into [the] human capacity for knowledge was the conviction that some of the questions the mind of man was apt to run into but was not fit to deal with were just the questions that led to intolerance, persecution and even war, so that recognition they were beyond our abilities would conduce to toleration and amity. It may serve much to the quieting of disputes and improvement of useful knowledge if as Locke said "We confine our thoughts within the contemplation of those things that are within our reach of our knowledge and launch not out in that abyss of darkness."[3] Locke's assault upon innate ideas had a practical motivation. Ideas that were "innate" were because of that fact immune from examination and criticism. Belief in them was a bulwark of factitious authoritarianism. To be able to trace the origin of our opinions and beliefs to the conditions under which they arose gave us a powerful weapon for estimation of their worth. And when Locke notes that his theory that the direct subject of knowledge

---

1. [John Locke, *Essay Concerning Human Understanding* (1690), bk. 1, ch. 1, sec. 7.]

2. "Fitted" and "adapted" are almost keywords in Locke's essay. [John Locke, "Epistle to the Reader, " in *Essay*.]

3. [Locke, *Essay*, bk. 4, ch. 3, sec. 22.]

consists of ideas is such as to place in doubt the existence of "external things," he contents himself with saying that our assurance of their existence was as wide as "our happiness or misery; beyond which we have no concernment of being or knowing" since "it is sufficient to direct us in the attaining of the good and avoiding the evil which is caused by them"—that is by the "existence of things without us."[4]

II

The influence of cultural conditions upon philosophy is exhibited in a large way in the coincidence of the first systematic expressions of the new science with the first systematic formulation of an attempt to break loose from beliefs that in one way or another had been standard in Europe for two thousand years and more. It is displayed on a smaller scale in the different ways of stating the problem of knowledge that were produced in different political and religious climes. The continent of Europe, especially in the peoples most influenced by Rome, the Latin countries, were more intimately saturated with the Greek-medieval tradition than was Great Britain. It was in these countries that the Church retained the larger need of political power in alliance with Government. Descartes, who was even a more thoroughgoing rebel in "intellectual" affairs, in scientific doctrines, than Bacon himself, disavowed, on behalf of his philosophy, that it had any bearing direct or indirect upon "practical" affairs. The revolution in science made it the first rule of his provisional moral code "to obey the laws and customs of his native land and to hold steadfast to the religion in which he had been brought up." He looked for improvements in the arts and especially in medicine to result from acceptance of his ideas in natural science, but kept entirely away from any suggestion of moral and political bearing. The arts of engineering were further advanced in Latin countries than in Great Britain at that time, and engineering had a long and honorable mathematical background and record. The industrial arts in which the latter country took the lead were of an empirical, i.e., experimental nature. Such considerations as these ones have a good deal to do, I think, with what is known as the "rationalistic" and theoretical coloring of Continental philosophy. Spinoza had a specifically ethical end in view in his philosophy. But it is characteristic of the tenor of Continental philosophy that he regarded improvement in *knowledge* as the agency through which the desirable moral goal was to be attained. In society at large it was to come gradually as a kind of by-product, although a necessary one as far as the revolution in knowledge of Nature for which he stood made its way. In the interval obedience was the rule of conduct in all political matters, overthrow of constituted authority being the worst of

4. [Ibid., bk. 4, ch. 11, sec. 8.]

evils, rational belief being free in that it is rational in those who attained to right understanding and therefore "inner."

There are technically adequate reasons for calling British philosophy empiristic in its statement of the problem of knowledge and the solutions it proposed. But "practical," in the sense in which that word is traditionally opposed to "theoretical," is a better name, "better" because more penetrating and instructive. I have mentioned the fact that the divergence of Locke from Descartes is rooted in the confidence the former puts in the "outer," and that his theory of experience and his "empiricism" are derived from this fact and his accompanying distrust of the "inner" save as a set of powers for handling the effects made by the outer. It did not root in any hostile attitude to "reason." I add the following to quotations previously made: "Reason must be our last judge and guide in everything."[5] Descartes's attack upon the syllogism as model and method of knowledge outdoes, on the other hand, anything Locke said about it.[6] And while Locke's account of the origin of mathematics differs widely from that of Descartes, he is equally sure of its inherent certainty, and being certain, truth and that it is the "workmanship of the understanding," although exercised upon *materials* supplied from without.

While Francis Bacon, to go back to a pre-Cartesian, avoided conflict with specifically theological beliefs, by adopting the doctrine of "two-fold truth," one of human affairs and the other of divine (a position espoused by some scholastics), yet his chief purpose is to effect a wedding of science with human art, because of which "knowledge is power" and the arts of command and administration of natural forces enter upon an assured and constantly advancing course. The practical intent of Hobbes's interpretation of the new science (which he adopted in its most "mechanistic" shape) appears in every page of his writings. With respect to Locke, the problem, then, is not so much to account for the practical aim and tenor of his doctrines as it is to explain its highly restricted character when compared with the confident and almost unbounded sweep of the systems of Bacon and Hobbes. My hypothesis on this point is that the change is due to the intervention of the religious-political wars which were such a feature of the seventeenth century in Great Britain as well as on the Continent. The Glorious Revolution of 1688 brought the struggles to a close, but by means of an experiment in

---

5. [Ibid., bk. 4, ch. 19, sec. 14.]

6. In the usual sense, in which "rationalism" means trust in human powers of judgment to attain truth if not *against* supernatural revelation than at least as judge of the authenticity and authority of what purports to revealed truth, Locke is more thoroughly "rationalistic" than is Descartes; it is particularly in matters of religion that "reason is out last judge and guide" accompanies his statement that "whatever God has revealed is certainly true" with the statement that "whether it be divine revelation or not, reason must judge." [Locke, *Essay*, bk. 4, ch. 18, sec. 10.]

temperate mutual toleration and compromise [rather] than by clear victory of any one contending force. Locke's writings are a classical expression of what is best in the result achieved. From his day to that of Herbert Spencer, Great Britain saw no attempts to construct all comprehensive systems such as mark the course of philosophy [on the Continent].

Whether this explanation be correct or not, there can be no question about the predominantly practical intent of Locke's writings. While his *Essay Concerning Human Understanding* reflects everywhere the influence of the "incomparable Newton," his problems did not derive, save incidentally from Newton. The book itself is the doctrinal counterpart of that group of writings to which the *Letters on Toleration, The Reasonableness of Christianity,* and *The Treatises on Government* are the other members. This central fact stands that in the passage Locke himself wrote about the origin of the *Essay.* "Five or six friends," he writes, "meeting at my chamber and discoursing on a subject very remote from this, found them selves quickly at a stand, by the difficulties that rose on every side. After we had a while puzzled ourselves, without coming any nearer a resolution of these doubts which perplexed us, it came into my thoughts, that we took the wrong course: and that before we set ourselves upon inquiries of that nature, it was necessary to examine our own abilities, and see what objects our understandings were, or were not, fitted to deal with."[7]

. . .

I shall say something about the nature of problems in general. For a clear view of the conditions under which problems come into existence and take the special forms which mark off one problem from another will greatly facilitate consideration of the problems of philosophy with which we are to deal. For the main point regarding the existence of such conditions is that problems have definite connections and can be understood only in terms of what they are connected with—the fact of connection extending to their occurrence, existence and to the specific terms in which they are formulated, a matter that regulates the way in which they are gone at and hence regulates the terms in which "solutions" will be sought for and formulated. The import of this "main point" will probably be most readily gathered by saying what it negates, namely, the notion that there is such a thing as problems "in general," or without relation to conditions outside themselves.

The rather common notion that problems exist directly *per se* and are given is a belief which finds easy explanation within the scope of restricted fields and as a practical matter is innocent of harm when confined to

---

7. [Locke, "Epistle to the Reader." This quote has been completed by the editor.]

them. But when it is converted into a matter of general theory it gives rise to a fallacy which is highly harmful both in itself and in its connection with affiliated doctrines. For it leads to the assumption, tacit or avowed, that the existence of a problem is simply an affair between something termed "mind," knowing subject, consciousness (the particular name here is of no importance), on one side and something called "object" on the other side.

A competent worker in any specialized branch of science, such as astrophysics, physical chemistry, relationships of electrons, protons, neutrons, is dealing with a field in which, at any given time the subject matter at hand is such as to offer recognized problems to further research. The same is true of any field of technology undergoing rapid, deliberate development. In the state of the science or art as workers are inducted into it, there is no harm in saying the problems are "there" or are "given." In a working sense, the statement is correct. There is a body of formulated propositions which are accepted and there are certain phenomena which do not hitch or jibe in the state of the science, or certain recognized needs, demands, which are not met or met economically in the existing state of the technological art. The discrepancy, repugnancy, clash which is noted constitutes a given problem. But this fact is so far from justifying the notion that a problem is simply a matter or affair between a knowing mind in general and an object to be known in general that it proves the contrary: The relatedness or relativity of the occurrence and differential terms (or content) of a problem to definite, specifiable, or concrete conditions.

The surprise often expressed at the fact that savages, or members of some contemporary group *we* regard as backward or wrongheaded, entertain beliefs so obviously in conflict with facts no sane mind can help seeing is such an illustration of the failure to place the origin and content of problems in their proper context as to be worth examining. For it illustrates the fallacy that arises when we transfer the kind of "givenness" of problems under the restricted conditions mentioned over to the theory of problems in general; that is, without limiting conditions. It rests upon the supposition that being a fact is an inherent character and is therefore something that is directly perceived or at all events that *should* be so perceived if the perceiving "mind" were what it ought to be, and that the incongruity of a particular opinion, idea or belief with fact is also what is, or should be, directly apparent. Both of these assumptions are contrary to fact. Events, occurrences, happenings are not in and of themselves, or "inherently" (absolutely or out of connection) facts. To take an event as fact is to take it out of a swirling dumb anonymity and give it *public* rank and status. It is to entitle it a member of a specific order in definite connection with other members. For to term anything whatever *fact* is to confer upon it a *rightful* claim, the *authority*, to determine belief and decide the conclusion to be reached in a given field of subject matter. To be a fact is to be a *noted* event; it is an event which is *acknowledged*, that is an event whose *claims* are owned or assented to. Such admission or countenancing is a *commitment* from which something follows. The notion of an admission devoid of consequences is nonsense. Since the something in question is specifiable or namable, not just anything at large, or "any old thing," to be a fact is to exist in described or describable connections, not in lonely isolation. A fact is always a fact of specifiable use, function or intent connected with other events having similar rank in a specifiable system.

Otherwise stated, an occurrence, even one of intensity in close proximity to an organism equipped with organs of sense and brain, is not only not identical with an observation but also is no guarantee that an observation will take place. The latter depends upon the claims to acknowledgment the occurrence puts forth and that in turn is a matter of existing occupations and customs. In respect to actual matters, as distinct from theory in the abstract, it is commonplace that observing, noting, does not place in a vacuum merely because something called mind, or consciousness, or a nervous system is there. A layman is not expected to see what an expert sees in the case of a power-loom, a piece of scientific apparatus or a complex blueprint, nor is a savage fresh from the bush expected to see even in a wire strung along on poles by the highway what a person habituated to telegraph and telephone sees there. In concrete cases, we recognize the dependence of the event of observing and of *what* is observed upon the antecedent existence of a constellation of habits, including attitudes of belief operating as facilities, resources.

The next step in understanding the matter of that observation of an event which gives it rank as *fact* (which is a precedent condition of noting the clash, incongruity or incompatibility which constitutes a *problem*) is that the existence of such conditions as those spoken of just said to be necessary is determined under and by social conditions including language, or the meanings current as means and material of communication. The true statement that we know (observe) *with* what we have known (that is, learned) needs to be supplemented by recognition that what is learned is a function of the social group and groups of which one is a member. This implicit fact is in the use of such words, as well as in the illustrations given about the conditions of occurrence of certain kinds of observation. But the fact needs to be made explicit. We are familiar, in some cases only too much so, with the existence of sects, parties, denominations, factions, schools, cliques, sets, economic classes, "organizations." We are also aware that each one of these consists of human beings who in that particular capacity are followers, adherents, votaries, devotees, partisans. Slight reflection makes [one] also cognizant of the fact that the groups in question are what they are because of formulated doctrines, creeds, tenets, platforms, etc., held by the members of the group, which they later accept and are supposed to be loyal to. These cases are cited because it is so obvious in their case that the belief that determines what is admitted and excluded as facts and the manner in which observation is carried on (including deflections and distortions under the caption "carried on") is a matter of group, constitution and behavior.

Now in spite of the case that in some of the cited cases, especially those of the groups with which we do not agree, the kind of influence exerted upon what is observed and believed suggests undesirable, objectionable qualities, I have used these cases because their somewhat extreme character illustrates the sort of thing which happens in all cases, including those which are regarded as highly desirable. For the contrast between the undesirable and the desirable is not that of determination of belief-constellations (and consequent facts and problems) in one case by socio-cultural conditions and in the other case by mind or intellect free from any such social influence but is that between habits and the attitudes which are characteristic of the methods used by different groups. The term partisan, for example, has acquired in ordinary usage a distinctly unfavorable signification. It signifies a kind of blind, unreflective, obstinately prejudiced, or perhaps fanatical adherence to the tenets of a group. But in the etymological sense of the word, all of us are partisans in that we are parts along with others, of groups which are with respect to their "parts" wholes of a sort. In this sense, to be a partisan is identical with being "social by nature"; and expresses the conformity to the statement that no human being can live by and to himself and remain normal. The unfavorable signification of the name is due to the nature of the group in question, its hard and fast views and the rigid conformity exacted of members.

For the cultural relativity of beliefs, facts and problems is far from meaning that they are all, on that account, of the same value. On the contrary this fact of relativity is an indirect way of calling attention to the differences which exist in the attitudes and practices of different cultural groups as to the methods and criteria by which their beliefs are respectively reached and modified. For instance, the objection which is ordinarily brought against what I have said about "Fact" is that it rests upon confusion of what is *taken* to be fact with what is *"really,"* what is *taken* as fact may be deceptive, fanciful, fictitious, mistaken, illusory. Assuredly no one can deny that many things once regarded as facts and as truths are now seen not to have been factual or true. But the conclusion to be drawn is that just the opposite from that which is often drawn.

. . .

[We may distinguish] between the customs determining methods and tests for belief in groups whose custom is that of maintaining custom and tradition intact and the groups whose customs include that of breaking and re-formation of custom.[8]

A number of conclusions follow. From the scientific standpoint, the "problems" of groups whose chief concern is to maintain their doctrines, as means of maintaining their own prestige and doctrines, are intact *pseudo*-problems, although they constitute genuine *social* problems, since their perpetuation is hostile to formation of a society [whose] operations are marked by greater intelligence. The history of some organizations proves that it is possible to develop great skill in perpetuating and extending the power which they exert over the beliefs and level[ing] the conduct of their members. It proves also that whether or not the advantages accruing to the leaders because of possession of power were active factors in the original production of the beliefs and the groups, they usually come to play an important role in keeping them alive and influential.

. . .

[There are groups] that pride themselves upon being modern and advanced, which consistently employ methods of inquiry and test and which accordingly contemplate with equanimity the possibility that industry will effect change, even great change, in beliefs already held, yet these groups exist side by side, intermixed with, groups of the other sort whose conduct is systematically directed to maintain their influence over their adherents by protecting their beliefs from change which is more than incidental and trivial. And I do not suppose that any will deny that while the groups habituated to scientific method exert great influence in certain fields, yet are quite restricted in comparison with the fields in which the other type of beliefs exert predominant influence. For the very word "science" suggests to most persons a technical, specialized subject matter, not a way of ascertaining facts and formulating and solving problems in every aspect and phase of human concern. More particularly, while it is admitted to possess quite properly, influence in "practical" affairs of a *material* (that is to say, economic) sort, the prevailing social belief is that it is an interloper in "practical" matters in which moral issues are involved[.]

. . .

[That in] certain fields—notably that of industry, business, and commerce—they exercise an enormous influence (the consequences of which

---

8. [Marginal note: "Somewhere the methods of tenacity, authority, compatibility of reason."]

spill, willy nilly, over into fields supposed to be none of their concern) but yet have made little headway in permeating the attitudes and habits, the spirit, of society and social interests as a whole constitutes, I believe, the very heart of the fact our life is carried forward within an immense body of established institutions, dogmas, customs and rules which are not of *our* creation and which do not correspond with the needs of our actual life.

For this reason it may be said that *the* social problem of modern life is precisely that of breaking down the walls now dividing the habits, attitudes, and methods of operation of the part of society that is engaged in scientific inquiry from those of other, less-specialized, and [so-]to-speak more humane groups, by means of thorough permeation of the latter with the spirit, the will or intent, that defines science.

III

Even today the saying that the special [sciences] make assumptions regarding principles (such as space, time, matter, causality) which they do not themselves warrant or justify and which accordingly it is the business of philosophy to investigated passes current as wisdom. The idea these principles or categories mean just and only what they *do* in the methods and conclusions of scientific inquiry so that the way to investigate them is to ascertain the service, if any, they perform in the conduct of scientific inquiry, is somehow ruled out in advance as a sort of crass philosophical philistinism. The one impossibility is that the operations of inquiry in observation, experimentation and test should bring their own adequate credentials with them.

Theoretically it is conceivable that the "problem of knowledge" should have taken the form of ascertaining how far antecedent assumptions about the nature of things to be known, about matter and mind, were capable of standing up under the impact of the methods and conclusions of the new knowledge. To some extent, that is what did occur. But there always remained certain principles and truths of a completely foundational nature which were unerringly and incorrigibly known in and of themselves, not as conclusions of inquiry and without having to undergo a test in the course of continuing inquiry. Even today we find teachers of philosophy who under the color of modernity appeal to the Aristotelian dictum that "Nature is intelligible" and who then proceed to apply the Aristotelian notion of the intelligible as a fixed criterion or "norm" by which to adjudge science even though the actual results of the [*illeg.*] science in physical, biological and social knowledge have no relation—save that of logical contrariety—with the forms and essences that define the "intelligible" for Aristotle. That "the intelligible" is synonymous with what is found out in patient, continued searching investigations is again a thoroughly crass position from the standpoint of philosophy as higher knowledge of that which is truly real. The firmness with which it is held that what is "known" before any operations of specific knowing are undertaken is so indubitable that it serves as standard and norm by which to pass upon the knowledge-status of the results of these actual and concrete undertakings and is indicative, from the standpoint of actual knowledge, of the hold of deeply rooted institutionally established habits. For the only things that are taken for granted as exempt from critical inquiry are precisely such habits. There is no doubt that many of the old first and ultimate principles show wear; attrition has operated. But since they are habitual attitudes, not rational principles, the only thing which can completely undermine them is the formation of new habits—specifically, such habits as incorporate within themselves as taken for granted a matter of course the results and conclusions of competent inquiry.

The course of modern philosophy, to summarize the outcome of previous discussions, presents then a confused mixture of enduring habits and slow attritions. It pictures a social scene in which there is a secure command of the values of neither the old nor the new. The most obvious effect as far as philosophy is concerned is its progressive divorce from science, a tragic separation that has led philosophers to claim for philosophy that it is a higher kind of science, concerned with Reality per se, while the "special sciences" occupy themselves with particular phenomena. In the older Greek-Roman-Medieval scheme, science and philosophy were one. The union was not technical or merely formal. Because of the union, the astronomical, geological, physical, biological, psychological and historical beliefs that formed the world-picture were integrated with moral-religious beliefs about the origin and destiny of mankind. The offspring of the union was the "law of nature" which was the proper norm of all positive rules and regulations, domestic, economic and political. When science and philosophy parted company, nature and the natural science which was supposed to report its "real" structure ceased to be the support and warrant of morals, while at the same time, as the new methods won victory after another in special fields, its applications in matters of industrial production, distribution, and methods of communication revolutionized the relationships of human beings to one another. Philosophy not only broke with the science of nature, but it claimed jurisdiction over science in a way which was an effective obstacle to efforts to utilize its methods and conclusions on behalf of humane and moral guidance. At the very time when philosophy because of its split with science was losing authority, it retained enough influence to prevent science from exercising the kind of regulation which philosophy had commanded in its heyday. In the [illeg.] in which philosophy became socially impotent, it became the fashion to proclaim the complete neutrality of science with respect to all human concerns that were not in a field set apart as "material." At the time in which philosophy separated from philosophy, it also separated from that everyday or commonsense knowledge which is chiefly, in effect exclusively, concerned with affairs of human moment—of what to do and how to do it—the technological inventions and applications which were revolutionizing industry being supposed to be by-products having no connection with science in its chaste purity. If it is paradoxical that the problem of the possibility of knowledge flourished at the very time when the practice of knowing had for the first time struck out in a secure path, it is equally paradoxical that the doctrine of knowledge as a body of self-contained propositions (or facts or truths, the mode of statement having no importance as long as the doctrine of seclusion was maintained) flourished at the time when in fact scientific knowledge was transforming human occupations and modes of association. Perhaps at some time in the future historians will be puzzled to account for this fact. Until recently there was a kind of complacency about the situation which may justly be called smug. And even today the school that most vehemently proclaims its addiction to science and its opposition to metaphysical philosophy, insists upon making the sharpest kind of separation between scientific propositions and the interests and concerns which actuate social behavior—pursuit of science itself included!

. . .

But the difficulty is far from confined to professional philosophy. Because of intimate connection of the Greek-medieval philosophic tradition with the moral-religious education of the West, words such as mind, subject, self, object, in fact all the words imbued with what is supposed to have psychological reference and force, carry a heavy load of directions and cues which are hostile to formation or theory of knowledge on the basis of the present actually accomplished state of knowledge. And it would be easy to cite many cases to show that scientific inquirers, the very ones who are engaged in building up the structure or extant knowledge, are as much under the domination of traditional uses of words as are the most case-hardened epistemological philosophers.

Under these conditions, it is probably well to begin with conclusions that are generally accepted among scientific inquiries in the fields in which they do their work unless they are withheld by early education or some other irrelevant factor. I would give first place to those developments in knowledge which put man irretrievably within the natural world. Since, however, *natural* and *nature*, especially *naturalistic* and *naturalism*, are among the words that owe the heaviest debt to old beliefs, it is necessary to particularize.[9] To say that man is in the natural world is then a way of saying that all events big or little that are or that can be characterized as human occur in connection with events investigated in other branches of inquiry, and are to be themselves investigated with any and all aids supplied by knowledge of these other events.

For reasons that have been set forth, the import of the statement just made is most conspicuous and most easily grasped on the negative side. It demands that inquirers turn their backs completely upon formulations of knowledge which are made in terms of any kind of relation or connection which is taken and treated as peculiar to knowledge, whether it be called relation of mind-matter, subject-object, self-world, individual-others, consciousness within—things without, brain—not brain, or whatever. It applies to assigning a *unique* position (though not of course a distinctive or specifiable function) to the nervous system just as much to perception and reason. There is no decision in advance as to whether such words as are just mentioned have in any place in description of knowledge or what that place may be. What is settled by the postulate of this sort is that issues are to be decided by the results of observation of *events-in-connection*, with no antecedent preference for this or that class of events save as a preferred position is established *by* what is known, and above all that there be no ruling out of any class of events whatever in advance of the results or inquiries of the type which has proved competent in acknowledged fields.

The basic proposition in a theory of knowledge which shall be consonant with the aforesaid point of view and method is that knowledge is an event. For only as an event can it be in-connection-with-events and be subject to inquiry by the method pursued in the case of other better-known events (better known at present than the event of knowledge itself)—the method, indeed by which it has been shown that inquiry is successful when its subjects are viewed and handled *as* events-in-connection, not as substances, essences or natures, and not as "objects" for a subject, mind, self, or consciousness.

The word-form "knowledge" does not lend itself to use of the article "a" nor to use in the plural form, which uses are required in speaking of events. When it does not stand for a collective body of learning or information, it comes close to being an abstract noun. The word-form "knowing" is also rarely used in the plural and with the article "a." In addition it is even more bound up with traditional significations, such as "mind, knowing self, subject" which carry a heavy load of doctrines that need critical examination, than does "knowledge." I propose then to revive for the moments two

9. For example, "naturalism" is identified offhand with "materialism," without the slightest trace of critical examination of the word "matter."

word-forms that are obsolete, and speak of knowledgings and knowledg-
ments in analogy with ac-knowledging and ac-knowledgment.

I begin by saying that knowledgings are events in the same sense in which
conversing, telling stories, studying, plying a trade are events in connection
with other events. And by the phrase "in the same sense" I intend at the
outset something more negative than positive. I intend to rule out (until and
unless its presence is substantiated by observation such as is employed in
other subjects) the view that there is [something] "unique" about knowledgings that sets them apart[.]

. . .

It would be, accordingly, a false simplification to divorce the problem of
knowledge in its relatively specialized and technical sense from the broad
moral problem of the place and work of knowledge in the social matters
which for the moment may be summed up under the heads of authority
and value. What we try to do with knowledge is deeply affected by what we
believe it to be; we shall not attempt to have it accomplish a work foreign to
its nature. Clear vision of what the methods and subject matter of knowledge are now doing and not doing in social life, and of what they might and
should do, is not possible as long as our belief-attitudes toward knowledge
are themselves clouded and twisted. Practically no one doubts that with
physics and chemistry as aids we can work in certain fields what once would
have been miracles. Very few persons have much confidence that scientific
methods and results can be effective and fruitful resources in what lies outside of fields which most people today would call "material." I do not think
we can decide why this striking difference of attitude exists without taking
into consideration relics of traditions that comes to use from a relatively
prescientific and pretechnological culture—relics that are not fossils nor yet
just survivals. I mention two or three matters by way of illustration. As long
as the subject matter of the physical sciences is taken to be that of an inherently "external" and "material" world, instead being "physical" because of
the type of behavioral inquiry-technique which determines its conclusions,
to urge anything like its systematic use in humane or moral subjects would
be taken to be equivalent to reducing the latter to materialistic terms with
evacuation of everything distinctively moral or humane. And in effect that
would be its actual tendency. And as long as psychological subject matter is
supposed to be "inner" and "private" and is framed to accord with that basic
"principle" as premise, the gap between it and the transactions that need
guidance by systematic knowledge of human-beings-in-society is uncross-
able. To state the same point in a more concrete form: *The* social bond is
communication. Yet according to the current theory, based upon the notion

that man as uniquely private and inner in essence is set over against the world in particular and one man is set over against other men in general, the "meaning" and substance of words, as language, consists of "thoughts" which are then clothed for public consumption in sounds or, in the case of written language, with visible marks. The theoretical background of what has called itself "individualism" in economic and political affairs is furnished by this same psychology of the self as intrinsically "inner." Nor can the force of these cases as illustrative evidence be disposed of by saying that they are merely "theoretical" and without much, if any, practical bearing. For this view would be tenable only if the theoretical statements were not reflections of social attitudes. If the latter are important, then their formulation, even if otherwise otiose, has at least the effect of calling attention to the habits lying back of the words and the way they operate.

IV

Introduction of new methods in natural [science] produced in general a new kind of picture of the world and man and, in particular, a vast number of processes which radically altered the terms upon which human beings associate. Even if the conflict of the new picture of nature had not so conflicted with that one which was sanctioned and propagated by official institutions that a crisis was produced in the beliefs that supply the raw material of philosophical inquiry, the multitude of "practical" crises generated in human associations by application of the conclusions reached would have given a new turn to the problem of knowledge.

In the abstract, two different facets of the present problem of knowledge may be distinguished, one of which would not be a concern of philosophy save in a rather conventional sense. It is theoretically possible to frame a theory of knowledge based upon and in terms of the conclusions of an extensive survey of the methods actually practiced in the entire set of sciences from the A of anthropology and astro-physics through all the letters of the alphabet down to the Zed of zoology. The net outcome would be a generalized methodology. But taken in itself, that is apart from comparison of its contents with those of traditional theories of knowledge and apart from the question of their bearing upon the issue of methods to be employed in locating problems and projecting policies connected with future direction of human behavior, there would be nothing especially philosophical about such a methodology. It would be rather a somewhat specialized branch of learning. And it is doubtful how much value it would have for workers in the various branches of scientific inquiry. Upon the whole, they would presumably go on using the methods that had proved successful in the past with such modifications as are suggested by ingenuity [to satisfy] the requirements imposed by new problems. The following passage of Samuel Butler's is fairly indicative of the attitude taken by workers in the field of the sciences to general theories of knowledge: [Quote missing.]

The question may, however, be raised from quite another standpoint. The question of the method of obtaining knowledge is as urgent and important from a general social standpoint as it is, relatively, unimportant from the standpoint of science as a specialized occupation. From this former standpoint, the problem is central and crucial in a theory or philosophy of the conduct of social affairs. It does not need much observation to note that they are conducted by a mixture of habits which congealed in earlier different conditions; appeals to superior force, political, economic, military; dependence upon various sorts of officials, misnamed authorities; shrewd manipulations undertaken under cover, and improvisations of policy having their source in happy—or unhappy—thoughts. The methods and conclusions of science also play a part, becoming notable in some matters, negligible in other, and for the most part more humanly important, affairs, the most conspicuous example being, I should say, the great and ever-growing extent in which the standards, rules and regulations, directives and cues of production in industry are supplied by scientific methods and discoveries in contrast with indifference exhibited toward these methods in respect to the human consequences of the industrial set-up. It is in the social context thus determined that the theory of knowledge takes on philosophical significance. Its urgency and moment are increased because the leading principles of historic systems, couched in "epistemological" terms confused, obfuscate, divert and pervert inquiry into the issue instead of serving to give it fruitful direction.

. . .

The impact of the broadly human problem of knowledge is not within knowledge as a specialized field. It has to do with transaction and interactions carried on between what is known and what is done and to be done in the entire range of human concerns. The non-technical, non-specialized frame of reference of the theory of knowledge is formed by the place it occupies, the functions it exercises, [and] the consequences it produces in the customs, institutions and policies which seriously affect the course and conduct of social affairs. More specifically, the liberal and human aspect of the theory of knowledge has to do with the connections or interactivities that take place between knowledge as one set or system of social events and other sets or systems, whether loose or "organized," of social events—such as are set apart more or less reified under such names as industry, business, politics, art, international relations, public health: Everything, in short, which, in the words of Jefferson, falls within the compass of "life, liberty, and the pursuit of happiness" on the widest and the narrowest human scales.

As was earlier indicated, it is not a matter of very great importance whether the name "philosophy" is applied to an inquiry of this type, concerned with projecting policies as to what knowledge can and should do [and] not with laying out the field of knowledge or adding to its contents—save as such questions, enter, under given social conditions, into determination of the conditions which at [a given] time and place are directing and deflecting the search for knowledge and the humane, liberal, or moral uses to which its subject matter is put. What is highly important is that there be some kind of systematic critical inquiry that is occupied with just this sort of question, and it is to it that I would apply the name "philosophical theory of knowledge."

. . .

To say that this sort of question[—that of physical, economic or political force or manipulation hostile to the scientific method is philosophic—]is to recur to the stand already taken about philosophy and the relation existing within it between moral issues on one side and logic and a general picture of nature on the other side. It does not mean that philosophy can or should settle the issues involved; that can be accomplished only by continued co-operative action. It means that a certain kind of systematic inquiry may clarify the issue, show how behavior in the concrete may come to closer grips with it and indicate plans that operate as working hypotheses in present scientific investigations.

I recur also to the matter of the emphasis carried in the word *"present"* prefixed to the words "significance of the problem of knowledge." There is no intimation that the problem of knowledge is an eternal philosophical problem. There is so much in current customs as well as in those of past periods that no stretch of [the] imagination can regard as a product of intelligence, that is of inquiries using the best available methods of examination and test, that we readily tend to set custom and intelligence in opposition to each other. But as is intimated in what was just said that opposition is a sad commentary on the quality of prevalent customs. The issue at stake is how far customs can become intelligent, or how the sets of customs that form behavior which is scientific in its traits can be integrally incorporated in other forms of habitual behavior.

. . .

We now frequently hear or read the statement that "science" is socially and morally neutral with the attendant implication that this neutrality is an inherent property of scientific subject matter. The statement will repay analysis. In the first place, it smacks of continued use of definition and classification by means of essential forms which has been abandoned in, say, physics and is rapidly giving way in biological subjects. In the next place, as in all cases of use of the method of inherent forms and natures, it means that the subject matter in question has been artificially cut off from its connections: that "science" has been reified into an entity in and of itself. In other words, it amounts to saying that when scientific subject matter is cut loose from its social connections, it is taken to be something which it is not. And like other erroneous statements of fact, it does not alter the fact though it does seriously confuse and frustrate the events in which facts are dealt with. For the scientific material goes right ahead having social consequences since it is one social event among others. The fact that the revolution in industrial production, transportation and communication both stimulated the scientific revolution and proceeded apace because of it should suffice as illustrative evidence. And the oft quoted fact that much the same scientific subject matters may be used as means for destroying human life and for saving it instead of proving, as it is supposed to do, that "science" and human beings are two different and independent affairs proves that at present social conditions constitute a very mixed affair which accordingly breeds humans who are inconsistent to the point of contrariety in their behavior. And when science is seen for what it is, a form of human being, instead of being first chopped off and then reified by projection into a void, the incompatibility is seen to be without knowledge itself.

. . .

It is noteworthy that among the four higher liberal arts, mathematics served as buttress of the dogma of fixed and immutable truths which was so fundamentally important in connection with the theology of the Church. For mathematical axioms and definitions were assumed to be ultimate, fixed, and self-evident truths, and therefore the infallible authoritative foundation of all other forms of knowledge. The other higher liberal arts, music, and astronomy (which included all forms of natural science) were also servants of the Church in theory and in practice.

There are two outstanding features of the scholastic educational arts, arts now held up as models for liberal education today. One of the traits is that all of them depend not only upon a strictly literary material but also look backward—a course only too slavishly followed by those now urging return to the standards and subject matter of Greece and the middle period. The other trait is the unquestioning and uncritical acceptance of fundamental truths as already in our possession and as the firm and immutable foundation of everything that can be known to be true and hence can serve to give guidance to the conduct of life's affairs. Since the problem is a social one, it is one that can be faced and settled only in social behavior, certainly not by philosophy as a special undertaking. But the situation has nevertheless something definite to say about philosophy. Philosophers have at least some responsibility for clearing away the elements of confusion and conflict that are a legacy from its past. And positively, if it is to have a future instead of living upon and by its past, it has the office of making articulate, as far as reflective inquiry can do so, the constituents of the present problem, and of indicating possible plans, of the nature of working hypotheses, to guide the formation of policies to be socially tried.

The remark that was incidentally about the past problem of knowledge does not signify that as a philosophical problem it was ever anything but a social problem. It is rather a reminder that the quality of the social problem has changed. A few short centuries ago the social problem was that of obtaining conditions in which new methods of knowing, hostile in effect to powerful institutionalized customs, could obtain the right to be publicly expressed and taught. The social problem involved is not one that can be separated from the political-moral movement in behalf of freedom of conscience in matters of religious choice, and freedom of inquiry, speech, and publication. At that stage, the problem of knowledge was a phase, an urgent one, of what is now embodied in our constitutional law as "civil rights." Nothing creates [more] issues of necessity for new direction than success: so much truth we may concede to the Hegelian dialectic. The success of the scientific movement in its own special and technical fields has radically shifted the social problem about knowledge. A passage from Samuel Butler's pertaining to a change in his personal attitude toward science may be transferred, with considerable instruction to a general change taking place between the seventeenth and the twentieth centuries with respect to the status of the problem of knowledge. [Quote missing.]

When engaged in science as a going concern, men do not need to concern themselves with its "foundations." They can go ahead. Science has demonstrated its success in its chosen field. It might seem then as if the older problem of the possibility of knowledge, the "epistemological" problem, would be disheartening. It maintains, however, something more than a professional and professorial interest because the division between "inner" and "outer," between man and the rest of the natural world, between what is merely material and what is fine and noble, is deep set in our institutional habits. The layman is likely to have a feeling of fatuity when he runs across a philosophical formulation of the problem of knowledge stated in terms of an "external world" and of a mind or knowing subject (or mayhap a brain) that is withdrawn from the world and is "inner" (for otherwise there would be no point in prefixing the adjective "external" to "world.") The formulations of epistemology of Descartes and Locke to this day have to accept some responsibility for keeping alive the sense of a gap between man as knower and the world as that which is to be known. But that responsibility is a minor one. It exists only as far as systematic reports of a split embedded in institutional beliefs tended to harden and perpetuate the conditions that philosophers reported in generalized terms. The very person who finds the philosophical formulation to be fatuous has the conditions it formulates in his own make-up. Many a college teacher of philosophy has developed an art of skillful cross-examination that demonstrates this fact.

. . .

The narrow signification, far from eulogistic in its implications, that has come to be attached to "moral" and "ethical" is a reflection of the conditions that create the negative aspect of the present problem of philosophy. The relatively academic phase of the matter appears in the acceptance, now an academic convention, of the separation of ethical theory from political and economic theory; a separation still made, although the earlier separation of the economic and the political is breaking down by the very stress of conditions. The human phase of the matter, underlying that which I have called academic, is illustrated in two important and correlative matters. One of them is manifested in the generally accepted separation of good and evil in an alleged distinctively *moral* sense from good and bad in their generic sense. The other matter is manifested in the belief that morals are primarily a matter of *personal* character and disposition in a sense of these words which gives to what is called "social morals" (or ethics) a special and separate subject matter. The flavor of the hortatory, or moralizing and the moralistic, and even of endeavor to regulate the conduct of other persons by laying down rules they *should* obey so clings to morals that one almost hesitates to use it in discussion of ordinary matters in which human values are directly and indirectly concerned. Yet there was a time when "moral," when prefixed to any subject, was equivalent to "human." The contrast or distinction conveyed by use of the adjective was that of the distinctively human from the distinctively *physical*. Politics and political economy were moral subjects not just in conventional or academic designation but because their subject matter was of human concern. This meaning was still uppermost in Great Britain in the eighteenth century. Adam Smith defined moral philosophy as an inquiry into the happiness and perfection of a man, considered not only as an individual but as member of a family, of a state, and of the great Society of mankind—and it is worthy of note that this definition occurs in his treatise on *The Wealth of Nations*. Moreover, according to moral philosophy, Smith included the material discussed in this book as its own fourth branch, the other three parts being "natural theology," "ethics" (in the narrower sense discussed in his *Moral Sentiments*), and jurisprudence as the theory of *justice*, especially with reference to its "natural rules" as the foundation of positive law.

Undoubtedly, the tendency towards specialization manifested in Smith's own treatment was a factor in subsequent limitation of the broad human field of *moral* to what Smith called "ethical," just as his *Wealth of Nations* contributed powerfully to subsequent setting apart *political* economy, and then of economic subject matter as something independent of politics—involving of course the reciprocal independence of political subject matter and of law from that of economics. The story of specialization amounts to that of separation, and the later rise of sociology as an attempt to bring into a "synthesis" subjects otherwise separated, is an interesting phase of cultural history whose details lie outside the present theme. What is pertinent, and in a highly significant degree, is that setting the subject matter of physical knowledge apart as a separate realm, that of the so-called external or objective world, was directly reflected in the idea that physical knowledge functions in human affairs only in connection with appetites, needs, desires, transactions, that are "material" and hence are within the competency of at least an external application of physical knowledge, so that "moral" subject matter is completely above and beyond any intercourse with natural science save one which is thoroughly harmful since, by definition, it is wholly foreign to the nature, essence and all properties of what is the moral. We do not lack for moralizing and moralistic utterances about the "moral" necessity (that is, the duty or obligation) of bringing economic matters and the relation of nations with one another under control by moral law. But the fact that achievement of this indispensable task is left as a matter of sheer "oughtness," and we are offered two mutually exclusive alternatives as the only methods by which the *ought* in question can be converted into an *is*—the only ones, that is, as long as the use of science and its potential applications in guidance of social change are ruled out in advance. One of them is conversion of a sufficient number of "individuals," the latter words being a secularized equivalent of souls. The other alternative involves giving moral authority, with appropriate practical power to enforce its authority to *an* institution. In so far the connections that bind morals to social arrangements are recognized. But the fact that authority and accompanying power are given to a separate institution—the Church—and that institution one that owes its right power to a supernatural agency, is another illustration, a sufficiently striking one, of the exact point under consideration.

It is none of the business of discussion of the present theme to indicate, even in outline, the contents of a moral theory that is framed in terms of human values and dis-values as the latter are generated and destroyed, promoted and retarded, by concrete arrangements of all forms of association, familial, industrial, political, international, by friendship, by education, by literature and the other arts. The fact is that development of a theory of this kind is hampered at every turn by isolation of natural knowledge.

. . .

The isolation in question[—of science from social matters—]is that which is involved in the generally accepted notion about the nature of economic subject matter, as it is set forth in the following definition of the science of economics: "Economics deals with social phenomena centering about the provision for the *material needs* of individuals and social groups."[10] The idea stated in the definition is accepted as an idea because it conforms substantially to the actual isolated state of economic phenomena in present society. I do not know how any more convincing evidence of the present isolation (in the humanly significant sense of isolation) of science in social matters could be found than that provided by the fact that the changes which have been wrought in society by the application of physical science (changes so vast that they are called quite properly "the industrial revolution") can be asserted as a matter of undeniable fact to be concerned with "the *material* needs of individuals and social groups." The reason the separation of material interests from moral (that is strictly humane) interests goes not only unquestioned but for the most part wholly unnoticed is because the separation of the "material" from the "ideal," that is from the concerns and ends which mark human life off from what is ranked as merely material has been carried over, without criticism, almost without attention, into the world *called* "modern." And up to the present the revolution which has occurred in the field assigned to natural science has confirmed rather than shaken the isolation of "material" needs, transactions, results and ends from those that are moral because definitely human. For the limitation of the field of *natural* science to the physical; to, that is, the *material* constituting what ancient philosophers called an order or grade of Being and what contemporary philosophers call a "realm" has its exact counterpart in social life in segregation of its economic phenomena under the name of "material" from other human concerns—and this in spite, to repeat, of the vast change in all concrete human relationships that has resulted from the revolutionary change in industry and commerce.

---

10. The opening sentence of the article on "Economics" in the *Encyclopedia of the Social Sciences* (1931), vol. 5, p. 344.

It is a historic fact that the position and significance held by and ascribed to the "material" was fixed in Greek philosophy by inherent contrast with what was called rational and ideal. It is a historic fact that medieval philosophy confirmed and deepened the tradition thus established by transforming the ideal and rational into the "spiritual" as the essence of the divine, and also of the human as far as the human has retained the impress of its divine source. Modern science has completely transformed the properties by which the physical is described and defined. But the inferior place assigned the material has persisted. In addition to being base and low, "matter" was also potentially dangerous. For the natural appetites, in their connection with the body, with the flesh which is carnal, are the representatives of the physical in the human constitution, and they tend by their own nature to resist the authority rightfully possessed by reason, and when permitted to do so they usurp its place. Moral theory as far as it has retained the standpoint of the old tradition has accordingly been a partner of economic theory in maintaining the segregation of science from the "higher" (that is, the moral) aspects of social life. It has proclaimed that the moral law and the ends it prescribed *ought* to govern man's lower nature and the economic behavior and relationships in which that nature is expressed. But isolation of the methods and conclusions of natural knowledge has signified in its practical consequences that the "ought" in question is purely external. Attempt to employ the methods and conclusions of natural knowledge in the human values generated in the processes of living together so that the economic organization of society may liberate those values, making them more secure, and more widely shared, is ruled out in advance. In fact, now that the possibility of natural knowledge in social affairs so as to render them intrinsically tributary to human values is occasionally seen and tentatively promulgated, there rises a chorus of voices to proclaim that the larger part of the evils from which society now suffers is caused by "science" having encroached upon higher domains from which it is properly (that is, by the metaphysical-theological tradition) excluded. In consequence, evils and troubles which *are* due to the operation of science within an artificially restricted technical field and to its arbitrary exclusion from concerns of the highest human importance, are pointed to as a warning against trying to develop and apply methods which would be effective in mitigating and removing these evils.

When the story of modern philosophy is viewed in connection with the relegation of the science to nature to a separate field, the determining consideration is retention of the controlling premise of classic philosophy, namely, that of the unique and privileged relation of knowledge to reality. While the proper subject of supreme or "scientific" knowledge was conceived very differently in medieval theological philosophy, this assumption retained its fundamental position and was transmitted in full force to the philosophical agents of the new scientific movements.[11] It is possible, without an arbitrary twisting of history, to connect all the features of modern philosophy which represent the projection into it of alien and distorting factors to the failure to observe the incompatibility of this assumption with the working postulates of the new scientific attitude and method—that is, with the hypothesis that determined the *practice* of knowing in distinction from its theoretical formulation. The first and most direct consequence was the substitution of two orders of "reality" for the graded hierarchical qualitative order of the Greek-medieval tradition. Since the subject matter of natural science was physical there had to be another psychical or mental order of reality to include and take care of everything that was not physical. This "bifurcation" (which was a complete split rather than a bifurcation that was a branching-out from a common root) furnished the premises, which of necessity rendered the problem of knowledge an *epistemological* problem in the special and technical sense of that word. This problem is central in the secondary, derived aspect of the modern philosophical tradition; it is that with which students become acquainted in books and lecture course which isolate the history of philosophy from its cultural context.

· · ·

Above natural and moral philosophy in rank as knowledge stood first philosophy (as *they* stood above the seven liberal arts or sciences) known also as "divine philosophy," theology, metaphysics, since its subject matter was ultimate reality; or Being, that is, completely such, lacking nothing, depending on nothing, and the unconditional condition of everything in existence. The subject matter of all Nature and hence of all knowledge, in the Greek-medieval tradition, was qualitative. Moreover, *all* natural changes manifested movement to ends in which their real nature and true essence (of Being) was fulfilled and made manifest for and in rational demonstrative knowledge. Hence, first philosophy, as just this knowledge, was the highest or complete science of the real Being of Nature; in that capacity, it also gave a rational account of the lower forms of knowledge in their correspondence with lower grades of natural existence, thus doubly rounding out the system of knowledge.

---

11. While the supreme subject of knowledge (its "object" in the post-medieval version) was above nature in medieval and was the natural culmination of nature in Greek metaphysics, nevertheless the statement of Aristotle that theology and "first philosophy" were one enabled the former to suppose it was continuing the Aristotelian system in spite of its radical change of emphasis.

The fact that the subject matter of the new science was deprived of qualitative and teleological traits had then as its consequence, given the position that the essential and exclusive business of knowledge is disclosure of the constitution of the Real (disclosure of which defines truth), destruction of the established view of the more than friendly, the inherent intimate relation of philosophy and science. Persons adverse to the claims put forth on behalf of philosophy will regard this break as liberation of science from bonds that had kept natural knowledge enslaved to a despotic power. But the effect upon philosophy (including the philosophic theory of knowledge) was that it was stopped from employing the methods by which natural knowledge was advanced. The method of experimental observation by which natural knowledge was winning its victories could not be employed by philosophers because that method was relevant only to "reality" antecedently defined as merely and wholly physical. I see no reason for denying that the emancipation of science which was involved was of great advantage to its progress in technical matters. But it was at the expense of relegating scientific material to the position of isolation from integral vital connection with and intrinsic bearing upon humane and moral issues. That it assigned "absolute truth" to philosophy as its subject matter, and fixed its connection with the body of natural sciences as simply that of "justifying" assumptions (so called) made by the special sciences (such as the nature of space, time, substance, causation, etc.) by exhibiting [them] on philosophical grounds not accessible to the sciences themselves, their connection with "ultimate reality" may seem to be a matter of importance only to philosophers. But the fact that human beings in their human capacity, in their habits and outlook, were confirmed in treating the method and conclusions of natural knowledge as at most having connection with and bearing upon only the lower "material" concerns of human life, was a matter of immense human importance. And this segregation is the entire practical or moral content of the view that by their nature—that is by the kind of "reality" with which they deal—the sciences at best achieve but "relative" and "finite" truths in opposition to the higher truths by which men must live. At the same time, subject matter which was set apart by definition as truly philosophical from *direct* fructification with the body of scientific knowledge, since all the latter could offer philosophy was the technical problem of how science was possible anyhow, and the further technical problem of "proving" its right to "assumptions" it has to make but cannot itself justify. That this segregation of philosophy is in large measure the cause of increased popular disregard of philosophy—if not contempt—is a point that hardly needs to be argued. Disregard for a particular type of philosophy has thus resulted in disregard for philosophical inquiry of any and every sort. It is one thing that men have no particular concern for philosophy which by its own definition of itself is extremely remote from *direct* connection with human concerns and human values.[12] The disposition which now increases in strength almost daily to have recourse to external authority to procure guidance in meeting serious issues which is the natural counterpart of an abdication of philosophy, which is the result that follows its break with natural knowledge and natural methods of obtaining knowledge, is another matter. For no one who observes present tendencies can fail to see that the confused mixture and half-way outlook of professed modern philosophy is providing a powerful argument to those who are now proclaiming with increased confidence that the only course open is return to the metaphysical-theological philosophy of the past with its fixed and ultimate truths, claiming authority to regular all human conduct and not subject to question and criticism.

If the subject matter of physical science is a distinctive realm of "reality" (as it must be if the traditional view of the equation of knowledge and the real is accepted), then its separation from philosophy compels the latter, if it is to put forth a claim to be knowledge at all, to insist that it is the highest, the supreme form of knowing on the ground that ultimate reality is its subject matter. It must also assert that the method of knowing which characterizes it as unique, as isolated and exclusive, is its subject matter. Unless it holds to a distinction between things-in-themselves and things that are merely appearances, between noumena and phenomena, it abandons all claim to have any subject matter—unless it is willing to surrender for once and for all that tenet of classic philosophy which equates knowledge and "the real." And it is obvious without argument that as long as it holds that it has a subject matter completely independent of natural knowledge, a subject matter beyond the reach of the latter, it is committed to claiming possession of a mode of access to which is its own peculiar or private property. The role of intuition and the a priori in philosophy is accordingly neither accidental nor secondary. The *words* may not figure, but their absence is a matter of slight importance since what they stand for is assertion of the existence and rightful command on the part of philosophy of a method or way of knowing that is different from that of common sense observation and natural science.[13] It is a strange fact that the moment any truth or principle is said to be seen or grasped by "reason," at that moment it ceases to be subject to

---

12. Its concern being the highly indirect one by dialectical method of proving the right of *Value in general* to exist and to be respected.

13. The statements of the text do not involve any denial that philosophers who have held the doctrines in question have as matter of fact hit upon hypotheses and enunciated principles in the course of their writings that are clarifying and fruitful. They refer to positions these philosophers are logically committed to; in practice they get away from them and make valuable contributions.

critical examination and test by evidence. That is to say, it becomes exempt from operations and conditions which in every day matters and in science define being rational.[14]

While the contrast between claim and achievement, particularly the contrast between settled achievements in science and the disturbed and controversial state of philosophy, results in the indifference to the latter that has been mentioned, there is an alternative. The variety of philosophy which defines knowledge in terms of conclusions reached by the use of operations that prove themselves to be progressively cumulatively confirmed competent by success, (including their own continued self-correction) in dealing with problems of any sort as they actually arise is not involved in the predicaments (called *philosophical* problems) that are inevitable when knowledge is defined in terms of privileged connection with what is called *the* real. It aligns itself with the procedures of the ordinary man and the scientists to whom "real" means whatever is substantiated in concrete cases as worthy of credence in distinction from errors and illusions that have been or that might be entertained: as in a given case a white fabric that is seen at dusk is "real" in contrast with an unreal ghost—since competent inquiry—knowing—obtains adequate evidence in support of one proposition, not in the case of the other. The existence of a particular body of knowledge [is justified] on the ground that it provides solutions for a general type of problem. In the present state of beliefs, the especial task (or "problem") of philosophy is to determine the type of problem for which "physical" subject matter provides material means of resolving, including a statement of how and why it is this special (and specialized) material is capable of functioning in this manner. There was a special reason why the qualification, "present state of beliefs," was introduced in the previous sentence. Once the task is accomplished and its conclusions generally accepted, there would no longer be a problem for philosophy in the existence of the particular kind of subject matter called physical. The result would be a part of the cultural capital, of the resources on hand, that can be employed in dealing with other problems as they present themselves. I see no ground for supposing we should run short of philosophical questions if it were generally admitted that such questions are temporal and hence relational, not timeless and absolute. As long as there is incompatibility or conflict among beliefs which affect important ends and policies of social action, and upon which, accordingly, men honestly divide; there will be occasion for a kind of inquiry which will employ the methods and conclusions of the sciences

14. A byproduct of this peculiar use of "reason" is that philosophers who question and object to the peculiar use of the word "reason" are then said to be anti-rationalists and anti-intellectualists! The dogmatism involved in setting up a special organ and mode of knowledge precludes the comity that is generally supposed to exist among fellow-workers.

as far as they are pertinent, but which will concern *what is to be done* and reasons why it is better to do it, not events which have already taken place.

Projection of old attitudes and doctrines into distinctively new movements and beliefs has done more than split philosophy off from natural knowledge. As far as theory is concerned, it has set up a separation, amounting to an impassable gulf, between the practical interests, occupations, regulative attitudes of every-day living (including of course their actual consequences in and for further living) and the distinctive subject matter of scientific inquiry. Reference was made in the previous chapter[15] to the "two suns" of Descartes—that of astronomical science and that of which rises, brings us light and causes us to get out of bed and go about our business in the morning, sets and brings darkness and sends most of us to cease work and to rest at the close of day. The fact that the latter subtends a small angle of vision in comparison with landscape about us (or even with household furnishings) in contrast with the incomparably larger size of the sun of astronomical science is the especial point made by Descartes. But in fact the matter is only one incident in the contrast between what enters vitally into the processes and consequences of human living and a subject matter regarded as if entirely out of connection with the latter. The "problem" of deciding which of the alleged two "objects" is the real one, or in any case of finding out how their respective existences are to be "reconciled" in view of their extremely diverse and seemingly irreconcilable features is still with us. It is a relatively meager output today that does not discuss the two tables, one of the molecular-atomic-electronic etc., one of physical science the other the table at which we sit, which holds books and various furnishings and from which we take our food at meal time—a table that is marked by qualities not found in the scientific material and that serves ends, effects consequences, foreign to the latter.

It does not require much skill in dialectics to discover there is something better with the usual statement of *two* tables—or whatever. From the physical standpoint, there simply isn't any *table* at all. There is a certain swirl of electrically charged particles which extends indefinitely. But one can read all the physical science there is in existence and nowhere come upon a table or anything of the nature of the table in the subject matter preferably formulated in terms of mathematical equations and other functions.[16]

---

15. [Located in chapter 5, "From Cosmic Nature to Human Nature."]

16. I do not say one cannot find it in the writings of men professionally occupied with physics when they nourish themselves at the table of philosophical remnants as not yet thrown into the ashcan.

From the dialectical point of view one might as well make a philosophical problem out of the fact that we can and do talk about tables, and what we say about tables has neither color nor size nor can it be sat by nor be used to support articles. It is possible the subject matter of physics like language is *about* things which enter into the resources, uses and enjoyments (and the obstructions, disutilities and miseries) that are the constant and inescapable qualities and characteristic features of the human life-process. If such be the case, then the subject-matter of natural knowledge stands in vital connection with all the things which are summed up in and by the title, *value*.

It might seem as if the preoccupation of philosophy, never more marked than at the present time, with reconciliation of alleged competing demands made, on one side, by the things and events of daily life and on the other side by the special subject matter of physical science was of no particular significance except to the scholars and teachers who happen to like that kind of occupation, since men in general go their way passing back and forth from one to the other with no sense of a chasm being crossed or any problems save the *practical* ones of attaining a scientific statement of some event that affects life—whether the heat by which our bodies and homes are warmed, the light by which we see to conduct our affairs, or the diseases from which we suffer—and of applying, by means of some invention or technological improvement, what is found out in the further course of life-experiences. Moreover, that the first of these matters, obtaining scientific formulations, deserves the name *practical* quite as much as does the second is evident in the fact that obtaining physical knowledge is a social pursuit or occupation, a division of labor socially maintained; and that the pursuit in question, the actual conduct of inquiry into nature, is an affair of resources at hand, obstacles in the way, devising instruments and techniques and plotting a series of transactions extending far into the future. For no matter what views are held about "mind," "intellect," or "consciousness," it is human beings at work in studies, libraries, observatories, laboratories, in mines, fields, and forests who produce physical knowledge as other human beings in other places, laboring with other instrumentalities and specialized procedures, create other products more tangible but hardly more visible or audible than physical formulations and mathematical formulae. And the transactions of one set of workers, like those carried on in other pursuits, are conditioned at every point by means of resources which are socially transmitted and culturally determined.

Examination of the existing situation discloses, however, that the import of the issue involved is far from being confined within the circle of those who occupy themselves professionally with the problem of the relation of physical subject matter to the operations, interests and materials of living. For the back-and-forth movements between the two which were just mentioned are far from being carried on freely or with the completeness that is possible. That such is the case is not, of course, the doing of philosophers. It is itself a social-cultural event having historical conditions that account for its occurrence.

· · ·

For instance, in economics the limitations are least marked at the end of the scale that is most technical, that conventionally labeled "production" and are most in evidence at the human end, that of consumption. Or, placing the matter in its own frame of reference, isolation of production of goods from processes of consumption and from the human aspects and consequences of the latter is involved in the habit of treating the former as it were complete in itself and treating consumption as a kind of incidental by-product.

The point I wish to make is so well exemplified as to be demonstrable to those who will reflect upon the implication of the fact that mathematics and physics are *"pure"* when they are taken as complete in isolation, while the operations and technologies through which they bear human fruitage are *"applied"* science, in a sense (as examination of current literature about science will clearly show) in which *application* means something externally and extraneously added. For I do not know what better proof of isolation could be given than that supplied by the well established habit of treating science as so complete in itself that the human uses to which it is put are extrinsic to it. In fact, while the words "pure" and "applied" are for all practical purposes synonyms in reference to the matter in hand, yet if I had only used "pure" I would have been thought to employ the proper eulogistic word, while "isolation" calls up considerations that evoke a certain uneasiness about the present standing of science and about the function to be assigned to it.

I doubt if many people would deny that the social uses which are now served by the material of physical knowledge are determined by institutional factors and conditions which had their origin in the pre-scientific epoch and which have not been internally much modified by the rise of science. The decadence of the feudal regime and the rise of the capitalistic regime were undoubtedly facilitated by the new movement in science and, in turn, the technological modes of production and distribution which operated to effect the overthrow of *overt* feudal institutions undoubtedly stimulated the new science; possibly to such an extent that they and their fruits were the chief factor in furthering its triumph in a limited field over powerful foes. But the attitudes and habits that directed the new technological resources into the economic framework called capitalistic were fixed and controlled by institutions which long anteceded the rise of both the new science and the new technology. One can believe, for example that there is an element of truth in the view that there is a genuine connection between the rise of capitalism and of Protestantism. There were features of Protestantism, or at least of conditions in the towns and countries that favored its growth, which gave the blessing and sanction of religion to financial savings which were, or were supposed to be, the material base of capital, as that was the condition *sine qua non* of introducing new forms of industrial production and exchange. But religious blessing upon abstinence and sacrifice was an old story. From one point of view the transfer of this blessing over from its old objects to new relatively mundane and secular ones represents a social mutation. But the factors which cause sacrifice and abstinence to be regarded as so intrinsically virtuous and desirable as to merit blessing from on high were "rationalizations" of institutional conditions of economic inequality which long anteceded both Catholic and Protestant adaptations of the underlying principle. And, as a matter of a larger scale illustration, no one would deny that in the feudal regime (and in that which preceded it) special privilege and command of the work and service of others were institutionally established features. That old habits, such as are exemplified in the cases just cited, exerted a controlling influence over the social forms expressed in the new capitalistic industry is as basic a fact as is the stimulus and direction given the latter by the new physical knowledge. Actual social events have been, and still are, a confused mixture of the consequences of habits that regulated the period before the rise of science and those formed, in a limited field, since its rise.[17]

But *authority*, the ascription of rightful power, to regulate the human uses and ends, the values to which the new science has been put through the medium of the new technology, has for the most part remained in practical attitudes and beliefs whose formation and authority long preceded the rise of modern modes and conclusions of knowing. This statement constitutes the significance of the view that the theory of knowledge in general and of natural science in particular, as they are expressed in modern philosophy,

---

17. [From Folder 53/15: "The new science has been, in other words, the source, or *author*, of the new technologies which in transforming industry, commerce and business have also transformed the face of society. Absence or suppression of conflict signifies non-existence of a problem; presence of a problem means that its terms are fixed by relationship to beliefs previously current in a given social group. Hence the structure and quality of these groups decides the kind of problem that arise and are given attention. The greater the *authority* in a given society of custom and established institutions, the more the problems and solutions that arise offered for them move within a predetermined circle of beliefs, consisting, as has been said, of fitting them into that circle with the minimum of change in its structure. And by *authority* here is signified a power to regular belief is more than sheer power because it embodies the active assent and loyalties of the members of a group. As long as it commands consent and fidelity, the power which represents a group is taken to have the *right* (or indeed the duty) to determine what shall be, and cannot be, a problem and how the terms composing [the] problem shall be stated and dealt with."]

had reflected and to some extent confirmed and justified this state of affairs by doctrines which represent a complete isolation of the subject matter of physical knowledge from *other* social subjects and materials. Institutional opposition to the new science was so powerful that, especially in continental Europe, it unconsciously induced representatives of the new science to protect their still young and immature efforts by proclaiming their isolation from all social consequences, save in matters of general "material" convenience and ease. This fact helps account for the particular form that was taken by the philosophical doctrine of knowledge. If the men who fostered the course are in need of an excuse for adopting the evasive means they employed to protect the new knowledge from being crushed in infancy by its powerful antagonists, the situation warrants exercise of charitable judgment on our part. But the facts of this case but strengthen the position which holds that the outstanding philosophical task of present-day philosophy is to indicate the place and function of knowledge as a rightful social power, an authority, in determination of the conduct of other social matters. Or, to speak in language which does not seem to accept the current views which convert knowledge into a kind of independent entity, the present task is to show how those attitudes and habits which constitute *knowing* in its actual effective practice (and which thereby determine conclusions reached) can be extended beyond the technical limited field in which they now take effect. In one of its aspects, this task involves breaking down barriers which the course of modern philosophy has itself build up. It involves, that is to say, the critical examination of the premises which gave rise to the *problem* of knowledge as that took form in the seventeenth century, and a similar examination of the various doctrines put forth as solutions of that problem. This negative aspect of the work to be done is, unfortunately, a condition of the positive work to be done.

V

In conclusion, I recur to the opening statement about the kind of unity that exists in modern philosophy. This unity, as was said, is one of *problems*, the doctrines put forth as solutions being divergent to the point of conflict and sheer contrariety. The diversity of systems lies on the face of the historic record. But it is logical as well as factually historic. There is nothing paradoxical in saying that the diversity of conclusions is the logical outcome of community with respect to the terms in which problems were stated. In the concrete it signifies that the dominant problem, that of the source, ground and conditions, and the nature and limits of knowledge, was stated in terms that contained elements so arbitrary, they permitted and encouraged extraneous factors to decide the course that was taken in setting up solutions. Diversity and conflict are the outcome whenever the conditioning factors of a situation are so indeterminate that outside preferences and other irrelevant matters have to be resorted to in effecting a settlement.

The evidence for the statement just made is contained in previous chapters. The terms in which the problem of knowledge was stated, by all schools, were indeterminate and contained arbitrary factors because they were set prior to and independently of the operations and conclusions that constitute knowing and knowledge as they are now conducted and constituted. The theories of knowledge which were put forth were not based upon the observed facts of knowledge, as a theory of eclipses, say, is based upon observed facts; on the contrary the theories had to be accommodated to outside "first principles." These pre-determining principles have been mentioned in the course of the previous discussion. At a minimum, they consisted of identification of knowledge with what is inherently or its own nature indubitable and of identification of such certainty with truths which are "necessary and universal," known to be such in their own self-evidencing constitution by direct inspection or "intuition" or derived, if they constitute true knowledge, from premises thus known. They consisted also of belief in the inherent correspondence of knowledge with Being or Reality at large, an innocent sounding assumption when stated in the abstract but which in the concrete means that conclusions reached in the course of actual inquiries have to be tested, as respects their standing as knowledge, by standards and "norms" set in advance of inquiry and independently of it. It consisted in belief in a knowing self, ego, or subject, the seat and organ of knowledge, equipped with a variety of power or faculties (later attenuated to states and processes) to whose structural constitution the conclusions of specific inquiries had also to conform if they were to be entitled to rank as knowledge.

When it is said that a procedure such as that just summarily described is bound to contain elements too arbitrary to control conclusions that are reached, there is postulated the possibility and desirability of an alternative procedure of a very different sort in forming a theory of knowledge. This alternative procedure, as has been intimated more than once, is that of basing the theory of knowledge on facts that are ascertainable and verifiable by the actual and behavioral conduct of knowledge, and upon conclusions reached in this form of behavior. It is altogether probably that this statement will call out the objection: "Yes, but how do we really know that the operations and conclusions in question *are* really knowledge?" For the sake of understanding the position here taken, it is to be hoped that that kind of a retort will be explicitly evoked. For it illustrates how deep-seated, even today, are the assumptions out of which arise the "premises" of the problem and theory of knowledge in modern philosophy. I mention here more as a matter of making clear, by sharp contrast, the nature of an alternative procedure rather than for the purpose of refuting the view which is fundamentally involved in the objection just brought forward. But, knowledge for knowledge, which has the better claim? Conclusions developed and tested in continuous patient inquiry in mathematics, astronomy, physics, physiology, in the whole set of sciences from the A of anthropology, through all the letters of the alphabet to the Zed of zoology, or first principles or ultimate truths of a very general nature alleged to be "known" in advance of any inquiry whatever and to which the results of the whose scheme and scope of inquiries constituting science have to be accommodated if they are to pass muster? Knowledge for knowledge there are those, among whom I place myself, who prefer to take lot with the former. But it is more directly pertinent in the present situation that the one making the objection ask whether it does not rest upon the assumption of the unquestionable nature of "real and true knowledge" and other assumptions closely akin to those listed. If so, he can then place himself in which one of the various epistemological schools he prefers: phenomenalistic and agnostic, empiristic, rationalistic, idealistic, realistic (of different brands of each) and so on: thereby illustrating what was said about the failure of the terms in which the problem is first stated to direct and regulate the terms of the procedure by which solution is sought for.

Further, by way of conclusion, I remark that the drastic nature of the criticisms passed is wholly grounded upon conditions of knowledge and other forms of cultural behavior which are comparatively recent. Given the comparatively sudden injection of the new knowledge of nature and especially of the new approach and outlook involved in obtaining and formulating it into the body of customs, institutions, allegiances or beliefs that formed the culture of Western Europe, especially in the matter of the fusion of the old cosmic science with imagination and emotion through the medium of morals and religion, and I do not find it possible to imagine how any very different course could have been taken. But I believe we now have at command the means by which there may be projected the pattern of a set of beliefs that are not dealt out and kept apart in a maze of reduplications—inner and outer, self and world, mind and body, active force and passive material, sense and reason, materialistic and idealistic (means and ends), fact and value. And I further believe that the state of confusion and conflict in which we live, without the settled advantage of either the old or the new, renders urgent the beginning of a new endeavor systematic in quality. For at best it will take a long time of cooperative effort to execute the endeavor.

PART TWO

VIII. The Supreme Human Art

In passing from discussion that for the most part is concerned with the past state of philosophy to discussion of what is now possible and needed, a start may well be made by noting the direction in which modern doctrines have made the most advance in spite of entanglement in alien doctrines that reflect the slow and halting course of institutional change. This direction of advance is conveyed, at least by contrast, by the general sense of writers modern in tenor that there was something hidden and occult in the older views. Stated in positive words, there was a sincere and energetic effort to get things out into the open, into the public air and light of day where they are open to inspection on equal terms by any and all who are properly equipped. Upon the side of actual behavior, the so-called practical side, the change of attitude is manifest in the era of explorations and discoveries which, beginning in earnest in the fifteenth century, are only drawing to a close in expeditions to the polar regions in our own day. And the vastly widened knowledge of human beings in their customs, institutions, practices, outlooks, languages that constitutes anthropology and other social studies, falls in this context, at first as hardly more than a by-product.

In a somewhat more technical fashion, the use of all kinds of apparatus and artificial devices to break through the crust of custom falls in this context. By their aid is continually brought to light a vast range of data of incredible minuteness and equally incredible temporal-spatial extent: incredible that is from the standpoint of what was accessible before the ever-multiplying invention of the instruments and techniques of observatory, laboratory and mathematician's study. Zest in discovery as distinct from zeal in proof is a mark of every significant modern philosophy of no matter what school. The working motto of one and all was: Get everything out into the open where it can be seen and examined.

II

Chapters of the first part of this work have discussed the harmful influence exercised upon the development of a theory of knowledge that should accord with the actual practice of knowing and its conclusions by beliefs that were incorporated in the structure of the culture of the Western world. Or, if one prefers to turn the matter around, they contain an exposition of the injurious effect of the injection of the conclusions of modern natural science into the system of moral-religious beliefs that were embodied in the institutions of Europe. It makes no difference, for present purposes, from which point of view, that of the old or the new, the development of modern philosophy is looked at. The important thing is that given the incompatibility and conflict of the old and the new and given the persistence of habits that have become intimately integrated into emotionalized imagination as well as institutionally incorporated, it is practically impossible to see how the course of modern philosophy could have been substantially different from that which it has taken. At the same time, history is an ongoing process. The fact that a period of confused mixture seems to have been, historically and humanly speaking, inevitable does not prove that it must endure forever. The state of confusion and conflict has, indeed, now become so apparent that it invites, on the one hand, organized effort on one side to effect a general turn to the theologically motivated beliefs of the medieval period as the way out and on the other side an organized effort to elicit from the movements that are genuinely modern in science, politics and technology their working postulates and report them in a form free from confusing admixture with alien elements. There are plenty of signs that the former movement is under way; social tendencies and forces that were on the defensive have taken the offensive, [with] the tragically disorganized and uncertain state of the world, domestically and internationally, giving them their opportunity. It will, in my judgment, perpetuate the present state of confused conflict and delay the needed clarification and reconstruction to meet this reactionary movement on the ground of that kind of "liberalism" which is an expression of the very conclusion that has to be cleared up. Something much more radical is needed.

· · ·

Instead of telling how the persistence of earlier beliefs diverted and twisted the course of modern philosophy, we may shift over to an attempt to tell in what direction modern philosophy attempted to move, and then attempt to list the main problems it has left as a legacy—not, indeed, as the problems with which philosophy must now cope but as material from which indications and suggestions may be derived.

Any attempt to tell the direction in which modern philosophy has tended to move lands us at once in a highly controversial field. It involves interpretation, and a kind of interpretation that is sure to be affected by one's own standpoint and preference. In view of the diversity and clash that attend the story of modern philosophy (indicated in fact in my own statement that the modern unity of philosophy resides pretty exclusively in its *problems*), the search may seem to be a futile one. However, I shall venture upon the undertaking. I believe that the most characteristic thing about modern philosophy, taken in its own terms, has been an intent to get everything out into the open. The attack of practically all seventeenth-century philosophers of whatever school upon what they took to be occult is in point as evidence. It is good evidence of their desire and intent, whether or not the things they took to be occult were actually so or not. The attacks upon what seemed to them to be secondhand "authority" points to the same conclusion.[1] Descartes accompanied the rule that only intuition and deduction should be depended upon with a warning against occupying the mind with "what others have thought." His advice that we begin by reducing every obscure proposition step by step to those which are simpler until arriving at those "absolutely simple" and then reverse the process so as to arrive step by step to those more complex throws more light upon what he meant by "intuition" and deduction than reams of elaborate disquisition. Get everything into the open and check at every step to make sure nothing has furtively crept in and note at each step the interval between it and the simple. That he took mathematics in general and his own analytic geometry especially as the models for these operations is, so to speak, the local and particular aspect of modern philosophy. His emphasis upon the absolute necessity of transacting business only with the clear and distinct if there is to be knowledge is the shared and public aspect of modern philosophy.

I hardly need recur to the evidence that Locke's standard and method for determining what is legitimate and secure and what is dubious and illicit is of precisely the same nature. Find that which is so simple that it is hence clear and distinct and then proceed by steps each of which is so simple that it also is open to direct inspection. His motto is "one step at a time and watch your step"; then you will know just the degree of certainty or of probability that belongs to your final conclusion. Aside from "want of ideas and want of a discoverable connexion between the ideas we have,"[2] the cause of ignorance is "want of tracing and examining our ideas," and this is the one cause which it is within our power to remedy. And in his definition of demonstrative reasoning, it is noteworthy that he adds

---

1. [Dewey's handwritten insertion: "Something about exp. and Bacon-Hobbes."]
2. [John Locke, *Essay Concerning Human Understanding* (1690), bk. 4, ch. 3, sec. 28.]

"visible" to the traditional "constant and necessary" qualifications of the kind of "connexion" between ideas which defines what is truly demonstrated. And when Locke joins in the contemporary chorus of depreciation of the syllogism, he does it on the ground that it is useless if the mind has not already directly discerned the connection of each term in reasoning with that which preceded and followed it, and it is worse than useless, a source of entanglements unless each step of proof has been discovered and then they have been "layed out in clear and fit order so that their connexion and force is clearly and easily perceived."[3] The complaints of "learned ignorance" that were rife from the days of the Renascence onward, get an emphatic statement in Locke's "[Quote missing]." The remedy is within the capacity of every normal human being. Get every idea that is entertained out into the open where it can be inspected with equal care and examine its agreement or disagreement with any and every other idea it becomes connected with.

That typically eighteenth-century philosophies were known in Great Britain as the *Enlightenment,* in France as *l'Eclairissement,* in Germany as *Aufklaerung* and are facts almost too pat for our purpose. But the all but everywhere repeated contrast of the "dark" that was passing and the "light" that was becoming ever brighter and brighter is surely evidence of something in the desire and intent of the period whether or not it was justified by actual events. The case of the good Bishop Berkeley is subtler than that of the French *philosophes* with their zeal for bringing everything to the light of sense and reason which they so inextricably linked to each other, and correspondingly better evidence with respect to the point being made. In the case of Berkeley, the decision as to whether the "objects" of ordinary perception or of science and conception owned the superior reality was so easily decided as to be no serious problem at all. He did his best to live up to the motto he wrote for himself in his youthful Commonplace Book: "Mem—in all things to side with the mob."[4] This slogan has a queer sound when put in juxtaposition with that popular notion of his philosophy which is presented in Johnson's belief that is refuted by the simple act of kicking a stone. For Berkeley, the "reality" of the stone and of the qualities that constitute the stone which was had by seeing, handling, or kicking it was the starting point—though not the terminal—of Berkeley's theory. What he denies was the existence of a "substance," named "matter," back of the perceived interconnected qualities which, according to him, *are* the stone, and the only stone there is. Locke's "new way of ideas" had logically reduced the "substance" which was supposed to support perceived qualities

---

3. [Ibid., bk. 4, ch. 17, sec. 3.]
4. [Berkeley, *Life and Letters of George Berkeley* (Clarendon Press, 1871) 420.]

to a fantom; Berkeley exorcised the ghost. Locke had said that our knowledge of particular things consisted of a combination of simple ideas, such as size, weight, solidity or resistance, ductility and fusibility (as in the case of *lead*) with "the supposed or confused idea of substance, such as it is," as "always the first and chief." And when he came to deal more explicitly with the meaning of his "such as it is,"[5] the best he could do was to say that after we have noticed that "certain simple ideas go consistently together,"[6] and after we have given their combination a single name, then, "Not imagining how these simple ideas can subsist by themselves, we accustom ourselves to suppose some *substratum* wherein they do subsist and from which they do result."[7] But "anyone who will examine himself concerning his notion of pure substance in general, will find that he has no other idea of it at all, but only a supposition of he knows not what support of such qualities as are capable of producing simple ideas in us."[8] In short, the only *"clear* idea" we have of such things as "a man, horse, gold, water" is that "of certain simple ideas coexisting together." And Locke explicitly adds that the same thing is true of the substance called *spirit*, when that is placed beneath operations like thinking, knowing, doubting, willing, as a support to hold them and a cause to produce them. Although Locke himself continued to believe in the existence of such supporting substances his words are in effect an invitation to do away with it. Berkeley accepted the invitation as far as "matter" is concerned, and Hume went him one better, adopting the same course with reference to an underlying soul (or spirit) substance.[9] Locke anticipated Hume as far as abolition of an underlying substantial self is concerned, insisting that *consciousness* of the continuity of past with present ideas was a sufficient warrant of personal identity, and the only warrant accessible to knowledge. When Berkeley read Locke, he found "matter" as an underlying substance to be but a shadowy ghost awaiting exorcism. When he got rid of it, the Cartesian problem of the two suns, and the Lockeian problem of the two substances of gold, one a set of ideas that go together, and the other an "external real constitution" held together by an unknown substratum, also disappeared. There was one order, the order of perceived things. The difference between connections of qualities which actually "go together" and those which are fanciful, being made by our own minds, was to be determined on the basis of constancy or regularity of connection, and hence by the dependability with which one could be taken as a predictive sign of the coming of the others [with] which it was bound up. There is, accordingly, a

---

5. [Locke, *Essay,* bk. 2, ch. 12, sec. 6.]
6. [Ibid., bk. 2, ch. 23, sec. 1.]
7. [Ibid.]
8. [Ibid., sec. 2.]
9. In his discussion of the "self," already mentioned (*ante,* p._).

sense in which Berkeley can be regarded as the first to be aware of the full force of the attempt to get rid of everything not open to observation—a fact testified to by his substitution of connections among observed events for an unknown underlying substance. This line of thought when it is followed out suggests that scientific knowledge as far as it is to be distinguished from ordinary knowledge furnished by direct perceptions is the result of search for and discovery of an order of signs which are *uniformly* and *permanently* trustworthy, enabling us thereby to distinguish between connections of events that are fanciful and those that are "real."

Only a slight knowledge of the writings of Berkeley is needed to show that in the previous account I have taken great liberties with them. The liberties however are not in what is said but in what is not said, in what is omitted. The actual, historic Berkeley interpreted Locke's ideas as mental and perception as the exercise of a mental power. Since he regarded the current Newtonian science to be "materialistic" in tendency and in effect (although not in intent) a bulwark of atheism, he asserted that since the system of signs was that of "ideas" which were mental and since its uniformly constant order proved that it was not the product of *our* minds, it had to be understood as a Book written by supernatural Mind—a Mind which had conferred upon his creatures faculties enabling them to utilize the order of signs for what Locke called their "necessities" and, of greater importance to reason from the Book to its divine author. In short, he retained, with a certain intensified emphasis, that part of the medieval tradition about spiritual mind as knower and about an ultimate substantial cause that lent itself to its theological bias. In consequence instead of acting in the way hypothetically suggested above, as forerunner of a theory of knowledge in accord with the actual practice of knowing, he more than any other author crystallized and precipitated the epistemological problem as a controversy with "idealists" and "realists," with (different) schools of each sort. The positive cues his doctrine contained went unheeded. Not even the theologians paid much attention to his new way of proving the existence of divine creative mind. His virtually entire historic effect was to so deepen the interpretation of Locke's "ideas" as themselves "mental" (a step Locke himself did not take) as to render the question of the "existence of the external world" an outstanding philosophical problem.

I have already referred to Hume's abolition of an underlying spiritual or mental substance. It was a move in the direction of getting rid of that which is "occult" because incapable of observation. Hume also did more than any other one writer to render untenable the identification of causation with the operation of entities called *forces*, and to enforce the necessity for a definition of causation based upon that which is capable of observation. In so far he did yeoman's service in promotion of the kind of philosophy that is based upon having all data and operations open and aboveboard. But, unfortunately, Hume's anti-theological and anti-clerical interest was more influential in determining his actual work than was his positive acquaintance with and concern for scientific knowledge. His denial of both material and mental underlying substances carried with it, logically, a complete elimination of all grounds for regarding observed events as "mental." He kept himself so completely within a *literary*-philosophical tradition, reinforced by his theological skepticism, that it did not occur to him to draw the only conclusion consistent with his premises and declare that observed events and their connections are entirely *neutral* with respect to any distinction that can be drawn between "physical" and "mental" and that *if* such a distinction is to be drawn, it must be drawn upon grounds that are *extrinsic* to the observed data. But Hume cannot be justly subjected to censure on this account since none of his successors, until the time of William James (in his later period) noted the conclusion—which as a matter of consistency clamored to be noted. That a professed skeptic like Hume never dreamed of questioning the inherently mental character of the immediate data of knowledge is one of the most convincing proofs to be found of the grip exercised by traditions when once they have been embodied in habits. In net result Hume, like Berkeley, emphasized and intensified the "epistemological" quality of the problem of knowledge:—that is to say, that attitude toward knowledge which is controlled and set by looking at it as a relation, of unique type, between a knowing subject (or its states and processes) and external objects—a phrase which is pleonastic from the historical epistemological point of view, since "objective" and "external" became synonyms.

Because of the influence of Hume upon Kant and of Kant upon subsequent philosophy, it is necessary to say something also about Hume's treatment of causation. As has been remarked, so far as his skeptical attacks were directed against the notion of "necessary connexion" which is to the action the product of some outside "force" (heat, light, electricity, life, as entities), his influence is all to the good. But Hume carried his legitimate attack upon force and upon *necessary* (that is *inherent* and inviolable) connexion to the point of denying any and all connection between events except that which was the order of an "association of ideas." From Locke's insistence that being a *simple* "idea" was equivalent to being an *independent* "idea" he drew the logical conclusion that every idea was an existence. The bonds that tie one to another were, accordingly, factitious; not being "necessary"—they were arbitrary. Sympathetic interest in natural science would have led him to dwell upon systematic observation as the means of determining the kind of connexion observed events have with one another in space and time in virtue of being themselves temporal-spatial. But adherence to the Lockeian literary tradition of separate "ideas" forced him to treat space and time as principles of separation instead of connection. Such connexion as seemed to exist between them was a matter of associations set up by habit or custom;—to which he gave, as his uncritically accepted prem- ises required, an "inner" (later called subjective) interpretation.[10] Locke's concern for inherently certain materials for knowledge terminated, ironi- cally enough, in wholesale skepticism regarding the possibility of any valid scientific generalization.

There is no phrase oftener quoted in histories of philosophy than Kant's remark that it was Hume's skeptical doubts about causation that awoke him from his dogmatic slumber. Prior to this awakening he had taken for granted the direct applicability of Cartesian rational conceptions, including substance, causality and mathematical relations, to "external objects." The difficulties raised by Hume in the case of causality led him to question the whole scheme. Upon what grounds can be certain of this applicability? At the same time, Kant was a devoted adherent of Newtonian physical science. He felt that the very foundations of this science were shaken unless it could be shown that and how mathematics, and the conceptions of substance and causality are applicable to physical subject matter.[11] I have no intention of going into the details of the Kantian system—about which an entire library of volumes has been written. With respect to the main features of his theory of scientific knowledge, it suffices to put side by side the problem presented to him by Hume and his devotion to Newtonian science. The former had shown him that there was no ground for the basic postulate that was common to the systems of his continental predecessors: That rational conceptions—such as substantiality and causality—are applicable by their own nature to external objects. He saw that the same reasoning applied to the inherent applicability

10. In the passage quoted from Locke (*ante*, p.) regarding the "natural correspondence and connection" of our ideas with one another, "natural" as "bounded in their peculiar be- ings" is set in opposition to "another connection of ideas wholly owing to chance or custom." This kind of connection he expressly terms that of "association of ideas." Instead of the ideas being "allied by nature," "custom settled habits of thinking in the understanding" and hence "Trains of motion . . . once set a-going continue in the same steps they have been used to." And he goes on that "this *wrong* connection of ideas in themselves loose and independent" is capable of extorting great force "in setting us awary." [Locke, *Essay* bk. 2, ch. 23, sec. 6]. Hume had his cue readymade. It required only a moderate amount of skeptical disposition to see that according to Locke's basic premise *all* ideas are "loose and independent." Hence he drew the conclusion that only *human* "nature" with is "mysterious tie" of habit connects what is observed.

11. It will be recalled that the title of Newton's chief work is *"Mathematical Principles of Natural Philosophy."* Kant could not regard the possibility of shaking the foundations of Newtonian with the nonchalant insouciance that marks Hume—who probably did not take his own arguments very seriously outside of theological matters.

of mathematics. In addition Newton had held that no theoretical views, no matter how consistent or developed among themselves, could be accepted in natural science until the actual existence of "objects" corresponding to them was proved by actual sense-perception. Kant did not dream for a moment of accepting the Humeian idea that uniform and necessary connections among objects were the consequence of irrational activity on the part of a knower: that is, of the mere casual and accidental action of habit. Why, however, should they not be the manifestation of a rational principle in the knower, universality and necessity being the traditional marks of the presence of "reason"? This mode of solution met and overcame Hume on the latter's own ground. It accorded with the tendency of eighteenth-century thought (especially strong in the case of Hume) to glorify the possibilities of human nature at the cost of what had previously been assigned to cosmic nature. If qualities and purposes had been transferred from the latter to the former, why not complete the work by carrying over also reason and rational conceptions and giving them their seat in the mind from whence they became efficacious in knowledge when and by, *in the very operations of knowing*, they brought material furnished by the sensible side of human nature into connections that were uniform and permanent? There was no need to take seriously Hume's reduction of the power of human nature to institute connections to mere habit and custom when everything testified (especially in the advance of Enlightenment in the eighteenth century) to rationality as the essential attribute of man. To Kant, moreover, it seemed virtually self-evident that one could discover the structural elements of rationality by inspection of the terms of traditional logic, the latter parting with their merely formal character and becoming positively effective in knowledge of "objects" when they operated to bring the otherwise chaotic matter of sense into order. Since both sense-material and rational bonds of connection centered in man, all the constituents of knowledge were within the possibility of ready control—after Kant had shown the way.

As far as sensible material was concerned, both the empiristic and the rationalistic traditions had already transferred it from cosmic to human nature, from the physical outer order to the inner mental order of events. Kant learned from Newton (even more than from Hume) the necessity of material derived from sense-perception to check and test the validity of theoretical material used in attaining knowledge of nature. What he learned in this way sufficed to loosen complete dependence on rational conceptions. But it in no way disproved the existence of the latter nor their presence in scientific knowledge: to have questioned the latter would have been at [the] time to question the "laws" of the natural order disclosed by Newton. The success of the latter's Natural Philosophy could be most readily interpreted as the result of the combination of mathematical principles, such conceptions as substance and causality and the material of sense-perception. It is not implied that Kant constructed his system by consciously borrowing from Newton. It was enough that the Natural Philosophy of Newton, which seemed to his followers to have provided an eternally valid picture of the very constitution of Nature, supplied the exact pattern needed by Kant when he was awakened from his rationalistic slumber and yet remained a loyal disciple of physical science. For the problem he had to face when confronted by the conjunction of the Cartesian tradition and Hume was precisely that of determining how sense and reason, perception and conception, can cooperate in creation of valid scientific knowledge. Newton's science, with its insistence upon verification of all theories by materials obtained through observation and its equally constant use of emphatic mathematical principles, supplied him with a working demonstration. Since for the first time in human history there existed a scientific system both comprehensive and detailed, there were was also in existence for the first time in human history a definitive model after which to pattern a theory of scientific knowledge.

It cannot be said, however, that the system of Kant carried to completion the strain of philosophy which tried to bring all issues and their deciding factors out into the open. In the scheme of Locke the "outer" things which acted to imprint upon the mind simple ideas as evidence of their existence and operation were at least solid Newtonian particles with definite physical properties; Locke never questioned his belief even though the results of their operation were such as to create the problem of how they could possibly be aware of the atomic masses which produced them. The Kantian scheme brought the space and time and the physical particles of Newton within the scope of directly observed phenomena and might in so far seem to be an advance. But it did so at the expense of setting up two ultimate "occults," two ultimate unknowables. One of them was the "thing-in-itself" which caused the indefinite manifold of sensory qualities that were brought into order by a priori forms of perception, space and time and by a priori categories of conception. It effectively displaced "matter" as underlying substance and as causal force. Whatever could henceforth figure in science as matter had to consist of definitely stateable mathematical relations among observed traits. But it replaced matter as causal substance by something more completely and inherently mysterious which could not even be said to be a cause, since cause was now defined as an observed connection among observed phenomena and which yet somehow was the source of the sense-material which was organized or synthesized into an order of observed "objects" by means of a priori forms and categories. Soul, spirit, any entity or force that could be called a person, were also abolished in the Kantian scheme. But it too was replaced by a mysterious unknowable center of the forms and modes of a priori synthesis, through which chaotic sense-material was ordered into a world that could be known. As unknowable, because unobservable, it could not be identified with the minds of individual human beings, the latter being "objects" *in* the observable field, and in any case too frail and transitory to carry the load of creating the known world. Not being Berkeley's divine mind operating through human bodies, it was to Kant but a logical center of reference in the system of knowledge which at the same time was the locus of all kinds of "synthetic" or organizing activity.

That such an incoherent scheme remained for a century and more at the very focus of philosophical discussion would seem to justify the most disparaging estimates of philosophy that ever have been uttered were it not for one consideration: These two ultimate unknowables are the inevitable logical ghosts of the "outer" objects and the "inner" subjects in terms of which the entire traditional theory of knowledge has been framed. The incoherency in the system was too obvious to escape notice. Its immediate effect was to instigate an attempt to reduce the two unknowables, the outer thing-in-itself and the inner noumenon to a single principle. This movement culminated in one direction in the Irrational Will of Schopenhauer and in the other direction in the Rational Absolute Spirit of Hegel. In both systems, the Cartesian principle of the priority and supremacy of the Inner came to a climax—save that it was no longer inner since it had swallowed and digested the outer. It might seem as if the net result would have been to establish that which is wholly neutral to the distinction of inner-outer, subjective-objective, self-world as the sole subjectmatter which is observable and verifiable, thus completing and thereby bringing to a close the struggle to get rid of the "occult." But that phase of the Greek-medieval tradition which found in the "spiritual" and it alone the source, seat, and authority of everything which is worthy and is capable of giving direction and instruction in the conduct of life and society with the "spiritual" was so strong that both the intent and the effect of the "unifying" movement was to restore to "Reality" by way of an analysis of the conditions of knowledge of the ideal-moral-rational features which the classic tradition had assigned to it by means of its analysis of the conditions of Being. Hegel's boast that his system set forth in terms of non-supernaturalism all the truths traditional Christianity had set forth in terms of the supernatural, with the appeal of the latter to imagination, is hardly correct historically. But it expresses intent of a movement to give all unworldly and super-worldly factors and attitudes a secularized reformulation, thereby conserving or "saving" traditional values. In attempting to accomplish this work by analysis of the rational and "spiritual" conditions of knowledge, he brought to a culmination that phase of the continental philosophical movement which strove to effect a re-interpretation of theological philosophy by means of a union of Greek and Post-Renascence philosophy.[12]

Kant himself pointed the way to the efforts of his German successors to establish a harmonious union of the inner and outer upon the basis of that which is inclusively "spiritual." Kant's theory of scientific knowledge has attracted so much attention that there has been a tendency to regard his writings on law, politics and morals and his sketch of a philosophy of history as secondary, if not afterthoughts.

. . .

[H]is theory of literally infinite and absolute value of every human self would have been taken to be the central principle of all his philosophy, and in this case the operation of *a priori* forms of space and time in perception and of the a priori conceptual categories of the understanding in linking events together by "scientific" (that is, necessary and universal) bonds would have been taken, as a matter of course, to be manifestations of the operation of this "spiritual" self—spiritual because outside of temporal-spatial conditions. At all events, Kant left the relation between the scientific and the moral in such a state of tension as to invite his successors to construct a unified "absolute" spiritually idealistic system of cosmology, which, by the road of analysis of the conditions of knowledge, was held to contain and support the values inherent in the Cosmos of the Greek-medieval scheme. Reason and rationality, with their traditional necessity and universality, were no longer primarily in the cosmos and secondarily in man. They resided primarily in Mind and Spirit, absolutely in an Absolute Mind and derivatively in the human self or subject. Their presence in the natural and physical world was not original and indigenous but borrowed and dependent. There was no need to fear encroachment upon higher and ideal interests of natural science. The triumphs of the latter, when rightly or philosophically viewed, were but manifestations of the advancing movement of the Spiritual Agent. In Hegel's phrase, it was one part of the march of God in the world.

The net outcome of idealisms of this general type is ironically paradoxical. On one hand it did away with the walls which traditionally separated man

12. Spinoza and Leibniz had previously attempted something of the same sort. Spinoza's connection was, however, with medieval rather than with Greek thought save as Arabian influences had brought the Philosophy of Aristotle into relation with medieval Jewish philosophy. Roughly speaking, his work consisted in effecting a junction between the latter and "modern" scientific ideas as they were expressed by Descartes. Leibniz attempted to "Reconcile" the teleology of Aristotelian cosmology with contemporary scientific mechanism and Protestant "individualism" by means of a theory of an evolving manifestation of inner forces.

from the world, the "inner" from the "outer," the "self" from others. In this respect, it replaced a disjointed scene and invited inquiry to deal with the constituents of an open world on their own behalf as observation might disclose them. It could be interpreted, without doing great violence to its tenor, as attributing to social culture practically all that tradition had assigned to a separate "mind." But on the other hand the scaffolding of traditional ideas by means of which the picture of one world of interconnected events had been constructed was so conspicuous as to be dominant. It effectively concealed from view the naturalistic-cultural components of the picture. In effect it restored "the truths" of the traditional system on the ground of an allegedly modern approach. As far as logical form is concerned, a similar irony attends the so-called subjective or empirical idealisms that emerged from the doctrines of Berkeley, minus his theological reference. With the abolition of a separate "outer world," the *raison d'etre* for an "inner" world also vanished. But the hold of traditional beliefs about mind and a knowing subject was so strong that the outcome was that the scene in ceasing to be outer was treated as one consisting of associated sensations, percepts, or projected states of consciousness. The force of old habits is perhaps most conspicuously exhibited in the schools of positivism and phenomenalism. Nominally they eschewed metaphysics. Actually they constructed their systems on the basis of acceptance of unknowable things-in-themselves which so acted upon mind, or upon the organism, or upon the brain within the organic body, as to create phenomenal appearances to which knowledge is confined.

Nothing has been said in the foregoing about "realistic" epistemologies. The epistemological postulate that knowledge is an affair of a relation between subject and object unfortunately gets the better of the alleged realism, which in many cases amounted simply to denial of the "idealistic" conclusions that what is known is of the same "mental" nature as the knowing subject. The triumph of the epistemological premise over the desired "realistic" conclusion is displayed in full measure in "representative realism." It took over the Lockeian double order of inner and order, and held with him that "things" are now only through the intervention of ideas or some mental state, its "realism" consisting in assertion that nevertheless the latter are capable of standing for or "representing" external real objects. Even when writers took cognizance of the conclusions of science, they usually contented themselves with substituting the brain for mind, and contemporary philosophers of repute have shown great ingenuity in propounding theories in which brain events are said in some case to stand for "external" events in a way that affords a sure foundation for knowledge. Writers professing psychological behaviorism have produced systems in which the strength of the old tradition is displayed in the fact that "behavior" is reduced to changes taking place *inside* the organism, with complete neglect of the non-existence of an organism save as one event in a world of connected events. Upon the whole, it can be said that while the prevailing tendency is way from overt dualism, yet its dead hand still holds philosophical discussion in its grip.

The prestige of schools of idealism and representative realism has, for example, been much weakened in the last few decades by the rise of a school of direct or "presentative realism." Members of this school (which has a number of sub-varieties) hold that knowledge is a direct, unique relation in which the knowing mind directly confronts "objects," grasping them without the intervention of any mental state. The rise of this school is readily accounted for. Knowledge has made such vast progress in the concrete that an air of unreality hangs about inquiries into conditions of its possibility. Knowledge is *there*, constantly growing in extent and in refinement and precision. In addition knowledge of the operations of chemico-physical processes and of the dependence of what happens upon them has reached a point where it is extremely difficult to think of "mind" or consciousness exerting a quasi-physical influence upon "objects." The epistemological *problem* extends to be reduced for member of this school to accounting for errors, delusion and illusion, and to discussion of how perceptual knowledge of ordinary objects is to be reconciled with scientific knowledge of physical objects. Nevertheless the discussion of the theory of knowledge is still carried on in terms directly derived from the epistemological tradition. This fact determines the very definition of knowledge as a direct unique relation of knowing subject and object known. There is doubtless a potential advance in naming this relation direct, instead of indirect. But the hold of tradition is exemplified in the fact that knowledge is defined in terms of the epistemological formulation. It remains the central and determining feature. I submit that if the influence of traditional epistemology were wholly eliminated, the work of genuine realism would consist in framing a theory of knowledge on the basis *not* of a relation between subject and object (no matter who either of them is defined or described) but of connections that are found among known events. For what possible course remains when all trace of the traditional epistemological formulation is dispelled? Until this course is followed, the philosophical theory of knowledge will continue to embody traits of modern life which illustrate the condition of wandering between two worlds, without the assured benefits of either one by itself.

The sort of philosophical theory of knowledge that would be based upon genuinely modern movements and that would be consonant with present needs, emerges, I believe, in some bare outline from the sketch just presented. Getting rid of the inheritance from a period that was relatively pre-scientific and pre-technological, whatever else may be said about its merits, is but the negative face of turning to the extremely difficult work of positive construction. Even the negative phase of the work, that of discharging the load we carry because of traditions that have entered deeply into the culture of the Western world, is difficult to accomplish.

IX. Things and Persons

As we have seen, the theoretical notion of persons and selves which has come to us from tradition is an interpretation of observed facts in terms of beliefs about souls and spirits formed in primitive conditions. It is now possible, probably for the first time in history, to form a theory about them based on the conclusions of the sciences of biology, anthropology and cultural history. Moreover, current philosophical ideas about personal selves represent deposits from some four strata. Intellectual energy that might, if the historic slate were fairly clear, be devoted to production of a theory in conformity with observed facts is spent in controversies about the merits of these different views or to the attempt to form a satisfactory theory by means of selection and arrangement of their constituent elements. The first of these views, the basic one upon the whole, is a fusion of the Greek idea of the non-physical intellect and the Christian idea of the immortal soul. The product of the fusion is the belief that personality is a supra-empirical or metaphysical spiritual entity. According to this view, it is a reversal of the truths to form an idea of personal selves on the basis of observed natural facts. We can observe the outward, the physical, form of John Smith and Susan Brown, but their "real" essence is so immaterial that it is grasped only by an act of spiritual faith or pure intuition. This type of view contains a number of varieties within itself, varying all the way from the affirmation of the theological doctrine of the immaterial soul as the essence of personality at one limit to the Kantian construction of persons as rational super-enforced ends in themselves and hence members of a transcendental metaphysical order [at the other].

The second heritage from past history represents a re-editing of the old idea of mind and soul on the basis of an interest in epistemological philosophy. Intense pre-occupation with the "problem" of the possibility of knowledge had a decided limitation of the view of the self as one of its results. The self was thought of as simply the knower, the cognitive centre and agent. The effect of this school of thought is identifiable by the continual use of the word "subject" thought of as the knower of "objects," and set over against them as of such a different nature as to create the epistemological problem.

The third historic heritage is provided by the "individualistic" movement which flourished in the British Isles and France during the latter half of the eighteenth century and in the first half or three-quarters of the nineteenth century—and in the United States as far as there was any philosophy independent of theological concern. This view was an offshoot of the view of the self as the knowing subject, extreme emphasis upon the separate and socially exclusive character of the subject being due to the political and economic doctrines formed in the earlier stage of "liberalism." This emphasis was, nevertheless, implicit in earlier views. The concern of Christianity for the salvation of the soul did not bring to open expression what was involved regarding the separate and independent nature of the souls whose fall, redemption and ultimate eternal bliss or condemnation constituted the central drama of all nature. The extent to which the Protestant revolt in its early stages deliberately insisted upon the immediate relation of the individual soul to God has received *ex post facto* exaggeration. But the elimination in some Protestant sects of the necessity of institutional mediation, and the multiplication of sects due to differences of creedal opinion of personal leaders operated in the direction of individualism, especially in connection with political [and] national ties and antagonisms and with new economic tendencies. Then the rise of the new astronomical and physical science was obviously occasioned by a few persons who broke away from the Aristotelian and medieval tradition. Under the influence of the Catholic Church, science as well as religion was institutionalized. The new science was so outstandingly the work of men who actively opposed the "science" enforced by institutional backing and prestige, that it could readily be looked upon as indicative of an intrinsic opposition between the "individual" and the "social." Political revolt against oppressive governments in Great Britain, the United States, and France, spreading in nominal form at least to other countries, stood out as an awakening of the sense of the inherent value of individuals, and as far as the *social* was identified with the *institutional* was further evidence of the right and proper inherent independence of *the* individual from the social. Even as early as the time of Descartes, knowing mind and self are treated as synonyms, a course followed by thinkers as unlike [him] as Berkeley. The fact that this was done without feeling the need for any explanation or justification is probably evidence that sudden breaking away from long established beliefs is felt to be the manifestation of the individuality of the knowing subject.

The fourth is that expressed by Hume as follows: "[Quote missing]." While this view in this extreme form is chiefly notably for the adverse reactions it evoked, yet there is close affinity between Hume's view and the view that "consciousness" is not only that sure and indubitable (because self-evident) [object] of which there is knowledge but is also the organ of such indirect knowledge of everything "eternal" as is conceded, on the ground of one or other epistemological theory, to be possible. This view of "consciousness" as *the* only certain cognitive agency and the self-revealing organ of its own contents was the product, on one hand, of refusal on Lockean empirical grounds to admit anything of an "occult" order, such as an underlying mental and personal "substance" and, on the other hand, of the Greek-medieval doctrine that no knowledge whatever is possible save on the basis of self-evident truths which carry their certification in their own contents; that is, on their face. Even today the main industry of the British "analytic" school has, as its chief source, the doctrine that inference cannot possibly yield knowledge save when it is derived from propositions that are non-inferential or true in and by the intrinsic nature of their terms and the relation between terms. Hence the anxious and prolonged search for "data" of this self-warranting type. The fact that scientific knowledge is inferential and that, in its case, premises are of the nature of hypotheses and postulates which are proved (trusted) by the consequences that result from their experimental application has had no generalized effect. It would be hard to find better evidence of the point already made; namely, that "modern" philosophy is confused and inclusive because it is an attempt at union of old and new beliefs which are inherently incompatible. Incidentally it is to be observed that this total reliance upon "consciousness" was a product and also a working cause of the "individualistic" movement. For nothing can be more completely private and inherently exclusive than "consciousness" as it was viewed in this so-called empiricism.[1]

When the idea about personal selves is framed on the basis of subject matter that is authentic, because verified in observation of actual connections among actual events, the obvious starting point is the behavior of organisms in their interactivities with environing conditions. Even when observed subject matter is confined to vital behavior (that is, behavior with regard to qualities having a cultural origin) racial and generic traits are found in intimate association with individual traits. Sheep are sheep and dogs are dogs, and so with all animal and vegetable forms, each "after its kind." But shepherds know the several members of the flocks in their severalty; they can tell them "apart," i.e. individually. Cat and dog owners and lovers are

---

1. The part played by identification of the "individual" self with the knowing subject in evocation of the German philosophic movement from Kant to Hegel and Schopenhauer receives attention in connection with another topic.

deeply resentful of any suggestion that their special pets do not have certain distinctive qualities of their very own. The point in calling attention to this commonplace is because of the evidence it gives that "individual," like "racial" and "generic," is an adjective. And the adjectival force is itself derived from an adverbial force and function.[2] The spatial distance between animals undoubtedly facilitated telling them apart. But things as like each other as "peas in a pod" are spatially separate. Different qualities in *ways of behaving*, in their connection with one another, are the ground on which sheep are individual to their herdsman, cows to their farmer, cats and dogs to their owners. And the phrase "in their connections with one another" is included because single traits, as single, are generic. All dogs bark, many are affectionate, and many are ugly, and many have about the same size and coloring, etc. But different generic *ways of acting* combine to yield something unique.

Observation of vital behavior. A theory of the qualities constituting anything such that it can be "told apart," or in its severalty as such, when based upon observed material will note that temporal continuity, or seriality, of behavior is an indispensible element. This temporal aspect is involved in animal life whether the latter is viewed phylogenetically or ontogenetically. With respect to the latter, it is now agreed by almost all competent students that classifications are properly framed on the ground of descent from common ancestry or involving the temporal continuity called *heredity*. But species and genera are also told off by differentiations occurring in the course of development. Differentiation and generification, if I may be permitted the use of that word, are both aspects of one and the same phylogenetic process. With respect to ontogeny, it should suffice to note how completely anything that is recognizable and describable as an individual qualification is a historical or temporal affair. Anything occurring instantaneously is at best an interruption of continuity of behavior; its character with respect to both generic and individual quality can be told only as the event gains form by being connected with [what] went before and what comes after as to be a sequence in which what is otherwise only a *succession* of incidents forms a *history*. The import of this statement may perhaps be most readily gathered by reflecting upon what constitutes biography whether of a brute or a human being. In fact, merely to say that a given account is a *life* of someone is enough to affirm a continuity in which events are interconnected. The life of Lobo the wolf, Jumbo the elephant, and John Doe the man cannot even begin to be related in terms of events that are not treated as growing out of

---

2. A surprisingly large number of fallacious philosophical views originate through conversion of qualities of activities (expressed linguistically by adverbs) into adjectives and then hypostatizing adjectival functions into nouns, the latter being then taken to stand for sheer entities. The "concept" of "*the* individual" constitutes one of the most harmful of these philosophic errors.

preceding ones and [into] those that follow.[3] And "out of" and "into" in this proposition are warranted to be taken in the most literal sense of seamless continuity the words can possibly bear. When an event, say that of birth, is mentioned as if its meaning was complete in itself, the content of a life-career is "understood": if that fact is not expressly mentioned it is because it is so intimately involved in the significance of what is told expressly that it is taken for granted a qualifying context. In short, the proposition that states, say, date and place of birth is potential and proleptic in force. The fact that every aspect, phase and detail of a biography must be related as having taken place in interactivity with environing conditions which evoke the act and which carry it forward into execution is an exemplary instance of the position herein taken about vital behavior and experience. Any view that takes "individual" to be a noun standing for something by itself in-stead of as an adjective qualifying a complex object which has meaning of its own without the qualification is dependent upon ignoring facts which force themselves upon anyone [who] thinks even casually of the biography of any human being—in fact it is so dependent upon failure to take account of these facts that it provides convincing proof that the view is a dialectic development of some dogmatic preconception.

What has so far been said applies to what is meant by individual quality in the case of any living creature. It does not at all cover what is conveyed by the word *personal*—also an adjective of adverbial force that in philo-sophical theory has been converted into a noun. For the serial histories that are marked by the combination of qualities that constitute an observ-able *uniqueness* of differentiation can be qualified by the further adjective "personal" only as they modified by cultural-social influences. Being indi-vidualized in the observation and descriptive report of another being is not the same thing as having the *sense* of individuality in connection with that other being or of one's own self. And [it is only in] this sense that anything can be called personal.

The Supreme Court of the United States has declared that, for a specific purpose defined in law, a corporation is a person. That fact that the court decision represented a definite economic trend favorable to the interest of finance-capitalism, and that its intent as well as its effect was to curb the power of state legislatures to enact statutes imposing certain burdens upon corporations, does not nullify the value of the declaration as an illustration of the strictly cultural status of the category of personality. When the doctrine of the personality of the "state" was put forward by a particular school of philosophy, the intent was doubtless to glorify and magnify the authority

---

3. The bearing of what is involved in temporal continuity as a prerequisite of the principle of *identification* upon "causality" receives later consideration.

of national state by transferring to it some of the prestige and glamour that had formerly been attached to kings who ruled in virtue of divine right. The "spiritual" properties which, according to the theological-philosophical tradition, inhered in personality, resulted in a kind of political mysticism, ensuring greatly the aggrandizement of political rulers. But since it was well known that corporations have no soul, it was not possible to apply to them, in their capacity as persons, the mentalistic-spiritualistic conception of personality. The only reasonable alternative was to recall the etymology of *persona*, the mask worn by the actors on the ancient stage. To be personal, in this respect, was identical with assumption and execution of a certain role or part in a definite group, the group in question existing and acting as a special group within an inclusive society and acting not merely *before* an audience but *to* them in a social exchange, receiving some sort of reward in return for services rendered.

I would not rest a conclusion upon an etymological fact even in its intimate connection with a historical-social fact. But the instance is used to illustrate the *representative* function and capacity which organic behavior takes on in and because of interactivities with environing socio-cultural conditions. In principle, there is no difference between the result of transformation effected by representative capacity in this case and that of souls which, because of the consequences of their social use in determining further behavior of the shared type, gain meaning in virtue of their strictly representative function. For when sounds become words, the original qualities of sounds (or marks on paper) are completely subordinated to the meanings they bear, the meanings in the process of communication being themselves derived from the way they operate and the results they effect in maintaining and promoting conjoint or shared activities, whether cooperative or competitive.[4]

The cases previously cited of specific representative function in human association, such as authorized agents, priests, trustees, elected representatives in lawmaking bodies, guardians, are cases directly in point. To possess and exercise an *office* is to be representative and the history or development of offices, or representative functions, is the history of transformation of biological traits into traits constituting *persons*. The case of the parental function is typical. Biologically parenthood may be merely the begetting or the bearing of offspring. Even among some animal forms, the male becomes the provider of food over a period of time and the female becomes directly the nurse and nurturer. Biological traits of this sort are prototypes of the offices that create the properties which provide the traits which constitute being personal until the nature of something with *responsibility* for performance

---

4. War and competition (*concurrence*) in sport and business are cases of shared, conjointly participative interactivities.

of the functions comes into existence on the part of progenitors and something of the nature of a *right* to protection and nurturance on the part of offspring. Then the execution of a biological function becomes an office, and an office takes on rudimentary moral quality. As in so many other cases, theoretical doctrine executes an inversion of actual order. Instead of moral relations existing because human beings are intrinsically persons, they become personal because of the rise and development of offices having at least rudimentary moral qualities. And this change from the biological to the distinctively human and moral takes place not just under social conditions but *because* of influences, pressures, and commendations (approvals) occurring in group and communal life. The case is similar to that in which, instead of acts being approved because they are virtuous in and of themselves, they become virtues because of the responses in others they habitually evoke; just as men are worshipped not because they are gods but become gods because of the reverence and adoration which is accorded them.

The exactness of meaning "responsibility" carries in relatively advanced social groups in which enforcement of authoritative legal regulations [is practiced] has given sharp definition to the meaning it did not have in earlier stages of culture. What we have primarily to think of is the fact that, in even the most primitive social group, there are demands of a habitual [kind] made upon human beings which they are expected to carry; that short of demands there are customary expectations that, in certain types of situations, certain kinds of actions will be engaged in and that fulfillment of these expectations is attended with commendation and other signs of approval (which in unusual cases cause a man to be a hero), while non-fulfillment calls out coldness, frowns, disesteem, if not overt imposition of penalty. These types of response have only to become customary to be recognized as obligations, and their performance to be a duty. The time comes with growth in social complexity and increased range of intelligent behavior when folkways are not the whole of morals; when expectation comes to include what is called "inward disposition," because, on its distinctively reasonable aspect, it is recognized that an habitual attitude is the surest guarantee there is for habitual compliance with group requirements and loyalty to group customs which make for social well-being. It is in and because of interplay among expectations, demands, fulfillments and evasions, with accompanying praise and blame, reward and penalty, approval and disapproval, that modes of behavior take on acknowledged social importance and become representative of social values; that is, of activities which are taken by the group to be important for group welfare and perpetuation. Human beings as the bearers of these representative functions, or offices, come into possession of the properties that describe a *personal* being.

Inherited cultural traditions have produced the belief that experience is inherently personal, and what is even more harmful to the cause of sound understanding is "personal" in a sense which ignores and denies the fact that qualities which are personal are social in origin and operation. The belief in question takes the following form. Whenever experience is mentioned with the doctrinal respect it merits, someone is sure to ask, "Whose experience?" The question is asked with a certain triumphant emphasis, as if it would be seen at once, without argument, that "experience" must be *yours* or *mine*, and necessarily in a private and exclusive sense of "you" and "me." Were such the case, it would follow that experience would be incapable of furnishing the ground for any belief deserving the name *knowledge*. An experience that was only mine could yield only opinions that are private to me. The belief, in any case, contradicts the theory it is supposed to accept for the purpose of the conclusion drawn. For the theory that experience is the source and test of ideas would be self-refuting unless it held that the meaning of such terms as *yours, mine*, "his" etc. is to be determined on the basis of experienced subject matter, not the nature of experience on the basis of some preconceived notion of what is meant by "you," "me," etc. In short, the use of "mine" implies they are my private property. It might as well be supposed that when I speak of "my [experience]," *experience*, not *you* or *me*, is the decisive factor. What has been said does not preclude the legitimacy, under certain circumstances, of qualifying the meaning of "experience" by, say, the adjective "mine." The case is similar then, in part, to what is said when one remarks "My idea is thus and so"—a remark that, instead of implying that all ideas are intrinsically my private and monopolistic possession, implies that as just mine, it is subject to correction by the observations and ideas of others. In other cases, the use of this qualifying adjective signifies the acceptance of responsibility. "Yes, that was undoubtedly *my* idea or proposal, not yours, that brought about this state of affairs." In general, the phrase "I think" is equivalent either to "That is the way it *seems* to me," a phrase indicating uncertainty (or perhaps a disclaimer in the interest of modesty of appearance) or I am willing to stand by and take the consequences that result from acting upon the idea. In any case "I" as here used is strictly correlative to "you" and "they." That is to say, one word has no meaning except in correlation with the other *within* a social situation. In the cases when acceptance of responsibility is involved in [the] use of "I," the initial occasion is the social act of being held accountable by others. When something unfortunate happens (less often than when something fortunate occurs), other persons say, "That is your doing" or "That is your fault." There is double meaning to these remarks: exculpation of the one making the remark, and indicating to the person that whatever objectionable consequences are produced should be borne by him. In any case, only slight observation of development of children is required to show that the meanings and sense of "I" and "you" arise together, each increase in the definiteness of one being followed by a like change in the other, both distinctions emerging from the same non-personal matrix.

Nowhere is the force of the old belief that mind is a kind of separate existence set over all else in nature more evident than in the doctrine frequently advanced as to how it is that we come to believe in (or have an imperfect sort of knowledge of) the existence of other persons than ourselves. The doctrine in question is that the belief is due to inference by analogy. We "know" (so it is affirmed) that our own existence consists of feelings, ideas, desires, volitions—or perhaps better expressed that these and other [modes] of self-knowing "consciousness" constitute our inmost veridical self. We note that certain results follow when we act upon the states or processes of conscious. When we see that similar results are produced by certain objects, *and by just those objects alone*, we conclude that the bodies in question have a constitution similar to that which we "know" constitutes our own selves and their mentalistic contents. The doctrine is so roundabout and so flies in the fact of observable facts of development of human beings from infancy into maturity, that were it not for the theory uncritically accepted from old tradition, it would be inconceivable that anyone should hold it. But given acceptance of and belief in that tradition, whose original is the notion of an immaterial substance called *soul* or *spirit* the view in question as to how we come to have the idea of other selves of the same general nature as ours presents about the only available way out.

Before taking up the grounds upon which we make a distinction between persons and things, I shall say something about the *common* material out of which both of these objects develop. One of the elements of the "analytic" psychology inherited uncritically from the old mentalistic tradition is the separation that has been set up between the sensory and the emotional or affective qualities of behavior. This matter was touched on earlier in another connection—that of division that is currently admitted between objects of knowledge and objects of impulsive tendencies expressive of need, desire, attraction, repulsion, etc. The present point is allied to that one, since so-called sensory qualities, especially those had in listening to sounds and seeing colors, have been associated exclusively with the cognitional aspect of experience. But the complete separation which is set up between sensory and affective qualities involves an error that is, so to speak, less doctrinal and more directly one of observation of facts. Affective qualities are just as *sensory* in their organic or vital content, as to both origin and function, as are the qualities of taste, smell, contact qualities of heat, cold, hard, soft, smooth, rough, and those of seeing and hearing that belong to things seen and heard. The difference between them is simply that the latter represent a progressive physiological and functional differentiation and specialization within the background of body-sense as a relatively undifferentiated whole. This statement concerns a matter of observable facts—facts which are many in number and mutually support one another. I mention some of these facts. Phylogenetically, the total body-sense develops first; and in large measure the ontogenetic development of the nervous system recapitulates the order of development of the race. Moreover, observation of conditions which are indispensible for the maintenance of organic life, as well [as] of its development, shows why this is so. Any form of an organic structure which develops and operates without the control of the processes and requirements of the whole organism is an injurious abnormality—as is shown by the case, say, of cancer. The affective qualities of the body-sense supply the sense of being alive, keyed up, save in cases of some abnormal strain when the sensory quality involved is as capable of fooling a person about his own condition as irregular qualities mediated by eye and are capable, when they have unusual emotional tone, of deceiving him about some object in the environment. Euphoria is an extreme case of the former sort of being led astray by "sensations." Normally, our sense of health, of vitality, of buoyant energy and cheerfulness and hence of confidence are manifestations of the general body-sense or what used to be called "common sensation." Emotional depression is the quality of lowered vitality of the organism as a whole and oftentimes of a feeling of incapacity, which in serious cases becomes what psychiatrists call "withdrawal from reality." But of more significance in the present connection is that those emotional states in which the entire body is most directly and intensely involved provide the background of mood and temper, which color, often dye, *every* experienced emotion. The matrix of body-sense is more than a background out of which emerged, in the far distance of our animal ancestry, the more special senses and their emotional traits. It permeates them through and through in the present manifestation, including the cases in which "intellectual" properties are relatively the conspicuous one. No form of psychiatric disorder is so outwardly calm, so free from overt strong emotive manifestations, so argumentatively rational, as paranoid states. The form of reasonableness is maintained in spite of "objective" evidence to the contrary, because the dominant state twists everything seen and heard in behalf of its own maintenance. The emotional quality of some of the "special sense" is notorious. It would not be necessary to mention tastes and smells were it not that, while their affective quality is a matter of general knowledge, no use is made of this well known in framing the general theory of sensations, or sensa or sense-data. For were the fact grasped in its own import, it would bring at once to an end the notion that sensa (etc.) are simply independent entities inherently "cognitive" in nature. The more obviously emotive character is, of course, in line with their being nearby differentiations of body-sense, as well as most intimately connected with the essential vital behavior of food-getting, detecting unseen and unheard prey and foes, etc. For persons whose main occupation is writing, reading, scientific pursuits, etc., the ear and eye, the latter especially, are means of getting and communicating knowledge. Hence the justified tendency to regard them as preeminently the "intellectual" senses, and also the unwarranted tendency to ignore their immediate affectional force, or at least to reduce it to a kind of after-effect. The existence of the arts of painting and music is enough to convince a person not hopelessly prejudiced by doctrinal pre-commitment that in fact it is the other way; in their primitive stage, sounds and sights are primarily emotive and they acquire their definitely intellectual force in the course of their utilization as signs of environing conditions and hence of the kind of interactivity in which to engage.

I have indulged in a somewhat extensive exposition of facts which, taken one by one, apart from an attempt to draw a generalized inference from them, are all but commonplace. The purpose is to set forth the behavioral background and underlying ground of the view that the observation of some objects as persons or selves and of other objects as things is framed out of a material that is generically the same in both instances—a view from which follows, negatively, the total uselessness of the view that we have an original intuitive knowledge of our own "ego" and then arrive, by means of analogical inference at belief in the existence of other similar creatures.[5]

My next step is to carry what has been said over to statement of the theory that, in fact, the idea of equal selves, whether mine, yours or theirs, is constituted out of directly experienced or had emotional qualities of behavior. The beginning is made by recalling two considerations, one of them a familiar commonplace: i.e., the indissoluble union between emotion and some kind of activity. It is not necessary to go as far as Hume went when he said that reason is and must be the slave of passion. Indeed, it is unfortunate that the exaggerated form of Hume's statement has been the cause of a great deal of ignoring of the element of truth his statement contains, thereby maintaining the vogue of the dogma of the intrinsic separation of "intellect" and "emotion." The word *slave* is a word indicating a strictly

---

5. It may be well to recall that this view is the result of union of two views for which there is no empirical evidence—that is, no support in observable facts. The views in question are, first identification of the self with the knower *as* knower and secondly the identification of the knower with "consciousness," a view which was intended to uphold, in a much changed environment, the Greek-medieval doctrine that knowledge means *certainty* and that it is attainable only when there are self-evident and self-evidencing "truths" as premises.

one-way movement, from master down to a servant who is servile in his abject submission. The fact is that the consequences of emotionalized behavior when they are noted and are referred to their source (that is, are subjected to "reason" as *intelligent* behavior) modify the original immediate and, so to say, brute "passion." In this case *reason* and *passion*, to continue the quasi-personification of the complex of traits to which these names are given, are partners in a common enterprise instead of one being master and the other slave. In this enterprise, *passion* gives to ideas and beliefs the force required for their execution. Otherwise they are as idle as the painted ship upon the painted ocean. The cases of so-called ideo-motor activity are in fact purely mechanical, with no present ideational constituent whatever, save in those cases whether at the very outset some idea is sufficiently affective in its own quality to start a mechanism, formed by habit, in operation. But an idea, when affective in quality, determines the direction taken by the executive behavior in question—a fact hypostatized when ideas and affections are separated in the statement that ideas (or "reason") directs, in the sense of ordering as a command, the course taken. There is probably no aspect of the general tenet of the "inner" and the "outer," the "internal" and the "external" set over against each other, than the aspect in which emotion is taken to be something occurring confined within an inward soul, mind, self, consciousness, or whatever. The intrinsic falsity of the view is [all] the more significant in that the emotional qualities of acts performed and attitudes displayed come, under the influence of membership in a social group, to be referred to a self as an essential constituent of its own being. A child becomes aware of anger or fear because, in the interest of social control or guidance of his conduct, it is ascribed to him as something he can be held to account for by parents and by other persons acting in representative capacity. No child ever lived who did not at first take fearfulness, hatefulness, attractiveness, irateness to be an inherent attribute of some situation. Only because of instruction, advice and reproof by others does he learn to refer the qualities in question to himself in a special way. And the lover who is fortunate continues to find some person of lovely constitution through and through. The state of affectionate bliss is drawing to a close when he characterizes the situation in which he and someone else are involved as a matter of an expression of some inward state of his own—and this takes place when a similar inward feeling is ascribed to the other person.

The other point to which I call attention is again notorious—familiar in and of itself. Although, in its case also, the recognized fact is not thought worth acknowledgement in general theory. That is the all-over quality, the all-or-none quality of that which is emotional. And this all-over pervasive quality is not at all a matter of the intensity of a passion. It marks a faintly emotionalized piece of behavior as well as one strongly affective. One is, so to speak, irritable, sad, joyous, fluctuatingly hopeful and fearful *all over*—as long as one is that way at all. What is proved by this fact is that an emotional quality is the manifestation, and potential mark, of immediate total organic or vital engagement in interactivity. In distinction, a predominantly intellectualized mode of interactivity has mediate, relatively remote, reference to life activity as such. In its own terms, during its occurrence it involves specialized action on the part of some special structure—hand, eye, ear— and with quite extensive subordination for the time being of many of the constituents of complete immediacy of behavior. In short, it is *partial*, discriminative, analytic. It is because of immediacy and totality in immediacy that emotional qualities are the material out of which personal selves are formed. Furthermore, the view that the material of experience is, generically, of the same sort as is the material in experience from which *things* progressively emerge is simply a manifestation of the fact that in both cases the material experienced is of a *sensory* order. *Specific* difference within generic identity is indeed great. The difference, moreover, is not quantitative, but qualitative, just as is the distinction between persons and things, although both are *objects* and, as such, generically alike. The difference is that between sensory qualities mediated by the organism in its entirety and sensory qualities dependent upon a predominant involvement at the time of special organic structures. There is no way I know of by which argument in discourse can prove [this] to those who doubt or deny the strictly sensory character of the experienced materials constituting the emotional aspect of behavior. The idea that the commotion and excitement, the driving urge to be doing something with and to surrounding conditions can be anyway given a primary location in the brain or central nervous system has no scientific support. On its face it seems laughably absurd. The nervous "seat" of the emotional is the autonomic nervous system, both anatomically and physiologically, and the connections of this system are with such vital functions as circulation, breathing, digestion, secretion, ejective or eliminative bodily apparatus and the act, and accompanying motor steadiness. It would be strange beyond belief if the eye and ear and hand were capable of expression of sensory manifestation in expression, while sudden disturbances of the regular functioning of [these organs] were incapable of expressing themselves in any sensory form.[6]

From the beginning of human experience, some human beings must

---

6. I add that while the James-Lange theory of emotion seems to me, with certain modifications, essentially sound, its acceptance is not required by the position here taken. The ideas of the intrinsic connection of emotion with the organism as a whole, and of its recognition with sensory reports of certain fundamental attitudes, is all that is necessary.

have noted differences of behavior in what, from a much later standpoint, are termed persons and things. All observable differences are differences of quality—even those of quantity could not be sensibly noted (though they might be grasped in idea) if they did not make some immediate difference in quality. It was on the basis of qualities of behavior that sheep were marked off from goats, and both from cows and so on indefinitely. It was on exactly the same basis that certain events were finally given the status of things and others of persons. If at first sight it seems strange or forced to hear that the differences of trees not only from other forms of vegetation but of different kinds of trees from one another and of the varieties of oaks from one another, and [so on] down to the individual trees are differences in observed qualities of behavior, it should be recalled that their behavior is a matter of interactivity with factors provided by human behavior. When the theory of perception is brought up anywhere near to the present date, as respects anatomy and physiology, to say nothing of matters of coarser and more direct observation, it will be a commonplace of that theory that the qualities we note are responses to different ways of our behaving as the latter are in true adaptive responses in conjunction with environing events perceived by qualitative differences made. The hardness of a stone does not force itself upon us; it is experienced in consequence of an interaction of an object with pressure exerted directly or indirectly by ourselves. The sound of a church-bell or of a locomotive-whistle is experienced in virtue of certain active adaptations of the motor mechanism of auditory apparatus. We listen *and* hear; and similarly we look *and* see. Listening and looking are modes of vital activity that involve the motor adjustments found in every activity. The property of interactivity is, moreover, of equal importance upon the side of organic action with respect in identifying and discriminating events. Differences in quality are marked to and by us in the degree in which [there are] different kinds of response. The principle involved in this consideration is of particular significance with reference to the ordering, coexistential and sequel, of a number of qualities—a matter of prime importance for perception of things since it is such conjunctions that constitute an object, which is an ordered assemblage of qualities not either a single quality nor a chance miscellany of a number of qualities. Every event and object has a figure, *eidos*, form; its qualities are *patterns* and the patterning is determined by the sequential pattern of our adaptive behavior. While pattern is most readily noted in connection with the consecutive order that characterizes every effective life-activity, a variety of contemporaneous elements of a perceived thing fall into pattern. It is physiologically impossible to find a single case in which the most transitory perceptual experience is of a single quality. The response the body may focus in the hand, eye, ear or nose and the result is that the thing as perceived is centered or focalized—an illustration of the principle under discussion. But it is physically impossible to suppress lateral bodily activities, and if it were possible the quality perceived would be completely useless from a behavioral point of view. (The mechanism for producing hypnotism is precisely that of production of an abnormally extensive isolation of some sensory response with a kind of temporary paralysis of the organs usually attending its operation.) In fact, all that is required is to note [that] the factuality of the account just given of the formation in observational experience of different things by means of their action upon our bodily organs and the response of the latter to them, is negative. It is to get freed from two traditional systematic misconceptions: the *passive* reception of "sensations" and the originally singular and simple nature of the latter.[7]

I commence my further discussion by mentioning a matter which taken by itself is of no special theoretical significance. Everyone, I am sure, has known somebody, usually a woman, who is noted for the quickness and accuracy of "intuitive" estimates of the characters of the people with whom she (or he) comes in contact. Careful observation of these unusually gifted sons will show both high sensitivity and high responsiveness. I add the latter word (either would suffice) to make it clear that by "sensitivity" I do not have in mind that egoistically centered easily "hurt feelings" that are often identified with sensitiveness. This kind of sensitivity is abnormal, since it is the outcome of repression of the "natural" outlet of responsive action. [A] previous situation has blocked or clogged normal avenues of expression, and has, as we say, driven the person in upon himself. There are, however, some persons who do not express their reaction in an immediate and overt doing, and yet do [fail to] adopt the just mentioned relatively morbid course. They make constant partial responses visible to others, if at all, only as slight facial expressions and slight bodily muscular readjustments and convert the qualities which result from their own incomplete overt responses [into] material out of which to form an estimate of the person who has called them out. There is a series of delicate subtle fluctuations with every change in what the other person says or does. But also long practice has enabled them to translate the qualities thus occasioned into a prompt and accurate estimate of the attitude involved in the other person's behavior. As Spinoza said, Peter's idea of Paul, when known, tells about Peter as well

---

7. The Gestalt school of psychology deserved much credit for its intelligent criticism of the "separatist" school and for its insistence upon the patterned or configured nature of all experienced objects beginning with those of perceiving. But I believe they have also done a disservice, due presumably from the German epistemological tradition in the doctrine put forth to account for the occurrence of patterned objects. It is enough to reference to the intrinsic coexistential and sequential patterning, which patterning is a practical necessity for and in maintenance of life.

as about Paul—sometimes much more. The reason is obvious. It is in terms of the qualities experienced by Peter, because of his interaction with Paul, that Peter forms the Paul which is *his* object. It is not, of course, literally true that men—and women—judge others in terms of themselves. For the activity of the other human being in a transaction has some determining effect on the qualities experienced; a mean man may have an act of generosity forced upon his grudging recognition. But since the resultant qualities are immediately experienced through the effect made on each participant, one's own share in their production is sufficiently overweighted to account for the truth in the common saying.

If in the previous discussion, the words "men-women" had been used instead of "persons," it is probable that what has been said would receive readier acceptance. For the former words are, so to speak, experiential on the same level as the words, "things," "events." They are free from a certain aura that clings to "person" and "personality," probably from their association with use in a religious or a sentimental moralistic context. And as matter of fact, "person" stands for something more than "man" does; it stands for *man* plus a special representative power that has evolved in social groups in which jural relations have received a fairly high degree of enunciation. Perhaps the fact that in most modern societies "voter" has meant more than "Citizen" just as "Citizen" has fuller meaning than "alien" may suggest the kind of difference. A voter must be a citizen, but the citizen to be a voter must satisfy certain further socially defined conditions. Similarly a person must be a human being, a man or woman, but must also possess additional capacities that exist (operate) only in a group in which there exist such relational functions as formulated liabilities, rights, duties, and immunities. When we speak of human beings as persons in the case of certain primitive groups, the attribution is not metaphorical as it is in the case of personification of, say, animals. But the word is used to designate a potentiality, rather than something as yet actualized. The same thing is true of infants in the legal sense of the word. In some pagan and most of early Christian literature, it was debatable whether women had souls in their own right and consequently whether or not they were persons. In the case of chattel slavery the same controversy has taken place regarding men and women held as slaves. Aristotle quite expressly reduced domestic slaves to the status of things since they were, with social sanction, employed as useful tools for accomplishing the ends of others—like other domestic utensils. The recognition that *all* normal human beings are persons potentially is itself the product and mark of a great moral advance in the constitution of human society.

It is probably fairly easy, preconceptions put once aside, to see that human beings are discriminated from other animals by the qualities of their behavior, and even yet easier to see that men are differentiated from women on the same basis. I do not underestimate the value of figure in its ordinary sense but that it counts because of its connection with specifiable modes of activity (interactivity) is evident the moment we consider the most perfectly formed wax dummies. It is not so easy perhaps to perceive that the qualities which are differential, given the common base of qualities belonging to all bodies, are the emotional ones. Yet if it once be admitted that emotions are appreciated by sensory means, while different emotions are told apart by the presence in experience of different sensible qualities, exactly as, say, apples, peaches, and pears are told apart, it is hard to see what other conclusion can be arrived at—provided, once more, the inherited idea of a separate mentalistic stuff be surrendered. The *total*, all-or-none, quality of the sense of anger, fear, love, hate, together with the gradations down to the highly specialized visual sense and the parallel gradation of the intellectual capacities of these "special" senses, should be given decided evidential weight. If one thinks of another human being, one thinks first of a body of a certain form, engaging in certain movements of the body as a whole, of posture, of facial muscles. But, when this is all done, what more is there in the way of qualities by which to differentiate the body in question from other bodies save the qualities pertaining to the behavior of organic bodies in communicative association with one another? Add to this question one further one: What means is there in any case by which bodies, objects, can be distinguished from one another save by sensible appreciated qualities? After all, the strongest argument that can be put forth in the end for the position here taken is its complete congruity with the accepted theory of perceptual identification and discrimination of *all* objects, and so a little more will be said on that topic. First, I assume that there is admitted the falsity of the two ideas of sheer passivity on the part of the organism and of single separateness in the occurrence of sensory qualities. The positive basis of these admissions is the fact that continued life-activity is an affair of the engagement of the organism as a whole in interactivities with environing media, that specialized structures and functions occur in the case of more complex living bodies for the sake of and as a part of a given continuing life-process. Sensory events, "sensations" physiologically speaking, have the special function of redirection of activities when changing environing conditions demand re-adaptation in behavior. It is a curious error to suppose they are stimuli to initiate action as if nothing were going on before—as if the organism were wholly quiescent until stirred to act from without. A living creature is a set of active energies more or less organized in connection with one another, and by the nature of the case these energies have, as a rule, a certain direction; toward food, a mate, or a lair, or away from an enemy, for example. But no environment is uniform for any animal of any degree of complexity and variations in it, spatial and successive, demand pretty continuous re-direction of the activity, usually slight veerings and tackings but occasionally shifts of considerable magnitude. Sensory structures and events exercise this interstitial and intermediate office as respects the course taken, the direction pursued, in the sequential continuum of life-activity.

Perception of the *qualities* of these conjunctural vector events is of the nature of any and every perception; whatever "mystery" or as yet unsolved problem there is about it concerns not the perception of hard, or red, as the quality a specific interaction of an organic process and a changing condition of the environment, but the occurrence of perception or being aware of anything whatever. Since the sensory event itself occurs at a certain juncture and has the function [of] redirection of activity, nothing could be more absurd [than] the account that used to be given in psychological texts of such experiences as perception of an object like an orange. The first error was the assumption that the object was built up in experience bit by bit, mosaic like, out of independent qualities of seen color, felt textures, smelt odors and enjoyed tastes. Not one of these occurred at any time save in a context of definite connections, so that there is a certain rudimentary patterning or "configuration" from the start. In the second place, because of the continuum of interactivities constituting the life-process, it is contrary to fact to assume the object, the rudimentary orange, has any existence in experience disconnected from that of other things. I do not mean of course that an orange does not come to be experienced as different from a lemon or an apple, nor that a single orange is not distinguished in a pile of oranges or on a tree. I mean that (i) in every such case, the thing perceived is perceived in a definite spatial and temporal context—in, so to speak, a "world" of which it is a part—and for the time being the central part. I mean also (ii) that this definiteness of perception, which confers a certain qualitative singleness or individuality to what is perceived is the outcome of frequently repeated discriminations and re-conjunctions, each one of which occurs at its own date because of a certain genetic state of affairs with reference to what went before in a life-course and serves to determine what comes next. It grows out of the previous experienced field and is, as it occurs, a factor in the forming of the further experienced field—which is always in consequence a moving field—but not a mere flux.

As was said earlier, the purpose in inserting this account of the relation of the occurrence of sensory events in the case of "special" senses, when the experienced result is perception of some non-personal *thing*, is to indicate that there is no difference in procedure when the original sensory material is the *total* organic sensory condition due to the engagement of the living creature as such in an interactivity with its environment and the outcome is perception of personal objects. Instead of first perceiving a *body* in the narrower material or physical sense of the word we first see a body in the sense of an animal or human body. The stripping away of "tertiary" qualities[8] is an accomplishment, in the degree in which the experienced result is perception of objects as inanimate and merely material, the bodies first experienced, in the original matrix of a relatively undifferentiated field, gain properties due to the contrast effect. They are living, and, in the case of human beings, personal in some rudimentary sense. Neither "persons" nor "things" would have the distinctive meaning they bear if they did not gradually differentiate out of a common background in a kind of polar contrast with one another. Just as perceived things, even in their singleness, are experienced as part of a larger world, so in the case of persons, both with respect to one another and with respect to connections of persons with things. The whole history of reflective thought shows no idea more contrary to observed facts than the notion that "solipsism" is the original "datum" of experience which either has to be accepted or, if and since one cannot get rid of the sense of its inherent absurdity, circumvented by some feat of ingenious philosophical technique.

---

8. [Dewey's note to himself: "Quote Santayana in footnote."]

X. Mind and Body

I

The remark made earlier about the conversion of words of adverbial force into an adjectival trait, and then, what is much more harmful, the conversion of the latter into a noun, applies especially in the case of "mind." A qualification of behavior which is of the utmost importance as a distinctive, a unique modification of some kinds of interconnected activities, is erected into an entity. Primitive notions about the soul, anima, at least related it to observable phenomena, those of breathing, the heat and motility of the living body, the latter to every appearance self-initiated and self-guided, and the absence of these traits from the animal corpse. In Greek philosophy (at least in Aristotle and in Plato when not in his Pythagorean mood), the psyche was definitely the active principle of life. No incongruity was felt in speaking of the "vegetative psyche," since plants are living bodies. The animal soul was also identified through a set of connected observable traits, capacity of locomotion and going after food and mate being the most obvious. But in addition to the lower animal souls, marked by self-protecting and acquisitive tendencies, there were outgoing and, so to say, generous impulses: bravery, defense of young, concern for the pack, etc. When man was defined as the *rational* animal, nothing was further from the intent than to define him as purely or even mainly rational. "Rationality" was the *differentia* of the human genus. The power of the body to take in and digest food proved that he had a vegetative soul; other features of his behavior show that he has animal psyche, in both the lower and the higher aspects of the latter, some persons and some racial groups, the Greeks and especially the Athenian, being marked by an unusual proportion of the higher. Relatively speaking, the northern barbarians, the Macedonians, were characterized by the *spirited* qualities of the psyche; the eastern pleasure-loving peoples by a predominance of vegetative and lower, getting and absorbing, traits. Different proportions also characterize different classes within a given community. The trading class exhibits for example domination by lower animal traits; the soldier-citizen class, as in Athens, manifests the spirited psyche; the rulers, especially lawmakers, are as such or ideally characterized by the supreme rational psyche—for law is universal (as distinct from the personal mandates of despots which are particular) and so rational.

I have no desire to make out that as respects psychological matters, Greek thinkers anticipated recent behavioral psychology. But it is true that with the exception of an occasional outcrop of the Pythagorean strain and of quasi-mysticism, their standpoint was, in comparison with the later theory of the soul (psychology), naturalistic and based upon observable events of a crude sort. One has only to compare popular Greek ideas of the state of psyche after death with popular Christian ideas of immortality and heaven and hell to note how much closer was the former to ordinary facts of nature, while the Christian ideas were framed definitely in a certain non-natural moral interest—association, as was said earlier, not with nature but with a drama enacted by *wills* human and divine. It would be interesting to show how medieval theological metaphysics preserved, in spite of predominant supernaturalism, elements of the Greek philosophy which maintained a certain hierarchical gradation and continuity between underlying "material" structures of nature, through plants and animals up to the human soul in its original constitution; the fall of man the divine incarnation, sacrifice and potential redemption being, as it were, superimposed climactic supernatural events. The Galilean-Newtonian physics deprived material or physical nature of all the traits which made it possible for nature in that "lowest" form to serve as the base of the ascending hierarchy. It cut all ties which connected psyche and reason with the natural occurrences and structures studied in physical science. Mind and nature stood over against one another as polar opposites. The resulting "epistemological" problem has already been discussed at some length. But since the body was a part of physical nature, the crisis produced by the emergence of seventeenth-century astronomy and physics also generated the "metaphysical" problem of the relation of mind and body.

Descartes wrote that he identified the *soul* with *mind*. The modern reader is usually not prepared to notice the revolutionary import of this statement. It is likely to be passed over, as far as the identification goes, as utterance of a mere truism. In fact, it means that Descartes deliberately eliminated from his theory of the constitution and operation of the "soul" the elements which had for at least two thousand years been its genuine and important, though not complete and sufficient, properties: Namely, everything connected with life and the phenomena of sustenance, growth, movement and motor impulse, and even sensory qualities as conditioned by the body. Descartes's statement of the negative implication of the exclusive identification of soul with *mind* is familiar. It is that all psychological and vital phenomena whatever are *mechanical*: that is they are purely physical in the new sense given that word by the new physics. A single example may suffice. There is no difference *in principle* between the beating of the heart and the circulation of blood (not, however, known at that time) and the action of a pump in moving a fluid. That is to say, the two phenomena are to be explained by exactly the same method and by use of exactly the same strictly mechanical principles. The soul in short became strictly spiritual, immaterial, operating by powers that had nothing to do with the forces which operated in "outer" nature and accounted for what occurs there. Matter is extended, mind is non-extended; matter is compound, and constantly changing its special form, mind simple and indestructible; every physical body is inert or is moved from without, mind is self-moving; matter is devoid of every capacity of thought, mind *is* thinking or consciousness, inherent or in and by its very substance—and consequently it thinks *always*—a position which Locke criticized vigorously, though without seeing how intrinsically necessary the idea was in the Cartesian system. The problem of how mind could act upon body and body upon mind was, given the premises regarding the essential being of each, imperative. Given the dualism of mind and matter (which has found its way into popular beliefs and even seems to many persons today to be a direct deliverance of common sense), how can mind "move" the body to action as surely it *seems* to do in every case of acting upon a decision or carrying a purpose into execution? And how can bodies, "matter" generally, act upon the mind, as surely seems to occur in every case in which the latter forms ideas of what is going on in the physical world? Using language sanctioned by traditional discussion of this problem, "interactionism" of mind and body seems to be one of the indubitable facts of our experience; perhaps the most indubitable, since it is exemplified in every item of knowledge we obtain about the world and in every act in which we deliberately move any structure of the body and produce the changes we wish in things about us. Yet "interaction" of mind and body is naturally impossible because of the inherent nature of the two forms of Being.

I shall not take up here the different types of "solution" to the problem that were propounded. What is relevant here is the state of cultural conditions, especially from the side of physical science on one side and moral-religious beliefs on the other side which generated the *problem*. For it is the conditions which form the problem (thereby evoking the need for solution as long as the conditions are accepted) that require examination. The simple fact is that the commonsense view never held in the past nor holds at the present—the idea that *mind and matter* act upon each other, or that states of "consciousness" act upon physical bodies (including one's own) and the latter impress themselves upon consciousness or upon something immaterial. What is believed is something very different. It is with traits that are personal that beings, persons in short, act upon and are acted upon by other things, inanimate and impersonal as well as personal. The action takes place in both instances through bodily media. But the activities constituting the behavior of personal beings have distinctive qualities, qualities so distinctive as to be unique in comparison with the traits and connections of traits assigned to "physical" bodies. It is John Smith and Susan Jones who interact with environing things, not disembodied "minds" or "souls," and their kind of interactivities in which, as human personal beings, they engage, are qualified through and through by traits which, when they are abstracted and converted into entities, are called percepts, ideas, purposes, aims, desires, deliberations; in a word, being aware of what one is about in its connection with what is going on in the environment: i.e. Being intelligent. Everyone knows that intelligent behavior differs from stupid behavior, and comprehensively intelligent behavior differs from that involving narrow insight. This fact is as evident as that idiots and imbeciles do not behave like persons of average gift, not the latter like persons of remarkable sagacity. Rarefaction of ideas, plans, desires, foresight, intuitive sizing up of situations, into a super-tenuous immaterial stuff is, in short, the source of the metaphysical problem of "interactionism," and of rival theories of occasionalism, parallelism, automatism, epiphenomenalism, etc. And the rarefaction instead of being an original datum of commonsense is the product of that complete separation of the mental from the vital which was made at a particular historic and cultural juncture. During the seventeenth century natural science ejected all overt animistic traits from its proper subject matter, and yet it retained beliefs about substance and essence, and about the "dead" nature of underlying substance called "matter" which had been derived from the earlier poetic view of the natural world. There resulted an insight into the mechanical connections of events which produced in an inconceivably vast access of control over movement, light, heat, electricity—in short, over all kinds of natural energy. But because of uncritical retention of portions of pre-scientific cosmology, the mechanical relations which were noted instead of being placed in the proper context, were erected into another kind of metaphysics.

. . .

The first consideration to be attended to in discussion of this topic takes us back to the opening sentence about conversion of words of adverbial [force] into terms having adjectival force and then the erection of the subject matter involved into nouns; the consequence being that of behavior erected into an independent activity. *Mind* and *mental* do not stand for things which are inventions of psychologists and philosophers. They stand, as has already been said, for important properties of activities open to observation, the characteristics of which are so distinctive in comparison with other kind of observed events as to demand special recognition. The case of the word "mind" is an instance of a considerable number of cases in which idiomatic usage is a surer clew to meaning than is sophisticated theoretical interpretation. There is an obvious reason for the existence of such cases. Idiomatic usage is determined by the experienced need of noting and recording distinctions of events which are important in actual management of affairs; in, this is to say, the effective conduct of life. Philosophical interpretation has often subjected this primary significance of observed facts to the requirements of some extraneous preconceived theory—frequently theological in nature. In the case of idiomatic usage, there is, accordingly, no ground for surprise when "mind" is used as a verb, i.e., to designate a certain kind of behavior, while the context shows that the activity so named is one of interactivity of the organism with surrounding conditions. Children are familiar with the injunction "Mind me" or "Mind what I am saying to you." The mother or nurse who utters the injunction is familiar with the necessity for minding, caring for, children. The cook minds the bread or cake baking in the oven. The word *minding* in these cases is equivalent to an attentive act, an act of *caring for* which involves doing something with or to surrounding circumstances, and hence, truistically, involves organic action, that is, *the body.* As long as we take our clew from and find our relevant data in observable facts, we are bound to employ the kind of *behavior* exemplified in the above words as the subject matter on the ground of which to form a theory of mind and mental.

It was said that *minding* is equivalent to an attentive act in the sense in which "act" involves an organic body doing something (or getting ready to do something) beyond the limits of its epidermis. It is necessary to emphasize this particular meaning of the phrase "attentive act" because were the phrase "act of attention" used, it is virtually certain that *attention* would be understood to mean a separate power or faculty itself *mentalistic* and not a mode of vital interaction. That is, it would be taken to be just a case of a pure "psychical" activity exercised by soul, mind, or consciousness, instead of observable properties of a distinct kind of organic behavior, I shall accordingly engage in a somewhat detailed analysis of the nature of attentive behavior. The military command "Attention" hardly furnishes an adequate example. But it is worth mention because of its obvious implication of an action performed in specific reference to environing conditions. If we start from less specialized cases of attentive behavior we find they involve the quality of *care*, and of *care* as an overt act performed or to be performed involving *care* in its two senses of *caring for*, doing something to protect or promote the person or thing cared for, and *caring for* in the emotional or affectional sense of liking, loving, being solicitous about. While both of these meanings are integral and inseparable in cases of attentive behavior, it will serve the end of clarity to consider them separately. "Have a care" is equivalent to *"Mind* your step," "Look *out;"* it enjoins a certain kind of action; a kind, be it noted, that cannot occur without observation of the kind of conditions the act is to deal with and modify. The emotional quality of the attentive act, that of care in the sense of solicitude, anxiety, fear, even worry and subjection to a burdensome unwelcome load, corresponds to the constituents of the situation that make it necessary to look out, to exercise care, caution, in deciding what to do. For the situations in question are such as to involve the one who needs to exercise care in undesirable consequences; the course of action required is one which will affect the *issue*, the outcome, of what is now going on. Observation is demanded so that the kind of overt act may be performed which will avert bad consequences that are likely to occur without an intervening act which so changes conditions as to prevent their later occurrence. When the quality of anxiety, of worry, is emphatically conspicuous it is because of [its] conjunction with the importance of what will later issue with great uncertainty as to the possibility of being able to perform any act which will alter conditions in the direction of a favored or desired outcome. In popular speech "apprehension" is used as a synonym for a mild state of fear of an unpleasant issue due to uncertainty as to the state or nature of the outcome or the possibility of doing anything that will seriously affect it. While this meaning contains an exaggeration of the emotional quality at the expense of cool or "intellectual" observation and grasp of conditions, of actions which are involved, this popular usage is a valued warning against the epistemological view which excludes any and every quality of practical reference, of inherent connection with action, from its theory of the nature of apprehension. As soon as any act entitled to the name "apprehension" is regarded as behavioral, instead of as an "inner" mentalistic act, the affectional quality is as much its intrinsic property as is its intellectual or cognitive [qualities].[1]

---

1. Ever since Aristotle tried to prove the inherent superiority of exclusively theoretical action, characteristic according to him of the philosophic class, over the activity of every other class, including that of rules of the state, I think it must be admitted that the desire of "intellectuals" to magnify their office has played, subconsciously, a role in maintaining the belief that "pure" intellectual activity, where *pure* means free from all emotional and practical connection, is a condition both possible and representative of the ultimate ideal.

Behavior which is marked by the qualities characteristic of minding thus has all the traits which, when they are discriminated, are called volitional, intellectual and emotional. There is care in the sense of concern for the issue; there is the need of observation of conditions in order to determine or decide what to do, the latter constituting the so-called act of will. It is worthwhile in this latter connection to note the case in which *minding* means *obeying*. It contains an element of personal arbitrariness so emphatic as to unfit it for service as an exemplar. But the demand for conformity to an environing condition that is involved in obedience is but a one-sided emphasis of a quality found in all minding as attentive behavior. Laws, rules and regulations are *observed* when action occurs in accord with what they prescribe. The property of behavior involved in minding as obeying is that insisted upon by Francis Bacon in his doctrine that obedience to nature is the prime condition of power to command its forces. Demand for obedience is an expression of a certain authority properly exercised by actual conditions over the formation of ideas and beliefs. On the negative side, it contains (markedly so in the case of Bacon) a warning as to the need of freeing the act of observation from all preference for one conclusion rather than other, whether the preconception or prejudice that operates is an "idol" of the personal or the socially customary orthodox type. Positively, it expresses the need of supreme respect in all cases of knowing; of acknowledgement of the authority of actuality; of the vast importance of readiness to submit to what natural conditions have to say and to teach. Experience of the causes that have led beliefs astray, in matters great and small alike, testifies to the necessity for that attitude that bears the significant name of *admission*. We have, to speak metaphorically, to let events in, and there are so many obstructions in the way to their admission that the attitude of submission required is radically different from that of passive acquiescence. The obeying or submission, the "objectivity," involved in minding specific conditions (or the "world" generally) is an art attained only by discipline and through prolonged practice. The quality that marks off the attitude involved is that which in another context is called fidelity, loyalty; the kind of *conformity* required represents an ideal which it is morally incumbent to strive for but which is never wholly attained.[2] It is the rarest and most difficult to achieve of all kinds of honesty, namely, intellectual integrity.

The submission or obedience involved is that which is emphasized by every form of "realism," artistic or philosophical. It is, however, a common unfortunate practice of professed and professional realisms to assume that

---

2. Only a preconceived theory can lead to the notion that mind or consciousness or the knowing subject is "naturally" of such an inherently cognitive nature that errors, mistakes, hallucinations, have to be specially accounted for as unnatural abnormalities.

the conformity to conditions which is necessary if observation is to serve its purpose, is final and complete in itself, and hence provides the full and adequate pattern for framing a theory of knowledge. In fact, it is required in preparation for the kind of action which influences conditions in a particular direction, that tending toward an issue regarded as desirable.[3] Two mistakes must be avoided in any legitimate realistic attitude. One of them is the assumption, whether tacit or explicit, that "conditions as they are" are static, or are all sensibly there: *there*, that is, in a way which renders them completely accessible to the senses at the very time of observing. Conditions are moving, changing. Observation contains [as] an indispensable part of itself an element of anticipation of what is *going to happen* and which accordingly cannot be touched, seen or heard (sensibly perceived), at the moment. Prediction is but an elaborate form of the anticipation of where and to what "conditions as they are" are tending. It is not a matter of some special theory about knowing to hold that all observation contains a prospective reference. The sole decisive matter is whether actual conditions are or are not in process. If one denies that they are intrinsically engaged in change then one can logically deny the operative presence of a prospective or anticipatory element in observation. By the same token one who does deny the presence of the prospective reference is committed to the view that things are not events in process but are inherently finished entities, without past or future. The emphasis which has been placed by science upon *causal* connections, turns out, when it is critically examined, to be the acknowledgement that process is so intrinsic to what is observed and observable that observing (and all knowing so far as it is admitted to depend upon observations) involves anticipation, and in so far, prediction of what is still to come.The other mistake, a common one on the part of professed realists, is the cognate assumption, open or covert, that the conformity or fidelity to actuality which is involved in observation (and knowing) is the sole and exclusive character requisite for its definition. It would, I suppose, be admitted without question that whenever one is in a state of uncertainty as to what to do in difficult circumstances, close observation of existing

---

3. While I am not concerned here save incidentally with the general theory of knowing, it may avoid misapprehension if it is now pointed out that in scientific inquiry of the strictest kind the observations to be made, the experiments to be performed, are controlled by reference to their bearing upon a future issue, a conclusion to be reached. This does not mean that some one preferred conclusion is the determining factor; such a view is the very negation of the scientific attitude. But it does mean that the activities of knowing in the concrete are relevant to an issue to be reached—to something which at the time is future. The notion that no element of desire is present is such a distortion of the fact that what is supremely desired is an issue or conclusion influenced by no other desire than that of arriving at a conclusion warranted by the facts of the case. Not the absence of something desirable but the quality of that esteemed as desirable is the distinguishing trait.

conditions is an important aid in reaching a decision as to what course to follow; that in fact such observation is the alternative to mere cut-and-dry methods. But any interpretation of conformity that takes it, as far as a theory or definition of the nature of observation is concerned, to constitute the complete meaning and content of that act, is bound to suppose that the act of observation takes place without any reference to what is to be done; that need for effecting a decision as to later matters exercises no influence in determining selection of what it is observed or the interpretation put upon it. According to this view, an act of observation takes place with no purpose or intent save just to observe, and after it has occurred, that which is observed happens somehow to act as a means in coping with the difficulty as to what and how to act. The way out of this somewhat absurd conclusion is recognition that the observing which is done is in fact the initial stage of deciding what to do and is influenced throughout by the existence of the practical predicament and the intent to find a successful way out of it. This way of viewing the matter does not eliminate the factor of conformity; it does not reduce its importance. It but takes the *conformity* out of the inane void in which it dwells as long as it is taken in a literally wholesale fashion. For when it is so taken, its fulfillment imposes upon observation the impossible task of duplicating every item and every quality of every item of the situation, a task as meaningless, moreover, as it is impossible of execution. For the point of an observing act is that it be selective, a condition which involves an end to be reached as a criterion for guiding and testing the selections made. As a matter of fact, if the question were simply whether the need and desire of determining, when one is in practical straits, the best thing to do influences the whole course of observation, determining just what is observed and the weight attached to it, I fancy there would be few indeed who would not take an affirmative answer for granted—to the extent of surprise that such a silly question was asked. What is not noticed is that the affirmative answer renders the kind of conformity or fidelity to fact which is involved subject to a highly important limiting condition; a limiting condition which is fundamentally important for the theory of the nature of observing (and knowing) because it proves that the conformity in question is not final and complete but is for the sake of something else, which is of the opposite nature of submission, obeying, conformity; namely, the subjection of existing conditions to activity that achieves an end in view, that carries out an experienced concern.

That in any act of observing there is tension between need for conformity or submission to conditions "as they are" and need for giving, by an action performed, a different direction of movement to these conditions that they would otherwise take (that is, if left to themselves) is proved both by factual and by general theoretical considerations I begin with the latter. A simple organism lives in a simple, that is, homogeneous environment. Changes, of any moment, in the direction of activity are, therefore, not needed. The state of equilibration of organic and environmental energies is sufficiently constant so that crises of re-adaptation do not occur. If some, any, mighty change in conditions does take place, it is simply catastrophic in its effect upon living creatures of a simple nature. In the case of higher organisms, re-adaptations of greater or lesser scope are required at frequent intervals. Now that which is an act of readaptation or readjustment with respect to environment is re-*direction* of energies with respect to the living creature. This redirection is by its nature a state of tension, or conflict of opposite tendencies. The activity, the course of action already engaged in, has momentum or inertia. It tends to persist; by its very being it is a process of *going on*. On the other hand, a change of conditions instigates or evokes a different mode of action in order to effect functional adaptation to changed conditions. Both tendencies co-exist. Organic action is, quite literally, pulled different ways. There is on the part of the action of some organic structures a tendency to continue in the course in which they are already engaged; on the part of other structures or organs there is activity responsive to new conditions. This tension is prefigured in animal behavior marked by curiosity; organic or vital behavior is simultaneously in a state of attraction towards and repulsion [from]. Potential drawing near or search and potential withdrawal or flight contend for supremacy. As long as the state called curiosity is dominant, some degree of action in one direction or the other may be temporarily dominant. But it is tentative, and so to say, experimental. Instead of being final and conclusive, it is subject to reversal with change of intensity in the stimuli that evoke, respectively, movement toward and movement away. This *wariness* is the organic prefiguring of the tension that constitutes *awareness* in the case of human beings.

I return now to concrete cases of observing. If, with a tinge of metaphor, one constituent of attentive behavior or minding is called submission or obedience when, with slightly more metaphorical quality, its other constituent may be called subjugation of conditions, rendering them subordinate by means of overt activity to maintenance of the life-process, tension or conflict then takes place between these tendencies in contrary directions. It is in place to again refer to Francis Bacon. He proclaimed obedience to nature on behalf of subjection of nature to humanity, to the desirable ends of our common human life. There is the same possibility of erroneous interpretation of this highly generalized view of knowledge as in the case of particular acts of observing. The attitudes or acts of submission and conquest may be regarded as wholly independent of each other, the practical subjection *of* natural energies to human ends coming in some mysterious way the exclusively "intellectual" and completely cognitive act of knowing in the form of subjection to natural energies has occurred. It is surprising that optimistic deists have not used the principle involved in this view's part of the proof from design of the existence of an outside supernatural arranger of things. For it is hardly possible to find a more striking instance of belief in a pre-established harmony. It does not seem to be noticed by the epistemological philosophers, who are aware of the effect of "theoretical" knowledge in bringing natural energies under practical control (science), that the view which separates knowledge as purely theoretical from any practical reference renders the demonstrated beneficial effect of right knowing upon practical activities (displayed on a large scale in the new technologies that have grown out of modern physical science) either completely mysterious or proof of the miraculous intervention of an extraneous designer of nature. If one is willing to begin with simple cases, it will have to be admitted that in their case the act of observation, including that phase of it which is most concerned to permit environing conditions to speak for themselves, is conducted with reference to an activity which will modify existing conditions in a sense favorable to the living agent. Such a simple case is found beyond peradventure when a man who is endangered by the factors of a situation in which he is involved observes as closely, faithfully and accurately as possible just what the conditions are. In this case it will, I fancy, be conceded that observations of "conditions as they are" signifies, with respect to its faithfulness, the kind of observation that notices them in that capacity and that the survey of them genuinely conforms or corresponds to them in the degree it indicates the kind of action that will tend to prevent occurrence of the anticipated harmful issue. If it is thought that the example used is loaded, it should be recalled that the statement is equally true of observations made in the course of a strictly scientific investigation, conformity or faithfulness of observation meaning in this case that events are observed in their bearing upon the end in view of reaching a warranted conclusion. The specific content of desirable and harmful differs from that of the illustration just given but not the principle involved. Whether one approves or not of the use of the word "tension" in description of what occurs in observing it will have to be admitted, I think, that there is a peculiar ambivalence or duality in every instance of observation. Accurate seeing of what is already there, noting the *fact* in the sense of what is already done and over with, is not the same process as anticipating what has not yet come about, and nevertheless although the two processes are incompatible, they must occur either simultaneously or in quick oscillation. It seems proper when the matter is stated psychologically to say there is tension between the *sensible* and the *ideational*, the peripheral and the central, constituents of observation.[4]

The existence of vital tension, in the sense of opposite tendencies each of which is pushing to control the over act that will take place, is clearly presented when we consider another meaning of "mind" that philological records show has been constantly involved in the word.

The anticipation, which is an integral aspect of the act of observing, cannot exist without something to draw upon different from the subject matter of immediate sense perception. This subject matter has its source in organic retention of the organic results of previous experiences or interactivities: the principle of habit. Recall or re-membering is required to make the material available in the anticipatory aspect of observation. Otherwise there is simply an immediate overt act on the basis of habit, with no discriminative noting of conditions involved. The presence of this constituent of recall functions in producing conflicting tendencies for control of activity. For if the recalled element in its literal original form obtained complete control there would be complete assimilation of existing conditions to those in which a habit was formed, thus nullifying the force of the novel elements that evoke observation. On the other hand, if it is completely crowded out by the organic activities involved in present sense-perception no element of anticipation could occur. The present of this element of tension is implicit in the common distinction of mechanical memory and total reminiscence from "judicious" memory. For the latter involves re-adaption of the recalled subject matter to meet the requirements imposed by existing observed conditions.

The connection, in general, of the foregoing discussion of minding and attentive behavior with the theme of the chapter, the relation of "mind and body," is extremely simple and direct. Its net import is that human behavior has, under conditions that can be observed, the set of qualities which, when they are discriminated from the properties of physical and vital behavioral connections, are called, collectively, *mental*. And the statement does not mean that mental or psychological qualities replace physical and vital properties. It means that the observer of human behavior takes account

---

4. From the standpoint of psychological statement it is necessary to observe the distinction existing between "perception" (with the term "sense" understood) and observation. We cannot observe without sense perception but the latter occurs, automatically so to say in the case of familiar objects when observation does not take place. The latter involves even in the case of familiar things act of *exploration*—in order to judge just what the familiar thing, recognized or "apprehended" on sight as stone, tree, approaching automobile, etc. will *do* under the other circumstances of this particular situation. Identification of observation with one of its constituents, sense-perception, is one of the psychological fallacies that has played havoc in epistemological philosophy.

of certain properties that are not relevant to the problems studied by the physicist and the physiologist, there being no way to define "physical" and "vital" or organic save in terms of conclusions reached in these branches of inquiry. It is one of the bad results of erecting the metaphysical dualistic separation of two orders of existence that those persons who see the un-verifiable nature of the idea [that] there is such a thing as a separate purely unearthly psychical kind of existence then find themselves obliged to deny the distinctive "reality" of qualities that are other than physico-chemical. This denial is as much a mark of subordination of observable facts to a pre-conceived metaphysical dogma about a substantial entity called "matter" as is the doctrine of a separate order of existence termed "spirit," soul or mind. That mental qualities manifest themselves only in certain chemico-physical and biological conditions is a fact of importance, but it provides no reason whatever for denying the distinctive and unique character of these qualities when they do occur. Aside from the animistic and theologi-cal beliefs that lie historically and culturally back of the belief in separate mental existence, a doctrine once taken to be scientific but recently shown to be non-scientific has played a part in the generation of the metaphysical problem and its various "solutions." Only recently in the history of natural science have the categories of *energy* and *event* displaced, in descriptions of natural phenomena, the categories of *substance* and things as *entities*—mak-ing it clear that the proper use of *thing* is as a term of *discourse* as when we use the words anything, everything, nothing; or use "thing" as a synonym of the Latin *res*, an affair or concern, that is, a situation having a certain qualitative unity, with nothing implied as to its entitative nature. After long centuries of habituation, it is not surprising that most persons still find it "natural" to think and speak in terms of static things instead of in terms of behaviors and processes. When "mental" and "material" are thought of as forms of *being* in a sense in which "being" is said over against acting, or is shoved under *energy* as its bearer, it is almost inevitable that the problem of the relation of mind and body should become a peculiar metaphysical one, to be dealt with in the interest of "Matter" either by denying the distinctive genuineness of mental qualities; by reducing "matter," as in metaphysical idealism, to Mind in imperfect manifestation or partial apprehension; or by the various metaphysical solutions that have been offered with respect to *interactionism*. It is only when the problem is seen and placed definitively in the context of things as energies, events and process, or in terms of modes of *behavior* in the widest sense of that word, that it becomes capable of intelligent approach and discussion.

In view of the dignified status occupied in philosophical discussion it is, however, not enough to leave the matter with this general statement. It is desirable, probably necessary, to discuss the matter in terms of the specific relation of the nervous system and the brain to behavior having the qualities of minding, the complex of qualities called collectively "mental." As far as animals below man are concerned, most persons would not need argument as a condition of believing that the brain is an organ of adaptive behavior. It is only with respect to man, and with respect to him chiefly among philosophers, that the brain is regarded exclusively or mainly as the organ of *knowing*, or more absurdly yet the "seat" of mind. When the body in general and the nervous system and brain in particular are taken for what they are, organs of vital behavior, the problem is not how "matter" can give rise to mind, how psychical volition can move physical muscles, nor how physical nerve-processes can get translated into "mental" sensations and ideas. The problem is one of strictly scientific inquiry. It is to be solved, like other scientific questions, by continued observation of what actually takes place. It is to discover the characteristic or definitive differences between behavior in the way of searching, finding out, and other modes of interactivity of organic and environing energies. This general problem breaks up into dozens of special questions of what special roles are [played] by the various parts of the nervous system in constituting which [*illeg.*] of seeing, hearing, observing, remembering the differences in question. The problem is much more difficult to deal with than is the problem, say, of determining just what and how the heart or lungs do in determination of vital behavior. But in principle it is the same kind of a problem. I cannot insist too strongly that the traditional problem of the relation of mind and body and the alleged need for choosing between the various solutions offered (epiphenomenalism, parallelism, automatism, occasionalism, pre-established harmony, insoluble mystery, etc.) are wholly the result of acceptance, as premises, of the belief of two radically different orders of existence. Moreover, the "monism" involved is not of a metaphysical sort but consists simply of recognition that the phenomena in question are behavioral in nature, behavior having the qualities, and as many different qualities, as observation determines it to have under different specifiable conditions of interaction.

As far as the actual problem of inquiry is concerned, the main responsibility of the present discussion, of any discussion from the philosophical point of view, is to point out its nature and the historic-cultural causes for its misconception. There is no responsibility for anticipating the detailed solution that will be worked out in time by scientifically controlled experimental observations. But inquiry has already reached a point which makes it possible to indicate the direction which the solution of the question of the function of the brain adaptive behavior will take. The obvious starting point are the facts which are known about the central and intervening place of cerebral structures in institution of indirect, new, and complex responses of motor activities to sensory stimuli. The inadequacy of the so-called "reflex-arc" theory has already been shown. There is no such thing as a succession of disjointed motor responses to independent and disconnected sensory stimulations. The maintenance of life, the continuity that is of life-activity demands that the motor response play a definite part in the institution of the succeeding sensory stimuli; the motor response controls sensory stimuli, or is *their* stimulus, quite as truly as the reverse control takes place; for the fact is that the requirements of vital behavior, as interactivity, controls both of them. The more complexly differentiated the organism and the more heterogeneous in consequence the constituent conditions of the environment, the more refined, delicate and extensive is the process of the formation of the motor responses constituting an adapting course of behavior. The brain, roughly speaking, is the organ through which action satisfying these conditions is brought about.

The work of the brain is sometimes compared to that of a central telephone exchange. A superficial relationship undoubtedly exists. There are incoming "messages" that have to be treated at a common centre so as to be relayed along a particular outgoing channel to one recipient out of a large number of "subscribers" each of which (or whom) is a potential recipient of a message from any one of the senders of a message. Hence the applicability of the *switch-board* analogy. The comparison breaks down, however, at a vital point. The telephonic central switch-board is a transfer-mechanism in a literal sense. It is its business to see that a message goes out just as it comes in; its sole function is to switch the electric disturbance already going into a particular wire. If the "message" is modified in any way whatever at the centre, the latter has failed in its office. The opposite is true in the case of the brain. If we continue to speak in the personified terms of the analogy with the central switchboard, it is its office to receive a large number of messages, each of which is too partial, too incomplete, to make sense by itself (i.e., to make sense from the standpoint of the interactivity to be finally attained) and to coordinate them so that a unified final adaptive action will occur, which is quite different from what would be done it any one sensory stimulus or a mere aggregate of them determined the motor outlet.

The behavior in which cerebral activity is directly involved is, in other words, deliberative behavior, and deliberative behavior is deliberate, that is delayed, as far as overt action is concerned. A common injunction to those about to engage in unwise conduct, because of haste, is "Stop and think." Now all intelligent, reflective behavior (that in which cerebral process are involved) involves a stoppage, an inhibition of immediate *overt* behavior; that is, of behavior which commits the organism to undergoing the consequences of an immediate interactivity with environing conditions. All observing involves an element of inhibition of direct overt action. When bodily habits are formed without adequate observation of conditions entering into the kind of habit formed (now generally as takes place because of the pressure at home, in school, and in industry for "prompt," that is speedy and thoughtless action), habits are "automatic": that is, they operate in a machinelike way. Only when a purpose and observation answering the needs of the purpose have entered into the formation of a habit will observation of the conditions under which it is to operate enter into the performance of an activity or will it be intelligent. The tendency to immediate action is so strong in most of the activities of daily life because of the social conditions under which they have been formed, that it requires a definite technique of deliberate inhibition to introduce intelligent guidance of what is done. Nor is this the whole of the story. Definitely intellectual or cerebral activity gets artificially disjoined from the behavior of the body in dealing with actual conditions. It is severed from what is more or less contemptuously spoken of as "practical" activity—although *practical* in its proper vital meaning is nothing more nor less than the whole conduct of life with respect to the medium, physical and cultural, in which one lives.

The "stopping" and inhibition involved in the delayed or deliberate activity in which the brain plays its due part is not to be thought of as complete cessation of action. The "stop" which is involved applies only to overt action. What happens is that energies are turned into *intra*-organic channels in consequence of which the organic set of conditions taking part in interactivity with environment are so modified that a new course of action is prepared. Deliberation is not just something which goes before overt action; it *is* that action in process of initiation and development. De-cision is the cutting short of the process of *intra*-organic activity which marks the readiness of that kind of action to pass into direct interactivity. It does not take an act of an outside entity called *will* in order to occur. It is the normal consummation of a the preparatory reformative process which takes place when cerebral processes are properly engaged. Initiation, ingenuity, inventiveness, are intrinsically involved. For novelty, variation is the essence of the situation in which the delayed action—the brain's functions—take place. The mystery that attends the matter is that such things as organisms and organisms with brain structures exist at all. But this mystery is identical with that of anything at all existing just as it does, what we call an explanation connects the particular existence in question with other existences. But in so doing it takes for granted that these other things exist just as they do exist. The *mystery* is that the world is what it is, and that applies to the wing of a bird, the occurrence of thunder and lightning, the existence of stones that are heavy and gases that are light as well as to the function of the brain in behavior intelligently adapted, to conditions in the interest of life in its most abundance sense.

This phase of the discussion will terminate with pointing out the legitimate meaning of purpose, plan, intention, when they are viewed in the behavioral context that has been sketched. They are too commonly hypostatized, just as is *will*. Indeed the erection of them into entities or forces is, ultimately, just one phase of the hypostatization of will into a force or faculty. Volition is a reality, but the reality in question is the entire content of the initiation and incubation of an intelligent action till it passes into that interactivity with environment that is, so to speak, the fate of every living process because it is that of which life consists. The denial of will in the sense of an independent extraneous force is justified. But it is one of the evils generated by belief in such a faculty that denial of the force is often taken to carry with it negation of the genuine existence of the qualities of behavior that popular tradition has hypostatized. The effective function performed by deliberation, of planning, of building up purposes is then taken to be illusory; they are said to be merely "epiphenomenal," whatever that may mean. In fact, an intention, purpose, end-in-view, plan, *are* the new mode of interactivity while the latter is still in process of formation—that is, is still in its intra-organic phase.

. . .

From the biological point of view, it is in fact superfluous to dwell upon the connection and relative subordination of the "intellectual" to overtly active doing and making. Given that point of view, it is now chiefly necessary to insist upon the fact that the sensori-motor nervous system operates in the service of life-activities which are what they are because of cultural conditions. For the influence of earlier views which treated the sense as organs of *knowing* has resulted in an *isolation* of the sensory system and its connections which still persists. It influences those who deny (quite properly) the competency of sense-material to provide knowledge. For their entire theory of the necessity of "rational" and *a priori* components to supplement that of sense-organs and sense-data is based upon isolation of the set organs and their structures from the genetic-functional place in the total extent of life activities. Only in this way can one account for the decisive effect of *social* environment upon what human beings see, hear, touch, taste and smell; how completely what are regarded as merely physical stimuli are transformed by the social setting in which they arise and operate. The qualities that are mediated through organic structural conditions in which sensory apparatus are involved are saturated through and through with values and uses they possess because of their social context. The "sensations" of red, hard, high note that figure in books are extreme cases of sheer abstraction conducted in behalf of some special problem. The quality actually possessed by the vents which are physiologically referable to eye, ear, hand, nose (in fact to some highly specialized set of physico-chemical processes) is always, in fact, the blue of the sky, of a ribbon, of a carpet, of a chemical reaction undergoing investigation. But while recognition of this fact marks an improvement over the treatment that isolates the quality by putting it in a total vacuum, it is still defective in failing to recognize that the sky, or whatever, is experienced as a part, focal perhaps but still a part, of an extensive environment which is socially conditioned throughout.[5] Appeal to reason or intellect in general, or whatever, to fill out the deficiencies of isolated sense-qualities is as pathetically incompetent to provide in its result the qualitative subject matters we concretely see and hear and touch and taste as it is gratuitously introduced in view of the environmental conditions interacting with those of the human organism every moment after birth—and indirectly before birth. An activity which is physiologically treated as sensori-motor, and psychologically is treated in the service it renders in knowing (even when including full recognition of the function of the involved motor-function) still represents *selected* subject matter. In and for the needs and purposes of daily life, the context in which it emerges and operates protects us from giving it a factitious artificial existence. When it is written about, it enters another context in which it is too easy to forget both its original context and the new context of investigation of a problem in which it now occurs. That among other properties the subject matter may have those which accrue from its being direct manifestation and enrichment of living itself, as well as being sensori-motor, cognitive, and hence instrumental to future living, naturally follows. I pass on, then, to discussion of some broader conclusions that are bound up with the temporal continuity of experience when that is viewed in terms of its identity with life functions.

Life *is* continuous from birth to death for any given human being and is continuous for mankind from generation to generation. This fact is so familiar that, in taking it for granted, we fail to appreciate the nature of the continuity which is involved. We even think of it as mere preservation or persistence in being, omitting from view the fact that life endures only when and because what is doing at a particular time modifies existing conditions, organic and environing, so that they contribute actively to the maintenance of a consecutive course of activities. Psychological analyses

5. Determination of a color-quality in terms of a certain rate of light-waves per unit of time, and/or in terms of certain specified nerve events is, ironically enough, itself but a highly specialized instance of social accomplishments in a given field.

have been couched largely in cross-sectional terms; in terms of snap shots, as if what happens in a very brief span were somehow more informative than observations of a span long enough to provide an idea of whence events are coming and whither they are tending:—in short, so as to give some hint of what is developing. A typical illustration is furnished by the current use of the *stimulus-response* category. There is no doubt that when it is taken as a kind of psychological unit, it marks an improvement over the isolated "sensation" and "ideas" that once were taken as units. But it is usually itself isolated, being interpreted after the pattern of the "reflex-arc" exhibited in the knee jerk or the winking of the eye when something approaches. The result is to chop living up into a succession of disconnected segments. It is as impossible to put them together to yield the process of living as it is to put Humpty Dumpty together again after he has fallen from the wall.

Such events as jumping when a loud bang is suddenly heard and jerking the hand away when something hot is unexpectedly touched are as near approaches as exist to the case of isolated stimulus-response action. They are of the nature of shocks. They take place when a sudden change in environing conditions evokes an equally abrupt change on the side of organic energies. The break and required switch are, however, relative, not absolute. They are not cases of initiation of activity as they would have to be if an isolated stimulus-response situation were an ultimate unit of behavior, but of *re*-direction of an activity going on, differing from what takes place in, say, a game of chess or even tennis in that the angular deviation of the required re-direction is greater. In the case of the sudden loud noise, the auditory apparatus has not been previously entirely quiescence nor have the muscles that execute the sudden jump been totally inert. It may be doubted whether any such thing as a completely monotonous treadmill activity occurs when we are awake. The occurrence of that which is new and different in some respect and in some degree is the usual thing. We expect some continuity of theme in reading a book but the continuity in question is not one of sheer identity or reiteration. It is a process of development in which something different occurs and has to be taken account of by re-direction of organic factors involved. In such instances as were cited as examples of shock the element of re-direction is greater in a given span of time than is usually the case, and hence the quality of shock. But its existence is evidence that the interruption-phase is more intense than is usual. The shock is the moment of re-adjustment in a continuum of activity.

Since living is an ongoing process it must at each stage of its existence serve, upon the whole, to modify *prior* conditions in a way that prepares conditions for *subsequent* activity. We may in times of stress act so as to jump from the frying-pan into the fire. We lose our heads; we give way to panic.

Under such conditions we act wildly; we strike out at random. That fact is evidence that abnormal breaks in the ordinary run of activity are adaptive in the sense in which "adaptation" stands for a functional fact: The capacity of activity performed at a given time to lead into subsequent activity by means of the change in conditions which are its consequences and the capacity of the subsequent phase of activity to grow out of the preceding one in a way which in turn grows into the next one.[6]

Were it not for the fact that psychological doctrines have been framed and psychological descriptions formulated without reference to the fact of their inherent connection with living, it would be superfluous to mention facts of the sort just stated. As the case stands, emphasis is necessarily upon the continuity which is that of movement, growth, development, in which change is continual but the changes form a *course* of activity. Temporal extension of psychological events—as in the case of anticipation and recollection—is often cited as a ground for marking them off into a separate order of existence. As long as the subject matter of physical science was taken to be instantaneous, since ultimately consisting of points in space and moments in time, the existence of hopes, plans, foresight, recall of the past and brooding over it, living in the past, etc., certainly seemed to place "mental" phenomena in a realm intrinsically set apart from the "physical." And when ground was had for assigning temporal duration to "realities" underlying the subject matter of physics, possession of intrinsic temporal qualities seemed to provide adequate warrant for treating them as basically "*vital*," or psychical, in nature—Witness the doctrines of Bergson and Whitehead as evidence. The doctrine of relativity has done away with the supposed scientific ground for marking off the "physical" on the ground of simultaneity and instantaneity, and this change directly bears upon the criterion that was taken to mark off a separate order of "mental" existence.[7] And wherever we are directly concerned with life-processes and functions we are confronted with a situation in which "past" has to be understood as *passage*, or as *passing into* something else, and the future or the "coming" as that which is coming-out-of. The theory which regards the psychological as a separate order of existence which is merely *inner* or *subjective* is the product of an attempt to combine the *fact* of past and future reference with the fiction of existence independent of interactivity with environmental conditions. Hence the basic significance of emphasis upon the intrinsic connection of psychological subject matter with life-behaviors, interactivity

6. It is quite possible, and unfortunately rather usual, to define premises in such a way that the existence of "adaptations" becomes a problem. But in fact, what is called "*adaptive*" is just the characteristic of continuity which marks living as such. It is the starting point, not a conclusion to be reached.

7. See, for example, A. F. Bentley [cite missing].

of organic conditions with environmental ones—qualified throughout by socio-cultural energies.[8]

In the previous chapter, it was pointed out that phases of imbalance and relative disequilibrium in activity occur in more or less rhythmic alternation with phases of re-equilibration and re-integration. Some connections of the theme with psychological matters were mentioned but the main purpose of the discussion at that point was to indicate the ground in actual experience for drawing the distinction (but not making a separation) of environmental and organic. In connection with the matter of interruptions, shocks, and continual need for re-directions, greater or less, in the course of life-activity, the theme has been recurred to in the present chapter. It is hardly possible to overstate the importance of the factors which are involved in connection with the psychology of emotions, of search (inquiry) in its comprehensive sense of examination, inspection, hunting for facts and ideas, reflection, turning things over, probing, testing, etc. Nor can the processes of effort, struggle, deliberation, choice and decision be understood except as they are placed in this context.[9]

Discussion conveniently starts from the matter of the connection of undergoing-doing-undergoing that is involved in interactivity of organic-environing conditions. The change effected in environing activities is undergone organically and in such a way as to modify in some degree its prior state (distribution) of energies. From one point of view, this alteration constitutes a *disturbance*, and in any case it is the equivalent of *need* for a re-distribution of energies which will effect a *re*-direction, lesser or greater, in the course of life-activity going on. To speak of a *crisis* seems extreme save as we think of a crisis literally, that is, in terms of a turning which may be slight but which is still a vector-factor. The need for this re-direction is the base, biologically, of tension and in-tension, of at-tention and in-tention. It is the source of the need every animal experiences for being on the alert, on the watch; the attitude which is the biological forerunner of anticipation, foresight, forestalling and planning. It is in these periods of reconstruction, brief or prolonged, that *habit* as persistent operation of conditions experience in the past is transformed into the behavior constituting re-collecting and re-membering. That is, the energies forming a habit are broken down into the special components that are likely to function in effecting a needed re-adjustment, the habit just as habit operating as it was originally formed

---

8. Were this the fitting place, it could also be shown that the "mystery" that goes by the name of the *transcendence* of ideas and of other agencies for knowing things which exist beyond the scope of the immediate moment, vanishes when the temporal, historic, continuum of living is duly taken into account.

9. That is to say, all the phenomena usually summed up under the head of *volition*.

and not being adapted in that state, to cope with the *here-and-now* environing conditions.[10]

A simple example, on the biological side, is found in alternation of hunger and satisfaction. Hunger is a state of organic imbalance constituting *need*, not, however, in a mentalistic sense, but as a condition of active uneasiness which manifests itself in search for foodstuffs—that is, for interaction with just those environing conditions which will re-instate a condition of equilibration. This biological aspect of activity when it is analyzed as a prototype will be found to furnish all the conditions and processes that describe search or inquiry in its most thoroughly ideational or intellectual aspect. The means in the former kind of hunting for what is needed are bodily organs; in the latter kind they are socio-cultural, consisting of sounds and marks which possess the capacity to stand for what is remote in space and time: that is, are linguistic signs. But in order to accomplish the function of re-adaptation, which will effect re-integration of living activity (the office for which they are called into play in the case of inquiry), they have finally to take effect through overt activities which modify environing activities. Discourse is use of qualities which we can ourselves generate—such as sounds and marks on paper—when we require them—to serve as intermediary agencies for bringing into existence a unified life-activity.[11] Literature or esthetic discourse is a case of the activity which is itself a direct manifestation and immediate phase of living, not having a preparatory and prospective reference. That it is fun, sport, a joy, to "think" or engage in reflective inquiry is evidence that one and the same subject matter is capable of being both a direct manifestation of life-activities, their immediate enrichment, and an agency in effective anticipation of subject matter which is spatially-temporally remote from the here-and-now phase of life-activity.[12]

Instead of developing at this point the connection of the theme of periodic alternation of imbalance and re-equilibration within life activity upon description of the emotional and volitional qualities of experienced subject matter, I turn to a theme which has played a primary role in the drama of historic philosophy. No question has evoked more attempts at solution or more controversy than that of the distinction and the relation of subject

---

10. It may be well to recall in connection with this general theme what was said about the consequences of increased diversity of structures and modes of organic action with increase in the intricacy and delicacy of their interactivities with one another.

11. To avoid misapprehension it may well be to say, explicitly, that *discourse* is here used in its predominantly intellectual sense.

12. The contemplative, meditative, non-"practical" aspect of discourse so much insisted upon in classic Athenian philosophy and by its religionist heirs is in part esthetic and in part a means of indirect preparation for accommodation, on the organic side, to later events—a kind of preparation carried to its extreme in Stoic doctrine.

matters that are designated by such words as sensuous—or more adversely, sensual—and ideal; appetitive and rational; impulsive and thoughtful; perceptual and conceptual; and, in more specialized contexts, flesh and spirit, the lower and higher selves. The subject matters indicated have to do primarily with the temporal range of factors involved; secondarily with the connected spatial range of factors involved. And although the names baldly set down suggest something disparaging if not evil in the case of the first term of each pair in contrast with the honorific meaning of its mate, difference or valuation depends in every case upon the concrete setting of the time element. When the immediate here-and-now phase is of controlling importance in the moving course of life-behavior, claim to superior valuation belongs truistically to it. When that which is relatively ulterior and terminal has [*missing*.] greater regulative power belongs to it. Everyday judgment recognizes that while it is possible and more or less common to sacrifice the future to the present, men also make their lives barren and empty by forever subordinating the present to a future—which never arrives, since what comes is also present. The history of philosophical thought is doubtless marked by the notion that difference in value is inherent and not a matter of functional position. In general this trait is explained by the wider tendency to neglect genetic-functional considerations. More particularly, it has arisen because moralists have been peculiarly sensitive to the harm wrought by yielding to the pressure of intense nearby unmediated forces to the neglect of what is good-in-the-long-run or what is reasonable. Philosophers being engaged in pursuit of reason in general have naturally magnified their office and depreciated the present and directly vital.

. . .

In a scientific experiment, the appearance of a given quality of extremely faint intensity may be of decisive evidential value under certain circumstances; namely, those in which it affords decisive evidence of *now-and-here* presence of a specified condition. No magic inheres in the mere presence of a "sense" quality. Whatever peculiar value it possesses it owes to its function as evidential. When the total situation is of a kind into which search for evidence does not enter, the question of the particular way in which a quality came to be experienced has no pertinency. When the need for evidence does enter in, then the question of its physiological source outweighs the question of its vividness and other immediate identifications.

Perceived material which is dominantly esthetic is, truistically, intensely sensuous. It is the more noteworthy accordingly that, in its case, the particular sense organ which is most directly involved in its production does not have the peculiarly privileged position it occupies in the case of observation conducted for scientific purposes. A picture is seen and *as paint* it consists of colors on canvas. Yet what the ordinary person sees is a scene, a landscape, seascape, portrait, or historical event. Colors are not seen as colors save as the spectator looks at the picture with the eye of another painter or as a critic or a student interested in noting how effects are produced. And the intelligent student will even in this latter case be interested in colors with respect to their arrangement, their relationships; when a special color area is particularly inspected, if it concerns the painting as a picture or esthetic product, the study has to do [with] its interactivity with other color areas in producing the total effect. Now when the fact that what is seen is a *picture*, or pictorial presentation, is duly taken into account, it is evident that while the biological activities engaged center or come to a focus in the visual apparatus, what is perceived is causally conditioned by the interrelated or unified energizing of a great variety of structures, cerebral, sensory (other than visual), muscular, circulatory, respiratory, etc. The richer and more intense the esthetic properties of what is perceived, the more fully are all the systems of organic functioning involved and the more completely and intimately they are interrelated. What the visual mechanism does is highly important but it is done only as one co-operative factor which in this case takes the lead in co-ordinating. If this account seems unduly elaborate, it may be called to mind that its meaning in the concrete is that color is seen as flesh, as jewels, as silk, as water, clouds, grass or whatever, and in "abstract" paintings as an arrangement of figured forms. It requires a special additional act, performed for a special purpose, to see color as just and only color. And when the painter in the course of painting does observe pigments on his palette and on the canvas in just this discriminated way, the discriminative act is not identical with an *isolated* one. The particular color is viewed as a contributing factor to an interconnected whole in process of construction. And just as a *single* quality is not that which is perceived, not even in the case of perception most emphatically "sensory" or a so-called act of "sensation," so that which is perceived is always much more than a single thing (now usually called an *object*) designated by a concrete common noun—chair, orange, tree, etc. A chemist who is intent in carrying on an experiment is concerned at a given moment all but exclusively with the appearance of a certain shade of color is concerned with it *in* a larger field and *as* a factor in carrying forward the investigation of a problem, possibly of comprehensive theoretical bearing, to a satisfactory conclusion. And similarly, if in ordinary non-scientific perception—a given "object," a tree, stone, or piece of silk—is the focal or centered object of perception at a given time, it is such as a factor in a situation that extends in space and time. Its physiological counterpart consists of a great variety of organs that are what they are because of modifications undergone in the entire course of earlier experiences and are at every point moving into the future: which is to say, have anticipatory reference.

The foregoing account is intended to show that the prima facie, "common sense" subject matter of perception, a unified variegated scene, earlier called a "little world" or a segment of an extensive world (using "world" in a purely colloquial sense), is entitled to figure in psychological doctrine as the beginning, the end and intervening material of any perception and that it is absolutely impossible to frame any description or analysis of perception, no matter how "sensory" it may be, that squares with the physiological and anatomical facts that come to any other conclusion. Upon this basis, it is safe to proceed to consideration of "sensations" as themselves *experiential* events instead of as physiological causal conditions of what is experienced. There is no ground whatever on psychological grounds for referring to a quality of red, hard or sour as a *sensation*; as has been shown, it can be called *sensory* only when [for] some special purpose it is important to determine the differential causal condition of its being experienced. Qualities were originally distinguished and identified (as far as they were not predominantly affectational in nature, like *sweet*, *smooth*, *bitter* or *harsh*, which were originally simple specifications of agreeable–disagreeable) in terms of the total things they qualify: sky-blue, grass-green, snow-white, raven-ebony or coal-black, blood-red, boiling-hot, gritty, velvety, etc. etc. Only by reference to the extensum or continuum of conditions in which they occurred could they be identified otherwise than emotionally. Nevertheless, there is sense or significance in referring to a certain phase or aspect of experienced subject matter as *sensational*. This sense is suggested by such colloquial expressions as "sensational newspaper," "sensational murder," etc. An exciting emotional quality is evidently involved. But the excitation in question has to be connected with an event experienced as having the quality of *shock*, in interruption of a relatively consecutive series of events. The temporal continuum is involved but, so to say, negatively; as being broken into, interfered with. "Sensations" in this sense are in no way whatever elements, constituents, components of anything *known*. With reference to what was previously going on, they are breaches in orderly continuity; with respect to what is coming they *may* serve as re-directions, as initiations of a change in direction, of *course* of action. A sudden loud sound may cause one to jump. If and when it is identified as a clang of a bell which is a fire alarm it becomes part of a perceived situation. And in this latter capacity it serves definitely as a pivot on which turns a change in the course or direction of ongoing activity. As thus placed (discriminated and identified) an original shock, or sensational event, functions as something other than sheer emotional excitation—such as, for example, the clang and scurry that induces the average man in the street to run to the scene of a fire for sheer immediate enjoyment of the total spectacle. Moreover, as a functional stimulus it depends upon the *situation* in which it occurs *as* shock or interruption. The loud sound perceived as an alarm, which at first may have induced simply a muscular reaction of a sudden jump, will have different con-sequences as it occurs in a crowded theater, in a home, or on the street. And these consequences will also be determined by the set of the organism and that in turn will be determined by organic modifications due to prior environmental interactivities—skills, attitudes, dispositions (and their negative instabilities), etc., which have been produced.

In order to bring out the point regarding the extreme difference that exists between an actual *experience* having direct *sensational* quality and a quality that is called *sensory* because of analysis undertaken for a purpose, I have used extreme cases for illustrative purposes. The important psychological consideration is that "moments" and moments of re-adjustment, of re-adaptation, of lesser intensity as interruptions and shocks, are continually occurring. If we use "crisis" in its literal sense, then crises are continual and normal occurrences. Just as walking is a rhythm of fallings and recoveries, so with the course of experience which has not been benumbed or fossilized in the direction of sheer monotony of routine. The rhythm of tensions and resolutions which marks watching the enactment of a drama or the reading of a well constructed novel is characteristic of the life process. We are thus brought back to the general principle of life-functions stated earlier—the fact that living, experience as an interactivity of organic and environmental factors, is a rhythm of doings-undergoings which presents a serial alternation of relative upsets and recoveries, states of imbalance and reintegration, unsettlings and settlements. The category of stimulus-response can be serviceable in psychological analysis but only when whatever is described in a given case is stimulus and as response is definitely placed in the specified context of the spatially and temporally extensive continuum in which it arises and in which it operates, a placing which demands detailed consideration of concrete conditions.

It is now a common procedure to speak lightly of the elaborate structure of epicycles erected upon cycles that was indulged in so as to square the Ptolemaic theory with astrological phenomena. That elaboration, however, has nothing on the traditional psychological theory of "perception." Having started with the fiction of sensations or impressions and gone on to their revival in fainter images and combined sensations and images with one another by means (at first) of association by similarity and continuity, and then gone on to combination by a kind of chemical fusion, and still coming short of anything like what is actually experienced, synthetic "thought" operating to introduce necessary and universal relations was brought into the picture. What is now held cannot be literally identified with the terms of this traditional scheme. To criticize the latter as if it were literally the old one might be regarded as flogging a dead horse. But to a considerable extent the changes which have taken place are changes in vocabulary with additions of new elements that have been forced upon recognition, rather than change in basic ideas. The organism with various physiological specifications may be substituted for the soul, mind or consciousness of earlier theory, but its separation from environmental conditions—especially from them as socio-cultural—repeats the chief defect of the old tradition.

II

The foregoing discussion is more closely connected with the genuine issues underlying division into so-called empiristic and rationalist schools than appears on the surface. If we frame our doctrinal account and definition on theoretic grounds supplied by and consonant with the actual conduct of scientific knowledge, there will be no doubt that the latter always involves a theoretical component; but there will also be no doubt that the meaning borne then and there by the word is wholly incompatible with the "theoretical" as a synonym for the *merely* contemplative and speculative. For it will be noted to be a word standing in conjugal relation to *practical* in the sense that word bears in connection with the indispensable place of experimentation in establishment of knowledge. For just as there is nothing which is worthy, from the standpoint of the conduct of scientific knowing, of being called experiment unless what is done and made is directed by something having the nature of suggestion of an idea, hypothesis, or theory (arranging words in an order expressing degrees of confirmation due to prior inquiries), so there is nothing of a theoretical or ideational nature which, from the same standpoint, does not demand, with the maximum of exigency, test and confirmation by the observable consequences of the experimental transactions that have been performed. Any reasonably unprejudiced examination of scientific knowledge makes it so clear that it is a product of close and indispensable cooperation of theoretical and practical constituents that it is impossible to understand their being set in opposition to each other (an antithesis so complete as to have been made the very foundation of two opposed schools of philosophy) save as we take express notice of historic considerations which are now extraneous and completely irrelevant. The fact that these alien and literally corrupting considerations are derived in direct decent from Greek-medieval doctrines renders the attention that has been given to historic philosophies a matter of contemporary import, not a piece of information about the past, gone, and over. Accordingly I shall say something in addition to what has already been said about the two strains sponsored respectively by Descartes and Locke, with especial reference to the point that the basic doctrines of the "empirical" school have their source in an exclusive emphasis upon factors and conditions of a "practical" kind, while the characteristic doctrines of the "rationalist" school spring from converting the role of the theoretical component of knowledge into an original and independent "faculty" of the knowing mind.

· · ·

It is a commonplace of historic accounts of modern philosophy that much of its course has been determined by opposition between two schools. One of them, the so-called rationalistic, has held that knowledge is impossible save through a foundation provided by an *a priori* factor: that is, by conceptions, principles, categories, proceeding from the Intellect, Understanding, Pure Reason—by something in short of the same general nature as the "innate ideas" of Descartes. The other school, the so-called empiristic, has taken the view that all knowledge is *a posteriori*; that is, dependent upon material supplied by "experience," in the Lockean sense of material furnished from without, the "mind" at most supplying only faculties or powers for combining and separating materials thus given to it.[13]

It needs but slight reflection to see that this aspect of epistemological philosophy is intimately and inextricably connected with the aspects discussed in the last two chapters. The controversies engaged in have issued from that identification of knowledge with something inherently fixed or "certain" that has already been discussed. Were it not for that kind of specious "clearness and distinctness" that is due to familiarity and that has the effect of placing some beliefs out of the reach of critical examination, it would be evident that neither school possessed an independently arrived at and independently supported notion of its own favored term. The "rationalists" did not frame their idea of reason and rationality on the basis of examination of actual operations or conclusions of knowledge. It has to fit into the preconception that any view, belief, or conclusion that involves *inference* or any kind of mediation is true (knowledge in the honorable sense of that word) unless it follows necessarily from premises which are known to be true by their very nature—or are self-evidently true. Given this preconception, there were facts—such as the importance of mathematics in scientific knowledge of natural events—which could be employed to support the doctrine that the

---

13. The words *a priori* and *a posteriori* appeared as designations at a relatively late periods. In moral philosophy, "intuition" has been the favorite word for name an alleged nonexperiential element.

first and fundamental truths which were indispensable, by definition, for knowledge to exist, were supplied from "within"—a convenient name which also served to escape from the need for observation of concrete facts upon which to ground a theory.

. . .

The two schools have, in fact, each derived its living from a capital stock provided by the weaknesses of the other. They have been too busy in pointing out these weaknesses as justification of their own doctrines to even dream of subjecting the philosophical premise they hold in common to scrutiny. Otherwise their theories about the subject matters respectively termed conceptual and a priori and perceptual and a posteriori would have been framed in terms provided by examination of the methods of inquiry which successfully yield knowledge.

Such an examination would have shown that material of observation (such as Locke rightly held to be involved in all sound physical knowledge) has been cumulatively proved by the advance of natural science to be indispensable. But it would also have shown that mathematical subject matter (such as Descartes set the example for insisting upon) is also indispensable. Having noted these facts, it would have been led to strive to discover just why and how they are both dispensable, and in studying that matter would have discovered two facts of such a fundamental nature that it would have completely thrown out, once and for all, the reference to antecedently given *inner* and *outer* orders, worlds, realms, or whatever. These two facts are: First, the premises which, as in the form of hypotheses or theories, function as general principles in a given inquiry and the data which function as factual material in apprehending and formulating problems and testing their solutions are, in these inquiries, both of them determined *in and by* the operations constituting scientific method—they are most decidedly not given readymade to knowing before it begins and to knowledge before that it is reached in the cases actually dealt. For anyone with firsthand acquaintance with investigations in physics, astronomy, physics, chemistry, biology, etc., knows that one of the outstanding difficulties and obstacles to be overcome is discovery of what are the *data* or facts of the case for the problem and inquiry in hand; that material first used as data has to be rejected and that new data has to be carefully and painfully sought for, and the capacity of actually perceived material to serve as data in the given case has to be proved into and trusted by every means at command, since no amount of certainty that something is actually perceived proves that this something is stable and legitimate data for the case in hand. That *some* data or other (perceived by means of the sense-organs as causal conditions) are an indispensable condition of knowledge arrived at in the sciences mentioned is itself a generalization from the vast multitude of special cases of inquiry constituting the historic advance of those sciences in secure range and precision.

. . .

The considerations just adduced make it possible to judge what elements in knowledge, "rational conceptions" on one hand and "experience" on the other, had a kind of remote reference to. But the words are so deeply infected by antecedent alien assumptions concerning "inner" and "outer," and well nigh three centuries of epistemological theory have so absorbed into themselves the results of the infection, that it is safer to drop the words, and confine discussion to the matter of the respective place and function of fact (in the sense of observed data) and of general principles (in the sense of hypotheses and theories) in knowing when the latter is so conducted as to terminate in authentically confirmed knowledge.

If we base our view and general theory of knowledge upon actual cases of knowledge, especially upon those of knowledge in such subjects as astronomy, physics, physiology, geology, etc. (the latter because especially their conclusions are the result of knowing which is carried on under conditions of peculiarly scrupulous care), it is evident that the properties defining knowledge are located at the end of inquiry, not at its beginning. We have to look at consequences, at antecedents; at last things not at first things; at outcome, fruits, not at originals. We short, we need to look to matters that are the opposite of those upon which the classic tradition is founded.[14] Nor is there anything strange in this fact since the classic doctrine was framed before there was such a thing as natural science in its modern sense. Substitution of the consequences of specific transactions for "first principles" that are set up before anything is done and set up in order to exercise complete control of whatever is done, has a close connection with knowledge (the bodies of subject matter constituting knowledge) as the product of a special form of technology. The analogy of the state in which beliefs exist prior to transaction of operations of knowing with the state of being raw or crude material, in which material exist before the application of other forms of technology, hardly needs emphasis. And while at the present day, many scientific

---

14. It would have saved a great amount of irrelevant and therefore futile "criticism" if present day teachers and writers in the field of philosophy had based their comments and interpretations upon the following statement of William James: [Quote missing.] Unfortunately they found it demanded less work on their part to base their views upon [what] they could read into the *word* "pragmatism" without engaging in the trouble of studying.

conclusions cannot be said to be raw—being finished goods as compared with beliefs about heavenly bodies, fire, air, lightning, magnets, the brain, heart and blood in, say, the sixteenth century—yet they are not finished in the absolute sense that they are outside the possibility of modification in further inquiry-transactions. The recent rise of relativity and quantum theories should, for example, serve as a notification that surprising transformations may still be in store, thus indicating that received formulations are, in a *relative* sense, but raw materials. There is, however, another matter in which comparison of knowing and knowledge with the materials, processes and output of knowledge with those of other technologies is highly significant. There is no technology which does not involve within itself a number of fairly distinct sub-operations as divisions of labor, these being so undertaken [that] they cooperate with one another in [the] production of finished goods and services. In the transactions which form the occupation and art of knowledge, search for facts to serve as evidence (that is, as directive cues and as tests) for in the conduct of inference is one such cooperative division of labor; the search for appropriate general principles, theories, "laws" together with inquiry to decide the most effective way of employing them in the given situation is the other division of labor the product of which works with the product of factual observation of transactions to institute a situation in which the original problem is resolved.

Indeed, we may go considerably further than this and say that in most cases of intelligent observation, the larger part of their subject matter is manifestation of transactions in which the vector component of interpretation is completely unified with that of direct perception—so that no differentiation of factual and ideational materials presents itself even tentatively for the time being. Only when and in the points where there is ground for questioning the validity (in general or with respect to its applicability in the case in hand) is there need for drawing the distinction of which we have been speaking with respect to the subject matter of observation. The broad distinction, which has been emphasized in the foregoing, is a generalization made regarding *functions* that for the most part are in direct cooperative connection. The generalization, moreover, is made by ex post [facto] reflection in dealing with the general theory of logic.

There may be readers who will infer from what has been said that there is doctrinal similarity between what has just been said [and Kant's view]. For Kant held that since perceptual material is "blind," chaotic and confused, and since rational conceptions are empty, some kind of union of the two elements is a necessary condition of the existence of knowledge. As matter of fact, the difference between the Kantian view and that here put forth is fundamental. Both views hold that knowledge involves union of observed data and general principles. But the grounds on which the position is taken are so different in the two cases that the superficially apparent likeness but emphasizes the radical difference. In the first place, Kant's doctrine starts with complete acceptance of the *outer-inner* primary and controlling assumption. Sense-material is "given" to the knowing mind or "subject" from without; the conceptual material is supplied by the mind from within. According to the position here taken, the distinction is instituted within inquiry as a means of resolving the problem that occasions it. In the second place, the difference between the two originally given materials is wholesale; only a surreptitious acceptance of the doctrine of pre-established harmony could account for the miraculous way in which, in actual cases of knowledge, the sensory (directly observed) and the ideational (theoretical) material fit each other.[15] Since the difference is *antecedent,* as well as wholesale, its existence does not account in any way whatever for the particular factual and theoretical subject matter which is operatively present in actual cases of knowledge. According to the position here taken, the two aspects of the subject matter of knowledge are correlative and together, since they are determined within and by inquiry with that result in view, so that their specific contents are checked throughout inquiry by their ability to function in resolution of the subject matter of the particular question and issue undergoing investigation.

Belief in a mind or "subject" within which receives impressions through the senses from "objects" outside has made its way from theological and philosophical sources into everyday attitudes to such an extent that to many persons it seems to be just a matter of common sense belief. On the theological side, the knowing subject (whatever name be given it (mind, consciousness,

---

15. Their lack of any intrinsic connection with each other accounts for the presence in Kant's theory of knowledge of what James called his elaborate "machine-shop," as Kant had to seek for intervening means that would soften the stark contrast between the two kinds of supposedly originally given stuffs. The inherent unreasonableness of the idea that materials proceeding from two antithetically different sources would or could so fit into each other as to terminate in actual knowledge was also the stimulus and occasion of the attempt of Kant's successors, Fichte and Schelling, to develop a philosophical theory according to which there was a single and common source. The result was what is termed "objective idealism," for according to Kant the only active factor in the constitution of knowledge was provided by mind, sensory material being passively received from "without." Moreover, the inherent unreasonableness of the notion that the "mind" of this that and the other human being could erect the structure of knowledge of an entire world of "objects" was virtually recognized in Kant's own system in a way that was an invitation to those who followed Kant to set up an "absolute mind" or "spirit"—which had the additional advantage that it could be identified with the God of traditional theology, while at the same time the theology involved purported to have a purely rational philosophical foundation so that recourse to the supernatural was not necessary—save as a way of conveying to the mass of men in the garb of imagination truths they are unable to grasp in rational philosophical form.

MIND AND BODY | 235

or whatever)) is an offspring in direct descent of an immaterial soul as agent and seat of knowledge.[16]

On the philosophical side, physical science has accustomed people generally to belief in material bodies that are outside the organic body and that act upon sensory-organs, eye, ear, hand (skin generally) and nerve endings, nose and mouth. This belief is supposed to be vouched for by physics on one side and anatomy on the other; it then blends closely with one aspect of the Lockean epistemological doctrine. The net result is popular acceptance of that phase of epistemological doctrine as if it were beyond need of examination. Or, to speak accurately, the popular interpretation of the physical and anatomical facts involved is itself to blend, product of the blending of the actual facts with a view like the Lockean.

In consequence a great number of people to whom formulated systematic epistemological doctrines seem to be fantastic exhibitions of the general futility of philosophy themselves firmly hold the beliefs which are the source of the doctrines deemed absurd. Every experienced teacher of "introductory" courses in philosophy is aware of how it is to start from beliefs held without question and lead students on from them into the epistemological problem and the various brands of various types of idealism and realism propounded in its solution. Accordingly I shall engage in a critical examination of the facts of the case, with a view to showing how arbitrary are assumptions which function as "premises" in the view just briefly summarized—and how far it is from any beliefs and attitudes meriting the name *common sense*.

The fact from which to start is the existence of *living* creatures constantly engaged (even when asleep) in interactions with their surroundings. Or, starting from the events that constitute *life*, living is a transaction which when it is analytically examined is found to be a continuous series of transactions carried on between *organic* structures and processes and *environing* conditions, one being just as natural and just as much manifestations of *integral* natural transactions those which take place between, say, carbon, oxygen, and hydrogen (in specifiable doses) in the case of sugar. Any person who begins with the transactions which constitute living, from the simplest to the most complex form, will appreciate the absurdity of the view that seeing is an event in which the eye (or the optical apparatus) on one hand and the physical vibration, constituting light, on the other hand are exclusively concerned. *If* seeing, hearing, touching, handling, tasting, and smelling were events of this isolated cut off kind, life would not endure, even if it

---

16. Peculiarly enough, in some contemporary philosophical (professedly psychological) and scientific documents, the "brain," or even the cortex, figures as the "inner" factor which receives the material of knowledge from "without" and then actively works it up into knowledge of the "objects" which used the impressions or sensations.

could get started beyond the shortest divisible interval of time. Consider the transaction which, as it goes on between the respiratory apparatus and the atmosphere, is breathing. That this function observes living as an ongoing concern is a proposition that hardly requires argument. Anyone has read accounts that state the results of scientific investigations of breathing is aware of the fact that the respiratory apparatus is so far from "acting" in isolation that the chemical-physical changes which compose it are constituents of a larger regulatory system so complex in extent and so minute in detail that it is still in process of study. And the student will also be aware that one important office of this complex regulatory organic apparatus is to carry on the respiratory transaction in such a way as to maintain a working coordination of *all* functions (circulation, secretion, nervous, etc.) which state—called homeostasis by Dr. Cannon—involves also keeping *environmental* conditions in a condition favorable to the continuity of living.

Were it not for the rigid hold exerted by the traditional theory of sensory perception, it would not be necessary to point out that the nervous system in general and the organs of sense in particular (optical, acoustic, tactile apparatus, etc.) function in the transactions that constitute living as a going concern in exactly the same way as do lungs, liver, kidney, etc. That is to say, they are organs of the living creature and their special operations are as much regulated by the total bodily economy in its interactions with environing conditions as are the functions of circulation, digestion, respiration and locomotion. Judged from the standpoint of what actually happens, as this is open to observation and is confirmed by physical and physiological knowledge, the notion that a single "object" or a set of isolated vibrations act exclusively upon a single sense-organ, say the eye, and that the single and solitary result is a quality, say red, variously termed a simple idea, sensation, sense-datum, or sensum, which constitutes an elementary unit of knowledge is, to speak frankly, a rank absurdity. For the quality in question, qualities generally, are neither, in their primary existence and function, modes of knowledge or forms nor items having to do with knowledge, nor anything which *in themselves* are sensory. As will be shown later they are termed sensory (a) only when the matter of their *causal conditions* is under consideration; that is, in a reference extraneous to them as immediate qualities; and (b) reference to causal conditions occur only in special conditions, namely, when it is an affair of determining the status of an existing quality with respect to its value as sign or inference of something else. Since the standing and worth of a quality as an evidential sign has to do with knowing, I take up for prior consideration the import of the statement that qualities, whatever the causal conditions of their occurrence as events, are *not* primarily affairs of knowledge at all, since they become such, under special conditions, as a derived and secondary use to which they are sometimes put. The most direct approach to discussion of this point is connected with the bald statement that the current view is absurd. For when one starts with the transactions which are life-functions, the interactions of the nervous system with environing conditions of sound, light, etc, are of the same kind as those of, say, the digestive system with the chemical physical properties of meat and vegetables. And on this basis the following facts are glaringly obvious: (i) The entire organism is engaged in the interaction, not just the optical apparatus in seeing or the moth and gullet in eating, although given interactions focus in these special structures. Hunger initiates eating and hunger is a condition of disequilibriation and need of the living creature. Taking of food is a step in the digestive process and while the latter centre, so to speak, in intestines and stomach, the products are taken up through the circulating system and distributed to maintain life-functions in their entirety—if digested material nourished only the organs primarily engaged in digestion (which of course does not go on save with the auxiliary cooperation of other vital functions), life would not long continue. In actual life-operations the processes of seeing, in which the nervous system and visual apparatus have immediate primacy, are strictly seeing. The living creature sees; it sees with and through the eyes.

. . .

The appearance of red, or a loud noise, a gritty feel, is no more of itself a case of knowledge than is a stomach-ache or a case of anger—which is also a set of qualities which investigation learns are consequences of a given interaction of specifiable environmental-organic conditions. It may be a mystery that interactions of a certain kind are the source of emergence of qualities. But if so it is the mystery that the world is what it is since the kind of a world in which we live is one in which interactivities of certain sorts produce the occurrence of qualities of certain sorts. Mystery or no mystery, there is no general *problem* involved unless one goes outside to inquire *why* a supernatural being created the kind of world that exists—and the proper theological answer to this question is that it is unwise and probably wrong, evidencing of sinful pride, for mortal creatures to ask such a question of its creator. There are *special* scientific problems involved. They are the question of what organic processes and structure and just what environmental conditions are involved in the intersections that lead to emergence of red quality or of color-blindness or of the qualities hot, cold, hard, soft, sweet, sour and so on indefinitely. As far as any *generalized* statement is concerned, the last word is that we live in a world of qualitative events and that their qualitative tonings, savors, etc. arise because of interactions, while patient, extensive, continued observation is capable of discovering connections between just such and such an interactivity and just such and such a quality.

I come now to the other consideration; namely, that there is basis, ground or significance in calling qualities in their own sensory, sensations, sense, or sense-data. We often use the phrase "sense-perception." It is possible, in fact a relatively simple matter, to give that phrase an intelligible meaning. In that case, the phrase signifies a perception having a subject matter into the *production of* which sense-organs play a part as causal conditions. Whether there are any perceptions whatever of which this does not hold—even perceptions or awareness of highly abstract matter—is a question of fact into which it is not necessary here to go, though the name "abstract" indicates that in any case the role of sense-organs is *relatively* indirect and weakened. What may be confidently affirmed is that the "sense" would not be prefixed to "perception" in the way it is prefixed were it not for events characterizing the history of philosophical doctrines. When perception was regarded as an instance or form of knowledge, and when especially it was regarded as an inferior grade as compared with "rational" knowledge occupied with First and Ultimate "realities," the prefixed adjective "sense" had an important—because differential—significance. It retains that significance only because remnants of the old tradition are uncritically projected into the existing state of knowledge with such confusion as a result that current philosophies instead of being able to take advantage of what is now known is kept discussing problems that are now artificial.

I doubt if it will be denied that *prima facie* what is perceived is an extensive field, which *as perceived* is a segment of a larger world—using "world" in its everyday non-technical sense. We wake up in the morning. If we see there is light enough to see anything what is seen is a room with its furnishings. Moreover it is perceived *as* a room of a house, and of a house located in a certain place and the locus of extensive occupational transactions. Anyone who wakes suddenly with sense of being in a completely strange place appreciates by the shock of dislocation and need for orientation that occurs the common sense character of what has just been said. Now this sort of thing which is just a commonplace example of the nature of what is perceived as long as we are awake constitutes a terrific philosophical "problem" from the standpoint of its complete divergence from what is to be expected from the standpoint of premises furnished both by the theory of the subject-matter of physical science as that of separate "reality" and by the theory of isolated elementary sense-data as the proper immediate material of perception. It is, on the contrary, just what would be expected when we accept and employ the view, suggested and warranted by present known facts, of living as a continuous transaction consisting of adaptive interactivities of a living creature with an extensive environing conditions; transaction in question having for its consequences qualities which are so connected, arranged, organized as to constitute a scene or situation.[17] The subject matter of these situations constitutes the world of ordinary "objects," employing that word to indicate what is indicated by common nouns—stone, tree, star, fossil, etc., etc.—*objects* in an idiomatic sense in distinction from object in the epistemological sense in which it involves reference to a "subject." These different subject matters are not in their primary existence, or "first intention," objects of *knowledge.* They are recurrent means—consequences, instrumentalities, and consummations of functions that make up living. They are distinguished and identified on the ground of what, in a given interaction, they do to us and we do to them. They are "objects" in the capacity and reference of being enjoyed and suffered, undergone and used or turned to account in the course of living. They are resources and obstacles in the carrying forward of the transactions that make up life. *As objects of perception* they not only are *not* isolated qualities but they are not sets or arrangements of qualities of the organs immediately engaged *save as* these organs are what they are in virtue of modifications undergone in previous interactions of use and enjoyment: that is, they are what they are by virtue of attitudes, tendencies, and dispositions that are acquired and now habitual. For this reason the larger part of the qualities (putting it in quantitative terms, which strictly speaking should not be done) express *potentialities.* A spade is not a *spade* in virtue of qualities conditioned by original and native sensory organs nor by any conceivable combination of physiological conditions of this order.[18]

There are no facts whatever to verify the Lockean notion that objects (of the kind mentioned or nameable by common nouns) are compounds or complexes or associated sets of a sufficiently large number of direct and simple qualities even if there were any such events as the latter. The qualities of a spade as perceived and named are the consequences that *would* result if it were used (or *will* result when it is used)—they are anticipations of what is future at the limited and limiting date of perception; and those of a *shovel* express the somewhat different consequences that result from use of a similar device that effects somewhat different ends. Because the organism entering an interaction is an organism of habits developed in prior interaction whose consequences were qualities helpful and harmful, used, suffered, or enjoyed, the qualities of things perceived later run out into the future so

---

17. To avoid misunderstanding, it should be explicitly noted that the existence of *situations* is the primary fact and that the above statement states the result of analysis of them with respect to the way in which the situations come to be.

18. The indispensable role played by social-cultural conditions in formation of habitual responses is dealt with in the next chapter.

anticipated consequences impossible of occurrence, were it not for habitual dispositions, are an integral part of what is perceived. The completeness and intimacy of the integration is what renders the quantitative characterization previously indulged unsuitable. For potential consequences, corresponding to habits that are operating usually override and transfuse the quality due to interaction of the organ primarily and focally engaged. That the optical apparatus is that which is primarily engaged when we see is a truism. But color, which is its special contribution to the perceptual field, may be and usually is a subordinate feature of the total scene. In the case of children, artists, and people of marked esthetic habits, colors and distinctions of light and shade tend to occupy in what is beheld a place comparable to that of the optical apparatus in the mechanism of perception. The reason that *seeing* is so often used as a synonym of perceiving and of being aware ("I see what you mean") is that the *body* sees through or by means of the eyes but not in a way that decides the perceived seen.

Cases of perceiving by the eyes in which color is a conspicuous feature, and yet the seeing is non-esthetic, may be used to illustrate the relation of qualities, which are causally mediated by sense organs, to knowledge. I may identify a book by its color; in that case when I look over library shelves in search of a particular book a given color is an especially prominent feature of the scene because it is a sign. Scientific knowledge is replete with instance of this sort. It suffices to note the way in which chemical substances are detected and identified in the constitution of suns indefinitely remote in space by colored lines in spectral analysis. We may confidently generalize from examples of this sort. Qualities that are immediately and primarily just the qualities they are as components of the world in which we live are used as evidence or signs of something beyond themselves. In this use they acquire a new status, of that of being instrumentalities of knowledge. When Locke managed to forget the extraneous theories which serve as the controlling premises of his theory of knowledge and spoke in terms of facts verifiable in observation, he traveled for a little while on a road that might have led him to a conclusion that would have given a turn to subsequent theorizing about knowledge quite other than that which it took. For in discussion [of the] question of "the reality of our knowledge" (its reality in general, not its veridical quality in actual cases) he wrote of qualities ("simple ideas" in his nomenclature) that by them "[We are] enabled to distinguish the sorts of particular substances, to discern the states they are in, and so to take them for our necessities, and apply them to our uses."[19] In other [words], qualities may be employed

---

19. [John Locke, *Essay Concerning Human Understanding* (1690), bk. 4, ch. 4, sec. 4.]

to serve as dependable signs in respect to both "theoretical" and "practical" affairs. Scientific determination of proper data—an extensive and difficult part of scientific method—is an endeavor to discover just what qualities are signs of just such and such events and the precise conditions under which they point to, signify and give dependable evidence. While this fact is of basic importance in respect to the traditional notion that "sense-qualities" are immediately and inherently known objects or else elementary unity of knowledge, it does not cover the whole territory.

I mentioned earlier that the word sense (and sensory) as a part of the phrase sense-perception has to do with an aspect of the causal conditions of the generation of the occurrence of given qualities. It is not part of the immediate existence or occurrence of any qualities to be *sense*-qualities. For qualities do not bring with them in their bare occurrence information about how they originate. Such information is a product of *ex post facto* investigation. Doubtless human beings learned at an early stage that light and colors were connected with the eyes and sounds with ears, etc. But not they had to learn the fact, and it is extraneous to the occurrence of a quality. In principle there is no difference between these cases and the extended inquiry that was found necessary in connection with, say, cases of color-blindness or the special functions of rods and cones in the structure of the eye. But this consideration does not explain just why it is important with respect to institute knowledge to reference to sensory conditions of production. The reason is not, however, far to seek. It is well nigh a commonplace that knowledge of causal conditions is the means by which we gain whatever degree of control we have over the occurrence of events. As long as knowledge was believed to be a matter of immediate intuitive certainty (whether directly or through a series of intuitively necessary intermediate steps) the need of similar control of knowledge (discriminating them from error, guesswork and arbitrary conjecture, etc.) did not present itself. The sole ground for prefixing "sense" to perception was, as has been noted, in order to discriminate the inferior type of intuitive knowledge from the higher rational type. One factor in the scientific revolution was, however, adoption as a working postulate of the belief that demonstrable evidence for the existence of specifiable physiological conditions, involving sense-organs, was a necessary part of the rock-bottom testing of hypotheses and theories. There is nothing in the intrinsic nature of any one quality that fits it to serve as evidence better than any other quality in the bare fact of its existence. The qualities that are characteristic of anger, fear, resentment, or awe were regularly used in one state of culture as primitive folk have ascribed rain to benevolence and earthquakes to rage as evidence in judging the nature of natural events. On purely general principles, there is nothing unreasonable in this procedure. It just did not work out as using qualities whose origin could be referred to specifiable participations of eye, ear, hand, etc. When the question of evidential force does not enter in one quality is as good as another—save esthetically or "emotionally." When the matter of evidence is fundamental, the question of the source of a given quality has been shown, in the course of [the] scientific method, to be of primary moment. More particularly, discovery of the direct participation of a specific peripheral nervous structure in the occurrence of a given quality is the best test there is—ultimately the *only* conclusive evidence that can be provided—of the *here-and-now* existence of any event inferred that is inferred on the round of existing qualities. Otherwise, the qualitative material used as evidence might have its source in a dream, in something read in a book, or something dimly recalled from a conversation.

III

When this line of understanding [treating knowing as a mode of technology] is followed the entire epistemological, subject-object, mind-reality, industry completely drops away. And this line is the only one that can be taken if the theory of knowledge is based upon knowing, as knowing is exhibited and made evident in scientific inquiry.

Doubtless many persons will balk at the idea of calling knowing as it takes place in the sciences a mode of technology. As far as this resistance is due to perpetuation of the belief that a theory of knowledge in order to be philosophical, must envelop the conclusions and methods of the sciences in a wrapping composed of definitions and criteria which are fixed by sheer intuition or some other mysterious source prior to and independently of all cases of knowing, nothing can be done until the old idea relaxes its grip. As far as resistance centers around the word *technological*, it may be said that any almost any word used at the present time is open to objection and that the main consideration is to be willing to face frankly the facts the word is used to designate. In the past, I have usually employed "instrumental" to designate the intermediate position and function of the subject matter of knowledge in the inclusive complex of the transactions constituting human living as a going concern. Events have proved, in the case of many persons, the word is so linked with linguistic uses that give *instruments* a mechanical sense, which perforce renders knowledge subservient to ends externally set that they have been unwilling and impotent to examine what was said to see what the word stands for, and the kind of liberal and liberating instrumentality which knowledge as instrumentality is shown to be by the analyses I have attempted to execute. I have no assurance that "technological" will not meet the same or a worse fate.[20] But there may be those not so ridden by verbal-associations that they can entertain the idea that knowing is an art; that it not *a* liberal but *the* liberal art; that the best exemplar of the art is the practices which constitute the fundamentals of scientific method; and, finally, that the significance of the method is so far from being restricted to physical subject matters that, from the standpoint of philosophy, one of the main (if not *the* main) reasons for taking the art of knowing as it is exhibited in the method of scientific inquiry as the data for framing the theory of knowledge is that the resulting theory will be a powerful tool (if it is permitted to use the word) in getting rid of the obstructions which now stand in the way of employing the method in free formation of beliefs that have decisive influence in [the] conduct of social affairs and transactions. The preceding sentences consist, unfortunately, of a number of clauses. Since, however, they are cumulative in effect, it did not seem possible to reduce the number and convey the meaning that is intended. A statement based upon negative features of the social situation may perhaps convey the meaning better. Scientific conclusions exert an immense influence upon formation and control of the arrangements and customs involved in the vast complex body of transactions and interaction which go on. But as has been pointed out, they take effect mainly in an area set as "material" because it is economic in nature. The interests and purposes which effectively regulate the uses to which industry, business and commerce are put and the human consequences that result from the use are for the most part a heritage from the pre-scientific age. That is, they have not been seriously affected by thorough and persistent intelligent examination; correspondingly, intelligence has not been systematically brought to bear to effect a constructive development of social policies and plans such as the conclusions and methods of science now render possible.

Fundamental and urgent social problems of the present time center here. As far as philosophy is concerned, its present task is to help bring to light or formulate the needs and obstructions that compose the practical problems and the resources which if they [were] systematically used would further their resolution. In saying this I am not arrogating for philosophy an inherent position of superior dignity; on the contrary, the implication is that anything which engages intelligence in this work is *ipso facto* in so far philosophical. The obstacle that most forcibly prevents attempts at execution of this task—and that blurs even the perception that it is the present task—is perpetuation of traditional views as to the problem of knowledge which, by diverting philosophical reflection into what are now

---

20. I may say that the example of the writings of Clarence Ayres has been influential in inducing me to make use of this alternative term.

relatively insignificant bypaths (whatever importance they may have had at an earlier time), effectively prevents the doing of what needs to be done. The view that, philosophically speaking, knowledge is one form, a central form, of technology does not mean that its subject matter and products are specifically similar to technologies exhibited in production of commonalities and services in the electrical industry or in transportation or application of bio-chemistry in agriculture. It means that knowledge is, first, a form of technology in the methods it employs in producing more knowledge and improving its own methods and, furthermore, is *capable* of being a technology in humane social guidance of technologies now called such but whose human and social consequences are left a matter of pulling and hauling of conflicting customs and institutions which are hardly touched by effective use of the method of intelligence at work. What I called the first affair constitutes the philosophical problem of knowledge in its narrower sense. The second matter defines the philosophical problem of knowledge in its wider human and moral sense. Its nature is indicated by the statement that is often made that "technology is indifferent to the uses to which it is put." As long as that statement remains as true as it is at present time, it signifies that something else is sure to decide the uses to which it is put—traditions and customs, rules of business and of law— which exist now because they came into existence in the past, superficially sugared over by moralistic condemnations and exhortations.

The two phases, the narrower and technical and the wider and human, of the problem of knowledge are intimately connected. The dependence of the second upon the first has already been indicated in on its negative side; that is, we have seen how the traditional statement in subject-object end-terms as an affair between a knower, individual, consciousness or whatever and reality, results in an isolation of the body of natural knowledge, since it results in the belief that there is a physical, merely material world or "realm" whose only possible human connection (save that of being object known) is with material and bodily needs, desires, transactions alleged to exist independently from and as a rival of man's higher nature. Opposing the rightful power of what is called the higher and spiritual self to lay down the ends and laws of conduct, this allegedly lower, appetitive, carnal, and sensuous "self" is morally subject to the sovereign rule of the higher. Discussion of this separation in morals is deferred for the present. We saw earlier that interpretation of the subject matter of natural science as a real world, the objective and external world in distinction from the subjective and mental order of existence as an opposite kind of reality, resulted in reducing everything which common sense takes to be the world, the total qualitative complex of things and events in and by which all human transactions, enjoyment and sufferings life, move and have their being, to relative unreality or mere appearance;—and this in spite of the fact that all the data and all the means by which conclusions about the supposed independent and physical "reality" are tested belong in exclusively the everyday environment.[21] The subject of [the] present discussion is, then, the bearing of the view here advanced upon the extraordinary doubling up of everything into two worlds, one that of science and the other that of the events and things of our everyday environment.

The view that knowing is one form of technological art bears directly upon the peculiar doubling up that is a necessary outcome of the traditional subject-object view of knowing and of what is known. The difference between crude ores deep down in the earth and a watch, telephone, or an automobile (as examples of selected specimens of the vast number of finished products which enter into the processes of living) is tremendous. What would be thought of a man who translated this undeniably immense difference into the problem of the relation sustained by two radically different orders of existence, one "real" and the other only "apparent," or in philosophical vocabulary "phenomenal"? The difference in question in the case cited is obviously that between raw or crude materials and finished (that is, refined) products. And while only the expert is aware of just *what* intervening operations have brought about the difference, everyone is aware that these operations exist and that they are carried by utilizing natural forms of energy, pressure, movements which bring together and separate them in ways by which they take on new properties, heat, electricity—separate them, the operations in question having themselves undergone, as materials, a long intermediate refining and preparation. Materials and energies both originated in the same world of nature; they never left it, the refining occurring by means of transactions native in nature and the finished products taking their place through time and in place in one and the same natural world, thereby meeting the needs which gave rise to practical problems, while the solution of these problems attained in refined materials and refined ways of effecting changes gives added significance and enrichment to human life. We have only to add to the points enumerated that the technological arts in question undergo a highly specialized intermediate development in which they are the concern of occupations carried on by particular groups of hu-

---

21. I omit in the above statement the alternative doctrine which takes the commonsense world to be alone "real" thereby shifting the epistemological problem over to the possibility of existence of the "external world" and the validity in general of physical science. The omission makes no difference in the present discussion since the premises that give rise to the "problem" and its two "solutions" are the same.

man beings whose transactions are more or less remote from both extracting the raw materials and employing and enjoying the finished products. Some of these intermediate occupations for example are exclusively occupied with invention and making tools and machines for further use. If their temporally intermediate and "instrumental" functional position were overlooked, and were virtually denied by being ignored, their special operations and products would be of necessity so isolated as to constitute the material of a problem so inherently and artificially self-made that various "schools of thought" would arise offering a variety of incompatible accounts.

No such problems arise because everyone is well aware that the independence and the kind of isolation marking operations relatively complete in themselves and remote from final application are for "the time being" in an interlocking inclusive *temporal* series. It is also to be noted that in the case of highly developed technologies, there is [a] definite place given to operations not concerned with production of agencies and instrumentalities, that they have the place and function of taking up and carrying on to the next stage the products of previous stages in an established routine sequence. There is, by definition, provision for a group of inventors and draftsmen occupied in transactions whose outcome is intended to produce the modification of component operations of an existing technology. As far as the members of this group are concerned their problem, operations and to some extent their materials are quite independent of any reference, *on their part*, to the matter of ultimate direct application, use or consumption. The fact that important industries today maintain laboratories carrying on research that are not all different from those carried on in laboratories of "pure" scientific research shows how far this independence *for the time being* can be advantageously carried, even from the so-called practical or utilitarian standpoint.

What has been said should protect the view that scientific inquiry is one form or type of technological art from being assimilated to the specific content of technologies already familiarly so designated—although it is highly probable that the association of knowing with "mind" and of technology with industries carried on for pecuniary profit will cause some persons to indulge in continued identification of the position here taken with the doctrine that knowledge is subordinated to gaining some fixed "practical" end of a private or "personal" sort. For in the case of linguistic, as well as of other, well-established habits, no change can be effected without some degree of willing participation on the part of those whose attitude is determined by the habits requiring modification. Those whose belief-attitudes are not already set beyond possibility of change will attach proper weight to the fact that all inquiry which moves in the direction of stable, because well-tested, beliefs involves a factor of *experimentation* in the observations, inspections, examinations, [and] analyses that take place. Observations conducted to obtain material to resolve the perplexities, predicaments, embarrassments, hindrances, troubles, dangers, that recur so frequently in the course of everyday transactions in ordinary affairs, are met by effecting some change in the conditions which determine what is seen, heard and handled from a simple modification of tension of the muscles that affect the acuteness and intensity of hearing (corresponding to cocking the ears on the part of animals) and those of the eyes to obtain a clearer, sharper and more accurate vision, up to bodily movements made to obtain location and position for seeing, hearing, touching, thereby refining the data upon which judgment is based.

It is a familiar fact that inquiries that are designated scientific employ a great variety of physical instrumental devices. Their use is the means for obtaining data sufficiently varied, refined, minute, and extensive, and (by means of attached devices of measurement) sufficiently accurate to guide formulation of problems, interference and testing. In comparison, the material of observations conducted by bodily organs without the aid of the devices of art, is too fixed, too coarse and crude, and restricted to carry investigation much beyond what is directly obvious to eye, ear, and hand. The reason that Greek-medieval science made so little progress was in part the absence of instruments and partly the unwillingness to use those which were available because they were connected with the low status of artisans. The lack and the refusal were the chief reasons why ancient "science" remained for the most part a dialectical affair. The scientific revolution on the other hand began and was carried forward by use of devices and techniques borrowed from industrial arts.[22] It would be a great mistake, however, to suppose that research in laboratory and observatory originated [the] use of experimentation as an inherent factor in deliberate modification of what is observed in order to obtain better control of the subject matter on which rest judgments that are formed. The changes that are instituted in ordinary perception so that material seen, heard, handled, tasted, and smelled will provide the more dependable material to serve as data and tests of judgments made in meeting the hindrances and perplexities which present themselves are of an experimental order. Effectuation of such modifications in what is observed is the only alternative to dull, stupid, routine acceptance of any conclusion that happens to offer itself. The transformation effected by extensive use of instrumental devices and techniques in investigation which take place

---

22. I have quoted elsewhere the following passage from the writings of A. N. Whitehead who cannot be accused of theoretical predilection for the practical and physical aspect of knowing: "In science, the most important thing that has happened in the last forty years, is the advance in instrumental design . . . These instruments have put thought inquiry upon a new level." [Alfred North Whitehead, *Science and the Modern World* (Free Press) 1925, p. 114.]

on the scientific level is indefinitely important. But it does not introduce experimentation as a novel, unprecedented resource.[23]

In both commonsense and scientific knowing, in short, there are conditions and factors fundamentally alike in form. The basic common character is the incurring of blocks, obstructions, conflicting tendencies (that is, presence of materials that call out incompatible modes of adaptive response) in the transactions which take place. The need for formulation of a problem and for measures to resolve it is common in both cases. The transactions involved in the two cases are very different in their specific contents and hence in their specific problems and specific measures undertaken to resolve them. But they are of one and the same form in respect to the considerations involved in framing a theory of knowledge. When they are viewed and examined in their own terms, instead of in terms derived from an irrelevant, because pre-scientific, set of belief-attitudes, there is nothing whatever in either of them to warrant, or even suggest, the doubling-up of "objects" which is a necessary consequence of the traditional wholesale subject-object, mind-reality epistemological antecedent assumptions—*antecedent* because they are drawn from a source prior to and independent of the conduct of knowing of any case that actually takes place, and observation of the operations of which knowing consists.

I cannot imagine that the most case-hardened epistemologist would suppose that the transactions of daily life would be facilitated or bettered if the sun that is described in astronomical science—taken epistemologically as the "real object" over against the perceived sun of daily life as a relatively unreal appearance—if the latter were completely to disappear and be replaced by the subject matter of the former. But his sole alternative to giving assent to this extraordinary proposition is his acceptance of the equally extraordinary propositions that all the transactions and operations which constitute living are sheer illusions. For if the question of "reality" is to be raised at all it does not concern the "reality" of the qualities and properties of the directly perceived sun but of the whole set and system of the transactions and interactions that make up the course of living. "Perceiving" being, from the standpoint of life behavior, simply one of a number of these *interdependent* and interconnected transactions. And if perceiving as one manifestation of life-behavior is eliminated as unreal, it is obvious what happens to the perceived materials that supply data and tests in "scientific" inquiries by way of their consignment to the limbo of illusions. Moreover, given the genuine or valid standing of the conclusions reached in scientific investigation of sun, light, the constitution of the organic body including its nervous system, it should be obvious that the sun as perceived is the result of their interac-

---

23. The inherent use of organs of sense and of muscles as agencies of obtaining data has, as is shown later, definite bearing upon the so-called body-mind problem.

tion in accord with accepted scientific conclusions, specific and generic.[24]

The preceding discussion has for its primary concern the task of outlining the grounds upon which scientific knowing should be regarded as a form of technology. Because of the obviousness of correspondence with other technologies, attention has been given to experimental operations (that is, those which deliberately effect change in a given direction) and to the indispensable presence of concrete agencies as means of effecting the changes required in order that changes effected may move in the direction intended—bodily organs in the case of everyday commonsense knowing, specially designed apparatus in the case of scientific inquiry. But the attention given these two points should not lead to the conclusion that they are fundamental and primary reasons for regarding scientific knowledge as a form of technology. They are derived and secondary. For they function in formulation and resolution of problems that arise in the course of ongoing transactions of a specifiable character—in contrast with the wholesale or at large conditions forming the premises of the epistemological problem and theory. Undertakings that are currently acknowledged to be technological start from a lack or need which the results of their operations satisfy or fulfill. The processes and the instruments and special techniques by which the task is accomplishment are means of achieving the fulfillment that conditions demand; they are not primary nor yet final, terminal. The movement in a given direction, which was mentioned, is movement toward production of means of satisfaction or making good a class of demands that recur because of biological-social needs. Grain produced by agronomic technology and bread [produced][25] by that of the baker are not a final end or termination; nor is marketing for a profit the outcome and *raison d'etre* of the technological operations. Use, consumption, application, of one sort or other is the outcome or consequence to which the series of transactions forming a technology is directed, and it determines the apparatus, the tools, machines and technical processes employed and the special kinds of modification to which original, relatively crude materials are subjected—corn is not subjected to the same modifications when the need to be satisfied is that of laundry starch as when the need is to provide grain to be further transformed into foodstuffs.

The considerations just mentioned indicate another sense than that already discussed in which science is a special or differentiated form of technology. The "original" state, that from which it sets out, is directly or proximately some flaw, defect, incompatibility in the existing state of scien-

24. A remark of Aristotle's about another matter is pertinent in this case. He wrote, [Quote missing.]

25. [Replacing "proceed."]

tific subject matter; indirectly and remotely it consists of the subject matter that is provided by the results of every day dealings with the problems that inevitably and continually turn up in the course of conducting successfully the transactions that constitute living—and not limited by any means to living in its narrower physiological *sense*.[26] Moreover, in the historical origins or beginnings, sciences arose, as previously noted, quite directly out of conditions caused by failure of existing subject matters to deal with satisfactorily, adequately, with the "practical" (that is, vitally urgent) problems of associated living as this was culturally determined in its specific forms at a given time. That the transition from crude primitive methods of dealing with the problems presented in cases of illness and medical wounds to method would [have been] completely out of the question were it not for the results of inquiry into anatomical and physiological and later into physical-chemical conditions is an illustration of this aspect of the matter. But this type of illustration (as has also been expressly remarked) is far from covering the ground in an adequate way. As long as anatomy and physiology were limited to problems and investigations determined by the subject matter of the kind just mentioned, the progress of science, as a technology, was slow, torturous and hampered. Subject matter involved was too coarse, too scanty, and above all too encumbered with considerations that were irrelevant and distracted to inquiry as an occupation its own (that is, its appropriate) concern, interest, aim, prepared materials, techniques and especially designed instruments. The great change in science came about when scientific problems were provided by subject matter which emerged as a consequence of the development of inquiry in its capacity of being inquiry. Socially speaking, this fact signifies the emergence of a group of human beings engaged in independent investigations, inquiries, researches, as an important mode of the social division of labor. And whatever be said, and be said truly, about the injurious results of the kind of specialization which has confirmed older traditional beliefs about the isolation of science from any save external accidental contact and intercourse with other social occupations and interest, there can be no doubt that the rise of inquiry into nature as a special occupation has been a condition *sine qua non* of the development of knowledge which is liberal, since not tied down to any special use or application. For any end or application that can be laid down in advance as a regulator of inquiry must in the nature of the case be the result of customs already established or at best depend quite directly upon conditions already in existence. If, then, the subject matter of knowledge as the product of inquiry is to be capable of originating new ends, instead of

---

26. Marginal note: "In some earlier writings, confusion persisted because of failure to discriminate with sufficient [*illeg.*] the two senses of instrumental."

merely increasing efficiency and economy of measures to achieve ends and uses already in existence. Just here is located the distinct quality of scientific knowledge as a form of technological art. It is the one form of technology which directly and systematically stimulates and promotes production of consequences, uses and enjoyments which constitute departures from previous conditions and even breaks in customary ways of doing things. The coinciding of an age of accelerated inventions with the period of growth in natural science is not a mere coincidence. Here is the simple explanation of what is otherwise a paradox—development of new ends, even more than assured ability to accomplish old ones, is an accompaniment of expulsion from the new science of the teleological factors inherent in the old cosmological science. The non-appearance of qualities in the subject matter of physical science (in its broadest sense) is similarly equivalent [to the] ability to regulate production of qualities either new in themselves or radically new with respect to the conditions under which they are now had in contrast with the state of affairs before the rise of a physical science whose subject matter consists exclusively of *relations*: ability to effect transmission of sounds to hearers at remote distances and to produce illumination by pressing a button being conspicuous examples.

XI. The Practical and the Theoretical

I

Certain assumptions regarding the nature of knowledge sense have persisted throughout pretty much the whole course of philosophical discussion. Certain other assumptions, used as premises in defining knowledge, account for that division into opposed schools that marks modern epistemological theory. The most important assumption in the first class is, in all probability, that which treats knowledge as purely *theoretical* in the sense in which that word is completely antithetical to *practical*. In the second class are the considerations that have produced the conflict of the empiristic and the rationalistic, the a posteriori and a priori, schools in modern philosophy—a division historically associated with its attendant separation of perception-conception, induction-deduction, particulars-universals, probability-certainty. The considerations involved in each group are connected with what has been termed the narrower and more technical sense aspect of the philosophical theory of knowledge. It is proposed in this chapter to develop the view of knowledge which was put forward in the last chapter by applying it to examination of the just-mentioned historic problems. The import of the view taken on these different matters will be clear when its various applications are put in contrast with the historic doctrines which have been advanced on the ground of the general view of knowledge that has been inherited, with only minor modifications, from beliefs that were formulated in the Greek-medieval period. Accordingly, the discussions of this chapter involve some going over of historical material for a second time, though from a somewhat different standpoint than that from which earlier discussion of the material was conducted.

The doctrine of the strictly theoretical or "intellectual" nature of knowledge will be first taken up, since it lies nearest to the material adduced in the previous chapter regarding knowledge as a form of technological art. But since *theoretical* and *practical* both have a variety of meanings and the ambiguity which results easily occasions misunderstanding and confusion, I shall first say what denial of the exclusively "theoretical" quality of knowledge does *not* mean. It is not in any way a doctrine about the attitude, motivation, or purpose of those who conduct scientific inquiries. It is necessary to make this point in an explicit and emphatic way. For adverse criticisms of the type of doctrine here presented have quite uniformly been marked by assuming that the position held about the method of knowing and the body of subject matter that results from competent investigations is a doctrine concerning a very different matter—the "personal" aim of scientists. The latter question is a *moral* matter. It is outside the scope of discussion save as the actual story of scientific advance has clearly demonstrated that interest in and effective concern for conduct of inquiry *as such*, or independently of the particular conclusion arrived (and even more, much more, independently of any special application or use to which that conclusion is put) is an indispensable condition of such progress. It is in this moral respect that inquiry should be "objective," liberal and "pure." Any theory of knowledge that is based upon observation and analysis of actual cases (instead of upon premises derived from an extraneous source) will, I believe, come to this conclusion. But transfer of a view about the attitude and aim of inquiries into the intrinsic terms of a theory regarding the method and subject matter of knowledge as such is a very different matter—the transfer comes with peculiarly poor grace from those who emphasize the complete independence of what is known from any and every "subjective" and "personal" taint.

. . .

The word *theory* has a definite meaning in scientific procedure, a meaning closely related to that of hypothesis. In this reference, theory is discussed in connection with the topic of scientific method. The word *theoretical* as it appears in the title of this chapter has a meaning determined by the tradition according to which the "theoretical" and "practical" designate two entirely separate orders of Being, the theoretical having a superior and indeed supreme metaphysical position. Modern philosophy has been chary of explicit adoption of this position in its ontological aspect, but almost as uniformly giving intellectual activity and its proper material a higher valuation than is accorded to practical activity and its appropriate objects. And, in general, the older metaphysical doctrine of the two has been approximated. For it is held that knowledge as exclusively intellectual (in a sense in which "intellectual" excludes all practical elements and reference) corresponds to "reality" while subject matter affected by practical considerations is so affected and infected by its connection with human interests as to be an affair of "appearance" in contrast with "reality." It is no part of the topic as it will be considered in this chapter to repeat what was said earlier about the cultural circumstances in which the classic tradition originated. I add, however, that rivalry was an intense factor in Athenian life and that it is quite likely that Aristotle's insistence of the superiority of the activity of philosophers to that of all other classes, statesmen included, was somewhat prompted by the contention of some writers of the rhetorical school as to the superiority of oratory as the chief civic force. And from the standpoint of professional interest, "intellectuals" in general and philosophers in particular have been wont to disparage the value of those engaged in practical action and to magnify their own calling.

The intent of the present chapter, however, is different. It is dual. First, I shall indicate, from the standpoint of experience as interactivity of organic and environing conditions, the meaning of "practical" and the various forms it assumes and is capable of assuming under different cultural conditions. Then I shall consider the sense in which an experience is capable of being peculiarly intellectual or theoretical in quality without on that account existing in a different realm of either value or Being from the practical. The discussion of the meaning of *practical* is fundamentally a continuation of the discussion of the last chapter, but it will take into especial account the ambiguities attaching to *practical* since their existence is a potent factor in rendering it subject to disparagement on grounds which, quite properly, win approval. It is in this latter connection that the effect of environment in its socio-cultural aspects is particularly important.

In discussion of the theme of the last chapter, the current state of the problem of mind and body rendered it appropriate to speak almost exclusively from the side of the body of the brain. In discussion of the *practical*, it is necessary to take other structures and functions of the nervous system into account. Not even the central nervous system, of which the brain is only one constituent, covers the entire ground that has to be considered. The backwardness of physiological knowledge, as well as the all but exclusive preoccupation of philosophers with the problem of knowledge, contributed to almost total neglect of the autonomic nervous system, the "sympathetic" nervous system, as it used to be called; or, when it did receive mention, to [the] limitation of discussion of it to a rather perfunctory reference to its regulatory capacity in connection with organic functions of digestion, circulation, secretion and elimination. Comparatively recent knowledge about its operations in connection with glandular condition and hormones has demonstrated its intimate connection with the emotional aspects of life-activities. The connection of the emotional with some kinds of practical activity is too obvious to be entirely ignored. But the traditional separation of the emotional and intellectual, the tendency to view the emotional as simply a force tending to interfere with the act of right knowing, has of necessity tended to continue the process of disparagement of the practical. For activity, personal and collective, which is animated by emotions and passions, apart from understanding and insight, cannot justly be rated very high. Any just estimate of the significance of the practical has to bear in mind the falsity of the psychological doctrine of divorce of the intellectual and the emotional. In abstract theory (as noticed earlier in another connection) the Christian doctrine that God is Love in his supreme attribute, as well as the importance given to sympathy in moral doctrine, has always pointed away from the glorification of reason. But official, as distinct from sentimental evangelistic theology has always tended to explain the idea in an esoteric sense; a course logically virtually inevitable in view of the emphasis placed upon orthodoxy of creedal beliefs as a condition of salvation through the offices of the Church.

From the standpoint of the central nervous system, the "concept" of the practical has been largely based upon actions of which the spinal cord and basal ganglia with a minimum of cerebral participation are the chief bodily agents. This is equivalent as far as it goes to identifying practice as such with its lowest, because most mechanical and least intelligent, form. This view of practice is embodied in the saying "Practice makes perfect," where "practice" stands for recurrent acts of sheer rote or repetition, and "being perfect" stands for ability to perform an action automatically—i.e., without giving it any thought at all. The actual proper function of the part of the central nervous system constituted by basal ganglia and the processes of the spinal cord is such as to color with a certain plausibility an argument in favor of the value of this type of mechanical action advanced on allegedly scientific grounds. But the argument in question rests upon virtually cutting off this part of the central system from the "higher," that is, cerebral, part. The function of prompt execution of intelligently chosen acts (those in which cerebral energies and events are involved) and arrogation of the function of original and final determination of the acts performed are two very different things. The first expresses the normal function of the lower centers; the second represents the state of affairs expressed in the "bad master" phrase of the proverbial saying "Habit is a good servant but a bad master."

The position there taken about the normal function of the structures and processes of the spinal cord may seem to be open to debate. For it will be argued that it, like all matters of *normality* of function, depends upon a

criterion which is or which involves a value-judgment. Since the physiological data involved are complex, I waive the question whether the same assertion would be made about say the functions of respiration or circulation
of the blood. The facts regarding the influence of the social environment in
production of mechanical reactions to stimuli are simpler and more accessible. Consider, for example, the effect of the average or traditional school
environment in its effect upon the attitude of pupils. The ideational or intellectual aspect of the transactions that occur is in effect monopolized by
the teacher and the text. What is demanded of pupils is reproduction, as
prompt and as accurate as possible, of subject matter which their own judgment has had no share in developing, and no share in appropriating beyond
the best method of its acquisition or the best method of giving the teacher
the impression it has been acquired. The constant demand is for "correct
answers," and this phrase means simply verbal statements which conform
to the statements of authors of textbooks and school-room instructors. The
emphasis put upon "prompt" replies in recitation periods means, of necessity,
the uttering of sentences in which pupils have not "stopped to think"—that
is, automatic repetition of statements "learned" by rote. "Attention" does not
go to actual subject matter but to anticipation of the requirements of the
teacher and the chief problem is how to get by. There is of course a certain
amount of exaggeration in what has just been said, but it cannot be denied
that the tendency of the conventional schoolroom is in the direction of
inculcation, as far as the material of instruction (also discipline) is concerned, of habitual attitudes in which mechanical reproduction dominates
intelligent adaptations to situations containing novel factors, which alone
evoke reflective or thoughtful qualities.

The case of the schoolroom is presented simply as an illustration of the
kind of social interaction that creates a separation of the practical and the
intellectual in which the former is reduced to a level which inevitably and
properly, as far as it is taken to exemplify the intrinsic nature of the practical,
[leads] to a highly disparaging estimate of it value. (As the same time, the
divorce reduces the "theoretical" to the state that accounts for the rather
contemptuous way in which men of action speak of "mere theory," and say
"it may be true in theory but is wholly impractical.") The illustrative material
is not intended to suggest that school instruction and discipline are main
factors in producing the split. On the contrary, their power to form attitudes
that maintain the bifurcation in being is derived from customs of action
and belief incorporated in primary institutions. The roots of the scholastic
practices in question are in the family, the church, politics and industry.
An attempt to prove this statement, rather than simply to present material
illustrating grounds for accepting it, would involve an extensive critique of

the institutions that have, upon the whole, formed the structural pattern of human relations through the ages. The traditional demand in family life for implicit obedience of the younger to their elders has undergone extensive weakening in the last half century. But it has existed far beyond the confines of the patriarchal family, and in as far as its weakening has not been intended by systematic strengthening of habitual attitudes of intelligent judgment, has doubtless contributed to the demoralization that leads superficial persons to clamor for return to old fashioned methods of discipline. In spite of the rise of Protestant sects, the influence of ecclesiastical institutions all through history has been to insist upon the necessity of unquestioning belief in creeds dogmatically laid down. Orthodox Christianity has enforced this demand by a claim to possession of the keys of the roads to eternal bliss and eternal suffering. The existing socio-moral environing is even now such, upon the whole, that extensive bodies of men and women act, as a matter of course without even thinking about it, upon the assumption that there in the most important affairs of life questioning, reflecting, intellectual activity, must cease at certain points, no matter how actively it may be carried on in matters that do not trench upon the reserved field. It is perhaps the most marked of the cases that justify the saying that chains which are completely habitual are so "natural" that they are not even felt.

The rise of democratic institutions in politics, and the corresponding decay of despotic government, has effected a certain widening of the area of intellectual activity in governmental affairs. Plato defined a slave as a person who carried out the orders of another person. The evident alternative is an active share in forming the orders, the ends and regulations to be executed. In idea, the freedom for which democracy stands is freedom of the mind, that is, of examination, criticism, involved in discussion, taking an active part in conference, communication, and decisions that determine general social policies and the ways and means of their execution. It cannot be denied that, in comparison with the regime of tyranny of the few and habitual passive subjection of the many, great advance has taken place. But when the scene is viewed absolutely or intrinsically, it cannot be said that beliefs and purposes whose formation in intellectual activity has effectively entered plays a very dominant role in shaping the relationships of human beings and the regulations to which conduct submits. In the first place, the amount of democracy now existing in the world, even of the mediocre type achieved in peoples having the greatest degree of self-government, is very limited, and recent events demonstrate how precarious is its existence anywhere as long as it [is not] everywhere a cherished practice. In the second place, the democratic ideal and practice have been for the most part confined to the sphere of government. This fact of itself is good evidence that the idea and working belief in it have not gone very far. For if the features and qualities of mutual consultation, free communication and respect for the experience of other persons is restricted to a special segment of life, it is impossible for it to have a deep hold. The peoples who have given totalitarianism free reign are the ones who have merely superimposed parliamentarian government with election of many officials upon feudal relations which continued to regulate the greater number of ordinary affairs and the substantial bulk of human relations. The rapid rise of fascism in Europe following a period in which its states had adopted forms of government nominally responsible to the people is enough to prove the superficiality of any movement when confined to a particular compartment of social life. It was not the inherent superiority of popular political institutions as a mode of government that occasioned a century of advance in that direction so widespread that it seemed to many to be inevitable and final. Its success and endurance in any country has been dependent upon habits of belief and action formed in non-political activities.

The fact that semi-autocratic methods have persisted in industry, and the fact that their maintenance there has reacted unfavorably upon political democracy, has received conspicuous attention. But emphasis has fallen exclusively upon the material aspects of the case. It has been contended, to be sure, that radical reconstruction of "material"—that is economic—conditions is, in the end, but the base for full development of the artistic and intellectual potentialities of human beings. But the material as means has been severed from the ideal as end. That is to say, there has not been anything approaching adequate recognition of the importance of the indispensable need for fostering the intellectual conditions of and factors in economic relationships.[1] In its bearing upon the present theme, the cultural conditions which produced separation of theoretical and practical qualities are both an original cause and a result of continuing the present state of political and economic activities.

As was intimated earlier, what has just been said is intended as illustration rather than as convincing proof of the proposition that socio-cultural conditions have been agencies generative of that separation of the reflective and the overtly active which has rendered the former comparatively impotent outside affairs designated material—as in technologies of material production as against creation of cultural technologies—and has rendered practical affairs relatively devoid, that is, of "ideal" and ideational qualities.

---

1. The reduction of the economic to the "material" is discussed in the next chapter. The matter is referred to here as part of the evidence that the intrinsic connection of "practical" activity with the reflective or intellectual qualities of action has had slight acknowledgment in the case of political parties, with the further consequence of serious retardation and distortion of the democratic idea.

So I return to the psychological aspect of the divorce of "lower" and "higher," or cortical, activities of the central nervous system. It is a familiar act that acquired activities are capable of becoming routine to the point of automatic execution; a fact which from the physiological side signifies that cerebral energies do not participate in determination of the act to be performed, the motor response being of the nature of a reflex arc. It is also a familiar fact that establishment of routine habits of this type is held by many to be positively desirable. The reason given for taking this position is that under such conditions the "higher centers" are released or freed so that they can be engaged in a higher type of action. A person, for example, may have established a habit of reading so complete in itself that he can read aloud with what seems to be understanding while his thoughts are wholly engaged with something quite remote from what he is reading. Since under existing conditions, especially in industry, a great deal of work is done which requires only the most perfunctory attention, this kind of "emancipation" comes to be regarded as the normal affair, without enquiring whether the conditions under which it is "natural" (customary) are themselves desirable.

What happens in such cases may be profitably contrasted with what occurs in cases of skills in matters into which variable elements enter. It is quite true that in all such cases there are sensory adjustments formed in the course of experience which are, up to a certain point, of the nature of the automatic cases. But there is also a decided difference. An etcher, engraver, acrobat, expert in billiards, tennis or golf, an author, scientific man in a laboratory, scholar in his library, would not get far without the immediate sensori-motor adjustments which carry out or execute the activities constituting the skills characteristic of the person well-trained in any given occupation. But when we compare these actions in their entirety with those of the persons tending machinery we find there is a property in the former which from the psychological point of view makes a world of difference. The difference is that each special motor response has to be adjusted not only to a prior sensory stimulus but also to the determination of the next sensory stimulus with a view to effecting a *continuous course* of action, leading to an *end-in-view*, carrying out a *purpose*, which controls each end-in-view or purpose constituent, sensory and motor, of the whole undertaking. In the case of the routine automatic act, the motor response also decides the next stimulus, since otherwise there would be no continuity of action and *a fortiori* no effective production of even the most material or physical result. But in the automatic act the continuity involved is of the nature of a chain in which each link is bound, in the literal sense of bound, to what precedes. The most direct sensori-motor adjustment of the expert in a game has to take account of some amount of variation in conditions.

The tennis player when executing the same kind of stroke (employing the same motor response) doesn't find his opponent always in the same place. He executes his stroke so as to catch his opponent off guard, in a position where it will be difficult for him to make an effective return stroke. A certain ultimate consequence as end-in-view, not a predetermined sheer mechanism, regulates the selection of each motor act no matter how mechanical the adjustment involved in its performance.

Now an end-in-view, a purpose, is present in experience in the form of an *idea* and the idea has to be maintained throughout the whole course. Here is the property that constitutes the great psychological (and moral or social) difference in question. An intention is something in process of accomplishing or achieving but neither as yet achieved nor yet having its accomplishment mechanically arranged for and guaranteed in advance. The idea in the case of tending or running a machine, executing a school task in what is called the most prompt and effective manner, etc., is formation of a habit which will of itself guarantee the production of a certain result. Uniformity of conditions, of stimuli and response, is the thing rated highest. The particular sensori-motor adjustments that are effected in the case of every form of skilled habit are, taken one by one, direct or immediate in the case of expert skills of the intelligently guided kind. But the particular adjustment employed at each step of the continuous interactivity is under the supervising control of the idea standing for the desired future consequence or issue. Expertness of execution is as much a desirable trait in the mathematician, artist or scholar among his books, as in a golf-player or plasterer. If [we] attend to the case of the former [we] obtain, however, a clearer idea of the subordination of the direct or mechanical adjustment to service in the moving development of a course of activity involving, at every step and stage of its growth, an end-in-view, or idea. The difference between the action of the spinal and basal ganglia and the cortical-cerebral marks a division of labor *within* an inclusive unified scheme of behavior; not a separation or divorce. At least that is the inevitable conclusion in case we rank intelligently formed and guided habits as more desirable, of greater value, than automatic routines. This conditioning factor is, of course, frankly of the nature of a value judgment. But so of course is the view that formation of automatic routines, with no connection of any sort with ideational (cerebral) qualities, is something to be cultivated in certain classes of actions performed by certain classes or strata in the community. In either case we come back to the question, previously discussed, of the socio-cultural conditions which are the underlying criteria in reference to which psychological attitudes, states, processes are formed. For no matter what importance is attached to original (native) impulses or "instincts, every *acquired* activity is formed under socio-cultural conditions which in turn are what they are because of the cultural habitudes of valuation incorporated in them, habitudes which both express and maintain the body of other customs constituting the social *ethos*."[2]

The position that it is normal, in the sense of the desirable and also of inherent physiological structures, that cerebral or ideational structures and processes take part of the order of all "practical" undertakings in which skill is involved, does not cover the entire question of the connection of the theoretical (the cerebral) and the practical—viz., that involving the motor activities through which interactivity is maintained and the environment qualified in behalf of the interests of human beings. The most important cerebral function has to do with *delayed* interactivity of some form of other. This function is engaged in the matter just discussed, namely the habits that constitute every kind of intelligently directed skill. For they can be brought into existence only when immediate overt action is inhibited, that is, postponed, long enough to permit linking up a number of diverse sensory stimuli so that there is constructed a unified, outgoing impetus to a new mode of action. The unnecessary and awkward bodily movements of a child learning to write form the material for a stock illustration in psychological texts when the subject of formation of habits is under consideration. It is not always noted that since they do not exist either before or after the formation of the new habitude, they indicate that a re-adjustment of customary sensory stimuli is in process. The twistings of the body do not occur previously because each sensory stimulus has its appropriate motor channel already laid out, so to speak. It does not occur afterwards because through the intervention of cerebral action various diverse sensory stimuli have been so coordinated as to determine a single but more complex or "synthesized" form of behavior than previously existed. The difficulty practically everyone experiences in undoing previously established habits of eye and hand, or, speaking in more fundamental terms, of observation of surrounding conditions and practical response to them in learning to draw illustrates the same point. The *undoing* in question means a breaking down of customary sensori-motor adjustments. During this disintegrative process and because of it, a variety of sensory stimuli are released which conflict with one another and create, except in persons whose habitual attitudes are already formed in an esthetic direction, a state of confusion, of mild daze and uncertainty as to what to do. Were this the place to follow up the topic by way of large-scale social illustrations, the widespread intellectual blur, hesitation and fog that attends periods, like the present, when reconstruction of institutions is taking place, might be pointed out. The benefit of whatever order inhered

---

2. See *ante*, p. ___.

in old customs is gone and that proper to newly forming cultural attitudes and standards has not arrived. In such periods, dogmatism and fanaticism are more rife than in the earlier period when institutions now under attack prevailed. For as long as a set of beliefs is so habitual as to be a matter of course, the beliefs are too "natural" to be experienced as dogmas. They are rather doctrines, accepted teachings. Nor under such circumstances do they seem to be imposed by any external authority. The personal habits of the members of a community are so permeated with the spirit of community customs the beliefs seems to be what their own minds and hearts would spontaneously choose. Such periods are the ages of faith—that is of unquestioning loyalties.

The ordinary and correct name for the delayed activities made possible by the participation of cerebral energies is deliberation, foresight and planning. What happens is not (as has already been shown) a cessation of activity but a direction of it into *intra*-organic channels. Various sensori-motor adjustments, along with the functions of respiration, circulation, glandular and autonomic action with which they are allied, have to rearranged, so as to be brought into new connections with one another prior to finding a new systematic coordinated motor expression. It is a great mistake to suppose that deliberation is, on the bodily side, an exclusively cerebral process. There are a multitude of partial, inchoate motor discharges going on, and there is some sort of sensory return wave from each one of them, and, on the basis of the affective or emotional tone accompanying them, rejections and selections occur until the tensions produced are so unified that they provide the energy that is required for a complete interactivity with environing conditions. The view that what goes on during deliberation and planning involves participation of practically all organic functions, instead of the brain alone, is proved as a matter of general physiological teaching by the impossibility of completely closing off cerebral activity but shutting down all the channels by which energies are transmitted to and from cerebral action. There is simply bound to be an inflow and an overflow. On the more definitely psychological side, the same conclusion is established by the fact that without sensori-motor participations (sustained in turn by vital organic functions) we should not be aware what we are thinking and planning. What we are aware of is always in terms of qualities that involve activity on the sensory side of organic activity. The extero-ceptor apparatus is, indeed, reduced to a state of minimal activity, no more occurring at the very periphery than will prevent that kind of absent-mindedness which made lode[3] his life. But the qualities mediated by the proprio-ceptor system

---

3. [This is as it appears in the original.]

persist; indeed, in all probability they are correspondingly intensified. In persons who are habitually of a deliberative turn, the proprio-ceptor action is confined almost exclusively to the nerve structures of the vocal apparatus. In other words, such persons think in and with words; it is evident that thinking in words involves innervation of sensori-motor tracts. Other persons, including "intellectuals," employ more imagery in their reflective operations. Some persons who deny the existence of psychical stuff have found it necessary to deny the existence of visual and auditory imagery, while mentalists have pointed triumphantly to their existence as final proof of purely psychical existence. The existence of imagery as an element in reflection is properly interpreted as a case of the existence of behavior in an inchoate partial state because still occurring intra-organically instead of overtly. The existence of imagery is, in fact, proof that deliberation is an intra-organic rehearsal of potential modes of interactivity, the "internal" (or spatial in a literal sense) rehearsal being in effect a trying-out of various lines of interactivity until that one is formed which best satisfies organic conditions as they stand at the time. Finally, in this connection it is to be noted that the motor aspect of intra-organic activity is not so completely inhibited that shrewd observation cannot gain an inkling of what is going on inside by means of postural changes and facial expressions. The pains sometimes taken to keep deadpan or immobile features is evidence that some outward motor change naturally occurs.

Deliberation as delayed interactivity, involving pondering, planning, comparing, recalling past experiences and their outcomes, is not put forward as exhausting the full scope of cerebral activity. If it were so offered, it might call out the objection that it involves a definite subordination of the theoretical (in the sense of *ideational*) to the practical, since deliberation concerns things to be done, courses of action to be adopted and pursued. The further function of cerebral activity will be considered later, but meanwhile I wish to say something by way of protest against an undue narrowing and hardening of the range and depth of the "practical" with respect to what is encompassed in deliberation. It is common to find that intellectuals, who are practically so protected as to feel aloof from practical concerns, reduce deliberation to *calculation*, the latter process being identified with search for means which will reach most economically and effectively some pre-formed end; the latter, moreover, being thought of (usually) as of a selfish and therefore restricted nature. Both of these traits are gratuitously introduced. There is nothing in the nature of deliberation to limit it to consideration of means to be chosen for an end already settled upon nor yet to ends that are unliberal. The contrary is the case. The primary business of deliberation is formation of new ends-in-view, reconstruction of purposes and plans which have previously directed behavior. And the fact that environing conditions, with which the course of action decided upon is to interact, are *social* is proof that every restriction of deliberation to ends that are predominantly egoistic represents a distortion or even violation of the conditions that are intrinsically involved in what is to be done. The fact that limitation of deliberation to calculation of means apart from consideration and reconsideration of ends tends in the direction of those routine forms of action in which participation of cerebral or confined reflective factors indicates that such limitation is set up in behalf of some special interest, instead of being inherent. It cannot be denied that existing social conditions, especially upon the side of economic activities affected by pecuniary factors, is such as to limit reflective deliberation as to what is to be done in industry and trade to calculation of means, "success" in business being the fixed end in view. Nor can it be denied that the habits formed incidental to pursuit and attainment of this end are such as to put a premium upon a narrow interpretation of success and "getting on" generally, or in every line of "practical" activity. But only upon the ground that the particular kind of economic and financial conditions that generally prevail at present at pre-ordained and virtually everlasting can these admitted facts be employed as criteria by which to determine the intrinsic nature of deliberation. As repeatedly happens in formulation of the psychological side of social doctrines and systems of belief, the cart is put before the horse. Attitudes and habits (so-called "faculties") which are products of current social conditions are taken to be original and native "psychological" constituents and are then employed to account for and justify the very conditions of the social environment that have created them. Such is the cultural origin and history of the doctrine that the sole "motive" of human activity is egoistic, and also of the somewhat weakened form of the same dictum according to which all deliberation is calculation about the best ways in which to effect merely personal ends. But with respect to the latter position, all but extremists of the school that has attempted to account for social phenomena by alleged original psychological factors (instead of recognizing that all psychological traits are in fact socio-cultural) have held that generous, outgoing, sympathetic or "altruistic" impulses are part of the original endowment. Or, putting the point in the context where it belongs, it is implicitly recognized that some social institutions already existing definitely promote, within certain limits, courses of activity and ends-in-view that have to do with a form of welfare in which a number participate. Instances of this kind are provided, for example, by family life and also by tribal and national life as far as what is called public spirit extends. Absence of both egoistic and altruistic motives are characteristic of the pursuit of science and art.

The fact that to *some* extent formation of new ends is involved in the very process of deliberation was brought out in the earlier discussion. All intelligent calculation within even the accepted system of economic relationships is undertaken in order to effect some change in existing concrete ends-in-view, the limitation already referred to consisting in the fact that these changes in concrete aims fall within outside bounds set by existing socio-economic conditions. It suffices as evidence to point to the fact that nowhere in materials and processes is invention of the new more consistently prized and practiced than in industry. Indeed, it is so highly esteemed that the existing economic regime is defended on the ground of the stimulus it gives to initiative, invention and enterprise. And any unprejudiced observer must admit that habits and institutions that are denominated "moral" are much more resistant to change than are activities within the range currently designated economic. The conclusion for the sake of which these considerations are adduced is, however, not the justification of the existing system but the proof they afford that all deliberation (even that occurring with reference to social conditions in which the *general* character of the end to be reached is socially relatively fixed) involves qualities of ingenuity, initiation, inventiveness of novel traits of ends-in-view. The actual problem here is, accordingly, a social one. What kind of environing conditions will most effectively stimulate and on the widest scale release these traits for full effective operation? In the degree in which nothing new is perceived and taken into account, planning is a superfluity. In the degree in which novel and unexpected factors occur and force themselves upon attentive behavior, courses of activity adapted to cope with them must be first pre-figured in intra-organic activities of reflection if future success is to be anything other than an affair at the mercy of luck and chance. In spite of the vogue of the doctrine in some circles at present, it is not possible to imagine anything more stupid than the notion that the influx of new factors that have produced present confusions and conflicts is to be dealt with by return to ancient doctrines, institutions and precedents: a consideration directly relevant to our contention that the basic trouble with "modern" philosophy is that so much of ancient origin and prescription is still mixed up with that which is genuinely new. The conservatism historically inhering in religious beliefs, reinforced by the alliances that have come into existence between the *institutions* that represent and protect religious beliefs and "secular" institutions having practical power, has seeped from traditional cultural conditions into the systematic theories which, under the name of philosophy, have attempted to interpret the new, and account in considerable measure for reduction of that acknowledged as "practical" to the level of the narrowly utilitarian. And one result is that the aspects and constituents of practice that are distinctively *moral* in quality are not seen to be those most in need of the kind of reflective action which occupies itself on the wide scale with formation of new values, purposes and plans on the base of thorough and systematic observation of existing conditions.

It does not follow, however, that reflective activity is confined to operations of the deliberative type, even when the wide scope and significant depth of the concerns that properly fall within the jurisdiction of deliberation is taken into account. Nor is the ground proper to deliberative activity fully covered when the temporal external of the delayed overt action involved is given due weight. For the extension of foresight, observation of present conditions has to be conducted with a view to determining consequences that are remote in time, so remote that they may not even come into existence during the lifetime of the one who forms plans of action concerned with them. Regard for the welfare of future generations is not a very high factor in determining the kind of deliberation which takes place. But it exists and by force of circumstances becomes of increased importance. However even when this factor is given proper consideration, the position here taken does not entail the conclusion that all reflective activity is deliberativeness even in the sense in which deliberation is concerned with most enduring and important interactivities to be carried out. It is not held that *intellectual* activity, that knowing, is not carried on for its own sake, though it is denied that the motive which animates those persons whose primary occupation is knowing can be egotistically converted into a doctrine concerning the particular pattern of behavior represented in knowing. It is contrary to fact to hold that interest in knowing apart from consideration of possible practical application has not played an important role in the development of the sciences. In fact, what is called "disinterested curiosity" has played an important part in development of even the useful arts. What has been applies first to the *conditions* under which intellectual and cognitive behavior develops, and then to the enduring *pattern* which is generated under these practical conditions. There certainly is nothing peculiar in the fact that an activity which comes into existence under certain conditions to satisfy a need due to those conditions is capable of being so enjoyed that it is kept up and developed for its own sake. The further problem now awaiting us is the question of *how* intellectual activity in the sense of "theoretical" develops out of the conditions in which deliberative behavior having practical reference originates.[4]

Greek philosophers said that science (which then included philosophy as its highest form) was a product of leisure. They omitted to note that with an indefinitely large majority of human beings leisure generates reverie and fantasy building. Men are sufficiently lazy "by nature" to enjoy idleness.

---

4. The thesis that the *pattern* characteristic of deliberation is maintained in scientific knowing is a topic of later discussion. See Ch. ____.

Idleness or leisure is a condition which arises when we are not under pressure from environing conditions to engage in doing something overtly. There are many theories to account for dreaming proper; that is the kind of cerebral activity which goes on during sleep. There is one constant factor in these diverse theories. During sleep sensory stimulation does not cease reaching the brain but it is no longer subject to control by the demands of any motor action which is adjusted to environmental requirements. The mechanism of adaptive behavior idles like that of a motor car with power still on but not used in effecting locomotion. The name "day-dreaming" thus represents sound popular insight. The energies and processes of the nervous system, brain included, are not annihilated in sleeping, and certain it is that during our waking hours its operations do not cease when we are not engaged in doing something in connection with surrounding conditions. Even when one is engaged in routine activities of the automatic kind demanding a minimum of cerebral guidance, the brain continues in operation and the result is day-dreaming. The case of a factory girl engaged in mechanical tending of a machine is fairly typical. Asked what *she*, as distinct from her hands, did all day, she replied that as soon as she had started a machine she married a millionaire and their adventures took her through the otherwise monotonous day. When a teacher in traditional school complains that the pupils do not "pay attention" she means that their attention is engaged with the more interesting train of images and ideas (if they may be called by that name) going on inside their heads. It is impossible to calculate the amount of floating reverie that occurs at any given time in the world. It can be truly affirmed that only those persons engaged in activities of a directive or genuinely productive type and whose mental operations are disciplined by the habits formed in such conduct do not spend more of their time in fantasy-building than in any other kind of ideational action. The facts involved are habitually ignored by all save psychiatrists and perhaps priests who have to listen to confessions of indulgence of libidinous imagery. The irksomeness of routine occupations stands in direct ratio to the amount of irresponsible idly-floating imagery engaged in.

Santayana is probably the only philosopher who has given much attention to the extent and intensity of experiences of this general sort.[5]

> It will be observed, however, that what is credibly asserted about the past is not a report which the past was itself able to make when it existed nor one it is now able, in some oracular fashion, to formulate and to impose upon us. The report is a rational construction based and seated in present

5. [A page of the manuscript is missing at this point. However, on the basis of the internal clues, we may infer and insert the missing quote. George Santayana, *The Life of Reason: Introduction and Reason in Common Sense* (Scribner's Sons) 1906, p. 39.]

experience; it has no cogency for the inattentive and no existence for the ignorant. Although the universe, then, may not have come from chaos, human experience certainly has begun in a private and dreamful chaos of its own, out of which it still only partially and momentarily emerges. The history of this awakening is of course not the same as that of the environing world ultimately discovered; it is the history, however, of that discovery itself, of the knowledge through which alone the world can be revealed. We may accordingly dispense ourselves from preliminary courtesies to the real universal order, nature, the absolute, and the gods. We shall make their acquaintance in due season and better appreciate their moral status, if we strive merely to recall our own experience, and to retrace the visions and reflections out of which those apparitions have grown.

When one notes the widespread neglect of this aspect of experience in philosophy as a whole one must acknowledge with respect the candor and acumen expressed in this view. But one will also remember that when a neglected fact is first clearly seen, it frequently looms so large as to shut everything else out of the picture. Upon physiological grounds it is quite impossible that the exclusive original office of cerebral processes and of "ideas," should have nothing to do with the environing and "objective" conditions of maintenance of life. Upon psychological grounds, it is impossible that "consciousness" if it were exclusively and completely of the dreamlike, irresponsible character described by Santayana should ever become "symbolic," representative of objects. Santayana himself writes (on the very page before the page from which the first quotation is taken), "Man's consciousness is evidently practical; it clings to his fate, registers, so to speak, the higher and lower temperature of his fortunes, and, so far as it can, represents the agencies on which those fortunes depend."[6] In passages like this he may be supposed to be talking about its later career; about consciousness as far as the factors forming the life of reason have intervened in order that anything approaching rationality may come to birth he is obliged to write: "The most irresponsible vision has certain principles of order and valuation by which it estimates itself; and in these principles the Life of Reason is already broached, however halting may be its development."[7]

---

6. [Ibid, p. 38.]

7. [Ibid., p. 54.] It is important to note that even as far as Santayana does assign to "consciousness" any representative function he uncritically follows the psychological Lockean tradition according to which that function is wholly one of registration. The preparatory, anticipatory aspect inherent in cerebral action is completely ignored. This neglect, systematized by Locke, is the source of the view that connects sensory qualities with representation of "external" things, instead of with appetite and impulse—the latter obviously having prospective reference. Greek psychological [theory] with its biotic motivation was wiser.

The object of these latter quotations is not the trivial one of convicting a philosopher of inconsistency. They are meant to indicate how it is possible to admit all that Santayana says or anyone else can say about the daydreaming properties of conscious experience and yet place them in their proper context. Cerebral activity has its primary and prime function as a set of intermediate processes in which new arrangements or adjustments are formed between a variety of disparate sensory stimuli and a unified mode of interactivity with environing conditions. But since not even the busiest is unremittingly engaged in overt doing and making and, since central nervous processes still persist during periods of idleness, there is a large field in which there occur a vegetative efflorescence pointed out by Santayana. Because of necessary conditions of the maintenance of life and because of the function of the nervous system and this maintenance, this phase of experience is secondary.

Hence it is not surprising that the most extravagant daydreams, the wildest fantasies, have a strange way of representing some aspect of the pattern of vital behavior. The deviations and distortions of reveries are pretty uniformly in the direction of construction of a more enjoyable or a more glorious career in the actual world and among actual human beings than hard cold facts have permitted to come into existence. The phenomena characteristic of even the insane manifest variations of what normally occurs in operations of organic-environmental adaptations and re-adaptations. When actual effort is brought to a standstill by obstacles, reverie rather than faith removes mountains; the cowardly are more courageous than heroes in dreams; the downtrodden attain positions of eminence; the neglected become conspicuously noted. Comparatively rare moments of enjoyment are repeated in imagination and anticipated with intense reinforcement. The material for fantasy building is derived from the things of daily "practical" experience, especially those of marked emotive quality. And the rearrangements of these materials effected in reverie are always in one direction. They redress failure and frustration; they embellish what is harsh; they magnify what is agreeable.

Even so, what has been said applies to the day dreaming which is an accompaniment of routine automatic behavior rather than to the reveries characteristic of the leisure whose normal action is of a productive character. Reverie has an important positive function to perform. It is an important agency in breaking through the inertia of habit; it serves to open new paths some of which may later be taken in action. I doubt whether any important invention involving great novelty has ever been made save after and because of intervention of reverie. The same thing may be said of the emergence of new hypotheses in science. Certain ways of "seeing visions" have always been recognized as conditions of significant advance. However, its normal, in the sense of regular, function is exhibited in the fine arts, when reverie bears the more honorific title of imagination. Any experience savored and enjoyed for itself is esthetic. Such experiences do not, however, of themselves constitute art. The esthetic becomes artistic only when its materials are re-ordered by doing something with actual materials, colors, sounds, words, wood and stone. Idealization that is a product of reverie is involved; it shows itself in the distortions of the material of ordinarily experienced objects which emphasize rhythm and symmetry. In them we speak of the normal in the sense of the desirable aspects of actual experience we may say that the normal lot or outcome of reverie is to be formalized, and that the formalization occurs only through acts that modify or re-arrange environmental conditions, acts that respectively constitute dance, song, painting, sculpture, architecture, etc. The environment is not modified in the same way nor for the same purpose as that which occurs in so-called useful or technological arts. But they have a use and value which indicates the lack, the defect, in the arts called useful as the latter exist and operate, upon the whole, in the existing stage of culture. For the use or service of the latter is more or less ulterior and deferred; the use of the fine arts in experience is direct and present. It is an intensification, here and now, of the qualities that cause the material of any experience to be preferred.

In short, we come again upon the determining influence of cultural conditions. Actual facts prove that it is possible for the implements or processes of arts that render direct service of a definitely material kind to have esthetic value, so that a useful art is at the same time fine. This fact calls attention to a social question. How far do existing conditions of production, distribution and consumption of goods account for the marked separation that now exists between fine and useful arts; or, more generally, for the existence of so many experiential constituents that are *merely* instrumental and not at the same time consummatory? That production exists for the sake of consumption seems to be a proposition worthy of acceptance. Why and how, then, does it happen that so much of productive activity is *labor* toil, so that economists have gone so far as to assert that no one would engage in productive work were it not for hope of some ulterior reward? And how does it happen that so much of consumption is gross, animal-like, meretricious, instead of being natural consummation of a continuing process?

The widespread existence of rites, ceremonies, overt activities of cults that follow upon the intervention of cerebral process having no direct practical connection is familiar fact. It affords indirect proof of the persistence of the sense of the original "practical" office and pattern of cerebral action that among primitive peoples (and today as well in respect to important issues not yet brought under human control) potency is ascribed to the performance of these formalized acts. We call this ascription *magic* when expressed in acts that no longer appeal to us today. It may be the expression of a devotion without which a successful issue is impossible when occurring in some great emergency today. The part played by immediate esthetic enjoyment in keeping up maintenance of stated ceremonies, with escape from the routines of ordinary life, cannot be ignored. But it is easy, on the other hand, to overlook the strong tendency in human nature to attribute to formalized activities the power to influence the course of events.

The net result of this particular portion of the discussion of the practical and intellectual is that in the full scope of the "practical" everything artistic must be included within it, just as the earlier discussion showed that all moral issues come within the scope of deliberation about choice of courses of action, whether on a broad civic scale or a narrower personal one. But what has just been said also forms the proper introduction to the interpretation of "knowing for the sake of knowing," or intellectual activity carried on for its own sake. For inquiry, reflective activity in general, is for a certain somewhat limited group of persons a kind of activity yielding immediate or esthetic satisfaction. Prejudices due to traditions which have divided experience into separate non-communicating, or water-tight, compartments alone stands in the way of recognition that for some human beings persistent reflective investigation is an occupation of the same order as the arts designated fine. While the number of persons who, from the standpoint of society, are called upon the make this particular art their professional concern is limited, it is highly desirable that all human beings be educated so that they are capable of finding immediate enjoyment in the ordered pursuit of ideas, entirely apart from any question of the use to which they may be put in behavior involving the environment. It is highly desirable that social conditions be such as not only to enable persons to enjoy this particular art, as well as those of fiction, drama, music, painting and architecture, but that they be such also as to afford everyone opportunity to enjoy the use of this art. For while experience shows that it is possible for specialized scientific investigations to occur in ways which are so completely out of gear with social needs and possibilities as to be civically and morally injurious, it also shows that the "theoretical" subject matter which has resulted has been the chief force in emancipation of men from customs and traditions holding them, otherwise, in unbroken chains. It is in this sense that theory is the most practical of all modes of human activity. But this result is a development without breach of continuity, out of the original more directly practical function of reflective action which finds its manifestation in deliberation and planning. Its occurrence and the high value attached to it is no more reason for setting the theoretical in opposition to the practical than the fact that an idle motor may race is a reason for holding that racing the motor is of a higher order than is using the engine to run an automobile.

II

Unprejudiced examination of historical conditions points directly to the conclusion that the notions of theory and practice which had the greatest vogue are reflections of social conditions affecting prestige and status. In Greek times, the idea of "practical" mirrored the low and unfree status of those who performed the necessary and useful work upon which rested the life of free citizens. Productive activity was in the hands of domestic slaves and of artisans who were not citizens of the community even if they were not domestic chattel. Under these circumstances, it was a "natural" conclusion that, on the one hand, *practical* activity was the kind of things which was so forced upon certain men by external necessities that it was inherently opposed to activity which was freely engaged in; and that, on the other hand, it had to do with and its end was fixed by things which were merely material, concerned with satisfaction of bodily needs. The activity of free citizens was on the other hand "liberal" because their material and bodily needs were met and satisfied by the activities of the lower class without their having to do manual and productive work. Relatively, at least, the activity of free citizens was concerned with ends that were "ideal" not material, while those of the class who were concerned primarily with *knowing* were completely ideal and free and liberal.

In short, the meaning of practical and theoretical was fixed by the sort of life that was open to and carried on by two different classes. "Practical" or productive signified the kind of activity appropriate to men who, being relatively relieved from these pursuits, were free to devote themselves to what was inherently worthwhile.

One of the most interesting chapters in the story of human culture will, when it is written, be about the positions and functions assigned respectively to the hand and the vocal organs. The hand is erected into a symbol of that which is "material" and relatively unfree. Think of the hand in social terms and you think of "hands" who work for others even though they are not slaves; you think of manual labor or the running of machines; only rarely does one think of the hand in terms of what is done by a painter or sculptor, by an artist occupied with creation of products that carry an intrinsic meaning and value with their own presence.[8] Speech, on the other hand, has been taken to proceed from "within" rather than be enforced, like manual

---

8. In Greek, even Athenian, civilization, all artists were relegated to the lower mechanical class. To play a musical instrument was the business of hired persons; free citizens listened and enjoyed the product of the work of others.

labor, from without. Free communication is the intercourse of free men in their leisure time.

. . .

[The Greek] identification of rationality with linguistic forms, together with the highly disparaging view of the kind of knowledge obtained in the industrial arts, gave the conclusions reached a specious finality. As Greek culture in its original and vital form was submerged and overwhelmed in that of the Alexandrian and Roman eras, the fixed linguistic forms took precedence over any vital subject matter that had been contributed by Greek acuteness and restless curiosity of observation. When the semi-barbarous peoples of the Middle Ages reached the point in which independent intellectual interest revived, ancient literatures (including of course the authority of the scripture and records of church councils) contained so much that was far in advance of anything in contemporary culture that language took on a new and, in effect, sacred and unquestionable prestige. The three linguistic arts grammar, rhetoric, *and* logic (definitely conceived and treated as a linguistic art) were viewed as the only organs through which the four subject-matter arts, mathematics, could properly be approached.[9]

In a social setting much less liberal than that of Athens, language, especially the written languages by which the records and wisdom of past ages were transmitted, was given a position in such supremacy that one of the chief marks of the awakening modern spirit was the assault directed against words. There is hardly a writer of the centuries from the fifteenth to the seventeenth who does not condemn traditional learning and the methods inspiring it on the ground that it substituted words for things, the substitution moreover being of a kind that conferred upon ancient writings the authority which properly belongs to observation and firsthand experience. They felt the evil to be so great that they reacted to the opposite extreme, overlooking the unique service which language performs. As so often happens, the reaction perpetuated, in a reversed form, the very evil against which it protested. For it became a commonplace, present in texts that are current today, that "language is an expression of thought"; of thought, that is, which exists readymade as a mental "inner" something independently of language and communication.

---

9. At the present time, a group of the theologically minded educators, with their pattern of thought set by medieval philosophy are urging almost that all the ills of present education are due to abandonment of the trivia by our educational institutions. It is not surprising that they also repeat the sayings of Aristotle about the illiberal and merely technical character of "practical" arts, with inclusion of natural science since it now employs the agencies and instruments of those arts. It is worth recalling in this context the following passage of an English scholar, who certainly was not moved by educational prejudice in favor of practical arts. Canon Hatch wrote: [Quote missing.]

In fact, ordered discourse does more than preserve and transmit the funded wisdom (and foolishness) of the past. It is the only agency by which reflection, inquiry, is liberated. Were it not for the invention and use of symbols, we should be tied down to conditions immediately present; there would be no escape from the pressure exerted in direct interactions with things of the immediate local environment. It is through the agency of words that the present is brought into fruitful intercourse with the past and the future; that imaginative experimentation is rendered possible. Apart from words, past experiences are available only as they have entered into habits that are settled, fixed; by means of words, combinations are induced in which what has happened takes on a new and freer significance. Invention, projection of the new and different, depends upon ability to observe and take account of what is not locally and instantly present, and language is the sole author and administrator of this ability.

In other words, the attack that was made upon words was directed, if the actual facts had only been perceived, upon a state of culture that was enslaved, as far as its basic beliefs were concerned, to external authority. Instead of being a summons to put "things" in the position that had been usurped by words, it was in reality a challenge to independent active use of all available resources to foster discovery, exploration, invention, and construction; all of which were undertakings that involved a break with the habits of belief and language that had dominated Europe for centuries. It is not without significance that "experience" underwent a reversal of signification at this time, its classic use (retained even by Hobbes) was to designate the products of custom; namely, the kinds of knowledge that resulted from repetition of useful acts, and the sanction of "practical" in opposition to knowledge arising from insight into causes. In the sixteenth century it began to be used as a name for knowledge due to vital personal initiative and participation, in opposition to beliefs that were secondhand because resting upon the authority of tradition. Even the Lockean identification of experience with material "mind" receives from "without" has a certain positive significance if it is interpreted in cultural terms—That is, if taken to represent the inrush of new social movements that were outside the traditions that formed the understanding or "mind" of Institutional Europe.

The mistake of Greek philosophers was in later periods a powerful factor in keeping knowledge and the operations by which knowledge is attained subservient to external influences proceeding from Church and the feudal order of society. But the mistake did not reside in the doctrine that there is an inherent connection between language as reasonably ordered discourse and knowledge. It lay, rather, in the fact that discourse-knowledge, if that word may be used, was set off as theoretical knowledge and the latter was completely isolated from "practical" knowledge which was nonetheless the only strictly *factual* knowledge that existed. For the industrial arts, in order to achieve success in satisfaction of human needs, had to develop and adopt methods which correspond to the operations of nature. Men who worked in wood, stone, leather, iron, bronze and gold, who sowed and tilled the land; who navigated the sea; who tended the body and healed disease, had to adapt their courses of action to conditions set by nature, instead of by grammatical syntax. Of necessity they discovered a multitude of facts about natural materials and natural processes. And if the analyses which were made of *Logos* had been used to arrange and order the rich factual material provided by the practical arts, the scientific movement initiated in the fifteenth and sixteenth centuries might have got underway twenty centuries earlier.

For, by itself or in isolation from principles of order and system capable of being supplied by study of discourse, the factual knowledge built up in the course of pursuit of the arts did not constitute *science*. For particular facts by themselves do not constitute a science, even if the facts are indefinitely numerous. A science is an affair of *form* as well as of material; of generalizations as well as particulars; of systematization that promotes inquiry carried on for the sake of inquiry and not for the sake of attaining an end or result outside the scope of free inquiry. The limitation—from the standpoint of *science*—of the technological arts of the Greeks did not proceed from "practical" factors [but] entered in an influential way into the methods by which natural facts were discovered. For after all, taken innocently or neutrally, without prejudice, "practical" signifies simply operations of making and doing, and apart from social conditions that affect injuriously the kind of making and doing carried on at a given time and place, there is nothing about them to suggest a cause for disparagement and contempt. The limitation proceeded from the kind of use to which the results of the practical arts were put. They were confined to uses which, relatively speaking, were technical and illiberal, being thus confined not because of anything in their own nature but because of social-cultural conditions.

For as far as a given social regime is so constituted that the products of industrial arts fail to be systematically employed in service of human life continually growing in fullness of meaning they are used for ends that fall short of being truly humane and liberal. They were used for such ends in the slave economy of Athens; they are used for similar ends in our non-slave economy as far as special and pecuniary ends or ends set by a limited privileged class control the uses served by the products of the "practical" arts.

At the present time, the representatives of the counterpart of what was "theory" in Greek philosophy are far from having it all their own way. On the contrary, men who pride themselves on being "practical" are vocal in condemnation of theorists, in spite of the fact that if they are engaged in any distinctively "modern" type of economic production and distribution, the very processes by which they succeed have issued from researches carried on investigators who work with the aid of theory, they speak scornfully of the latter as something idle and academic. But in philosophy it still seems obligatory to maintain a separation between theory and practice; the words by which the separation is set forth being "pure" and "applied" with higher rank assigned the former.

It is instructive to compare the meaning "pure" has when it is put, as it usually is, in flat opposition to application, or use, and the meaning it has (or would have) if it were defined on the ground of effective and humanly fruitful scientific procedure. Most of the industrial Athenian arts had a short range; it was concerned with a special nearby result. The technological arts of the present day are extended in space and time; they involve many sub-arts whose special products have to be coordinated. But the end-in-view in operations that themselves require a long time to reach completion may be specific and limited. Most technological occupations today are sufficiently complex so that it is found worthwhile to subsidize new investigations in the interest of efficiency. So far as the intent and the result of these inquiries falls wholly within the scope of a particular occupation, the inquiries involved may be called impure. But "impure" in this usage has no connection with use or application. It signifies that inquiry is carried on for the sake of a result which is not determined by inquiry itself; that, in so far, inquiry is predetermined by an end which is external and alien. In contrast, knowledge or science is "pure" when it is the outcome of knowing, of inquiry, conducted with an eye single to conditions which are set by the very process of inquiry. No one would deny that knowing is "impure" when the one engaged in knowing allows his investigation to be deflected by the fact that one conclusion will bring him more money or more fame than another by the fact that it will support some doctrine to which he was committed in. But just as *impure* has in such cases a moral meaning, so with the proper signification of *pure*. In its moral sense, it is an admonition not to allow the inquiry which is undertaken to be influenced by any alien considerations whatever. It has nothing whatever to do with whether or not practical factors (doing and making) enter into the conduct of the inquiry. It has nothing to do with the usefulness or applicability of the conclusion arrived at, save that, in any case, the width and depth of its applicability in human affairs is a measure of the rank and standing of the problem that evoked the inquiry.

These considerations bear out the proposition that "theory" and "practice" in their current use do not have meanings that are based on anything more reputable than prejudice and the preferences of a social class. They suggest the importance of getting discussion upon a plane as free as is humanly possible from the influences which have declined, upon the whole, traditional usages. It will do no harm, it will probably be useful, if, pending conclusions reached on the ground of an examination of tested subject matter in respect to methods and conclusions of knowledge, we manage to get along without using either word.

If we take a long view of the temporal progress of any art and science, we find that, in its early phase, its subject matter had spread in space and time. Even when the subject matter consisted of verified facts and not of fancies and guesses, the facts involved were spotty. They covered a rather narrow locality and a slight portion of time. Their spotty quality was the necessary result of the isolation, the lack of interconnection, inherent in any such situation. What was known about iron, say, might be well established as far as it went. But it did not go far. A few properties were made evident in smelting of ore, in blacksmithing; in short, in cruder processes of handling and working. But compared with present systematic chemical science in which knowledge of iron is based upon and contributes to knowledge of the whole class of substances called metals and this knowledge in turn is connected with knowledge of some ninety elements in a way that enriches both what is learned about iron and about air and water and oxygen and hydrogen, etc., etc., and what is meant by the spotty, the provincial and short-span quality of the facts known in the early stage of the subject is, I think, sufficiently obvious.

In short, interconnectedness is an indispensable trait of scientific knowledge and of technological art, as appears most clearly when their mature stage is compared with their early stage. Indeed, this trait is so familiarly known that to mention it is but to cite the commonplace that every science and every highly developed technology is a systematic network of connected facts and operations. Viewed in this setting, the change that has taken place in our own generation regarding the nature of space and time is but the culmination of the movement that has been going on steadily since the seventeenth century. Newton's *Principia* disclosed the connectedness of a number of generalizations that were previously independent of one another. The solar system became a system in the scientific sense of that word. But this achievement in astronomy, great as it was, was of highest importance in providing a model for all science in its demonstration of the interconnectedness of all phenomena. It is the more significant accordingly that in the Newtonian scheme time and space were regarded as "absolute"—absolved from any relatedness. They were empty containers: Space, of ultimate indivisible or individual substances, the atoms; Time, of the motions producing changes or events. Today space and time are in effect names for the indefinitely extensive web of interconnectedness that all events sustain to one another, an interconnectedness so complete that science is obliged to speak of space-time instead of space *and* time.

An intimate relation exists between the fact of interconnection and the function performed in natural science by what scientists themselves call *theory*. For if one examines what such terms as the theory of gravitation, of the electro-magnetic nature of light, of evolution (whether the Darwinian theory or the theory of mutations), one finds the term "theory" employed to stand for some mode of connection which certain phenomena are taken to sustain to one another. In this usage, theory stands for something taken to be factual; it stands for something whose right to the title "scientific" is to be tested by *observation* exactly as much as is the case with the claim of any particular phenomenon to be regarded as scientific fact.

In short, if philosophy frames its idea or definition of theory on the ground of what the word stands for in actual scientific practice, one finds one's self in an intellectual climate that has nothing in common with the philosophic tradition initiated by Aristotle and perpetuated in the antithesis of theory and practice.

If we take our cue as to the meaning of theory from the subject-matter to which the word is applied in the conduct of scientific inquiry, we find that it stands legitimately in contrast with something else, but that something else is not "practice" or the "practical." The distinction, the contrast, involved is one that obtains among facts; it is the distinction of fact as *general* and as *particular*. If one consults an almanac one finds certain predictions regarding eclipses of sun and moon. The events in question are dated; the almanac is for a certain year, and the events foretold are to occur at a specific minute of a stated hour and month. And the sun mentioned is not any one nor every one of the millions of suns that exist; it is a single specific sun—and of course the same holds regarding the moon and its eclipses. It is comparatively easy to get into confusion and controversy if one attempts to define *particulars* at large or dialectically. If we determine the meaning of the word by reference to cases like those just mentioned we shall escape the trouble we get into when we try to define "particular" on the basis of alleged psychological events called "sensations" or on the basis of an alleged metaphysical system according to which "particulars" represent a lower order of Being than do "universals."

Now while "particular" in the cases mentioned stands for an event occurring at a specified date and in a specified locality, *that which* occurs, the "what" of the case, the *eclipse*, is a general fact. It is a fact expressing a *connection* among phenomena, and this connection is formulated in the theory of eclipses; a theory which is only one aspect of comprehensive astronomical theory. That the distinction between "particular" and "general" fact does not mark an opposition due to isolation or separation but is a distinction of subjects that are strictly correlative (like, say, the distinction expressed in husband-wife) is proved by the fact that the productions made regarding the occurrence of particular events rest upon calculations whose subject matter and method are determined by theory.

If the case is as just described, it may be asked how it happens that "theory," if it is the name of a fact that is general and not limited to any given place and date, has a significance markedly different from that borne by downright *fact*? The reason is easy to find if we continue to take the conduct of scientific knowing as the model after which our view is framed. That which is a general fact when it is looked at as a *conclusion* is a method of instituting connections among facts that have not previously been included in the system. For in scientific procedure, the function that is served by what has been found out is the important thing. Scientific knowledge is always pressing forward. It is moved by a divine discontent. Conclusions reached are capital to be invested not beds upon which to repose. As a rule, the layman who is not in touch with scientific practice regards a general fact as a law and a law as something final. To the active worker in a field, it is a *theory*; that is, something with which to open now fields to inquiry, be setting new problems, and something with which to try to coordinate areas of knowledge that have not previously had fruitful intercourse with one another. As far, for example, as the Newtonian theory of gravitation was taken by scientific men after Newton as a law *and nothing but a law*, it operated as a barrier. The Einsteinian revision restored to the formula its function as theory.

In other words, in the actual conduct of scientific knowing, the quality of *hypothesis* belongs to every formula which expresses an interconnectedness among facts of particular observations. To give the name *hypothesis* is to call attention to two properties of a generalization: it represents a finding of facts already known for the sake of effective and fruitful further knowing, an instrumentality for invading what at the time is not adequately known; and it is subject to test and modification by means of the very facts which are brought to light by its use.

As far as the question of theory and practice is concerned, the import of the discussion up to this point is that significant contrast between them, even a distinction that has instructive bearings, drops out of the picture when our idea of the nature of *theory* is formed on the ground of verified observations of the actual practices of scientific knowing. The field is thereby left open for an unhampered and unprejudiced consideration of the meaning of *practical* in connection with the philosophical problem of knowledge. I shall begin the discussion with a brief account of certain biological considerations that bear upon pre-scientific everyday knowing—upon knowledge of the commonsense type which is even less systematic from the standpoint of ordered discourse than that of the industrial arts. Facts of a phylogenetic order prove conclusively that overt behavior comes first in the process of development of organic structure and functions. Before sense organs or central organs are differentiated, certain tissues (which functionally fore-shadow muscles) are developed which are directly connected with bodily movements. Motor organs having to do with that adjustment of an organism to environing conditions without which life cannot go on are phylogeneti-cally prior. Investigation of the development of central structures among vertebrates discloses that structures which have to do with "body-sense" as a whole, with maintenance of equilibrium and the relation of the body as a whole to its surroundings, constitute in earlier forms by far the great-est bulk of the brain; next in development are structures concerned with the "practical" senses, taste and smell, while organs for the "intellectual" senses, hearing and vision, are the latest to develop, gradually enlarging so as to vastly reduce the bulk of the organs of body sense in general. Psychi-atric findings combine with those of physiology and anatomy to exhibit the intimate alliance of the basic autonomic nervous system with the relatively specialized central sensori-motor system. The facts which are now known prove conclusively that the psychology of moralists who dwelt upon the appetitive and impelling quality of "sense" was much closer to fact than was the psychology of the philosophers whose concern with the "problem of knowledge" led them to view sense-organs as "gateways to knowledge" and the primary material out of which "ideas" are made.

The belief that "sensations" are units of knowledge was formulated in a period when anatomy and physiology were in an infantile state. The belief became so fixed that discovery of the structural and functional intercon-nections of sensori-motor organs and processes had little effect upon the philosophical theory of knowledge.[10] Any theory that has any respect for basic biological facts will be obliged to break loose entirely from the tradi-tional treatment in three important respects.

In the first place, it will give full credence to the demonstrated fact that all sensory events of sight and hearing, as well as of touch, taste and smell, are primarily connected with *motor* operations. We *look*—an operation involv-ing intricate muscular adjustments—in order to *see*; what is *seen* (that is, the

---

10. Probably the most convincing evidence of the correctness of this statement is furnished by contemporary epistemological "realists" who, having got as far as denial of the "mental" character of sensory qualities, still retain the notion that the "sense-data" or the sensa they put in the place of mental states are units or simple elements of knowledge in complete isola-tion from behavioral motor connections.

sensory changes following the motor processes) then directs a new looking that results in a new seeing, *and so on.* To a very large extent, the genuine import of the discovery of structural and functional interconnection of the sensori-motor was missed because the connection was interpreted as an isolated affair, each sensori-motor adjustment being complete in itself. This view was definitely formulated in the so-called "reflex arc" theory. This theory recognized in words the connection of the sensory with the motor, but the influence of the earlier unitary ultimate simple element theory persisted to such an extent that the function of each particular sensori-motor re-adjustment in maintaining the continuity of life-behavior as a going concern was overlooked and virtually denied.

For, and this is the second point, a given series of lookings—seeings—lookings, has the function or office of providing conditions for an *over* or relatively total change in the state of behavior. If, for example, we take the case of an animal watching at the entrance-hole of another animal, the watching consists of just such a connected series of lookings—seeings as has been described. The processes involved are however practically *intra*-organic. The whole *body* of the watching animal is *waiting.* In short, the watching is not done for its own sake. If the hidden prey appears, then the body of the waiting animal comes into play as a whole. It pounces or chases; the function for the sake of which the watching, the connected series of sensori-motor adjustments, took place is executed. Or, generalizing the point of this illustrative example, just as a given sensori-motor reaction cannot be isolated from the series of continuing adjustments of which it is a part, so the total sensori-motor series cannot be understood if it is isolated from the place it occupied, the function it subserves, in the total life-behavior as an ongoing concern in space and time.

In the third place, in the case of vertebrate organisms, especially in the case of the primates including man, central, or cerebral, structures intervene at and in every particular sensori-motor adjustment—and it is *by means of the intervention* of *central processes* that any given series of sensori-motor functions *subserves* life-behavior as a going concern. In short, when the matter is looked at from the biological standpoint (from that of anatomy and physiology) central structures and processes are *in*-*termediate and instrumental.* They provide the means by which particular sensori-motor adjustments are constituted members of a serial behavioral act that in effect looks ahead; that is preparatory, since it gives readiness to meet future conditions. As far, then, as processes of central organs are, biologically, the conditions of that which is *intellectual* in distinction from that which is sensory and motor, *knowing with respect to its biotic aspect* as a form of behavior is an operation of surveying of existing conditions of a sort which interconnects with planning for future conditions and for behavior adapted to those conditions.

What precedes is deliberately limited to *biological* considerations that must be taken account of in any theory of knowledge. The fact that a theory of knowledge must be *in accord* with biological conditions of behavior, that it must not contain factors which are openly incompatible with basic physiological aspects of behavior, is far from signifying that these conditions of themselves provide complete data for a theory of knowledge. More specifically what has been said does not signify that knowledge either should be or is subordinated to some specific mode of practice or all modes of practice put together. For there is nothing in what has been said that militates against knowing, inquiry, being capable of being itself an engrossing form of behavior, and thus itself a form of "practical" behavior.

In what precedes, it has not been mentioned that strictly biological behavior has in the case of higher vertebrates an aspect that may be called *esthetic*. When that fact is noted, we find that even on strictly biological grounds there is provision for development of knowing as a form of behavior as self-contained as is any other form of doing and making. Biological operations have a double status. They are means by which life is maintained and carried forward and they are themselves immediate manifestations, expressions, of life activity. In the latter capacity, they are *ends*, consummations, as well as preparatory and instrumental. For a period, behavior may be mostly or even entirely a means for obtaining food to maintain life. But there is nothing in that fact to prevent the eating of food, when obtained, [from being] immediately enjoyable as well as an indispensable means of keeping alive.

The reference made in the previous paragraph to the *esthetic* takes on concrete meaning when we note that with kittens, puppies, young lions and adult simians, as well as in the case of human beings, motor activities take the form of play. That is, modes of behavior which have to do, say, with chasing and seizing prey, are engaged in under conditions in which there is no prey to hunt and in which hunger, the normal stimulus to the practical activity of searching for food, is absent. When we consider the case of human beings, it is evident that such physically or physiologically primary activities as hunting, fishing, cultivating the land, as means for obtaining food by which to continue living, as fighting and mating, become sources of immediate intense enjoyment; enjoyment which as immediate is independent of any result to be obtained later.

In view of actual facts, a *generalized* distinction between *practical* in the sense of useful for something beyond itself and *practical* in the sense of an immediately enjoyed doing or making is strictly conventional—using that word to include that which is what it is because of existing social institutions. We have already had an illustration of this fact in the case of the Greek estimate of the productive arts. Under the given social conditions they *were* illiberal, and there was little upon which to base an imaginative projection of any other kind of conditions. Custom is not only second "nature" but those who live under its influence have no criterion by which to distinguish it from first and unadulterated nature. Athenian philosophers were quite right in associating the rise of the science and philosophy with which they were acquainted with the emergence of a leisure class. For the existence of a class which is relieved of the burden of making a living because it can live upon the products of an inferior servile class is a socially conditioned fact; the ability of members of the leisure class to devote themselves to the development of ideas as ideas, to creation of rationally ordered discourse, was a manifestation of economic-political conditions. But the customs, the institutions, involved in these conditions were so settled, were so much second nature, that the philosophers were quite unaware that the leisure which made their kind of knowledge possible was a sociological phenomenon. On the contrary, they assumed that it was a proper expression of the inherent cosmological constitution of nature. And in analogous fashion under the greatly changed conditions of the feudally and ecclesiastically ordered hierarchy of the Middle Ages, its class-organization was taken to be a manifestation of a theological metaphysics which providentially gave the occasions for exercise of the supreme virtues of charity on one side and of loyal obedience to constituted authority on the other side.

Only fatuous complacency, however, would lead anyone to confine illustrative material to ancient times. The social conditions which back up the relegation of whatever is practical to a relatively degraded position exist wherever the processes of *making* a living are isolated from the processes of *living*. The extent to which industrial operations (those of making a living) have been segregated in modern times from those which constitute *life*, in the eulogistic sense of that word, is well exhibited in the doctrine of classical economists. For they *defined* productive work as labor, and then defined *labor* as behavior which is intrinsically so onerous that it will not be engaged in save because of expectation of reward to be had in the future. It would not be easy to find a clearer instance of identification of the "practical" with that which is deprived of significance and worth on its own account. Philosophers of modern as well as Greek and medieval times have taken facts (which *are* facts only too flagrantly) of a conventional or humanly institutional and hence extraneous kind as if they were somehow inherent. The usual philosophical rendering consists of a rigid separation between ends which are said to be "ends-in-themselves" and other ends which we are compelled to seek for by pressure of external conditions but which "in themselves" are only means to things which are ends-in-themselves.

The notion that the difference between the "instrumental" and the final is intrinsic is due to the very nature of things or to the metaphysical and theological constitution of the universe is so firmly entrenched that facts which otherwise are notable are slurred over. The processes which distinctively mark the "fine arts" for example are no more consummatory than they are instrumental. The very existence of musicians, painters, sculptors, dramatists, poets, etc., is itself proof of the extraneous quality of the separation of things that are means from things that are ends—or, stated in positive terms, is proof that one and the same operation is capable of being indivisibly "instrumental" and "final." And even under present socio-economical institutional conditions one finds many a human being, labeled mechanic, who is an artist in his attitude to his work.

There is here not involved any denial of the fact that there has been and still is a division into activities that have their significance and value outside themselves in something that will follow externally from them in the future, and activities that are immediately worthwhile in virtue of their own qualities. The facts tell in the contrary direction all too plainly. What is denied is that the difference in question is intrinsic and necessary because of the cosmological or metaphysical or theological constitution of things. What is affirmed is that the difference in question depends upon and reflects social conditions; that it is of the same nature as the difference between slaves and owners, serfs and lords, hands and managers. As becomes more apparent every generation, every year, the problem of reducing the gap that now divides, the problem of effecting a coalescence of activities that are useful but that are engaged in because of external pressure and activities that are enjoyable and worthwhile because of their own proper qualities, is one of our main social problems.

This fact takes us back to the problem of philosophy in its inclusive human phase. It is not the business nor problem of philosophy to remedy the social evils which are presented in and caused by social divisions into a class that is instrumental in a somewhat menial and unfree sense and a class that directs the productivity of others and that finds its operations enjoyable in quality. The work to be done has to be executed by all elements of society working together; it is a *social* problem in the deepest sense of the word social. But philosophers have a distinctive part to carry in accomplishing this work. They have, at the very least, a responsibility for clearing up that part of the mess they have themselves contributed. They can make clear the error that was committed in setting *theory* as the highest form of knowledge in stark opposition to *practice* and *practical* knowledge. They can indicate the conditions under which theory ceases to be remote and otiose and becomes what Justice Holmes called it—the most practical of things. They can point out the conditions which keep practical affairs of the highest moment upon a relatively unfree or illiberal level, since they obstruct the use and application within them of available intelligence. In so doing, they will further production of a state of social life in which free theoretical knowledge and concrete practical application reciprocally support each other: The only condition under which the existing separation of science from morals and the separation of conduct in matters of highest human concern from authenticated knowledge can be overcome.

XII. The Material and the Ideal

The subject dealt with in this chapter is closely connected with the theme of the last chapter. In one respect, the contrast and opposition embodied in the title of the present chapter was the source of the early or Greek formulation of antithesis of the theoretical and the practical. For the primacy of the former in Greek philosophy was essentially moral; the superiority of that which is theoretical by nature is one of intrinsic value. The human being is shaped by that with which he occupies himself; with which he is characteristically concerned. In pure knowing the soul is occupied with things which are intrinsically higher, even to the point of being divine. In dealing with objects having no material taint, the mind is purged of the grossness, the coarseness, which inevitably results when it is occupied with what is material, since the latter is guided by appetite and has its origin in appetite and is directed to satisfaction of bodily needs. Food, drink, and sex-relations are the immediate objects of appetite. Acquisition of goods and money as the means of their acquisition are its indirect objects. Desire may be manifested in the field of human, that is, civic relations, and in that case has a higher object: Reputation. But such an object and the activities by which it is attained, even when of the nature of good citizenship and loyal defense of one's city, at the expense of life itself, are contingent and transient in comparison with the necessary and eternal objects of pure knowledge. These latter objects are purely ideal or rational, and in the process of knowing them the rational potentialities of mind are actualized. In this actualization the knowing mind takes on the qualities of that which is known and becomes in so far divine, enjoying bliss without alloy.

I do not see how "matter" and "material" could have acquired the disparaging and quasi-degraded signification that has attached to them except on the ground of the belief that they are completely severed from all "high" and intrinsically worthy objects and activities. Cosmological and metaphysical theories, which have systematically disparaged "matter," turn out, when looked at in this context, to be the results of converting alleged moral differences, difference of value, into properties of the very structure of the universe. Medieval Christian philosophy marks, in a way, a frank acknowledgement of this interpretation of Nature in its material aspect and constituents. For holding, as Greek thought did not hold, the world to be the creation of an all-wise, all-powerful and all-righteous spiritual Being, it could account for the gross, unmoral and anti-moral tendencies of outer and inner nature only on the ground of a corruption wrought by an evil act of human will.

I have already pointed out that on the basis of a naturalistic interpretation of known facts, the word "matter" as a general term has no standing of its own in philosophy. In natural science it has a definite meaning, associated with the need for a symbol to stand for qualities of events of the order of mass and inertia. It is obviously absurd to attribute any value-predicates, eulogistic or the reverse, to "matter" in this meaning. It simply stands for something in natural events it is found necessary to take note of in every physico-mathematical formulation. The fact that "spiritually" minded persons greeted with acclaim the false rumor that modern physics has entirely resolved "matter" into energy, merely proves the cultural hold upon belief possessed by direct projection of moral valuations into the total constitution of nature. For the word "spiritually-minded" as here used means those whose beliefs about the world have been determined by the medieval theologian version of Greek cosmology.

As was said earlier in another connection, in philosophy the word "matter" may be legitimately used to designate the sum-total set of natural events that condition whatever occurs in human experience. The word, although a term so general as to be abstract, is legitimate in this usage as long as the view prevails that human experience, as a whole or in specific parts, has no conditions or that it is "caused" by a non-natural physical or spiritual special force. In this usage, it is a term of general protest against a type of belief which is general in the sense of being widespread and influential. In its positive aspect, the word is as harmful as is that against which it protests when it too is erected into something that can be taken for a "cause," i.e., a force, in producing whatever exists. In its positive aspect, the word, as previously indicated, is of the nature of a precautionary advice to search for the *particular* conditions that account for or explain the occurrence of this and that and the other that, in the sense in which "account for" and "explaining" mean to bring the thing in question under control of actual formulation and prediction and of potential, practical, i.e., existential, control.

The word "material," if not the word "matter," has a meaning of this sort recognized in common speech. In this sense, *material* stands for that which is to the point, germane, weighty, "of serious or substantial import," in the language of the dictionary, and, especially in legal practice, facts of such a nature that they have a proper place in determining final judgment. In contrast, the *immaterial* is the flimsy, trivial, unimportant; in the case of the relation of facts to judgment, the irrelevant and "incompetent." The use of "material" (especially in the plural) as a noun is cognate. We speak not only of "raw materials" of physically manufactured products but also of materials of literary and historic art; of materials for reaching a conclusion, of human beings as material for factories, armies, or (sometimes) for citizenship. In short, matter as material as that out of which anything, whatever its nature, is made or constructed; its differential meaning being found in its contrast with the ulterior finished product *out* of it, or *from* it, by some human activity. In this sense, *material* is like *stuff* in the sense of provision for an activity that will yield a certain product. The subject matter designated by *matter* and *material* thus used is closely allied to the philosophic usage in which *matter* is related to but distinguished from *form*, since raw materials of every sort have to be formed—reformed (that is, re-formed or re-arranged) to yield a finished product.[1]

The bearing of what has just been said upon the problem of the relations of material and ideal is that while the issue of valuation enters in, the valuation to be put upon "material" is also dependent upon the facts of the particular case. There is no ground for either a wholesale disparaging, pejorative interpretation nor for an honorific, optimistic one. As a general term, "matter" is what it does in a given case and in the case of materials everything depends, as far as their value-status is concerned, upon what is made out of them. Science, for example, cannot get far without statistics but it is a commonplace that as raw materials of science they may be made to lie and, in any case, they have to be ordered, given form by being related, to achieve scientific standing.

The ambivalence of *matter* and *material* is significant. On the one hand, base, low, gross are synonyms for "material;" the word carries the morally disparaging sense that has been attached to matter in contrast with spirit through the ages. On the other hand, "material" is synonymous with the important, the weighty, with that which counts, with what is substantial.

---

1. This fact was perceived by Aristotle in so far as he identified matter and material with *potential*, at the same time holding that everything potential has its own *relative* form and actuality. It is difficult to say whether the ultimate form*less* matter of Aristotelian writings is genuinely his or a latter qualification. From the standpoint of the later theological tradition, this question, important as it is for historic scholarship, is not important—matter being that "without form and voice," inherently unordered and chaotic. In any case, the cosmology of Aristotle treats the potential and material as being *the* intrinsically fixed and hence inferior to the ultimate fixed actuality which in its own being is *the* superior, since it is purely ideal and rational. In other words, his theory postulates the *wholesale* fixed connection that is criticized in the text which follows.

An *embodied* idea is, from this point of view, a *realized* one, while from the other standpoint, it is one degraded to a materialistic level. The ambivalence in question is not explicable on the ground of anything inherent in subject matters that are called material. It can be understood only on the ground of *uses* to which the subject matters in question are put, and this affair is an expression of socio-cultural conditions. When there is a social division, a separation of classes in civic standing, esteem and prestige of the ground of occupations habitually engaged in, the materials involved in the habitual activities of the lower group share in the disesteem and contempt in which the class is held. They become "matter" par excellence. Historically, the activities of this "lower" class have to do (i) with physical things; (ii) they are carried on by bodily organs, largely manual; (iii) upon the psychological side, the senses, touch and sight, rather than ideas are the basis of control of what is done and how it is done; (iv) the activities are mainly routine, mechanically repetitious, and (v) they are performed under the direction of others and for ends in the formulation of which the workers have no share. This latter consideration is the most important one in determining the menial, quasi-servile quality of the occupations in question, and accords without a flaw with the four other traits mentioned. Taken together they serve to explain not only the dyslogistic meaning of "practical" and "utilitarian," but also the position assigned to whatever is *matter* and *material*.

The fundamental points of the foregoing introductory statement go contrary in important respects to current views and are far from being self-justifying in the present state of opinion. They are, accordingly, intended to summarize the position that will be set forth in this chapter rather than as an argument in its defense. The more detailed exposition of the opinion will cover three matters. First, a statement of the connections existing between material and ideal and subject matter in culture as culture. Secondly, discussion of the phases of the historic conditions of the split between lower and higher social functions in their direct affect upon philosophical formulations; third, a discussion of the issue from the standpoint of any naturalism consonant with present-day knowledge, that is, a naturalism which is non-materialistic in the traditionally approved meaning of "materialism." In beginning with the cultural aspect, I reverse the mode of statement adopted in the previous chapter, where theoretical considerations came first, and socio-cultural considerations were brought in by way of illustration and re-enforcement.

The discussion of the distinction and connection of material and ideal from the cultural point [of view] fittingly opens with a quotation from the article on culture from which a quotation was made in the opening chapter. In fact, the remark was made incidentally in connection with the quotation to the effect that the constant and inherent connection of material culture with certain non-material factors has a definite bearing upon the philosophic problem of the relation of mind and matter. The quotation follows:

> On all points of contact with the outer world man creates an artificial, secondary environment. He makes houses or constructs shelters; he prepares his food more or less elaborately, procuring it by means of weapons and implements; he makes roads and uses means of transport. Were man to rely on his anatomical equipment exclusively, he would soon be destroyed or perish from hunger and exposure. Defense, feeding, movement and space, all physiological and spiritual needs, are settled indirectly by means of artifacts even in the most primitive modes of human life. . . . This material outfit of man—his artifacts, his buildings, his sailing craft, his implements and weapons, the liturgical paraphernalia of his magic and religion—are one and all the most obvious and tangible aspects of culture. They define its level and they constitute its effectiveness. The material equipment of culture is not, however, a force in itself. Knowledge is necessary in the production, management and use of artifacts, implements, weapons and other constructions and is essentially connected with mental and moral discipline, of which religion, laws and ethics, rules are the ultimate source. The handling and possession of goods imply also the appreciation of their value. The manipulation of implements and the consumption of goods also require cooperation. Common work and common enjoyment of its results are always based on a definite type of social organization. Thus material culture requires a complement less simple, less easily catalogued or analyzed, consisting of the body of intellectual knowledge, of the system of moral, spiritual, and economic values, of social organization and of language. On the other hand material culture is an indispensible apparatus for the molding or conditioning of each generation of human beings. The secondary environment, the outfit of material culture, is a laboratory in which the reflexes, the impulses, the emotional tendencies of the organism are formed. . . . Artifact and custom are actually indispensable and they mutually produce and determine one another.

A little further on in the article it is said, "The organization of social groups is a complex combination of material equipment and bodily customs which cannot be divorced from either its material or psychological substratum."[2]

The passage quoted affirms that "material culture" is associated with at least types or kinds of non-material culture; namely, the existing system of

---

2. B. Malinowski, "Culture," in *Encyclopedia of the Social Sciences* (1931), vol. 4, pp. 621–22.

knowledge, of beliefs about value (together with all the processes by which these beliefs are formed and maintained) and social organization. The connection of culture with value-beliefs was mentioned in the first chapter in its bearing upon the significance of philosophy; something will be said later about its connection with social organization and the problem of "individual and social." The connection of knowledge and processes of knowing with culture is a pretty constant object of attention in consideration of all themes. Here in this chapter, we are concerned with a more general issue: The meaning assignable to "material" and "ideal" respectively in the light of what is known about culture.

In the passage as quoted the distinction as well as the connection of the material and non-material aspects of culture is set forth in a way which may give the impression to readers that after all material culture has a certain relative existence of its own and that non-material culture is complement. For a student of culture, the distinction is so important as to be inevitable, and the student is obliged for the purpose of study and for the purpose of conveying conclusions to others to set them apart as if they had a certain original independence of each other. The interpretation that follows goes a step further. It takes a position not explicitly authorized by anything said in the text, but also, as far as I can see, not contrary to anything in what is there said. This further position is that the distinction of the material and the non-material, while necessary in study and inquiry, does not exist in culture as that which is studied, save as it is itself a characteristic of certain cultural beliefs. What is meant by this statement is that (as the passage cited itself shows) that which is called material and that which is called non-material cannot and do not *exist* apart from each other; the distinction made between them is one of inquiry and discourse, not a separation in what exists. Belief in their separation is itself a constituent of the non-material aspect of some cultures, and, like other elements of this culture, is maintained and carried only by elements of the material aspect.

If we search for the criterion or principle upon which the distinction is made, we find, I believe, the clue is the passage in which it is declared that artifacts in their totality constitute the *effectiveness* of a culture. They are, in other words, the objects and processes that are selected or distinguished when inquiry is concerned to determine causally determining factors in [the] study of [culture] generally or some given culture in particular. It is true, as the text states, that ideas and practices classified on the non-material side interact and determine the production and use of implements, utensils and all kinds of apparatus and equipment, including that of stated rites and ceremonies. But it is also true, as the article also says, that they operate, or have *effectiveness*, only through material bases and vehicles. Language or speech is, in this connection, the exemplary instance. Meanings or ideas are the defining and differential characteristics of all words and combinations of words. They make speech, oral and written, to be what it is: language and not meaningless babblings and scribblings. But bodily activity and physical embodiment are the material aspects of language. They are not two things, meanings *and* material embodiment, passengers and a vehicle that transports them. Language *is* meaning and sound or visible form in complete fusion with one another while, as in the face of other cultural phenomena, it cannot be profitably studied or told about without their distinction and separate *treatment*, as far as *discourse* is concerned, of meanings on one hand and of focal and auditory bodily apparatus on the other.[3]

The illustrative material of instance which follows is not very important in and of itself but becomes such when used as illustration. As far as is known, every form of social organization has employed threats and promises, together with penalties and rewards, as instrumentalities of control of its constituent members. A certain amount and quality of *brute* force is involved. Yet even in the instances in which the latter element is least disguised and most apparent, the control aimed at and effected is of a different dimension, as far as its subjects are concerned, from that exercised over inanimate things. The threat of penalties to be inflicted in case of noncompliance with an order involves expression of [the] intention to employ physical agencies upon the bodies of those to whom the command is given. But what makes the threat operate is not present physical force (though of course physical energies are required in conveying the order and threat) but a *representative* factor, an *idea* of suffering and a psychological response to

---

3. [From Folder 53/15: "It is not necessary to deny the existence of non-material factors nor is a super-gaseous spiritual force demanded to account for them. The existence of language, that is to say of *meanings* of which material things are vehicles, suffices. Perhaps the easiest way to form an idea of the respective material and non-material elements in the cultural environment is to contrast events that involve bodily collisions through direct impact and consequences that occur because of interactivities of persuasion, advice, instruction, argument, and even the uttering of threats and the promise of regard. Language involves "physical" contractions of the vocal apparatus, expulsion of air, production of vibrations of air, etc. But these events are not language save as they communicate meanings and the meanings while non-material are not in any way "spiritual" in the sense of a peculiar kind of mental existence set over against physical existence.

With respect to the distinction and the connection of the respective constituents of material and non-material culture, *connection* is thus as intrinsic and indispensable as *distinction*. The system of values, ideas (meanings), and known facts and principles that exercises regulative influence upon the nature and course of human associations in cultural groups has no separate and disembodied existence. It exists *in* such activities as hunting, fishing, farming, mining, working of metals and wood, fighting, meeting in assemblies for discussion, and the making of the appliances by means of which these activities are carried on. Non-material constituents can be observed only in their material incarnations, not in themselves. A logos, a meaning, is made flesh, takes on material embodiment in every act that has cultural import."]

what is represented in the idea. The shrinking, the fear, that animates conduct is induced by anticipation of something not yet in existence. What is here illustrated—namely, that while physical energies as such act here and now, predications, anticipations, ideas and plans operate when things represented are not here and now present—has been one of the chief *empirical* factors (as distinguished from those that are metaphysical and religious) in producing the notion of an immaterial stuff or substance. Yet the fact that what is represented is of the order of language, being an embodied meaning, is in fact indicative of the nature of the distinction and the connection of the material and the non-material in experience. Moreover the illustrative force of the case cited may be carried further. From the valuation standpoint, many have urged that appeals to fear of suffering and hope of reward are appeals to unworthy motives. They would rely upon higher, more ideal motivations, through processes of instruction. The change of method does not, however, eliminate the material condition; it changes its character to one which is believed, human nature being what it is, to be more *effective* in the long run for establishment of good social relationships. On the other side, it is usual, if not universal, for those who bring coercive pressure to bear upon others to affirm that they do so on behalf of some "higher" good, perhaps even the ultimate welfare of those upon whom pressure is brought to bear. Even when the claim is insincerely made and is in fact a "rationalizing" cover for desire to maintain private and class privilege, it testifies to the presence of an "ideal," in the sense of *psychologically* operative, quality.[4]

Illustrations are by their nature limited in scope. They may, accordingly, obscure rather than illuminate the main point. This point is that culture, by and in its own nature, is a union of qualities and traits which, when discriminated in inquiry and discourse, are respectively called material and non-material. There are sociological treatises that attempt to explain social phenomena exclusively in psychological terms, just as there are political philosophies that try to explain the state in terms of a common Will or Reason that is struggling to realize itself. On the other hand, there are

---

4. Belief that *material* and *non-material* stand for two different substances or kinds of existence has been so long established in our cultural "heritage" and has been supported such powerful social forces that a proper vocabulary is lacking. The text quoted uses occasionally the word "spiritual." Denotatively, or with respect to the moral and psychological conditions involved, there is objection to the word. But from the point of view of traditional beliefs, use of that word may seem to express acceptance and endorsement of a metaphysical and theological dualism of "matter" and "spirit." Similarly, the word "ideal" used in the title of this chapter is open to serious misunderstanding, and hence may well be found objectionable. For "ideal" has a eulogistic flavor of something intrinsically higher than the material which stands in the way of taking it as a neutral term, the ideal of ideative, subject matter involving the presence of something of the order of *meaning*. Hence the terms *non-material and psychological* frequently appear in the text of this exposition.

theories that attempt to rule out everything save the material factors, as in the vulgar version of Marxism. The issue as between these two schools of thought is not even debatable, provided the social phenomena in question are defined in cultural terms. For when the identity of *social* in its human sense and bearing with the cultural is admitted, it has also to be admitted that material aspects of culture (the artifacts of the anthropologist) exist and act only in connection with that which is non-material; only in connection with knowledge, valuations and communication of meanings, while it is equally true that the latter exist in a social sense only through the instrumentality of a more or less complex equipment of material agencies. And, to repeat, the material and non-material are so fused or interpenetrated in culture that the subject matters in question represent only distinctions in inquiry and discourse, not separations in existence.

It follows from what has been said that the distinction between the material and the non-material is strictly functional or, with greater accuracy of statement, it does not *follow* but is involved in what has been said. What is meant here by functional will probably be clearer if its import is stated negatively. There is nothing which is such in its own existence that it comes to be labeled, as it were, either material or non-material, psychological, ideative. We name it one or the other according to the way it operates, while this latter matter, the mode of operation, is determined by the kind or quality of consequences that result. This mode of statement is sufficiently extreme to indicate what is meant by the protest to the contrary it will evoke. What, it will be asked in effect, do you mean to say that when we see a chair, a spade, a house, and recognize it for what it is, we do not know at once that it is material? Or that when we enter into a religious service, see or hear of a noble deed, or entertain an idea, we do not know as directly that the object is ideal, spiritual, or at least ideational? These questions bring out by way of contrast exactly the point that is intended. Chair, spade, or house are *meanings* as well as physical things. And this statement means more than that the *words* have meaning. It signifies that the things called by these names have meanings and that if we eliminate or exclude the meanings, the things in question are no longer spades, chairs or houses. If we substitute things like the flag of our own country, a crucifix, or a memento of a dearly loved friend, for the commonplace *chair* or *spade* and a temple, say Westminster in London or St. Peter's in Rome for *house*, it is probable that the meaning which is intended will stand out more clearly. In fact, if any work of fine art, genuinely appreciated as such, is substituted for the prosaic things first mentioned, it should be seen that the position taken is at least not self-evidently absurd. For if the object is a work of fine art and is appreciated as such, matter and meaning are so completely interfused that it will be seen, if the case is surveyed without a dominating influence from preconceived theory, that they are distinguished only in reflection—which, as reflection, is always an *ex post facto* affair. On the other side, noble deeds, religious rites and services, ideas are embodied[5] and, without this embodiment, they do not exist.

The notion that we identify objects and subject matters offhand, on the spot, as material or non-material is the outcome of a natural and, in itself, innocent mistake. We take the result of a series of experiences through which a habit has been formed as if it were an intrinsic property of an original experience. From a practical point of view the mistake is innocent because, practically, it is the fruit, the functional outcome, which counts; the experiences through which it was arrived are put to one side in the interest of clarity as well as economy. But the error is serious when in a theoretical, generalized interpretation we treat a product as if it were an independent, original and hence "natural" property which, moreover, is capable of being recognized on sight. The fact that some objects, those for example of the illustration just given, are taken directly and without question to be material and others to be ideal or spiritual shows how habits formed in a long series of experiences can cause one functional aspect of things to be so prominent, because of constant emphasis, that it finally excludes any other else from view.

The position just taken raises two questions which lie at the heart of the issue under discussion. If *material* and *non-material* represent functional aspects instead of being differences inherent in the very nature of things, it is incumbent that a reasonable account be given of the nature of the functions involved and how it is they are so pervasive in their influence as to constitute aspects as deep and as widespread as are designated by the terms *material* and *non-material*. This question does not cover, however, the whole ground. Suppose this first question is satisfactorily answered, we still have to face the question: How does it come about that the functional aspects in question, instead of being recognized for what they are, have been so completely misinterpreted as to be taken to be differences embedded in the ultimate structure of things? The answer which will be given to the first question is that the functions in questions are those of things in their capacities or offices as means and ends respectively: the distinction being a functional one since existences are in themselves neutral with respect to it and are placed in one class or the other according to the way in which they habitually function or operate in our experience. The answer that will be given to the second question is that while things which are used as means

---

5. That is, in some sort of object which is linguistic in the sense of being representative. See, *ante*, p. ___.

and things which are enjoyed as ends are in fact correlative or conjugate, customs and institutions formed under their influence have created a split between them, and that this socio-cultural split is the ultimate ground of the doctrine of the two-world view of material and spiritual.[6]

The statement that a profound cultural division is the source of the separation of means and ends and that this division is at the root, practically and philosophically, of the problem of matter and mind has without doubt a strange sound, even though it is the only view at all plausible if one takes the position that philosophical problems have cultural origin, context and impact. It is well, accordingly, to call to mind at the outset that the common popular use of "materialistic" gives the word a moral sense. In popular usage, a person is materialistic whose *behavior* displays the tendency to treat things which are means as if they were ends. The materialist morally speaking refuses in his action to subordinate material to moral goods. "Material wealth, material civilization, material needs," are familiar phrases. According to ordinary ways of judging, those persons are materialists who permit themselves to become completely absorbed in the activities and objects for which these words stand, no matter what their avowed philosophical and metaphysical beliefs may be. From another point of view, we find economic theory officially defined as a "social scientific discipline, concerned with the relations of man to man arising out of processes directed to the satisfaction of *material* needs."[7] The definition is accepted even though it is impossible to find any definition of material needs that covers the facts.

It is a matter of common information that materialistic interpretation of history is synonymous with an interpretation that finds, in the words of Engels, "The causes of all social changes and political revolutions not in men's brains, not in man's better insight into truth and justice, but in changes in methods of production and exchange."[8] The dialectical materialism of Marx is much too large a topic to be discussed here. But it may be noted that he criticized what he called "vulgar materialism" according to which molecular changes in the brain are the proximate cause of social phenomena.

---

6. [Paragraph cut by Dewey: "The subject matter of answers to the two questions is largely the same; their materials overlap and interlace. For the distinction and relation of means and ends, of ulterior and consummatory consequences and the agencies and instrumentalities by which they are attained is basically the question of the relation of the economic to the moral, and the split between the social elements which have been distinctively representative of the economic and the social elements which have been the supposed bearers of the moral provides the causal conditions of that separation between things that are taken to be merely instrumental and things supposed to be merely final that is the empirical source of the injunction of material and spiritual. Accordingly I shall first take up the story of separation of means and ends, postponing till later questions of their actual connection with one another."]

7. "Economics," in *Encyclopedia of the Social Sciences* (1935) vol. 5, p. 345.

8. [Friedrich Engels, *Socialism: Utopian and Scientific* (1880).]

He was concerned to prove, in opposition to the then reigning school of German idealistic philosophy, that the "ideal is nothing else than the material reflected by the human mind and translated into forms of thought."[9] The "material" in question is "material" in the sense of "the material conditions of life"—Marx's own phrase—rather than in the sense in which "matter" is used by metaphysical materialism. The reversal is primarily [illeg.] socio-moral theory in spite of the Marxist assertion of the elimination of moral elements. What is relevant to the present topic is the fact that when means and ends are completely separated, arbitrary choice alone can settle which one of the two extremes is to be assigned "causal" power. When, in fact, the material pole is, by commonly accepted theory, supposed to furnish all means, it would seem to be less arbitrary to tie causal efficacy to it than to attribute it to that which by definition is merely "final," that is, terminal. Consider, for example, the "epiphenomenalism" of Santayana, a writer assuredly far removed from Marxism. For while he continues the classic tradition of glorification of the ideal in complete separateness, he unites with it an explicit assertion of complete impotency from the causal point of view. Indeed, the popular conception of *"an* ideal" or *"the* ideal" dwells upon its utter remoteness, its very perfection providing a measure of its unattainability. In short, Marx's view is illuminating as a logical development of what is implied in the traditional theory of separation of material and ideal, whatever be thought of it in terms of the phenomena it is nominally based upon. Given the traditional dichotomy; given the idealistic metaphysics of the Hegelian type; given also the impressive demonstration of the social effects of economic forces which was furnished during the nineteenth century by the events of the industrial revolution together with the conclusions of the new physical science, it would seem as if a theory of the material and ideal were inevitable. Consequently, effective philosophical criticism must base itself upon questioning the fundamental premise—the separation of means and ends, material and moral.

We owe to Aristotelian writings the first completely generalized statement of the idea that there is an inherent separation of means and ends, the generalization being so broad in scope as to provide a fundamental category of interpretation. I quote two passages in which the principle is stated. "Some things are conditions of a worthy life but are not constituents of it."[10] The point of view expressed in this statement may be regarded as one implicitly postulated in the whole Aristotelian cosmological scheme. For while, as has already been said, this hierarchical arrangement avoided

---

9. [Karl Marx. *Capital.* Afterword to second edition (1873).]

10. Dewey's note to himself: "(Check up on this passage which is a paraphrase—not translation)"

the hard and fast dualisms of modern thought, it did so only by distributing hard and fast separations through a considerable stretch of classes of objects said to be marked off from one another by their natures and essences so that there are no passages of growth or development from one to one another. They are graded or ranked metaphysically with respect to one another on the ground of deficit and fullness of ultimate Being—a matter determined by degree of immutability. They are ranked morally on the ground that the higher the object in the scale of Being, the higher the type of activity that has commerce with it and the closer the soul comes, in this commerce, to realization of its own proper Being. Because of the fixed separation existing between different grades, each species lower in rank may be said to be a condition of higher grades (up to the highest or divine Being) but in no sense a constituent of them. For the constitution of higher orders is what it is precisely because their *constituent* determinants are of a different order, a higher essence. It is a condition then in the sense that in the entire cosmic scheme the lower orders of Being do not in any sense produce or cause the higher but that what is higher depends for its particular *metaphysical* status as higher upon what is lower, specifically, upon what the next lower in grade. Drawing for an illustration upon the point next discussed, we may say that just as animal life would not be possible without vegetable nor rational life without animal, and yet it is impossible for the vegetable to bring the animal into existence and for the animal to cause the Being of the rational, so the citizen-class of the civic community would not and could not exist without the material support (food, clothing, shelter, etc) provided by the working class, and yet the activities of the latter class do not in any way enter in or help compose or constitute the characteristic and essential activities that define the citizen-class—since, by Aristotle's definition, the citizen-class is the class whose material and bodily wants are so supplied from without that they have full leisure to devote themselves to the distinctively civic activities.[11]

Stated in terms of means and ends, the principle involved in the kind of hierarchical arrangement assumed by Aristotle to exist in Nature is that there is a kind of *means* which are wholly external to the ends of which they are the conditions. A scaffolding of a building may, for example, be a condition or external means, a *mere* means in common speech, of *erection* of a building, but it is no constituent of the building itself. Owing to extraneous conditions, it is necessary. But it is wholly indifferent to and outside of

---

11. It is, of course, equally true in the scheme of Aristotle that the scientific-philosophic class would not and could not exist without the activities of the citizenship class, since the work of the former depends upon an ordered and secure civic life, and yet citizenship activities do not in any constitute the essence and definition of scientific-philosophic activity and energy.

the idea that constitutes and defines a building as building. Were it not for extraneous and ultimately accidental conditions, no scaffolding would be required at any stage of proceedings, and the higher the object in the scale of Being, the more complete is the freedom of the object from any and all extraneous conditions and means. God, for example, has no need for any external prop or support. *That which is properly called material* consists precisely of the things which are external and means, extraneous to the real being of which they support and yet necessary to its *coming* into being. The relevance of the foregoing interpretation of means and ends is explicitly set forth by Aristotle in express connection with the thesis that "not all who are indispensable to the existence of the civil community (*polis*) can be re-garded as citizens (*members* of the community)." For he says, "When there is one thing which is means and another thing that is end, there is nothing *common* between them, except in so far as the one, the means, produces, and the other, the end, *receives the product*." Providing and receiving is a strictly one-way process. For to grasp the full meaning of this statement we have to recall the sense in which "product" is used by Aristotle, a sense contrasting with action and activity. The arts are concerned with production, while morals is demarcated form the arts in being concerned with actions. In the arts, it is only the product which has to be good, not the producer. Actions (that is, the subject-matter of morals, of the good and bad proper) are good or bad in and of themselves. Moral acts are ends, finalities, in themselves; industrial production, as "activity," is always subordinate to an end beyond itself.[12]

The direct bearing of this view upon social—that is, moral—theory, has been anticipated. But the point will have to be developed in order to illustrate the position which is taken regarding the indirect influence of the resulting social theory upon the whole conception of means and ends, the effect of their separation upon separation of the *material* and the *ideal*. Life, ac-cording to a passage in the *Politics* ascribed to Aristotle, is divided between business and leisure, war and peace, and actions are directed either to what is necessary and useful for us, or to what is noble. We have to decide between these upon the same principles as we decide upon what parts of the soul and their respective actions are higher and lower. "The end of war is peace, the

---

12. In Aristotle, as in the Greek estimation generally, no distinction in principle was made between artist and artisan; between architect and carpenter; between a painter of pictures and a house painter. The external product, not the "activity in and of itself" was what counted. These persons were quite literally servants of the community, not members of it. An orator and poet, on the other, dealing with words, relatively intangible and the media of ideas, were directly engaged in civic activities. They were citizens, because they were internal formers not external conditions of the community's existence. They had in typical Greek conception an educative function of the order of legislation.

end of business is leisure; the end of things useful is things fair and noble."[13] One who questions the finality of such dicta as these is usually understood to be one who affirms the equality—if not the superiority—of the merely utilitarian and "materialistic" to acts and objects "fair and noble" in themselves while still retaining the dualism involved in their separation. On this score, he is an easy victim. But what any intelligent critic of the position is doing is to question the desirability and the inherent necessity of the dualism involved. He does not question the existence of the split; it is precisely the moral inhumanity and the injurious social (moral) results or actual "ends" of its existence to which he directs his criticism. A society is better in the degree in which "useful" acts are also intrinsically worthwhile, because they have qualities that are rewarding in and of themselves, instead of the acts having to be endured, as best one may, because of some possible future "pay-off." The critic declines to take activities which have no significance or value in themselves as standard models for a large part, the necessary because useful part, of human action. He objects particularly to that view on the ground that it is once a reflection and "rationalizing" justification of the condition in which the "masses" find their activities subordinated to providing leisure and opportunity for "higher" things to a small "class." In short they reply affirmatively to the charge that their position is an expression of a value-judgment, while they point out that the traditional separation of ends and means from one another is also a value judgment. But this fact is not openly avowed; on the contrary, it is covered up and protected by armored metaphysical lining. This armor protects the moral judgment and social practice which are involved by presenting them as inherent necessities of the constitution of "Nature." Frank acknowledgment that the position taken, to whichever side it inclines, is one of the social morals would make it clear that the practical activity [is] to be decided in and by the course of social policy which is chosen and acted upon.

For the sake of adequacy of presentation I shall continue this aspect of the discussion by reminding the reader of some of the details of Aristotle's economic theory since these details give concrete illustration of the significance of the separation of means and ends; the origin of this separation in a specific form of organization of social relationships; and the identity of the issue involved in the separation with the separation of things material—necessary and useful—from things free, noble, and fair—or ideal. And since the habit of interpreting favorably anything found in the Aristotelian canon has supervened upon a period of reaction in which everything in it was given as disparaged a meaning as possible, I shall repeat in another form

---

13. [Aristotle, *Politics* 7.15.]

the warning just given. The over-kindly habit just mentioned tends to find in what Aristotle said simply an emphatic assertion of the subordination of the economic to the ethical. Hence it tends to command the approval of all who would uphold the superior claims of the ethical. It appeals with especial force to those who do not accept the modern doctrine that the economic is completely independent of the moral, and that the introduction of any socio-moral considerations into economic theory undermines the "scientific" character of the latter. So I repeat the issue is not the highly general one of subordination of the economic to the moral, but concerns that *kind* of subordination in which economic activities and relations (admittedly the socially necessary) are completely denuded of the qualities and traits that belong to ends that are of intrinsic value, while activities and relations that are "noble and fair" (i.e. intrinsically valuable) are placed upon a pedestal too lofty to have any reciprocal responsibility to the human conditions by which they are "produced" and supported.

The household is to Aristotle the proper, the legitimate abode of the arts, that is, of *productive* or economic activities. Every art requires implements or tools. These instrumentalities are either inanimate or animate. The latter include beasts of burden, slaves, domestic servants, and women. Even as bearers of children, women are *producers* in the technical Aristotelian sense, a tool, a means to an external end. Some persons are slaves *"by nature"* the one final standard and source of reasons that are so inherently rational they cannot be argued against. Hence it is as truly advantageous for them to live a life of subjection as it is for the body or for (domestic) animals. Upon the whole, Aristotle's views in these matters are "realistically" empirical. That is to say, he reports the socio-cultural state of affairs he finds existing but with the usual absolutistic assumption of the "rationalistic" school that certain things are so "by nature" and hence are eternal. Of course, it is not true that all economic activity was in and of households when he wrote, but it is true upon the whole that the subject matter of *political* economy is of different origin. The polis or community of free citizens was, of course, its own public finance or scheme of revenues and expenditures, but it was definitely a political affair, in the sense in which politics had to do with the polis, one of political economy in the sense in which Adam Smith and others have written of *The Wealth of Nations*. Aristotle's view was that "unnatural" trade, save as exchange of necessities that happened also to be superfluous in the hands of those who bartered them, made it easier to restrict legitimate economy to the household. Mechanics and artisans who were not clients of a household were in his mind less capable of a good life than domestic slaves. Since the latter could share in a reflected and vicarious way in the rationally ordered life of the head of the household.

It looks as if I had been engaged in a discussion of economic activities as one aspect of social life. In fact, special consideration of that subject is reserved for later treatment. What I have been concerned to show is that the class-structure of society, especially low social status of workers in things necessary and useful for the maintenance of life, personal and public, is the source of the separation which found philosophical expression in the notion of the inherent separation of things that are *merely* means, means one might say "in themselves," and other things that are ends "in themselves," and that the physical conception of the "material" in its divorce from the ideal or spiritual originated in this bifurcation.

I do not suppose that many persons today would deliberately uphold the idea that there are any such things as "means in themselves." It is too obvious that things, energies, come first and that they become *means* when purposefully employed in a human art for the accomplishing some result, attaining some end. We are too familiar with the spectacle of inventions of new arts and technologies, which turn previously unused things into means for ends, to take readily to the notion that some things are ends by nature. And in spite of the great lag in practice and of the attempt of totalitarian states to establish the idea that some races are inferior by nature so that their members should perform the service and menial tasks beneath the standing of a *Herrenvolk*. We are too familiar with the notion that all normal human beings are morally free, to take kindly to the notion that some class of human beings are means and only means in themselves. Arts among the Greeks were customary and hereditary. They were instituted by the gods or by semi-divine heroes according to popular belief, a belief which in the hands of philosophers was easily translated into the ideas that their materials and processes existed by nature so that their status as means and "material" was fixed. The readiest way in which to arrive at sympathetic understanding of an idea about things as means that to us is plainly absurd is to note that belief in the cognate idea of things which are *ends* in themselves is till indeed so current and highly influential that professional moralists and preachers of morals generally assume that the whole cause of the "reality" of morals is bound up with unquestioning faith in the existence of things which are ends in themselves, instead of those things being ends which are made such by human desire, purpose and endeavor at realization. For while it is admitted that such origin and status is appropriate for "lower" ends, the view applied to "higher" and controlling ends is said to result in moral anarchy. It requires a cool and detached mind to see that the logic, a logic of events as well as of discourse, that has ruled out the notion of means-in-themselves, performs the same emancipatory work of abolition for the notion of ends-in-themselves, because of the strictly correlative character of the two categories, sauce for the goose is sauce for the gander. The idea of ends-in-themselves, as over against that of *objects* which become ends in certain contextual connections, exhibited *logically* a monstrous lopsidedness as soon as the notion of means-in-themselves was surrendered. But, *practically*, it persists because of the assumption that habits must be unalterably fixed in all matters of moral import, so that the regime of invention and novelty found in all other materials and practical matters is completely irrelevant. The lopsidedness is thus the result of the fact that, when the doctrine of the separation of the useful and necessary (material) from the noble and fair (ideal) was formulated, social customs with respect to both means and ends were unaffected by invention, while now invention reigns almost supreme in affairs and relations to which economic value is assigned while it is supposed that moral values are too lofty to be a proper field for experiment and invention. It would be hard to find by searching a better example of our thesis that old beliefs have been so mixed with those that are the result of genuinely modern conditions that the word "modern" designates in fact a confused combination of elements all at war with one another.

If things, events, in and of themselves are neither means nor ends, but become one or other or both, under the influence of the social conditions which determine prevailing customs of use and enjoyment, the primary problem is creation of social conditions in which productive activities are such as to be intrinsically rewarding and refreshing and final consummatory activities are such as to be also productive—just as taking and enjoying food is productive of life as well as immediately enjoyed. The problem is one of social arrangements in their economic aspect and, as such, its discussion does not come within the scope of the present chapter. What is relevant to the present theme is the fact that intelligent naturalistic philosophy is by its very nature committed to the doctrine that natural events, as far as they are unaffected by entering into interactivity with human behavior expressive of needs, desires and purposes, lie totally outside of the categories of means and ends, while (and this statement contains the positive significance of the preceding clause) as soon as intentional or deliberate human activity intervenes, the means-consequence category becomes central. And in this statement the words *"any kind"* declare, in effect, that it makes no difference whether the activity in question is prudential, technological, moral, artistic, or scientific. That the first two modes of activity are guided by search for things sustaining the relation to one another of means-ends would, I suppose, be admitted. Opinions differ as to activities classified as moral; it is so generally believed that artistic and scientific modes of action are controlled by another category that the special impact of the thesis advanced concerned them.

XIII. Nature and Human Nature

Students of the history of thought are familiar with the fact that the words *subject* and *object* have undergone a change of signification so great that it is often said to involve a reversal. In Greek philosophy, *subject* was virtually synonymous with *substance*. Etymologically, substance was that [which] *stood* under and supported while *subject* was that that *lay* under and performed the same office of support. It was that in which properties and accidents inhered. The logical (and grammatical) usage in which a proposition (sentence) is said to consist of *subject* and *predicate*, and a certain independence, is attributed to things which are subjects in an ultimate sense, while dependency belongs to that which can only be predicated, recalls this original meaning. The use of "subject" in the expression *subjectmatter* is somewhat akin, as it is used as a synonym for the topic or theme of an inquiry or discussion. While substance and *subject* were words used to designate the thing in its own intrinsic being, *object* and *objectiver*, used to designate it when [it entered] as an existence into the sphere of knowledge; a subject was an object when and only when it was *thrown over against*, or in front of, the knowing mind. The word *object* took on its present prevailing use as a synonym for things or existence generally fairly early. Hobbes used the word in the middle of the seventeenth century as a synonym for "a body without us."[1] Transition from the older meaning to the later was easy and almost imperceptible in the case of object. For all that was needed was simply an elimination of a qualification. *Subject* on the contrary didn't acquire its present meaning, at least in any general philosophic usage, that of the knowing mind or the conscious ego, until the nineteenth century; as far as English thought is concerned, the influence of Kant seems to have been paramount in effecting the change. It is also quite likely that the older sense of *substance* persisted in the case of *spirit*, *soul*, or *consciousness*, while the conditions which brought about the rise of epistemology had rendered problematic the existence of any "external" substance.

The foregoing reference to transformation of the meaning of the words *subject* and *object* is made not for its own sake but to introduce discussion

---

1. Thomas[Hobbes, "Of Sense," in *Leviathan*, bk. 1, ch. 1.]

of the "subjectivism" which is said, with much truth, to be characteristic of modern philosophy. Since, however, the words *subject* and *subjectivism* are loaded with meanings derived from highly technical theories and since the purpose of this book is to discover the cultural source and context of problems and distinctions which have taken on technical philosophical meaning, I shall approach the topic with a quotation from Hume. [Quote missing.]

. . .

The word *humanism* is not used and yet there is a confident revival of the idea that man's nature, human nature, is the point from which all understanding of the world must set out and is that which is served in the end by understanding. The new physical science, the science of minute material particles moving in space according to fixed laws which are expressed in terms of measured extension, duration and motion, dropped, yet shut out, from nature all the qualities which, according to older science, had made that world admirable and noble and life in it of significance and value. From the point of view of this denunciation of [cosmic nature,] human nature provided a refuge. Values and standards of value which did not exist in nature as it was disclosed in physical science were the very substance of *human* nature. Yet human nature was also natural. That phase of modern science which had ruled out the supernatural, which was content with the reign of natural law, persisted in full measure. Human nature provided then an inexpugnable fortress as well as a place of refuge. Human nature is more than close to us; it is the very being of our very selves. It is immediately accessible; or rather it is self-illuminated and self-revealing. Not only did qualities and values expelled from physical nature—now only an *external* world—take up their abode in human nature, but they were so irrevocably and fundamentally at home in this new proper abode and at the same time so directly open to knowledge, that there was at last in our possession the foundation upon which the sciences and arts stand. [*illeg. sentence.*] And if in this interpretation I have suggested [*illeg.*] of optimism not justified in the case of Hume personally, I have not, I believe, gone outside the scope of the vision that inspired the new humanistic "rationalism" of the eighteenth century.[2]

---

2. [From Folder 54/1: "Having thus moved around to his actual starting point, Kant could develop a theory of art and esthetic values and a philosophy of law, social organization and history, which promised continuous constant movement in the direction of the final, though asymptotic, triumphant incarnation of the rational within the sensuous—or an elevation of sense, emotion and desire to the rational and noumenal level.

It would be difficult indeed to find a more thoroughgoing glorification of human nature *in its potentialities* and ultimate promise. Kant provides, in fact, a formulation in highly technical form, utilizing the material and vocabulary of the professional philosophical and

It takes more, however, than a new idea of human nature and a new confidence in its powers to account for the phenomena which, when formulated philosophically, constitute subjectivism. There is needed also a certain specific view of the nature of human nature. And I think I am safe in permitting a passage from John Stuart Mill to stand for this constituent as I have employed the passage from David Hume to stand for the other. "The laws of the phenomena of society are, and can be, nothing but the laws of the actions and passions of human beings united together in the social state. Men, however, in a state of society are still men; their actions and passions are obedient to the laws of individual human nature. Men are not, when brought together, converted into another kind of substance, with different properties; as hydrogen and oxygen are different from water, or as hydrogen, oxygen, carbon, and azote, are different from nerves, muscles, and tendons. Men in society have no properties but those which are derived from, and may be resolved into, the laws of the nature of individual man. In social phenomena the Composition of Causes is the universal law."[3] The idea that human nature is the "capital and center" of all scientific knowledge, of all justified beliefs in any field, is here supplemented by explicit resolution of the facts of human nature into facts about *individuals* in their alleged exclusively individual capacity. And an equally important consideration is that, while

---

metaphysical tradition, of the principle of constant social progress and indefinite perfectibility which animated the Enlightenment, although with an emphasis upon the necessity of a *moral* foundation and directive *moral law* that was quite foreign to French and British representatives of the Enlightenment: A strain that maintained close contact with the classical tradition in a way, however, which gave that tradition a turn that was not indigenous or intrinsic. For the intervening link was the conception of the Law of Nature in its jural aspect, having its source in Roman Stoicism, rather than in Plato, Aristotle or the Neoplatonists. This emphasis upon the juridical side of morals, upon duty and imperative commands, constituted also a connection with the enlightened despotism of Frederick the Great, and also, although indirectly with the pietistic side of the Lutheran dualism—for the dualism of Germany, it took form under Lutheran Protestantism was that of a Pauline conflict of flesh and spirit which was essentially and at bottom a *moral* separation, very different from that of France with its strictly metaphysical and so to say cognitive split of the extended and compound physical and the simple unextended spiritual.

But the promise of the ultimate victory of the cultural over the natural—in the sense of the original sensuous and appetite nature of man—had to have its roots in human nature as it now exists—otherwise no impetus to the steady if infinitely slow movement toward the final goal."]

3. Mill, *Logic*, Book VI, *Logic of the Moral Sciences*, ch. vii sec. 1. With respect to Mill himself, and in justice to him, it should be noted that he is engaged in discussion of another topic than the one under consideration in the text. He is trying to show, in opposition to methods which he considered faulty, that scientific treatment of the social phenomena demands what he calls "concrete deductive method," and the only ground he was able to see for institution of such a method is the postulate just quoted. Nevertheless, the fact that he saw no other ground for the use of the hypothetical deductive method, checked by observation than the one stated and the fact that he thought that ground was so obvious that it might be taken without argument, is sufficient justification, if justification be needed, for the use made of the passage in the further discussion of the text.

it is assumed that serious inquiry is needed in order to discover the laws of "individual" human nature, it is also assumed that the *existence* of individual beings with their natures complete in themselves apart from social connections is so self-evident that no argument on the score is called for.

The sociological considerations requiring attention are then the extraordinary cultural changes indicated first by the shift from cosmic to human nature and secondly by interpretation of the latter in terms of one being isolation of human beings from one another as well as the isolation of the human from physical nature. With respect to both of these points there has been a marked change in the century since Mill wrote and the two centuries since Hume wrote. We live in a time of partial reaction against each of the views that have been presented. Nevertheless while recognition of *social* psychology as an intellectual discipline is an event that must be dated post-Mill, it is still the common assumption that there is a psychology of individuals apart from their association with one another and that, moreover, this variety of psychology is the primary and fundamental science of human nature. The following from a recent writing passage has evidential value: "Man is born into two worlds. One world is a material world and is inarticulate. It cannot talk to man, write him letters of propaganda, or spin theories of social science. Man is interested in this world as the source of the raw materials upon which his bodily welfare depends. The reactions of man in this world and his experiences in it are the subject matter of *individual psychology*. The second world which confronts man is social. He lives in a community of people as well as in a land of corn fields and coal mines. This is so in the very nature of things. By his biological make-up man is destined to be a social creature. The utter helplessness of the human being through his long period of infancy and childhood makes his survival dependent upon the ministrations of other. . . . It is this social world, based on the relations of man to his fellows, which furnishes the subject matter for *social psychology*." The passage is noteworthy in that it leans far in the direction of the dependence of the "individual" upon "social" psychology and in so far reverses the usual tendency. Not only is it stated that man's biological make-up destines him for society, but right after the passage already cited, there is the following express declaration: "The delimitation, or separation, of social from individual psychology is not clear-cut. It is an arbitrary division created by specialists, interested in different problems in the study of man. The reactions of men to their natural environment are colored and determined by the social milieu which has bred them. In turn their reactions to one another are limited by their biological and psychological nature."[4] Certainly the "land of corn fields and of coal mines" (given

---

4. [Daniel] Katz and [Richard] Schanck, *Social Psychology* (1938), p. 1.]

as illustrations of the "world" with which the reactions and experiences that are subject matter of individual psychology) are social phenomena and the adherent of conventional views about psychology may be challenged to point out any reaction to the rawest of raw materials having psychological quality (which, that is, is more than strictly biological) which is not a reaction, itself socially shaped, to a socially conditioned object. It would seem, then, from the authors' own statement, that the separation of social from individual psychology is arbitrary in another sense than that stated in the passage quoted. Instead of being one created by scientific interest in kinds of problems and subject matters—a statement true of the distinction of psychology from physiology—it would seem to be the product of projection of ideas formed in a period that was pre-scientific, with respect to this especial field, into later attempts to be scientific in which the scientific properties of an inquiry are greatly hampered by entanglement with relics of earlier beliefs. In short, the positive aspect of the position taken seems to be that all the phenomena with which psychology, as distinct from physiology and biology, is concerned are transformations of original biological endowment which are effected by the sociological or cultural conditions in which human beings live. Or, stating the matter in another way, the "social world based upon the relations of man to his fellows" is not a world formed when beings who are "individuals" in some non-social or pre-social sense come into connection with one another. It is something which conditions the special relations they sustain to one another and in so doing conditions the reactions and experiences of each one in connection with the "material world" so that the "material world" is, as far as human experience is concerned, interlaced at every point with constituents of the "social world." Development of the position that all psychological phenomena are transformations of biological phenomena, which transformations are effected under the influence of sociological or cultural conditions is, however, a matter for later discussion. The point of immediate bearing upon the present problem is the fact that for a considerable period of time, influential views, popular and philosophical, purporting to be peculiarly modern, have assumed that human nature is such that it is adequately manifested in beings completely separate from one another and inherently independent of one another. The psychology presented in textbooks rests, whether the authors of the books are aware of it or not, upon this assumption. The entire introspective method takes it to be the fundamental postulate of scientific study of human nature. A movement calling itself "behaviorism," popularly supposed to exhaust the behavioral mode of approach, substitutes an isolated organism for the isolated "consciousness" of orthodox psychology, and even isolates the nervous system from the rest of the body, and in connecting, quite properly, thinking with language, more than undoes its good work by reducing the former to specific processes taking place in the vocal apparatus. A philosopher who is usually regarded as ultra-modern, dangerously so according to theological reactionaries, holds that "every object-word, in its primitive use, has an implicit ego-centricity, which the subsequent development of speech renders explicit,"[5] and since the language of physical science consists wholly of words having no ego-centric reference, the theory of knowledge is compelled to deal with the problem set by this contrast. And the assumption of primary ego-centricity is not relieved in this case, any more than in the case of Watsonian behaviorism, by the further assertion that the datum of primary or "basic" propositions (namely, those caused with the maximum of immediacy by perceptive experiences) exists in the brain. Given, however, the premise of isolated individualism, or, to use a word freer of ambiguity than is "individualism," of ego-centricity, there is a problem for philosophy that goes much deeper than the epistemological one just mentioned. Actual subject matter of all the sciences, physical science included, has advanced out of its earlier stage of relative impotency by means of adoption of descriptions in terms of *connections*. What but confusion on a large scale can result when it is held that the ultimate and surest truth, upon which rests the certainty of all actual "object" (subject matter) propositions, is that of total and absolute non-connectedness?

The problem directly before us is, in accord with the fundamental postulate of our entire discussion, the two-fold question of how and why from the cultural point of view the transition was made from cosmic nature to human nature, and how and why the latter was thought of in exclusively ego-centric or "subjectivistic" terms. In point of the facts of actual historical events, the sociological conditions supplying the material for answering the two questions are interwoven and interdependent. They may, however, be considered separately, at least up to a certain point. The considerations that furnish the answer to the question as to why human nature gained centrality has already been given as far as these considerations lie within field proximate to that of philosophical formulation. That is to say, the subject-matter of physical science was such as to exclude from itself all objects and all subject matter having any connection, direct or indirect, with qualities, ends, goods and evils, prudential or moral. Nonetheless the things of the excluded latter sort continued to exist and to determine our conduct to all appearances since they were, by definition, the only prized and desired things in experience. Human nature became then their locus, their abode. The two assumptions (neither of them proved) that knowledge has "Reality"

---

5. [Bertrand Russell, *An Inquiry into Meaning and Truth* (1950) (Routledge 1996), p. 127. Based on Russell's William James Lectures of 1940.]

for its object and that physical knowledge completely exhausts knowledge of the cosmic universe (with the exception of course of human nature) did more than institute complete separation between the subject matters of physics and psychology, or, as it was stated when put in traditional terms, between the physical and the mental. It effected the identification of the strictly human with that called mental and, also, with everything having meaning and value.

Why was it assumed that, in language the polar opposite of that of Juvenal, physical science must count everything human foreign to it unless and until everything distinctively human had been evacuated? And why was it that search for a sure and inexpugnable abode for the qualities which provided life with meaning and value led to creation of ego-centric instead of cosmic metaphysics? Any discussion that tries to answer these questions will find itself landed in the midst of the most striking amalgam of old and new, totally incompatible elements which is presented anywhere at anytime in the cultural scene. I begin with the physical side, that is, with the elimination of constituents of human origin and reference from the material of natural science, in that sense of natural science which excludes psychological and social phenomena, the sense that has come to be the prevailing one. The first reason for this can best be set forth in negative terms. It became evident at an early date in the development of modern science that accepted and institutionally authorized views about nature were conceived in human terms and that this fact operated as an outstanding obstacle in the way of general adoption of the point of view and method type of the new investigators, regarded as the only right one. So generally accepted at the present time is the position of this group that the last sentence seem to be an unduly pompous announcement of a fact now so firmly established as to be commonplace. Formulation and explanation of natural phenomena by means of attribution to nature of purposes and of tendencies to realize purposes is a piece of discarded anthropomorphism. Yet in the sixteenth and seventeenth centuries it was still the habitual and approved mode of procedure. It was so customary that it seemed to representatives of the new science to be *the* greatest single enemy that must be overcome before better methods could secure their opportunity for effective action, opportunity to develop.

This attitude is still so powerful that a statement suggesting the intrinsically human quality of natural science will strike as sheer sentimentalism, or worse, as obscurantism. Such would indeed be the case if the statement in question envisaged that kind of implication of the moral, or human, element in scientific subject matter against which the new science revolted. But in fact philosophical formulation of the grounds, the so-called first premises, and the content of the new physical science went far beyond elimination of moral or human qualities from the immediate subject matter of science, for this elimination was all to the good as subsequent development of science amply proves. For this philosophical interpretation set up a separation of the physical and the human so sharp and complete that it amounted to opposition, a view reflected in that sheer dualism which, in another context, created the epistemological problem already discussed. The causes of the division and dualism did not lie in the methods of the new science as they were actually practiced nor yet in the concrete conclusions forming its subject matter. They came from an extraneous source; namely, from uncritical acceptance of Greek-medieval ideas which were projected into interpretation of the new science although they were themselves both a reflection and a justifying ground of the very attitudes the new science was displacing. We have met these old ideas in discussion of other problems. They are, first, the notion that knowledge, especially in the form of science, has Reality for its object and subject matter, and, secondly, the notion of the dichotomy of the theoretical (in the sense of the intellectual and cognitive) and the practical. When the first notion was permitted to go unchallenged and was projected into interpretations of the conclusions of the new science, the facts designated by matter and by physical took on a strictly metaphysical meaning. It was the legitimate and indeed inevitable descriptive proposition that the characteristic subject matter of physical science is completely devoid of those qualities that render the things of direct experience useful, enjoyable and precious was thus converted into the metaphysical proposition that the "real world" or the "ultimate reality," as it is revealed in natural science, is of a kind that sets it in opposition to the kind of ultimate reality which is immediately revealed in "consciousness" of distinctly human states and processes.

There was a genuine problem involved in the scientific revolution. Instead of being either of an epistemological or metaphysical sort, it was the question of how and why it was that elimination of qualities, ends and values from the subject matter of inquiries into the natural environment did in fact promote so vastly and systematically the progress of science. Such a question would necessarily have developed into an inquiry as to the place of context and function of definitive subject matter of physical science.[6] Such an inquiry would have resulted in distinguishing the subject matter of this particular mode of experience, as interactivity, from that of other modes of experience, esthetic, moral, etc. But it would also have resulted in interest in fruitful interaction of these various modes of experiencing with a view to better control of their occurrence and enrichment of primary experience

---

6. The postulate here is that what the term "physical *world*" actually stands for is "subject matter of physical science," the only possible interpretation of the phrase free from injection of extraneous metaphysical ideas.

in its own processes. Nothing that has been said proves that the outcome of this interest would necessarily have been the institution of positive or constructive intercourse of physical and moral or human subject matters. But at least their complete separation on the ground of fixed a priori principles would have been averted. If conditions were present that favored the humanizing of science and the naturalization of human desires and purposes, they would at least have had an opportunity to operate free from barriers and inhibitions that were supposed to inhere in the very nature of science and to be justified by the first and ultimate truths that were the concern of philosophy.

The Greek-medieval belief that theoretical activity was as much above practical affairs as immutable Being was higher than things which alter and fluctuate added its force in support of the idea that the proper objects of natural science were of such a character as to be inherently opposed to all the traits that are specifically human. Time and chance were only too obviously forever busy in the latter. Uncertainty, struggle, rise and fall, ups and downs, are the common lot of mortals while physics was believed as to penetrate below the changes which appear on the surface of nature so as to demonstrate the majestic reign of universal and immutable law. The further away anything was from practical concern and dependence upon human intervention, the more assured was it.[7] In physical science itself, when the essence and fixed species of earlier cosmology gave way to law, the working of cultural inertia, the force of habit in intellectual matters, is exemplified in the fact that the "essential," or necessary, property of immutability was carried over in full import. Even when scientific inquirers were in fact devoting themselves to discovery of correlation among changes, they still spoke and wrote as if in effect they were only extending the ancient "concept" of fixity from the small number of (heavenly) objects to which it originally applied to all phenomena whatsoever. As a result the principle of "uniformity of nature" took on metaphysical instead of methodological meaning, although in fact even the latter was pertinent in a negative cautionary sense—a kind of warning against introducing the miraculous—rather in a positive one. Putting the matter more specifically, the word "correlation" in the phrase "correlation of changes" was assigned a strictly structural or morphological meaning. In consequence, the notion which was formed of the natural world

---

7. [At this point, Dewey made a note to transfer a block of text, but did not indicate where it was to go: "Even when the medieval view of the corruption and depravity of human nature yielded to a brighter picture, and change in human institutions was thought of as an opportunity for progress instead of as a sign of necessary degeneration, the desirable development was supposed to conduct man to the remote goal of a society in which human affairs would be so completely controlled by fixed law that further change would be as impossible as it would be unnecessary."]

was a nonsensical mixture of two contradictory, logically unrealizable, ideas. On the one hand, it is admitted that all which exists consists of changes. On the other hand, the world, fundamentally, is a completely rigid skeleton whose structural bones keep changes within fixed limits. Immutability of the relation of changes takes the curse off from the cha[*illeg.*]. The conclusion to be drawn, however, is not that the definition of law as correlation of changes is nonsensical or invalid. It is that *correlation* must be understood in a functional sense; that is, to put it baldly, as a means for achieving an end.[8] And while it would go beyond a conclusion that is justified by what it is said to affirm that the end in question is a human one, a functional interpretation at least rooms[9] for the possible rightness of that conclusion. But, upon the whole, the meaning that was given to the words "reign of law" in scientific and philosophical circles was only a technical version of the popular doctrine that phenomena occur in "obedience" to law, this popular notion being, in turn, a dilution of the medieval-Christian theological cosmology form by combination of Hebrew Will and Greek Reason in the idea of God as Creator. The contrast of the picture of the physical world with facts of human nature that were too obtrusive to be ignored is perhaps most evident if we compare the monotonous homogeneity and steadfast repetitions of the natural world in Newtonian cosmology with the vast variety and continuous turmoil of the human scene. The fact that scientific inquirers within the field of human phenomena undertook to reduce their seeming heterogeneity, novelty and unpredictably to expressions of a small number of fixed laws was not at all inconsistent with the fact that the contrast just mentioned was an influential factor in producing the split of nature into physical nature on one side and human nature on the other. It embodies the outcome of the new point of view created by expulsion of human qualities and from the old subject matter of science with retention of the old point of view according to which fixity, and hence the necessity and universality supposed to inhere in fixity, is the gauge of the ultimate "reality" of any existence.

These last pages have to do with the question why the interpretation of the findings or conclusions of inquirers into the environment were taken to be intrinsically and necessarily of a kind opposed to the qualities and properties characteristic of human nature. The answer given, in substance, is that these findings were taken, by those who attempted to give them a philosophical interpretation, out of any and all experiential context, and

---

8. [Dewey handwrote a text insertion, but it is not clear where it was to go: "It is a historical fact that in all metaphysics principles have been able to fulfill their assigned role only by being at once homogeneous with facts and superior to them in dignity."(Georgio Diaz de Santillana, "The Development of Rationalism and Empiricism," in *International Encyclopedia of Unified Science*, vol. 2, no. 8 (University of Chicago Press, 1941), p. 43.]

9. [Dewey's text reads "rooms."]

thereby converted into an independent "external" world. Instead of that designated by the term "physical world" being taken for just [what] it openly is in its own evident terms, namely the system of conclusions reached in physics (leaving the place of physics in human experience a question for further investigation), the system of conclusions was converted into a species of metaphysical Being.

XIV. Experience as Life-Function

I

propose to begin with [a] statement of general principles that may be regarded as postulates of the ensuing discussion; as, that is, of such a fundamental nature that they apply in all the themes and problems that will be dealt with. The meaning of postulates is to be gathered mainly from the consequences flowing from their use; these consequences also furnish the test of their value. What is true in general holds of the postulates that will now be stated. But the latter do not profess to possess any thing approaching the rigor of postulates in mathematical inquiries. Because of the subject matter with which they are concerned they are matters of the method of exposition of a point of view rather than of a method of demonstration. Accordingly as the present statement of this proceeds, attempts will be made to commend and sometimes to [bring] them to the attention of readers by comparing them and their bearing upon certain forms of contrary views that have been and still are influential in human life generally and in philosophy in particular.

The first postulate to be set forth is that, for the purpose of the discussion, *experience* is taken as a synonym for *living* or occurrence of *life-functions*. The second of the postulates is that *living* and *life-functions*, as the words are here used, stand for events whose nature is most clearly and fully presented in *human* living, a fact which is equivalent in general to recognition of the socio-cultural nature of the phenomena dealt with. The third postulate is that *psychological* theory or doctrine is concerned with the analysis and description of just these phenomena, which may also, taken collectively, be named *behavior* (with "human" tacitly prefixed). The fourth postulate, underlying and giving point to the discussion as a whole, is that a correct theory of *experience* in the sense just defined is a necessary means or agency for systematic criticism of the activities, including beliefs, which at the present time constitute any existing form of living (with, be it remembered, socio-cultural understood or taken for granted) and for constructive projection of the general aims and policies of such living. That critical and constructive effort of this kind constitutes *philosophy* is not so much a separate postulate as it is the focal point of the four postulates just set down.

The postulates are about a complex subject matter; and do not pretend to have the independence attributed to mathematical postulates. They overlap and run into one another. For their actual meaning and operating is determined by their bearing upon other and largely contrary views which are influential in contemporary life and which are connected in historical derivation, direct and indirect, from philosophical and psychological formulations of earlier states of social life; states in which scientific methods and conclusions, as well as industrial and political activities, were of a very different character from those now prevailing. Instead then of beginning with exposition of the matter of the first postulate, it will probably be found more enlightening to begin with a discussion that involves, mainly by way of contrast of present conditions, the second and third. Because of the influence of certain special traditions embodied in enduring habitual attitudes, it seems necessary to emphasize at the outset the fact that life-activities are so thoroughly saturated with qualities and properties due to socio-cultural conditions and energies that identification of biotic and biological with the results of physiological analysis and description is thoroughly misleading. The connection of what is involved in this statement with psychology is intimate. Current psychological theory adopted and incorporated conclusions reached in epistemological philosophy. By so doing it gave them a pseudo-scientific standing and thereby became a powerful influence in determining the subsequent course of the present, including philosophy.

. . .

The position here taken is, then, that the environment or "world" with which psychology and psychological subject matter is concerned is *social*, and in a sense in which social is profoundly affected by cultural conditions. It follows that the subject matter of philosophy is social when it uses such words as "mind," "mental," "sensations," "ideas," "reason," "imagination," "thought," "belief," and that all these words, used in analysis and description, stand for life-activities or behavioral events in which the environmental interacting partner can be said to be *physical* only in consequence of an analysis in which qualifying social conditions are deliberately dropped out, because of the nature of the special problem then and there dealt with. The underlying principle has to be applied in both directions. It rules out the existence of a *mental* or *psychical* apart from the socio-cultural in exactly the same way that it rules out the existence of a physical in separation. Anything [that] can be called determinately *psychological* (using that word to avoid the pitfalls of the words mental, intellectual, volitional, affective or emotional) is a transformation of physiological organs and processes wrought by and in socio-cultural conditions.

We shall first consider the environmental aspect. That utensils, furnishing, apparatus, weapons, tools, and machines and all connected arts and technologies having to do with adornment, food, shelter, war and social regulation etc., are energies [modified] in, by and for occupations and interests which are social may, I suppose, be taken for granted. That savage life developed out of that of the anthropoid apes and civilized life out of that of savage and barbarian because of processes and products which are included in what the anthropologist calls culture is, I suppose, also admitted by all those who do not introduce supernatural forces into their account of historical changes. Folklore preceded anthropology in recognition, for example, of artificial control of fire as a factor in determination of human life, and the Greek humanist philosophers who identified invention and technological and civic progress of the arts, with all that marks human life off from that of brutes may be called the first to appreciate the meaning of culture in transformation of natural energies into the home of man. The position here taken involves all these beliefs and more. It holds that the kind of significance exemplified in the everyday fact that *rain* has a different import for the farmer whose occupations directly depend upon [it than] for the city dweller to whom its direct significance is the need for carrying an umbrella or raincoat holds for all natural phenomena. The fact that all natural events were once clothed with properties of an animistic order does not mean the impossibility proclaimed in the theory that early man in his foolishness "projected" a lot of inner psychical events out into a physical world. In that events were directly and without sophistication in their actual social connections or, what is the same thing, without analyzing actual phenomena into terms of the physical; that the doctrines of the classic philosophic tradition, naturalistic in Greek and supranaturalistic in medieval philosophy were derivations from this primitive view has been shown. In this derivation one feature is maintained constant, and it persists wherever physical science has not performed the analytic selection the outcome of which are conclusions that have been *philosophically* summed up and recorded in the phrase "physical world" and the practical importance of which is so great that it is forgotten the idea involved in the phrase *is* philosophical (metaphysical indeed), so that it is taken to be a direct deliverance of common sense—practical importance being the common sense measure of the "real."

The actual fact of the case is that the very notion of a "world" which is physical and nothing but physical is itself a product of social factors. It is an expression of the scientific movement which is most readily identified by mentions of such names as Copernicus, Galileo, Newton, Boyle, Helmholtz, etc.

. . .

Writers who would regard the Cartesian theory of the function of the pineal gland as merely an antiquarian oddity, still endow the brain or even some "center" of it with the power of reaching out into an "external" world (now viewed as existing beyond the skin or perhaps the brain itself) which used to be ascribed to a power named intellect. Such persons should be those open to reception, for attentive consideration at least, of the hypothesis that mental phenomena represent life-functions of a physiological order transformed by interaction with social conditions involving language and its cultural products.

When we approach the issue from the side not of the *environmental* aspect as socially conditioned but of the *organic* as similarly affected, we can get a start in the fact that the human organism has an original or native capacity for making *articulate* sounds and that the structures which exercise this capacity are in such close physical connection with the auditory apparatus that the two mechanisms interact to render acquisition of language a "natural" achievement. In the process of achieving this result, nasal and labial structures of the vocal apparatus are organically modified, in the same way in which the organic structures involved in playing a musical instrument are modified in acquiring that form of skill. The fact that the bodily modification takes place under and because of social conditions as indispensable factors in its production and the counterpart fact that the native organism, when normally constructed, actively lends itself to the interactions by which its modification is effected. Ability to make *articulate* sounds is a prerequisite, on the organic side, of speech; the special point of what has just been said is that this ability, even in its physiological aspect, is a product of intercourse with others. Speech is something more than sounds made and heard, even articulated ones, because it is *intelligible*, a fact which, no matter how intelligibility be defined, is strictly correlative with the fact that its component have *meaning*, however that word be defined. The fact that meanings accrue to sounds during and because of social interaction and social interception gives the *hypothesis* that language as a socio-cultural medium is the source of the existence of meaning and of understanding-intelligibility factual standing; it satisfies the requirement that a hypothesis be made out of subject matter that is capable of independent observation. It would seem as if those who reject the supernatural component (the material "soul" and its various heirs and assigns) were at least committed to applying the hypothesis to analysis and description of all psychological phenomena until they arrive at an insuperable obstacle to its application.

The fact that definition of language as "expression or communication of *thought*" sets forth a secondary and derived function of language and not its primary office supplies indirect confirmation of the view that the social interaction of which language is an inherent constituent is the observationally verifiable foundation of *meaning* and *understanding*.[1] The statement, found in so many texts, that "language is communication of thought," of ideas, etc. (or worse yet that it is the *means* of expressing it) sets forth the notion of writers whose pre-occupation is so much that of *written* discourse that they have forgotten that language is primarily *spoken*, and is addressed not to persons at a distance until the phone was invented—not persons remote in space and time (as is literature and "letters") but to an immediate circle. When these ordinary and primary traits of speech are held in mind, it will be seen that the primary original and basic function of language is influencing and regulation of behavior of beings who are engaged in conjoint undertakings of friendly or hostile, cooperative or competitive quality.[2]

---

1. [From Folder 53/15: "This double charge of the present is expressed in language. Because the present carries what is going and bears and brings to birth what is coming, the present represents. It is momentous, not momentary. Everything called significance, meaning, value, import and importance, is bound up with the saying and telling in which the ability of the present to represent becomes present.

We take communication and language for granted and make a mystery, a problem, of knowledge. But it is from the event of language that knowledge and every event with which words—whether verbs, nouns, adjectives and adverbs indicative of mind—are associated stem."]

2. [From ibid.: "[In light of contemporary quantum theory,] it suffices to note that physical "elements" no longer exist and act in a void but that every scientific equation is a formulation of the [main] connection with one another and *as* so connected. (footnote: See A. F. Bentley's _____; Whitehead's writings are exceptional, almost unique in philosophy for its explicit perception of the many differences made in the traditional theory of experience and its relation to natural events because of the theory of physical relativity.) There is even a sense in which an electron is said to exist (act) "everywhere"—there can be no more extreme statement of interconnectivity. In the case of plant organisms, modern ecology has substituted intimate association, amounting almost to solidarity of life, for independent isolation. Zoology has brought out the significance of swarms, packs, herds, flocks and hives, to say nothing of symbiosis, for the behavior of unitary organisms. Recent physiological research has radically altered the earlier theory of cellular activity and structure, and while the idea of subordination of structural and morphological consideration to those which are co-functional has not completely won the day, the strictly anatomical standpoint has nothing like the monopoly of the field or prestige it once had. All along the line, the fact that everything that exists is in continual interaction with other things compels revision of the earlier idea of that which is *individual* and profound modification of the psychological and philosophical theories based therein. With respect to human beings, it would seem as if the facts of sexuality, reproduction, thoroughgoing dependence of the young, would have presented at any time the rise of the "individualistic" theories that had had such influence. The fact that such things were not even noticed is a tribute, not a happy one, to the power of ideas, when they are allowed to become fixed, to regulate observation to the point of preventing it. A variety of theories have

Realization of this basic fact should go far to dispel the notion that "thought" is something having an independent prior readymade existence which is externally garbed with words in order to be able "to go into society." This latter notion, derived in the main from scholarly and scholastic pre-occupation with written language, becomes then cause and effect of the category of "inner" and "outer" which underlies that "mind *and* matter," "subject *and* object," "individual *and* social." When there comes to be widespread realization of the force of the statement that is forthwith quoted there will also be an equally extensive revision of the category of inner mental and outer physical and all its congeners. "The meaning of words consists in what they achieve in concerted action, the indirect handling of the environment through direct action upon other organisms."[3]

What has been said does not imply that sociology is a branch of psychology nor yet that the latter has the same subject matter as sociology. The postulate involved, stated first negatively or by way of contrast, is that there is no separate order of existence which is the subject matter of psychology because of its inherent mentalistic or psychical nature. It involves thoroughgoing denial of the notion that there is one existential kind of events or "objects" with which physics deals and another kind with which psychology is concerned. It would eliminate from psychological description and theory the attitudes and categories that were uncritically taken over by it as an alleged science from

---

been advanced since the asocial theory of human beings in their severalty came into vogue to account for their coming together and forming society. Need of defense and the economic advantages of living and working together have been among the causes adduced. These special agencies are relevant to explanation of how and why association took on this or that special form. But there is no more need to search for reasons why men live, work and play in association with one another than there is to explain why "atoms" are themselves associations which enter into more inclusive associations. The only "reason" is that human beings, like chemical elements, are made that way. This fact does not in any way deny the distinctive character of human grouping nor reduce the immense significance of the features they uniquely possess. In a metaphorical sense, hydrogen may be said to "partake" in formation of, say, water, and conditions intervening between sun and earth to "communicate" light from the former to the latter. But *partaking* in the first case does not have the meaning which *participation* has as the bond of union in human society. Nor is *transmission* identical with sharing of meanings, with mutual understanding, and *communication* is precisely this sharing. A *community* is established by making certain attitudes, outlooks, beliefs, traditions, *common*, and communication is the process which institutes this result."]

3. Cited from the *Social Encyclopaedia* article by B. Malinowski titled "Culture" mentioned previously. Compare with this statement, the treatment of language by the same author in Ogden and Richard's *Meaning of Meaning*. If the point made in this *Appendix* had been utilized as the foundation of the doctrine set forth in its main text, the content of the latter treatment would have been much sounder than it is, and the harmful influence it has exerted upon subsequent "semantic" theories might have been averted. The extraordinary feature of the latter theories is that they treat the primary or social function of language, direction of conjoint activities participated in by a number of human beings as if it were something objectionable, if not quasi-pathological.

the epistemological philosophy of the seventeenth and eighteenth century. For acquaintance with historical events shows that persons who had no direct interest in the problem of how an immaterial "subject" could know and act upon material "objects" who often, indeed, expressed scorn for such problems as "metaphysical" in nature, nevertheless felt entitled to assume as a *fact* the existence of an independent inner region or "realm" which provided the material for psychology. Upon the positive side, it affirmed in what has been said that psychological phenomena are biological phenomena which have been so intimately colored or rather dyed by socio-cultural conditions as to have taken on the properties that mark human behavior and experience, qualifying them so thoroughly that they constitute the distinctions and relations made familiar in psychological literature.

Discussion has thus in effect come around to the first postulate mentioned in this chapter: Namely, that behavior in the sense of life-activities or life-functions is what is designated by "experience." While we cannot understand or correctly analyze the material collectively summed up in the word "experience" without taking account of the fact that life in its cultural aspects incorporates and qualifies biological functions, it is also true that understanding we have of psychological phenomena depends upon knowledge of general features of the kind specifically biological sciences are concerned with. For whatever is true of life in this selective narrower sense is true of the wide and inclusive sense; namely, human and social life, it being a matter of linguistic convention of convenience that "biological" is usually given a meaning that is restricted to what has physiological connections. The first thing requiring notice is that life-activities are cooperative interactivities of component factors to which the names "environmental" and "organic" apply. Were it not for the abiding effect of the doctrine of subject-object, inner-outer, subjective-objective, it would not be necessary to note explicitly that walking involves the earth as well as legs; breathing, the air as well as lungs; digestions, food-stuffs as well as organs for swallowing, transforming, circulating and eliminating, etc. The fact that inquiry is best conducted by means of division of labor, which is finally carried to a high degree of specialization, does not [_____] separateness or isolation of existence upon matters selected for study. The structures and processes constituting the respiratory apparatus can be investigated with a minimum of direct reference to the air and the muscular-nerve mechanism of locomotion is profitably investigated without explicit reference to the environing conditions that enable walking to take place by provision of resistance and support. In these cases, no one would deliberately suppose that the possibility of fruitful independent study is an equivalent or guarantee of independent existence on the part of the organic conditions involved. In their capacity of being *environmental*, exactly the same thing is true of atmosphere and of earth, or whatever, walked upon, or of water as the medium that enters directly into maintenance and conduct of life-operations.

In short, the terms organism-environment are simply *generalized* names which serve to summarize, condense, unify, a large number of particular interactivities, such as air-respiratory processes, ground-locomotor apparatus, food-stuffs-digestive-tissues etc. They do not stand for two separate and independent things which then somehow come into connection with one another and produce life-functions. On the contrary, in their status and capacity of being organic and environmental, they stand for results of analysis of primary life-activities. It is, undoubtedly, an easier matter to appreciate this fact in the case of what "organic" stands for than it is in the case of "environmental." Long ago Aristotle remarked that an eye is an eye in actuality only when engaged in seeing; since his time scientific inquiry had made evident the nature of the environing conditions that participate in actual seeing. What was said about the eye can be said about the *organism*; it is only *potentially*, save as [it is] actively engaged in interactivities with environment. Those who question this statement are those who believe in [the] antecedent existence of a vital "force." The present argument holds "life" is not entity or force; that life is *living*, and living consists of a number of interrelated activities or functions in which environing energies are operatively involved.

There will, in all probability, be more hesitation in the case of "environment" in acknowledging the fact that it is but a general name for a set of interacting conditions. The use of the noun, *environment*, instead of the adjective, *environmental*, is a contributing factor to misconception, as happens in the case of many nouns that seem to make an "entity" out of conditions which exist only in processes of active connection with other modes of energy. The use of "environment" as an equivalent of "world" in a sense in which *world* is wholly independent of life-operations is not, however, merely a matter of hypostization. There are certain properties of environmental conditions involved in human living that contribute to the misinterpretation. Advance in the scale of complexity of life-activities is a matter of extension of the spatial-temporal range of environing conditions. The conditions that are involved in the living of unicellular organisms are so nearly homogenous as not to take account of conditions at a distance in space or time. As organic structures are more and more differentiated, maintenance of the unity of functioning (without which living ends in death) is accomplished only by active inclusion of conditions more and more spatially and temporally remote. As an illustration, consider the effect of development of distance-receptors, eye and ear, as incidental with extension of the environing conditions that operate in the case of organisms having only structures of direct connect; consider the extension of environmental conditions that marks human living in its dependence upon recollections and memories, and the effect of written language in enabling human beings to "live" in ancient Athens, medieval Europe and far away South Sea Island or Arabia. Every new technology institutes a widening of environment. Knowledge of such considerations as these makes us aware that no fixed limit can be set to what is designated by environment. We are aware that it will overtly and explicitly extend further in space and time in the future than it does now. Use of the word as an equivalent of *world* in general, the *universe*, etc., marks a kind of confused recognition of indefinite extensibility. The force of the considerations just noted is increased, moreover, by discovery of the fact that conditions which are not openly and directly involved in existing life-activities are indirectly involved. It is discovered that the actual environment at a given time is not bounded by the horizon's edge or the arch of the sky: that, in fact, these conditions which are *immediately* present are the product of environing conditions are explicit or noted only because of conclusions of scientific inquiry reached much later. This sense of indefinite extension of "environment" is perhaps the chief factor in producing the notion that the things and events of "environment" can be viewed and defined as if they were independent of activities analytically referred to as "organism." For ordinary purposes this treatment of what is potential does no particular harm. When it is erected into the notion of two separate kinds of world, one *outer* and one *inner*, one *physical* and the other *psychological*, it continues and projects the harm done by the old beliefs, of cultural origin, that generated epistemological problems.[4]

The words "environmental" and "organic" are highly generalized, and to be available for interpretation of psychological phenomena have to be resolved in the numerous and diversified concrete inter-activities for which they stand. Even such as air and respiratory mechanism are too "general" to be useful save as it is noted that chemical and physiological inquiry resolves them into interactions of a large number of more minute processes having intricate and subtle connections with one another. Interpretations of experience in its scientific phase is given to ignoring the fact that in every case inquiry starts from a gross qualitative occurrence:—the rusting-of-iron water-engaged-in-quenching thirst, as medium-of-movement-of-rafts boats, or of-cleansing. The use of hyphens here is but a clumsy method of suggesting the incapacity of analytic language like English to name primary events in their experienced qualitative gross or macroscopic quality.[5] We

---

4. What is here said about the indefinite extensibility of the environmental is applicable, in another context, to the theme of "possible experience" as an inclusive category.

5. Languages of the "_____" type would, if they could be employed, serve the purpose of designating events of this primary occurrence. But they would be correspondingly unfitted

are so accustomed to the results of analysis of these gross "wholes" (analyses that are "practical" as well as scientific) that we are inclined to regard them as the "realities" of which primary events, are more or less artificial products, known in traditional philosophical discourse as mere *appearances* in contrast with *realities*. The original and direct function of such analyses is facilitation of control of the occurrence of gross events. *Fire*, for example, depends for its controlled experiential presence, or existence, on our ability to treat its occurrence as an interactivity of smaller interactivities, such as, say, the act of twirling a hard pointed stick in environing conditions of rotten wood, or the act of striking flint on steel to make sparks in close proximity to tinder. Ability to regulate, to guide and direct, the ongoing course life-experience, as well as furtherance or prevention of occurrence of this or that special event, depends upon breaking down the actual total event into a number of lesser events. But the history of human beliefs shows that two connected errors have accompanied the performance of this necessary task. As just suggested, the events which are analyzed into more minute events have been assigned a secondary degree of "reality," and the interactions in virtue of which the lesser ones constitute the original gross event are lost from view, or, what is even more harmful, are treated as themselves "simple" or elementary static entities.[6] It is one of the functions of philosophy to re-call us from the results of analyses, which are made for special purposes, to the larger, if coarser and in many respects cruder, events which alone have primary existence.[7]

The point just made is summed up in the proposition (i) that what is designated by "experience" is identical with life-activities or functions, and (ii) that these functions when analyzed are found in every case to be interactivities of factorial or operative components, which, when they are generalized, are referred to as respectively environmental and organic. Following out clews which are provided by examination of life-processes in their (or simpler biological) aspect, attention naturally goes to the temporal, biographic, historic continuum they constitute, a continuity which, however, for reasons that will be adduced, has to be described in connection with periodic interruptions or "breaks" that occur in its ongoing process. That living *is* a going, and an

---

for conveying distinctions and generalizations of a scientific nature.

6. The fact that *scientific* inquiry, that of the laboratory, as distinguished from that of the man in the street, store and factory, takes precisely these interactive connections for its distinctive subject matter is shown in a later chapter. But unfortunately the same zeal for isolation persists, with the result that philosophic reflection has treated them, as presented in scientific conclusions, as a special kind of "objects" contrasted to the point of opposition with ordinary things.

7. It is one of the merits of C. S. Pierce that he appreciated so thoroughly this aspect of philosophy. I quote the following: [Quote missing.]

ongoing, concern is as nearly *prima facie* evident as anything can be. It is worthwhile, however, to consider not merely the obvious fact that living endures from conception to death and from generation to generation, but *why* this trait has to be brought conspicuously to the front in the account given of it, and also *what* are some of its main features. Because living is an interactivity of environmental and organic factors, it involves phases that, relatively speaking, are *active* and *receptive*, and to which may be given the names *doing* and *undergoing*. Since activities which go on involve environmental conditions in their occurrence a crucial, comparatively slight modification of the latter necessarily takes place. In terms of the organic energies involved, we say they *do* something to the latter. In terms of participating environmental energies, *they* do something back; some aspect of the change produced in the conditions involved in the life of a given creature (conditions beyond the superficies of the body), effects change in what is undergone by the organism. The latter has to accept or receive, in some degree and aspect, the consequences of what it does in and hence to environing conditions. Change of position is regarded (correctly enough for practical purposes) as a change occurring in the organism rather than as a modification of the environment, since running out of danger or running into it by jumping out of the frying-pan into the fire, has such obvious beneficial or injurious consequence for the particular life concerned. But descriptive analysis has to note that the change effected in, say, locomotion, is an actual modification of the actual, the existing, environment; and that only because *conditions* in their capacity or function of *being environmental* have been modified is the organism concerned any better off or any worse off than it was before. A change that was completely limited (for its entire duration) to within the epidermis or shell of an animal would have no bearing upon its living as an ongoing affair. Changes occur in circulatory and digestive processes which may, for special purposes, be treated as taking place only inside a given body. But they count as processes of a live-creature only when they are viewed in connection with interactivities with environing conditions in which they latter undergo change and in consequence of which organic conditions, the agencies of subsequent interactivity, also suffer change, and so on continuously until a given life-processes terminates in death. In short, the temporal continuum of life-activities, when it is analyzed and described in terms of organic and environmental factors, must be regarded as continuous reciprocal doing-undergoing, in a sense in which the hyphen stands for inherent connection, in *both* directions, between what the two terms stand for.[8]

---

8. When the connection is successful—that is, effects maintenance of environmental-organic conditions that interact to continue life-operations, there exists the fact called *adaptation*. It suffices here to say that adaptation describes the traits of an actually occurring event

The more enduring phase of the modification that takes place upon the organic side constitutes *habit*, the latter being the name given to the conjoint modification and its continued operative existence. It takes the form of habituations, getting used, accustomed, wonted, becoming familiar to and with, environing conditions in the relatively passive, receptive *undergoing* aspect of living as interactivity and skill, ability, faculty, in its relatively outgoing, *doing* aspect. In another context there is much that might fruitfully be said about formation of habits, especially about the minor role of repetition (which is a consequence rather than a source of their formation) and the primary role of achievement, or success in accomplishment. I content myself at this stage of discussion with saying that operation of the latter factor in forming habitual attitudes has not only been much understated (mostly because illustrative material has been selected from scholastic and industrial conditions that are irksome) but has been treated as a peculiar problem, difficult to explain. The reason for the latter view is, of course, that the start is made from and with premises which substitute a number of isolated events, as simple independent units, for the actual life-continuum.

The point directly pertinent in the present discussion of habit, context, is that (i) it represents the modification which an organism undergoes in connection with what it does, and that (ii) it constitutes, on the side or aspect of organic conditions, the temporal continuum of living. Through habits, attitudes, dispositions, skills, formed in the process of interactivity with definite actual environmental conditions, past environmental conditions become conditions that continue to operate in future life-situations in which they are not directly there-and-then involved.[9] The counterpart modification of environing conditions is exhibited more conspicuously when we expressly observe human life-activities with respect to the socio-cultural environment involved than when we take account of the interactivities constituting the life of "lower" creatures. Birds make nests, beavers make dams, etc. But for the most part environmental changes made in the case of the animal of the last named kind have to do with changes of environing positions and locations. The live activities of human beings are directed to effecting enduring material environmental changes, and as intelligence develops these modifications, are planned with respect to their consequences upon later, much later, life-activities with respect to promotion of certain kinds

wherever life is going on; that any view which makes a problem *in general* out of the fact of its occurrence suffers from infection with false, artificially produced premises; and that *adaptation* is no more of an organism *to* an environment than they are of the latter to the former.

9. The bearing of this fact upon the existence of recollections and anticipations hardly needs to be pointed out. It is perhaps advisable, however, to mention that "retension" is not some kind of separate force or event but is simply a name for organic modifications wrought, with respect to their enduring or temporally continuous operation.

and averting and minimizing certain other kinds. One has only to point to invention and making of tools as means for having at ready command agencies for effecting future changes when the latter are needed as well as their use in occasioning immediately desired alteration of surrounding conditions. The fact that the difference between states of savagery, barbarism and civilization is constituted by the presence of cumulative consequences of prior life-activities in the institution of changes in environment that are available in here-and-now life actions should suffice to indicate the nature and importance of change in the environmental interactive factors produced in the very ongoing of the interactivity which is living.

Re-adaptations are almost continuously required in the course of living. Changes which are made in environmental and organic conditions alike may serve the needs of nearby conditions without meeting those which are remote, yet performance of actions that accomplish the first result may eventuate in plunging an organism into conditions for which habits formed in earlier conditions afford no preparation; conditions in which indeed the two sets of interacting energies are at odds with each other as far as smooth continuance of ongoing activities is concerned. Only in thoroughly stabilized and uniform conditions do activities that are adaptive at one time continue to serve maintenance of life. Unicellular organisms living in a homogeneous imagination do not have to face crises or struggle with emergencies. The more complex is an organism the greater is the variety of activities in which it engages and the more intricately are its diverse actions bound up with one another. Its environment is correspondingly spread out in time and place and contains a similar variety of factors which sooner or later have to be dealt with.

The net outcome is that the course of living is constituted as a rhythm of interactions that are balanced and unified and interactions that are in a state of imbalance and tension. Necessity for coordination is in direct ratio to the amount of differentiation of structures and division of work in existing operations. The greater the number of different structures the more intricate is the matter of their interdependence, and hence the greater the ease with which they are thrown into a state of imbalance. There is illusion further from fact than the notion that advance, progress, marks a movement into smooth seas and fair winds. Every movement that effects greater differentiation of organic and environmental conditions creates of necessity new problems of effective adjustment. Some things become easier and more automatic, but environing conditions become more difficult and the working mechanism is more easily thrown out of gear. Only when the new situation is treated as a challenge to courage and to inventive intelligence is the conclusion other than that all is vexation and vanity of spirit. And upon the whole the record of human history is the record, on the lower level, of stoical accommodation, in the attitude that what can't be helped must be endured, and, on the higher level, of responding when possible with good humored creation of new devices and methods, and when not with elevation of the scene to the heights of tragedy. However, it is not the extreme cases which here concern us. The point is the fact that states of imbalance or disequilibration are recurring normal events in the life-activity of human beings, and that they are attended with characteristic psychological phenomena. Every emotional quality is, for example, a manifestation of such a condition. Moreover, it is capable of being treated as a *sign* of an actual event just as much as is a sensory quality, the exclusive attention of philosophical and psychological students of knowledge to sensory-qualities, sensa, etc., notwithstanding. Foresight, anticipation and planning are directly connected with the intervening occurrence of these critical conditions.

. . .

But in any case it is the latter conditions which take the initiative in reconstruction or re-adaptation. In this ambivalent capacity, that of being obstructed with respect to activity then-and-there pre-ceding and being initial and initiating with respect to the turn taken by immediately succeeding activity, some energies are demarcated as organic. Other energies have the ambivalent status of being obstructive (thereby demanding re-adjustment) and the material conditions by means of which an indicated change of direction can be carried through in interactivity with initial activities. These features serve to demarcate certain energies as environmental.[10]

It should be plain from what has been said that the *distinction* of organic and environmental is not original and primary, but is the result of an act of *distinguishing* the ground for which is provided in the re-adjustive phase of an organic activity. The direct ongoing of life-functions knows of no *distinction* much less a difference amounting to a division. Even when it is said that life as a going concern is an *integration* of energies capable of being referred to respectively organic and environing conditions, there is danger that what is said will be understood to say that originally two different kinds of things somehow manage to be so thoroughly combined in an activity that the result may be called an integration, the word implying prior differentiation. What is actually meant is radically different. Living *is* the unity or integration; differentiations occur phasically and periodically within it and mark times of readaptation when continuance of life-activities requires change of immediate, then-and-there, direction. Because *awareness* in general is most acute in these recurrent periods, during these periods

10. The discussion in *Logic: The Theory of Inquiry*, pp. 27–34, may be compared with the foregoing. [LW 12: 33-41.]

we become emphatically aware of factors that are counteractive to one another at that particular time and yet have to be brought in to co-operating connection—as we walk for a long time without special awareness of either ground or legs and become aware of them both when something novel and unexpected emerges in the course of a walk, and as we are *differentially* aware of the mechanism of a motor car when learning to drive and when something goes wrong with its functioning and at the same time have to give special or differential attention to skills and resources that belong to us as initial means of re-institution of over-smooth functioning. Having become accustomed in these phases of intervening activity, in process of re-adapting to the distinction and these times being those of acute *immediate* psychological import (emotional, volitional, intellectual, in customary vocabulary) we form the habit of carrying over the distinction into all cases. Practically speaking, no harm results, and maintaining the distinction is a positive resource in [the] study of special problems. The great harm is done when this distinction, entirely genetic-functional in nature, is erected into a difference of kinds of existence.

The point that is last made should be suggestive of the potential in philosophical value of the term *experience* when it is used as a synonym for "life-functions" and life-activities as these have been described. That the word is dangerously ambiguous is obvious to every student of the history of thought. Indeed, analysis of it in the foregoing terms of biological activities (as culturally transformed) is engaged in as a means of avoiding some of these dangerous historic confusions and distortions. The last point made is suggestive because it indicates the value of having a term of comprehensive scope, one, moreover, which is not merely general or of extensive application but which is capable of special qualification as and when needed. "Experience" does not designate a kind of stuff, and most certainly not of mentalistic stuff. It designates an inclusive frame of reference. As such it serves both as warning and as guide. "Experience" as the most inclusive category of philosophic discourse is a warning that every distinction and relations that figures needs to be placed where it emerges in the set and system of ongoing life-functions and with respect to the way it operates in this connection. In its comprehensive function, *experience* denotes organic-environmental interactivity, and as a "double-barreled" term, in standing for both modes of experienc*ing* and that which is experienc*ed* it is capable of being used to protect philosophical discourse from that violent disjoining of the two which characterizes the entire epistemological tradition of modern thought: The subject-object end-term categorical relation. It may help us keep in mind that we are not just angry but mad-at-something the "something" in question being an intrinsic part of anger; that we do not just "think" and have "ideas" but think-of-and-about something and that "ideas" are suggestions or something which is nonetheless existent because future in time.

With respect to needed qualifications of the general term, we are habituated to discriminating *subject matters* in accordance with the ways or manners in which they are experienced. The fact that the influence of traditional psychology, based upon splitting up "experience" into two independent orders of existence, has resulted in speaking of what is thought of as concept and what is seen or heard as a percept, and what is directly sensed as a sensation (or is now more usual) as a *sensum*, does not destroy the values that reside in ability to discriminate experienced subject matters according to determination, *through inquiry* (not by alleged introspective magic) of the way it is experienced: that is, of the special psychological conditions engaged in a given interactivity. I doubt if any one would deny that it is practically and intellectually an aid to know that *this* subject matter came to be experienced by way of a dream; *that* one by hearing and now by recollection of what was heard, and *the other* subject matter by an experience in which the eyes and optical apparatus directly took part. Such characterizations are no part of what is originally experienced. They are as additive as is description of a man as a thief or a chronic loafer, or as is telling a child for the sake of its possible effect upon his future conduct that an act he has performed is *greedy* or *polite*. In one case as the other, the name given is [the] designation of an event in terms of connections, [the] grasp of which serves to provide great power of control over the occurrence and non-occurrence of the given event and, indirectly, of events of its kind.

It is a commonplace of scientific practice that "observation" occupies a privileged position and plays a crucial role. The proper way in which to form a correct idea of the nature of observation is, without doubt, to study (to "observe") observation as it takes place in best regulated cases of scientific activity: The astronomer in the observatory, the biologist at his microscope, the physicist in his laboratory, the geologist with his rocks, etc. But there are still so many pitfalls present in [a] report of what is then noted that the more extensively we can discriminate observing from other specified ways of experiencing and the more systematically we can unite with other ways in a comprehensive view, the less likely are we, to put it mildly, to go astray, in the account given of just how observed material functions in scientific inquiry and what are the conditions of origin of this material most conducive to its effective functioning. For example, it is still the usual thing to find "observation" analyzed and described, even in cases supposedly having to do with it as it occurs in scientific practice, in terms which utterly fail to take account of such things as its guidance by a sense of a problem, of the operative presence of need for an idea or hypothetical interpretation, of need for a particular kind of evidential data and a specific kind of subject matter as test of an idea. It may be that in the future we shall eliminate the remnants of epistemological psychology to such an extent that a systematic theory of experiencing, in which different ways of experiencing are discriminating and systematically interrelated, will not be required. That time has not yet come.

Irrespective of the matter of the use made of experience, it is needful, for both protection against errors that have been embedded in tradition and for guidance, that an extensive background and foreground be taken into account in all psychological affairs that are used in connection with philo-sophic discourse. For views that originated a long time ago in philosophies (which were themselves controlled by much older beliefs and attitudes) made their way into psychological doctrines and the latter were supposed to have "scientific" non-philosophical status and warrant. Thence they find their [way] back into philosophy and are used without even the remotest sense of need for criticism, to say nothing of thoroughgoing revision, as standard means of philosophical inquiry. There are times when I believe that the chief obstacle to genuine advance in philosophy has this source; these times are when I read writings of fine minds, exercising great academic influence, still engaged in threshing over the husks of epistemology. The need for reference to what I have called foreground and background can be met only by a method which is simultaneously genetic-functional. The method is genetic in that it attempts to place the subject matter dealt with in the context of the conditions under which it comes into existence—as astronomer, paleontologist, physiologist, and pathologist habitually do as the means of bring particular observed facts under assured control. The method is functional in that it indicates what the factual subject matter under examination *does* specifically when it comes into existence. Such words as *origin, genetic, functional, operational*, carry associations which readily lead to misunderstanding. The best safeguard I know of is to make sure that the subject matter under consideration, that to which the words apply, is inherently temporal and temporally continuous. If that condition is satisfied, there is hope that it will be seen that whatever is the matter under special investigation it has to be placed in connection with what goes before—a genetic reference—and what comes after, a functioning reference. Isolation of subjects from the context in which alone psychological events happen and have the properties which give them their significance is the curse of traditional and still prevailing psychological subject matter—at least as it figures in philosophic discourse. I can but believe that even the psychological specialist at work in his laboratory with animals or with per-sons who are mentally and morally disturbed will do more effective work when they have got rid of the burden they took over thinking it is a genuine heritage of intellectual wealth. Present-day philosophers would seem to owe their psychological colleagues at least a set of general ideas that will serve as instrumentalities in replacement of those that unwary psychologists have unwittingly borrowed from them. It is doubtful whether before recent advances of physics—in "field" theories—of biology, anthropology and other cultural subjects, there would have been available the resources required. Given the intellectual tools they have now put in our hands, we are in possession of the conditions that have to be met and satisfied in construction and use of a genetic-functional method.

II

Experience in the sense of the continuing course of life-activities is marked by alternation of phases. Looked at in the large and in their more extreme manifestation, the material of one phase supplies the stuff out of which are formed the dream of the Golden Ages that blessed the remote past and the Utopias and Millenia that are to come in the faraway future. Less mythologically, they provide the form, the framework, which is called an ideal when it is furnished with a content. In their more intense form they are the energy, zest and source of courage that are more than animal. The other, the alternating, phase is that of effort, of struggle. Contrast gives them and the times of unity their poignancy. Their occurrence is the stimulus and challenge to achieve again the satisfactions of unity and harmony. The latter brings with them something other than bovine contentment because they emerge as completions of struggle, as consummations won through conquest of obstacles, just as their own occurrence gives the times of effort what qualities of adventure and romance they possess.

What is of greater importance for a general theory of experience is that it is the predominant subject matter of given phases of harmonious interactivities which provide intervening times of interruption and need for readjustment with materials which impose the special demands they have to meet and set their concretely actual problems. For these times are just periods of interruption of continuity in general; they are interruptions of a continuum having its own uniquely constituted material. When one thinks of any actual course of experience as it is manifested in a given biography and in a given period of history of some actual social group, one can only be impressed with the power of doctrinal opinions, once they become currently accepted and a matter of custom, not just to distort recognition of actualities but to conceal them from any need for being recognized, taken into account, or even looked at. When one views even in the most general way the enormous diversity of experiences which the actual scene presents, the total incapacity of a small set of sense-data, no matter how supplemented by simple ideas and their combinations, to furnish means for constructing anything approaching in the remotest way the movement of events would seem clear beyond peradventure. The problem with which epistemologists have concerned themselves, that of deriving "physical objects" and the distinctive facts of natural science from sense-data and their most extensive complementary affiliates, pales into triviality compared with the task of constructing anything remotely resembling the scene of human history out of psychological materials which are available when these materials are taken in isolation from the course of primary life-activities.

The most conspicuous application of what has been said is its bearing upon a matter previously discussed—the notion that there is such a thing as "individual" psychology[11]; that there are events of a psychological character apart from interactivities in which socio-cultural conditions constitute the environment. The point is mentioned here, however, in its bearing upon the concrete subject matter, as to both material and operations, involved in readjustments. Adaptation, a degree of unification of interacting factors sufficient to maintain living [as] a going concern, is the primary fact and the content, as distinct from the form, of the critical phases of a course of experience as determined by the contents or subject matter of the unified phases. And the same is true, of course, of the agencies and procedures of the actions engaged in restoration of a unified phase. Situations of consummation determine the level on which the course of experience goes on; it determines the character of the ends to be attained in efforts at re-adaptation. As a generalization, this statement means only that a fish "aims" to live as a fish, an ox as an ox, a tiger as a carnivorous animal, a savage as a savage, and a civilized being as a civilized being according to the degree and quality of civilization that has entered into making him what he is. More specifically, it means that while only a general theory of experience can supply leading principles to serve as the instrumentalities of inquiry, subject matter must be derived from observation of social situations. Psychological theory can provide [the] framework but not [the] filling.

III

It has been pointed out that analysis (conducted for [the] sake of effectively dealing with special problems) resolves "experience" into certain ways of experienc*ing* and into certain subject matters experienc*ed*, the former constituting the organic components that dominate in an interactivity while the latter are environmental factors that enter most directly and conspicuously into the interactivity undergoing analysis. It was also pointed out that these

---

11. Unless of course whatever is denoted by "individual" is itself described in "social" terms.

considerations dictated the use in philosophic analysis of a method that can be described as *genetic-functional*. No matter what the problem may be, approach to its solution depends upon ability to state the conditions of experienced subject matter under which the material constituting the particular problem arises and the consequences that ensue, also in terms of experienced material in experiences. In short, the phrase "genetic-functional method" is a way of indicating, first, that philosophic inquiry gets ahead by placing the material of its problems in a *context*, and secondly, of announcing that this context consists of the material of prior and subsequent life-functions as interactivities. In so far, the method is not unlike that followed in every scientific inquiry, for any reasonable formulation of the "cause-effect" relation—which is the leading category of scientific description and interpretation—treats it as taking phenomena otherwise isolated and placing them in [a] temporal-spatial context that has continuity of extent.

What characterizes philosophic use of the common method is concern for the more general and enduring constituents of the context, those which are neglected and left unformulated in the formulations of specialized scientific statement, and moreover are left tacit just because they are so lasting and common that they are taken for granted. It is the business of philosophic analysis and description to make explicit the connections of specialized materials with what I shall call, without, I hope, too much risk of misunderstanding, the "world of common sense"—that is to say, the events and transactions which constitute everyday life experiences.[12] The social aspects and elements of environments are common in all experiences; they do not appear in explicit form in special-formulations. Qualities which are called interest, concern, intention, enjoyment (or the reverse), when they are abstracted, characterize the matter of firsthand experience. Science itself exists because of instinctive tendencies and impulses that are finally organized into an interested occupation. When it is said the task of philosophy is to place special topics, propositions, conclusions, lines of activity, etc., in an inclusive context it is indicated that such matters much be taken into account as well as the wider spatial-temporal abstract context, "rational" or "physical" in terms which the generality and comprehensiveness of philosophy is often defined.

Because everything experienced is determined by interactivity of organic-ongoing conditions, everything inquired into and discussed belongs in a field or situation. Fields and/or situations possess spatial and temporal *to-*

---

12. That the *connection* with which philosophy is peculiarly concerned is that with ends and policies that affect future social interactivities has been indicated in earlier chapters and will be taken up later.

getherness of the existences and events which constitute them. They are extensive and enduring. *"Togetherness"* as used here covers what is often named by the words connections and relations, and interconnections and relationships. I have employed a word derived from the word "together" because I want to avoid as far as possible prejudgment regarding the kind of way or ways in which things go and come together in forming situations. The notion of "relations" has often been played with dialectically in order to support some special philosophical conclusion. It has been used for example to try to justify the necessity of some kind of monistic scheme and block-universe. The word *together* involves denial of the existence of any such thing as complete isolation, and in so far points to a highly [_____] property of every experience as field [or] situation. But it leaves room for every kind of connection that observation discloses without the necessity of forcing them all into the Procrustean bed of some preferred type. It includes, for example, what James called the "each-to-each" or distributive type, and not just the "all-form" or collective type. It has room for what he called the "strung-out" kind of connection, provided observation finds it in its material. The spatially extensive and temporally enduring aspect of a situation may be regarded, if the above remarks are given full weight, as indefinite if we include in "indefiniteness" the vague shading off that occurs at the edges, which may contain things and connections that be will be focal and, so to say, bright and clear in other situations of experience.

It must also be understood, if misunderstanding is to be avoided, that breaks in and of connections that pre-existed at a given time and place must be admitted to be genuine components within a field when observation discloses their presence. There is possibly something verbally paradoxical in saying that discontinuities may occur within a field whose constituents are together in a way forming a temporal-spatial continuum. But the paradox, if there be one, is only verbal. Disequilibration in interactivities of organic and environmental factors occur and are the occasion of re-adjustments and re-arrangements. They function accordingly in bringing about changes of direction. To say that relative discontinuities exist within situations marked by continuity is only to say that the continuum of life-activities is such that it provides opportunities for changes which are qualitative not just quantitative. Disequilibrations, producing a state of relative indetermin-ism, produce those rearrangements of experienced materials which effect transition from one situation to another in a way which maintains their continuity in a life-history. Without these critical junctures there would be neither growth nor retrogression but only flat plateau of sameness. Without situations extensive in time and space within which re-arrangements take place so as to maintain adaptation in changing conditions there would be only a staccato succession of *disjecta membra*—without enough continuity to justify calling severed items "members."

These remarks about the ways in which components are together in a field are intended primarily to anticipate possible misunderstandings. They might almost be summed up in the view stated by James that difference is a mode of relation,[13] quite as much so as agreement, if we add that there are many forms of differing and of agreeing and that there are all degrees of looseness and tightness of connections in fields, and even in a single field. I come now to consideration of some general *properties* of situations which have to do with problems that have played an influential part in the history of philosophical discourse. I shall discuss characteristics of situations that have their source in the fact that a situation (every situation) is an interactivity of organic-environing factors, in which the contributions of the two are so fused, blended and consolidated that only outside analysis is capable of instituting the two terms, and even so, that retrospective and extraneous analysis has to be guided by the results of prior scientific inquiry in order to be able to attribute aspects of the situation to one rather than another of the two interacting factors.[14] The first generalized statement that will be made about a situation in its determination as an interaction of organic-environing energies is that a situation is marked by all the traits that are called esthetic, practical intellectual or cognitive,[15] when they are dissected out of the situations all of whose immediate qualities are so blended that they are no more one of the three sorts than they are of the other two. For I mean something more than that a situation has all three kinds of qualities. I mean that in the qualities that are immediately present are such a thoroughgoing fusion of all the characters are presented by the three words *epistemic, practical,* and *esthetic* that the latter distinctions arise only in consequence of analyses conducted because of pressure of problems lying outside the immediate situation. The fact that different schools of thought give such different accounts or descriptions of what it is to be epistemic, esthetic or practical is convincing, if indirect, proof that the properties by which they are marked off from one another are not the exclusive possession of different situations and experienced events nor yet common but separate properties of any one situation. Were either of these alternatives the case, the distinctive traits of each would so openly upon the very surface of what is experienced that the great diversity of accounts that exists in fact would be an impossibility. But

---

13. *Logic: The Theory of Inquiry*, p 54. [LW 12: 60.]

14. This is a generalized statement of the principle underlying the fact that to speak of a given quality as a *sense* quality, sensum, sense datum is to speak of it in its causal conditioning and not in its immediate present quality.

15. Because of various associations with the two latter words, I shall hereafter use "epistemic," not to be confused with "epistemological."

since they stand for distinctions that are deliberately made in the course of dealing with other problems, and are in that sense thoroughly artificial, different views about art, industry, morals, science which have a prior and independent existence will control the discriminative selections that are made as the ground of defining the esthetic, practical and epistemic. Hence the historic and existing diversity of views is just what should be expected. It is almost beyond belief that one who knows much of anything about the history of thought should suppose that the distinctions in question lie on the surface of "experience" or "consciousness," and hence are open to immediate uncolored and uncoloring inspection or introspection and report.[16]

In speaking earlier of life-functions, it was remarked that they are both direct phases of living, manifestations of what it is to be alive, and, since life is something which goes on, also are such as to prepare the way for future adaptive interactions. Proleptically or in anticipation of later developments, it may be said that even the simpler biological forms exhibit both preparatory and consummatory characteristics. The distinction is anticipatory because in the simpler forms every change that occurs is, in virtue of the simple fact that living is a temporally ongoing process, both a manifestation of the process a leading into next manifestation. In so far there is no ground for making a distinction into preparatory and consummatory aspects. In higher forms, for example, in forms provided with distance-receptors, distinction between contact-processes and processes that involve movements of search and approach as conditions of later contact-functions such as eating food and copulating with mates (and still more temporally remote production of young), provide ground for making a distinction between preparatory and consummatory. But at most it is a distinction of relative emphasis. As was previously pointed out, it cannot be denied that flight from a foe and approach to prey may themselves be such a direct expression of vital energies as to be enjoyed, nor can it be denied that the continuity of the life-process is such that the most emphatically consummatory activity does in fact influence subsequent life-functions and is therefore preparatory in a factual sense. As was indicated in the earlier discussion, the difference between sheer drudgery on one side and sheer enjoyments on the other marks an abnormality—in spite of the fact that it has been unwittingly used as a model for theories that make a complete break between what are then termed the instrumental and the consummatory, and between "values" called *extrinsic* and *intrinsic*.

---

16. The so called fundamental triadic psychological classification, *intellect, feeling, will*, is at a twofold remove from actual experience. It presupposes the one dealt with in the text and adds to it a hypostatization of distinguished properties into powers, adding a vicious artificiality to what may be a legitimate artifice in the case of discrimination of properties of subject matter into three kinds.

The fact that every situation is determined by an interaction of factors that analyze out as organic and environmental draws attention to the contributions which are made respectively by each of the two sets of conditions. The general *formal* statement that the situation has the qualities which are respectively called practical, esthetic and epistemic when *they* are carved out calls attention to the contribution from the organic side. The actual content assumed by these formal properties and the differing interpretations put upon them by different systems of thought lead us to consideration of the part played by environments.[17] I shall now deal briefly with the first point.

The word "practical" has such a variety of significations as to be ambiguous. It is here as a designation for certain qualitative aspects of a situation in the most neutral possible sense. The following definition, taken from the Oxford Dictionary comes close to conveying the gist of the matter: "Having or implying value or consequence in relation to action." Since "action" and "activity" are also words of uncertain, because varied, meaning in philosophical writings, and since some meanings set up an independent agent or force, "action" in a way directly contrary to the position here taken, the emphasis falls upon subject matter which is viewed in relation to the consequences which flow from, as when the words "doing" and "making" are taken in a neutral sense with no implication of *a* doer or manufacturer:—as equivalent in fact to "something doing" or *going-on* viewed in connection with its outcome. That all situations have qualities or qualitative aspects answering to the conditions set forth in this definition is truistically an expression of the fact that since living is a continuous process of adaptive interactions, what takes place at any given time must be such as to further subsequent life-functions or at all events be such as not to place insuperable obstacles in their way. Prospective reference is involved in every state and phase of the interaction which constitutes living, and this advance or anticipatory reference is bound to show itself in the immediate qualities of the situation which is produced. If we take an extreme example, the existence of situations whose subject matter is emphatically retrospective illustrates, directly or indirectly, the truth of this proposition. It illustrates it positively when the subject matter of the past (that which upon psychological analysis is referred to a way of experiencing called re-membering) forms the focally conspicuous part of the situation experienced in order to get guidance and instruction as to what to do—a case more usual than is generally recognized.

---

17. If we reduce the organic to the biological in the restricted sense of the latter word, leaving out of account the modifications and transformations affected in the biological by interaction with social conditions, then the role of the organic means of philosophic instruction is *purely* formal.

It illustrates it indirectly when recurrence to the past is nostalgic, for in such case there is always involved an element of escapism. What has been said does not imply in the least that qualities having to do with getting ready for the future, preparing for what is coming, need be dominant or even prominent traits of a situation. That the contrary is the case is proved by the existence of situations in which "esthetic" qualities are so predominant there is no explicit or verbalized or conscious reference to anything prospective. What is meant is that the continuity of life-function involves such interdependence of past-present-future temporal factors that every situation, including that which is most emphatically esthetic, has aspects which would not be there were it not for habitual prospective functioning of organic conditions in interactivities.

IV

[M]ovements in the arts of marked esthetic properties have often turned out to have such enduring consequences that they seem in retrospect to have been prophetic although there was no such intention in the original movement. The freedom from every kind of worry, anxiety, care, for the future involved in situations of a strongly esthetic character provides in fact a better hygiene with respect to the future than is anything pertaining to the *katharsis* of Aristotelian fame; its consequence is the more significant just because of absence of any *express* future reference. I would point to education deserving the name of education as in the same class with the esthetic. Educational situations which are most thoroughly and deeply educational whether for "instruction" or for "discipline" are those in which organic factors are so integrally interactive with environing factors that their educative import is not even suspected at the time. The experiences which lay deepest hold upon one, to use common parlance, are those that most deeply affect organic factors—attitudes, dispositions, habits—upon which formation of subsequent situations depends.

I have taken extreme situations for purposes of illustration in order to forestall the objection that there are experiences in which there are no traits or features that have to be described in terms of prospective reference. It is no more necessary for the validity of the position here taken that there must be such traits than there is that every condition and phase and aspect of an experience be in a state of focal awareness. That traits of which we are conscious are in many cases (I myself should say always) what they are because of factors of which at the time we are quite unconscious is a fact amply covering the present case.[18] Coming to the cases in which prospective

---

18. "Conscious" and "unconscious" are here used in their colloquial sense not in a philosophical sense which makes or tends to make entities, forces or agents out of them.

reference is an explicit quality of a given situation, I would point out that the position here taken does not involves the assumption of the existence of a power or faculty of anticipation, foresight, or prediction belonging to something termed a mind, self, person, or consciousness. Speaking in terms of psychological analysis, impulses and habits have momentum, they reach ahead. Speaking more generally, all living is a going-*on*, and futurity colors the qualities of any situation into which organic factors enter as components. As Whitehead has said speaking of experience "cut away the future and the present collapses."[19] Prudence may be nurtured into a virtue, corrupted into a vice—used or abused. But in any case the elements out of which policies, expediencies and plans are built exist in the very processes of animal life; indeed, they doubtless have roots in vegetative life. For without constituents of this sort the temporal seriality involved in living is non-existent.

It is not necessary to consider here whether politics and morals are more complexly developed forms of prudence, distinguished from what is usually labeled prudence by more extensive spatial-temporal mediation of environing conditions, or whether the difference of degree constitutes them of a different order. In any case, it *is* necessary to bear in mind the fact that they are concerned with extensive and enduring situations and that these situations have prospective outlooks. If a review of traditional and current theories of economics, politics and morals were here in place, it would appear that they often fail in both points. Followers of the Aristotelian-medieval tradition erect *prudence* into a separate faculty or power and adherents of the Protestant tradition do the same thing for *conscience*. In both cases, one factor, the organic as it is transformed by interaction with social conditions, is hypostatized because it is isolated from the situation in which it is one contributing factor. On the other hand, theories that strive to be "scientific" and to avoid the subjectivism of the type of theories just mentioned identify "objective" with *external*, thereby retaining the very dualism of internal and external that marks the theories against which they protest, and in the end substituting one kind of arbitrariness for another. Even theories of morals have managed to rule out the prospective reference of all behavioral situations by setting up "first" principles as all-controlling, by setting up "ends-in-themselves" which are antecedent because eternal, thereby accomplishing the miracle of eliminating from what are *called* ends all reference to consequences. That they then treat all theories of morals which operate on the ground of reference to consequences as low and unworthy follows as a matter of course. And it must be admitted that some theories of the latter type fail to see that consequences are always situational, and hence vibrate between

---

19. [Alfred North Whitehead, *Adventures of Ideas* (Macmillan, 1933), p. 246.]

the one-sided "internalism" of the hedonistic aspect of utilitarianism and the one-sided "externalism" of the institutional aspect of the same theory in politics and economics. When theories of morals neglect the future and prospective phase of all behavioral situations it is perhaps not surprising that economic and political theories have supposed that they are scientific when they confined themselves to what *"exists"* in terms which identify existence with what is over and done with, thereby failing to see that every economic and political proposition contains in fact a proposal about what should be *done* and is an expression of policy social in its sense of having to do with a *course of social behavior* to be adopted, the proposal resting ultimately upon preferences for some form of polity or social arrangement.

That the epistemic has a future reference in the case of what are regarded as "lower" non-scientific instances of knowing is, I suppose, generally admitted. For arts and crafts are traditionally relegated to the domain of the "practical," and the admission that knowledge in their case has to do with production of certain consequences is after all but a way of emphasizing the lower place of the kind of knowledge in the arts exhibit in contrast with the alleged timeless *reference* of even temporal *subject matters*, of scientific knowledge—a view which gives support whether so intended or not to the view that knowledge of the timeless or the eternal renders philosophy the supreme and culminating form of science. I do not propose to discuss in detail here the matter of prospective reference of the subject matter of all existential natural science. I content myself with saying that adverse criticisms of the view that such a reference is involved generally rest upon misstatements of the view. The commonest form of misrepresentation is that which converts a theory about the matter of subject matter in its epistemic or cognitive aspect into a theory about the motivation of the one engaged in knowing, thus reducing the theory to a theory that a scientific inquirer also has some "personal" end in view, the misrepresentation in question being supposed to be a more effective refutation in case the personal end is identified with some form of "material" advantage. This whole matter of motivation is in fact completely irrelevant to the position in question; the way in which it is lugged in suggests that the critic has not been able to eliminate "subjectivism" from his own theory of knowledge.

Criticisms in general (including that just mentioned) rest upon ignoring the fact that the prospective view of reference on the part of the epistemic defines consequences exclusively and completely in terms of *situations*, while the critic not being accustomed to inquire and describe in terms of situations reads into what is said his own view in which consequences are taken to be "internal"—labeled subjective and personal—or "external," labeled "objective." Having done this, "refutation" is an easy job. We are thus brought back to the main point and guiding principle: that the epistemic is *one* aspect of a *situation* and is an aspect of which in every directly experienced situation is blended with those called practical and esthetic when they are lifted out and formalized (formulated) for some special purpose. I know of no proof of the [belief] that every case of knowing begins and ends with and in situations and is regulated all the way through in its capacity as a transition from one situation to another since that of *demonstration* in the primary sense in which "demonstration" has the signification of *direct* pointing out and at, or direct exhibiting, showing, of what is there, as distinct from the derived sense of showing by reasoning or discourse. This kind of demonstration demands direct observation on the part of those addressed of what is pointed to else—a voluntary response not in the power of anyone to procure. If the observation in question is made I am unable to see how there will be any other result than that of the (1) primacy of experiences as extensive situations having qualities which evoke on the side of the organism as an interacting factor modes or ways of behaving which are capable of being so conspicuous, so dominant and em-*phatic*, as to constitute *know*ing as the leasing behavioral-phase; together with (2) the controlled transformation of the original situation into a situation with subject matter modified in specifiable respects.[20]

I add some remarks about the first clause of the last sentence in order to facilitate the performance of demonstration by those, of any, who are inclined to undertake it. Can any one imagine a cognitive operation which sets out from a sensation or datum in isolation, or from even a number of such elements provided they are supposed to have no connection with one another? Can any one imagine, with any enlightenment, an act of knowing which sets out with an isolated "object," or even a diversity of objects of totally disconnected from one another? I can only invite any who are interested to try the experiment of putting before himself for observation any case of actual inquiry, investigation, reflection, he may choose, provided he frees his observation from vestiges of antecedent psychological and epistemological theories. The outcome may be some objection to the *word* "situation"; I should gladly welcome suggestion of other words. But I am confident that whatever name is taken it will have the traits and properties I wish to suggest by the word *situation*.[21] I do not wish to repeat the earlier discussion; but no better illustration of building up theories of knowledge on the basis of

---

20. The latter clause is, of course, a restatement of what was said above in connection with the matter of future reference and consequences.

21. "Sights-seen" is an expression conveying the same underlying point of view. See the article by A. F. Bentley in *The Journal of Philosophy*, ["*Sights-Seen* as Materials of Knowledge." *Journal of Philosophy* 36 (1939): 169–81.]

acceptance (with some rehabilitation) of earlier popular beliefs about mind or soul can be found than that supplied by the present topic. The position here taken rests upon the simple postulate that a theory of knowledge and knowing is most likely to be successful if it be built upon observation of what goes on in cases which terminate in knowledge.

From the standpoint here taken, the chief problem does not concern the connection of knowing with situations whose prospective outlook affects what is known. The chief question concerns the evidence for the [position][22] that every situation having the qualities that are called esthetic or practical, when they are cut out, has also those that have cognitive or epistemic import. The need for calling up special evidence is not, however (in my opinion) derived so much from the facts of the case as it is from the state of theory. Philosophers have often been so preoccupied with the theory of knowledge that they have supposed that no treatment of art and esthetic experience was adequate until they had been reduced to the vehicles for carrying knowledge or "truth." Given their standpoint this procedure was the only way in which esthetic experience could be defended against the charge of triviality. I cannot think of any view of their dominant interest more uncongenial to artists and to those whose concern with esthetic matters is that of direct appreciation than this one. Naturally, it evoked their protest. The most immediately available form of protest took the form of emphasis of the emotional nature of esthetic experience. This emphasis often took the form of denying *all* connection whatever with action and "intellect." Reduction of the esthetic to a mere vehicle of some sort of scientific, philosophic or moral truth is such a violation of the qualities of immediate esthetic experience and of the creation of anything worthy of being regarded as enjoyed art that it is likely that the view that such art and experience contains the qualities that define "intellectual" affairs will arouse suspicion that an attempt is making to put over something extraneous. The suspicion will doubtless persist even when it is said that the according to the position here taken the qualities in question are in any case phases—that is to say em-phases, and that when the esthetic phase is so emphatic that the entire experience is named after it, knowledge-qualities are completely subordinated to the pervasive quality. But after all it seems necessary to cite but two lines of fact. I do not believe there is any artist of any kind who has not been intensely sensitive to the qualities of things and who has not in consequence been a keen observer of natural phenomena, and whose artistic productions have not been profoundly influenced by what he has observed, even when attendant emotional imagination has wrought great transformation. As far as appreciative experiences are concerned, it seems to be enough to

---

22. [Replacing "situation."]

call attention to the fact that the most convinced adherent of the theory of their emotional nature would hesitate to reduce them to sheer sentimental gusts, yet that is what they come to when all significances of the sort knowledge deals with are ruled out.[23]

It is my opinion that those who hold that observation of a sort appropriate to the subject matter dealt with is the sole method by which the data and tests of philosophic discourse can be obtained will not quarrel seriously with the substance of what has been said. Fundamental exception to the thesis that every situation is characterized by "intellectual," "emotional," and "practical" qualities is due to exaggerations, tending toward isolation, which are produced by one-sided growths in the environmental factors that enter into the determination of situations. This fact is most readily appreciated, probably in connection with the reasons why the esthetic experience is so often set off by itself—doubtless with the intent of honoring it but at the expense of denying any esthetic, emotionally satisfying and vivifying quality to the great mass of daily experiences. For existing social conditions on the economic side are such as to reduce to a very minimum the esthetic aspect of experiences had in the course of the daily occupation. The immediate aspect of activities carried on exclusively or nearly so for the sake of an "ulterior" end have as their directly enjoyable and satisfactory quality only in anticipation of the ulterior reward, and naturally that cannot saturate or even markedly tinge the traits and direct consequences of the intervening behavior. Then the absence of the esthetic element from activities connected with "making a living" (the predominant ones for the mass of human beings) is treated as if it were something inherent in all behavior having to do with the physical features of the environment, as work does. The large, probably much the larger, part of industry as it is carried on today is preparatory and "instrumental" in a sense in which the preparatory is isolated from direct consummation and fulfillment. Without its intention (as far as its grounds are concerned) the theory of separate kinds of experiences conforms to the type of experience that now prevails.

As has already been suggested, current understanding of the "practical" is profoundly affected by the cultural-environmental conditions just mentioned. It is identified with those experiences which are carried on for the sake of consequences which ensue only because of factors so external in their operation as to be, in effect, coercive. This is what happens when men and women (and oftimes children in school) do things that are not in any sense their own reward, and that are, moreover, of such a kind that the

---

23. There is something ironic in the fact that devotees of the view that all art as such is "abstract" and/or "non-objective" are the ones who *intellectualize* artistic production to the highest degree.

consequences for the sake of which they are done are determined by social conditions marked by great inequality of status, and hence flow from social conditions capable of great change, instead of flowing from the fact of association. It was virtually impossible, however, for the Greeks to imagine any other state of society than the one with which they were familiar, that of extreme difference of class status. This fact is manifest in the belief that slavery was "natural" since some human beings (not always completely identical with those who in fact held a servile position in a given society) were by their own constitution only instruments for ends outside themselves. But whatever ground the constitution of Greek society had for holding that certain experiences were "practical" and only that and for giving the "practical" a very long rank, we now know that the situation is of our own making, not in the "nature of things." Traits of experienced situations which are due to environmental conditions capable of change cannot be regarded as expressions of psychological conditions which are inherent.

While isolation of the "esthetic" and the "practical" (ultimately two aspects of the same basic isolation) are, as far as they go, reports of actual social conditions (and hence erroneous not so much as reports as in the assumption the difference inheres in nature or in the very psychology of experience), the same thing cannot be said of isolation of the epistemic element; of knowledge and search for truth. Knowledge and effort to achieve it have never occupied in fact a very distinguished position in the constitution of societies nor has the class of persons professionally engaged in knowing ever been given a place of superior privilege. When the intellectual class has held such a position it has been in the capacity of priests, and the fact that homage went to them in virtue of their being the guardians and distributors of the supernatural is indirect testimony to the revelatory [low] estate in which search for knowledge is held. It may truly be said that the prestige of science and the status of scientific men have greatly advanced during the last century and a half. But this is a recent matter; moreover, it is still doubtful whether such honor as is conferred is a tribute to their pursuit or to the utility of knowledge for the purposes of industry and war. A cynic might say that the separate and supremely high place given knowledge is an expression of the fact that intellectuals constitute the writing class and like others suffering from an inferiority complex have taken advantage of the position given them to over-compensate.

Index

adaptation, 325n8, 327–28
anthropological approach to philosophy, 3–14
Aristotle, 20, 44–50, 131, 322; appropriation by medieval church, 53, 58–60, 63; economics, 300–301; ends, 46–48, 299–300; knowledge, 97; matter, 288n1; naturalism, 45–46, 298; separation of knowledge and practice, 44–45, 48, 50
Arnold, Matthew, 92, 111–12
attention, 207–8, 214–15, 256. *See also under* mind
authority, 62, 72–76, 134–38, 162–63
Ayres, Clarence, 243n20

Bacon, Francis, viii, 70, 75, 112, 131, 134–35, 171n1, 209, 212
behaviorism, 11–12, 186–88, 216–19, 260, 308–9, 315
Bentley, Arthur, 319n2, 342n21
Bergson, Henrí, 222
Berkeley, George, 73, 74n9, 78–79, 90–91, 172–75, 179, 181, 185

Catholic Church. *See* medieval synthesis
certainty, 99–104, 114–20, 164
Comte, Auguste, 108
consciousness. *See* mind
consequentialism, 104–6, 126–27
contemplation, 44–45, 51–52, 229. *See also* theoretical

continuity, 324–26, 331–36
correspondence theory of truth, 94, 97, 164
cultural naturalism, xviii–xxxviii, 293–94
custom, xxiv, xxix–xxxviii, 14, 25–26, 43–44, 62, 65–70, 73, 76, 140, 148, 190

democracy, xv, 72, 74, 257–58
Derrida, Jacques, ix
Descartes, René, 70, 73, 75, 77–78, 112, 131, 134–35, 159, 171, 185; certain knowledge, 99–102, 114–15, 122–23; epistemological problem, 80–87, 89, 115–17; faculty psychology 82, 100–101, 115; mathematics, 81–83, 114–15
Dewey, John: critical social theory, xxxi–xxxviii; critique of his theory of culture, xxvii–xxviii; *Experience and Nature*, xiii, xiv, xix; *Logic: The Theory of Inquiry*, xxvi, 336n13; *Quest for Certainty*, xviii; *Reconstruction in Philosophy*, xviii, xxvii
Dewey, Roberta, xvi–xvii
Diggins, John Patrick, xxvii
Durkheim, Émile, 8

economics, 151–53, 161, 258, 264–65, 296, 300–302
education, 256–57

John Dewey (1859–1952) was twentieth-century America's premier philosopher, educational theorist, and public intellectual. He wrote dozens of books and hundreds of articles in areas of both technical philosophy and popular interest, including *Democracy and Education* (1916), *The Public and Its Problems* (1927), *Experience and Nature* (1929), and *Art as Experience* (1934). He taught at the University of Chicago (1894–1904), where he created the department of philosophy, psychology, and pedagogy and the Laboratory School, and at Columbia University (1904–52).

Phillip Deen is a visiting lecturer at Wellesley College. His articles on the history of pragmatism, the Frankfurt School, and contemporary democratic theory have appeared in *Contemporary Pragmatism*, the *Transactions of the Charles S. Peirce Society*, and the *European Journal of the History of Economic Thought*.